7.8

AN INTRODU...  ...URY

D1354012

An Introduction to Twentieth-Century Poetry in English

R. P. Draper

First published 1999 by
MACMILLAN PRESS LTD
Houndmills, Basingstoke, Hampshire RG21 6XS
and London
Companies and representatives throughout the world

ISBN 0–333–60669–8 hardcover
ISBN 0–333–60670–1 paperback

A catalogue record for this book is available from the British Library.

This book is printed on paper suitable for recycling and made from
fully managed and sustained forest sources.

10   9   8   7   6   5   4   3   2   1
08   07   06   05   04   03   02   01   00   99

Printed in Hong Kong

Published in the United States of America 1999 by
ST. MARTIN'S PRESS, INC.,
Scholarly and Reference Division,
175 Fifth Avenue, New York, N.Y. 10010

ISBN 0–312–21979–2 cloth
ISBN 0–312–21981–4 paperback

Contents

Preface   vi

Acknowledgements   viii

1 Introduction   1

2 Modernism: Pound, Eliot,
William Carlos Williams and Wallace Stevens   11

3 An Alternative Tradition: Hardy, Housman,
Frost, Kipling and Graves   33

4 Private and Public: Yeats and Lowell   60

5 Poetry of Two World Wars   80

6 Auden and Co.   98

7 'Black Mountain', and the Poetry of
D. H. Lawrence and Ted Hughes   116

8 Women's Poetry   138

9 Regional, National and Post-Colonial (I)   161

10 Regional, National and Post-Colonial (II)   187

11 Experiment and Tradition: Concrete Poetry,
John Ashbery and Philip Larkin   218

Notes   237

Select Bibliography   247

Index   289

Preface

I would like to emphasise two aspects of this book which define what I hope will be its usefulness to the reader, and, simultaneously, perhaps excuse its scholarly limitations. Both of these aspects are alluded to in the title, and, indeed, explain its slightly top-heavy nature.

Firstly, this book, as it says, is an *introduction*; it is designed for the general reader, including the A-Level student and university undergraduate, who is interested in modern poetry, rather than the specialist (though I hope that the latter would not find it entirely without interest). The aim is to create a map which charts the increasingly crowded and complex territory loosely called 'modern poetry', singling out what seem to me its main features, developments and writers. In doing this I have not found it possible, or thought it desirable, to include every significant modern poet (though I hope I have not omitted any of the really major figures). I did not want the book to become a mere series of names with somewhat perfunctory notes attached, but to have space in which poets and particular poems could be discussed at sufficient length for their character and quality to be conveyed to the reader. At the same time I have tried to be objective in the sense that I have not included or excluded writers merely according to my own personal preference. I recognise that distortions are nevertheless bound to have occurred; but I hope that the map remains at least broadly true to the situation as it is on the ground. (The inclusion of some writers in the Bibliography whose work is not discussed in the main body of the book may also help to balance up the account.)

Secondly, it is presumptuous nowadays to use the phrase 'English Poetry', unless one is confining oneself arbitrarily to poetry written by poets born in England; and it is equally presumptuous to write 'Modern Poetry', unless one is willing, and able, to write a polyglot account of poetry in French, German, Italian, Spanish, Russian, Arabic, Chinese, Hindu and all the other languages in which poetry has been, and still is being, written in the twentieth century. And for reasons which are sketched in Chapter 9 of this book, the 'English' of England, though still immensely fruitful and important, no longer has that pre-eminence in the production of English-language poetry that it enjoyed till the end, or towards the end, of the nineteenth century. There are significant varieties of poetry written in English within the British Isles, and even more significant varieties in the USA and the Commonwealth. Moreover, the situation is complicated culturally and politically, as well as linguistically. Hence the cautiously treading phrase in my title 'Poetry in English'.

Over and above these considerations, I have also tried to write a commentary which gives some flavour of the critical and cultural debate in which such poetry flourishes, and to suggest what relations it has to past traditions and what 'traditions' it is in the process of establishing itself. I cannot hope to have succeeded in all of these purposes; and in many cases I have had to be content to refer the reader to other places where such matters are more fully and competently discussed. (To attempt a book of this kind is to have it brought home how much one depends on a whole host of critics and commentators; and I would like to acknowledge how much I am indebted, not only to those mentioned in the Notes and Bibliography, but to numerous others, whose names, alas, I may even have forgotten.) But I hope enough has been done to constitute a useful outline map; and to provide an introduction that will stimulate the reader to further exploration, above all of the poets and poems themselves.

R. P. DRAPER

Acknowledgements

The author and publishers wish to thank the following for permission to use copyright material:

Marion Boyars Publishers Ltd, for the extract from Robert Creeley, 'Don't Sign Anything' from *Poems 1950–1965* (1966/1978);

Carcanet Press Ltd, for the extract from Iain Crichton Smith, 'Deer on the High Hills' from *Selected Poems* (1985); with New Directions Publishing Corp. for the extract from William Carlos Williams, 'Song' from *Collected Poems 1939–1962*, vol. II, copyright © 1962 by William Carlos Williams; and with University Press of New England for the extract from John Ashbery, 'The Lozenges' from *The Tennis Court Oath* (Wesleyan University Press), and *Selected Poems* (Carcanet), copyright © 1962 by John Ashbery;

Faber and Faber Ltd, for the extracts from Stephen Spender, 'Moving through the Silent Crowd' from *Selected Poems* (1940); Ted Hughes, 'Hawk Roosting' from 'Lupercal' in *Selected Poems 1957–1981* (1982); HarperCollins USA for the extracts from Ted Hughes, 'Crow's Nerve Fails' from *Crow: From the Life and Songs of a Crow*, copyright © 1971 by Ted Hughes; and Sylvia Plath, 'Ariel' and 'Lady Lazarus' from *Collected Poems* (Faber, 1981) and *Ariel* (HarperCollins), copyright © 1965 by Ted Hughes, copyright renewed; with New Directions Publishing Corp. for the extract from Ezra Pound, 'E. P. Ode Pour L'Election de Son Sépulcre', from 'Hugh Selwyn Mauberley' from *Selected Poems* (Faber, 1940) and *Personae* (New Directions), copyright © 1926 by Ezra Pound; with Farrar, Straus & Giroux Publishers Inc. for extracts from Derek Walcott, 'Omeros' from *Omeros*, copyright © 1990 by Derek Walcott; and Robert Lowell, 'Epilogue' from *Day by Day*, copyright © 1977 by Robert Lowell; Philip Larkin, 'The Building' and 'The Whitsun Weddings' from *Collected Poems*, copyright © 1988, 1989 by the Estate of Philip Larkin; and Philip Larkin, 'An Interview with *Paris Review*' and 'Introduction to *All What Jazz*' from *Required Writing*, copyright © 1983 by Philip Larkin;

Farrar, Straus & Giroux Publishers Inc. for the extract from Elizabeth Bishop, 'The Moose' from *The Complete Poems 1927–1979*, copyright © 1979, 1983 by Alice Helen Methfessel;

John Fuller for the extract from Roy Fuller, 'During a Bombardment by V-Weapons' from *Collected Poems* (Deutsch, 1962);

HarperCollins Publishers Ltd, Australia, for extracts from Judith Wright, 'Bullocky' and 'Remittance Man' from *The Moving Image* (Meanjin Press, 1946);

David Higham Associates Ltd on behalf of the author for the extract from Louis MacNeice, 'Soap Suds' from *Collected Poems* (Faber, 1966/1979);

Macmillan General Books for Thomas Hardy, 'Thoughts of Phena' and the extract from 'Overlooking the River Stour' from *The Complete Poems by Thomas Hardy* (Papermac, 1978); and for extracts from R. S. Thomas, 'Postscript' and 'Rough' from *Later Poems 1972–1982* (Papermac, 1984);

W. W. Norton & Company Ltd for extracts from e. e. cummings, 'ygUDuh' and 'here's a little mouse)and' from *Complete Poems 1904–1962*, ed. George J. Firmage, copyright © 1991 by the Trustees for the e. e. cummings Trust and George James Firmage;

Oxford University Press for the extract from Fleur Adcock, 'On the Border' from *Selected Poems* (1983);

Laurence Pollinger Ltd, on behalf of the author, and New Directions Publishing Corp. for the extract from Denise Levertov, 'A Tree Telling of Orpheus' from *Selected Poems of Denise Levertov* (Bloodaxe Books, 1986) and from *Poems 1968–1972* (New Directions), copyright © 1970 by Denise Levertov;

Random House UK Ltd for the extract from Robert Frost, 'Mowing' from *The Poetry of Robert Frost*, ed. Edward Connery Latham (Jonathan Cape, 1955).

Every effort has been made to trace all copyright holders, but if any have been inadvertently overlooked, the author and publishers will be pleased to amend further printings.

1

Introduction

'All coherence gone'

The twentieth century has been a century of enormous, and deeply disturbing, change. Yet it is the scale rather than the fact, or even the kind, of change that has been so remarkable. The English seventeenth century saw the beginnings of what we recognise as 'modern' in a change from the settled world-view and corporate sense of the Middle Ages to scepticism and individualism – a change reflected in the poetry of John Donne, who wrote:

> 'Tis all in pieces, all coherence gone;
> All just supply, and all relation:
> Prince, subject, father, son, are things forgot,
> For every man alone thinks he hath got
> To be a phoenix, and that there can be
> None of that kind, of which he is, but he.

These words can be matched with the celebrated lines in W. B. Yeats's 'The Second Coming':

> Things fall apart; the centre cannot hold;
> Mere anarchy is loosed upon the world,
> The blood-dimmed tide is loosed, and everywhere
> The ceremony of innocence is drowned;
> The best lack all conviction, while the worst
> Are full of passionate intensity.

Both suggest a tragic sense precipitated by the undermining of values and beliefs hitherto accepted as universally valid and permanent. But if the changing of the old order in the seventeenth century led to regicide and ultimately the rise of parliamentary democracy, for the ordinary common man life went on much the same as before. The disintegration proclaimed in Yeats's lines may be intellectually similar, but the consequences were already being felt far more widely, and on a much vaster scale, than anything known to Donne or his early seventeenth-century contemporaries.

'The Second Coming' was written in January 1919, less than three months after the end of what used to be called The Great War, but is now more usually referred to as World War I. This was war on an unprecedentedly international scale, involving not only all the European powers, but major world powers such as America and Japan. It was also a war of the common man, in which not only professional soldiers, but volunteers and conscripts from every walk of life were caught up, and in which the number of casualties was obscenely huge. 'The blood-dimmed tide' did, indeed, seem to have been 'loosed', creating something that was almost a literal rather than metaphorical condition in the trench warfare fought between the Germans and the Allies in northern France. The sense of disintegration was likewise made physically real in the dismembered bodies which littered the battlefields; and it had its social and spiritual equivalent in the sense of betrayal felt by many soldiers who had trusted the leadership of the 'powers that be' only to find themselves the victims of what seemed an incompetent High Command. Still more significantly, it was a mechanised conflict in which artillery, machine-guns, tanks and, for the first time (though not to be compared with developments in World War II), aerial warfare acquired supreme importance. Although hand-to-hand fighting and countless acts of individual bravery still played a decisive part, the experience of many soldiers was of passive submission to a death-dealing machine. At the Battle of the Somme, July 1916, when 20,000 men were killed on the first day, few of the attacking British troops ever came to grips with the enemy. They were simply mown down by the German machine-guns (which, ironically, were supposed to have been wiped out by the intensity of the preceding British bombardment). The traditional heroism of the individual soldier, as an eyewitness account graphically illustrates, went down before the impersonality of the machine:

> I saw from my post the first wave of troops scrambling out of their trenches in the early morning sunlight. I saw them advancing rapidly led by an officer. The officer reached a hillock holding his sword on high. Flashing it in the sunlight, he waved and sagged to the ground. His men, undaunted, swept up the mound to be mown down on reaching the skyline, like autumn corn before the cutter.[1]

The effect of this and similar experiences on the soldiers of The Great War is seen in the poetry of Robert Graves, Siegfried Sassoon, Isaac Rosenberg and Wilfred Owen. In the latter's 'Soldier's Dream' release from the fearful technology of war is what the soldier longs for. In his dream 'kind Jesus' deliberately jammed the guns and rusted the bayonets on both sides, 'ours' and 'Theirs', but God, who was 'vexed', gave power to the militant Archangel Michael: 'And when I woke he'd seen to our repairs.'

Such sardonic disillusion is characteristic. The satire implies a split in the once harmonious assumptions of a Christianity in which God the Father and God the Son were at one; now they are deeply divided, and 'God' has become no more than an apostatisation of the authorities who set, and keep, in motion an inhuman mechanism of destruction. In the minds of many writers the war became symbolic of a corrosive force which ate away the conventions and beliefs shoring up established society – a watershed dividing, as Philip Larkin's 'MCMXIV' suggests, innocence from experience.

That, of course, is a simplification. Larkin's poem paints a world of decent, almost pastoral, serenity changing after 1914 to something all the more appalling to the imagination for being expressed only in terms of what ceased to be rather than the horrors that were to come. The facts are more complex. The Great War was itself the outcome of a competitive struggle between the older industrial power of Britain and France and the growing industrial strength of Germany; and, as was to be even more apparent in World War II, the still newer industrial might of the United States of America had to be called in to the aid of the old before victory could be secured for the Allies. In Britain, in particular, a euphoric, and often deeply sincere, belief in empire-building (as a moral mission bringing the benefits of western civilisation to supposedly less enlightened peoples) masked a real decline in the economic pre-eminence which the nation had enjoyed as a result of its late eighteenth-century Industrial Revolution. Moreover, the tensions and strains associated with industry and empire were already evident in the nineteenth century in, for example, the economic and agricultural depressions of 1873–96, the wars against the South African Boers (1881 and 1899–1902) and the running sore of Irish Home Rule which came to a head in the Dublin Easter Rising of April 1916. (This was patched up after World War I by the treaty of 6 December 1921 establishing the Irish Free State, but on the basis of partition, which left serious problems that are still unsolved today.)

Conditions of poverty and overcrowding among the increasingly urbanised working class, exacerbated by periods of severe unemployment, led to the development of trade unionism and strikes such as those of the gasworkers in 1888 and the dockers in 1889. These in turn fostered the growth of working-class political movements which reached their most significant stage in the formation of the Labour Representation Committee (1900), which became the Labour Party in 1906, and eventually, in the post-war period, supplanted the Liberal Party as the main opposition to the Conservatives. From the points of view of the upper and middle classes these were disturbing signs of the old order changing, giving place to a new one in which their wealth and privileges seemed to be under threat – though it was often from individuals within these classes (such as the 'Fabians', Sidney and Beatrice Webb) that the intellectual and political leadership came in the struggle to improve social conditions and extend the parliamentary franchise. The Reform Acts of 1884–5 gave some working men the vote, but it was not till 1918 that both men and women were enfranchised (and full enfranchisement for 21-year-old women did not come till 1928). Women in Britain, following the lead already given by American women, had begun campaigning for independent rights prior to the war, upsetting entrenched conventionality with their militancy, and although they agreed to put their grievances in abeyance for the duration of World War I, by virtue of the work they did replacing men at the front they effectively undermined the male prejudices which decreed that they were by nature unfitted for tasks outside the home. What is now thought of as 'women's liberation' did not come until well after World War II, but it was in the first part of the twentieth century that consciousness, reinforced by practice as well as argument, of women's equality with men firmly established itself in the social and political spheres.

POST-WAR AND MODERNIST

After World War I Britain and the West saw further changes which continued the impetus of these pre-war developments and their acceleration by the war itself. Despite setbacks such as the Great Depression, which affected America and the whole of the English-speaking world in 1929–34 and brought with it mass unemployment, the standard of living for ordinary working people greatly improved compared with that in the nineteenth century. Yet the erosion of its imperial role left Britain as a medium power rather than a world power, uncertain whether the future lay with its 'special relationship' with America or as a member of the European Union, and its affluence declined *relative* to that of other Western countries. The USA, in particular, became the wealthiest and most powerful country in the world, though serious deprivation, especially (but not exclusively) among Native Americans and Americans of African origin, existed side by side with this prosperity, aggravating tensions created by racial discrimination. National self-confidence was high, however, among the bulk of the US population and increased after the World War II victories over Germany and Japan, surviving even the disillusionment with 'peace' created by the division of spheres of influence between the Soviet Union and the West, and the 'cold war' between capitalist and socialist economic systems which this generated. Sharp anxiety was felt about the destructive potentialities of nuclear weapons, on which the uneasy balance between the two great powers depended, but it was not until the Vietnam War, in which the USA experienced its first major military defeat, that American self-confidence was seriously dented. With the collapse of the Soviet empire in the late 1980s the USA was left as the only effective super-power – its problems more acute internally than externally.

America's problems are those of adjustment to the enormously increased control over man's physical environment which 'progress' (meaning largely technological-cum-commercial development) has made possible in the twentieth century. The advent of such things as the telephone, motor car, aeroplane, cinema, wireless, television and computerisation have speeded up communications and created a national and international awareness which, along with ever-increasing industrialisation and commercial activity, have radically altered people's sense of the universe in which they live. The traditional relation between the human and the natural has been effectively reversed. As Fredric Jameson suggests, in an argument about James Joyce's *Ulysses* and the city-based modernism which it represents:

> What is paradoxical about the historical experience of modernism is that it designates very precisely that period in which Nature – or the in- or anti-human – is everywhere in the process of being displaced or destroyed, expunged, eliminated, by the

achievements of human praxis and human production. The great modernist literature – from Baudelaire and Flaubert to 'Ulysses' and beyond – is a city literature: its object is therefore the anti-natural, the humanised, par excellence, a landscape which is everywhere the result of human labour, in which everything – including the formerly natural, grass, trees, our own bodies – is finally produced by human beings.[2]

This speeding up of change till it reaches a critical mass threatening irreversible consequences is what lies, for example, behind T. S. Eliot's inverted vision of a 'waste land' of city-dwellers herded into unnaturally close proximity, but deprived of the rituals and conventions of smaller, more organic, and more slowly evolving societies. A neo-pastoralism develops which, in the work of writers such as D. H. Lawrence and Ted Hughes, also becomes a critique of the evils of a deracinated society. (It is significant that Lawrence, though an English writer, had his closest affinities with certain American writers, saw America as the symbolic nation of modernity, and found his most receptive audience in America.)

Perhaps more importantly, however, consciousness of 'the achievements of human praxis and human production', whether regarded as a good or an evil, generates what might be called the 'arbitrariness' of much twentieth-century poetry – its consciousness of itself, not as an extension of natural processes (the 'art that nature makes' of Shakespeare's *The Winter's Tale*), but as another artefact in a world of essentially man-made productions. Here it is closely allied to developments in modern critical theory derived from the linguistics of Ferdinand de Saussure which emphasise the arbitrariness of the verbal 'signifier', its lack of inherent connection with the thing 'signified', and the pattern of contemporary relationships between words as they are used at any one given time rather than their historic derivation from earlier forms. The principle of relativity becomes all-important: 'both signifier and signified are purely relational or differential entities. Because they are arbitrary they are relational.'[3]

The relativistic view tends also towards the sceptical and demystifying. Language, and the literature composed from it, is seen as an elaborate, internally organised construction properly subject to intellectual analysis, but deprived of its quasi-religious status. One of the consequences of this view is 'the death of the Author'. Hitherto the individual writer, whose work is enshrined in the accepted canon of great literature, has been accorded high status for his almost superhuman skill in the creation of deeply meaningful texts to which he himself holds the essential clues. But in the approach exemplified by the French philosopher/critic Roland Barthes, this traditional respect has been devalued, and with it the common assumption of the writer as someone in complete control of what he writes. The very idea of authorship is seen as over-restrictive: 'To give a text an Author is to impose a limit on that text, to furnish it with a final signified, to close the writing.'[4] And in tandem with this downgrading of the Author there is a corresponding upgrading of the Reader – or rather Readers – whose multiple and subjectively various interpretations of texts are welcomed as democratically equal and open-ended.

Such a line of argument leads to affirmation of the man-made rather than the confirmation of a natural or divinely sanctioned authority, as is evident in Barthes's conclusion that the process is one that 'liberates what may be called an anti-theological activity, an activity that is truly revolutionary since to refuse to fix meaning is, in the end, to refuse God and his hypostases – reason, science, law'.[5] It is an argument appropriate to the complexity and uncertainty typical of a world where it can no longer be taken for granted that the universe is the creation of a purposeful and beneficent creator, and where almost all the traditional icons of authority seem to have been knocked from their pedestals. Yet the anxiety for reassurance manifestly persists. Much literary 'modernism' is, in fact, highly conservative, reflecting this deep, underlying anxiety and the desire for orderly structures, or the re-vitalising of decadent ones, to counteract it. But it also coexists with more liberal manifestations which seek to run with the tide of uncertainty, welcoming the breakdown of hierarchies and the deconstructing of ideologies as a benign chaos. These, broadly speaking, are the two camps, led by Eliot/Pound and Williams/Stevens respectively, which are discussed in Chapter 2 of this book. Paradoxically, however, the two camps are united in their search for changes in form and language which will more properly articulate the nature of the world as the twentieth century perceives it; and, equally paradoxically, in an increasingly democratic society they produce poetry which expresses the values of a sophisticated élite, and which in its deliberate 'difficulty' often seems aloof from, and even hostile to, popular culture.

The alternative tradition discussed in Chapter 3 produces poetry that is more accessible. But it would be a mistake to treat it – as earlier critics, carried away by the heady excitement generated by modernism, tended to do – as merely the perpetuation of Victorian forms and values unmodified into a poetic world which had moved on. Many of the writers within this alternative tradition were more radically subversive than their apparent conformity suggests, and their poetic techniques were often far from conventional. The most marked difference between them and the modernists is in their respect for the kinds of rhetoric, versification and syntactical completeness by which the thrust of discursive argument is maintained. In the work of these poets the disruptive forces of change into which modernists variously flung themselves with willed enthusiasm, or felt themselves being thrust reluctantly, were neither ignored nor underestimated, but harnessed to structures suggesting continuity with the past. If content did not pressure form into fragmentariness or openness, neither did form remain untouched by the potentially chaotic material it tried to contain. Often the tension between the two was poignant and in itself deeply expressive. Hardy, in particular, 'though certainly not an ideological modern*ist*, is emphatically a self-aware modern; and despite the obvious differences between his work, situated as it is in a national tradition, and that of the more internationally minded modernists with their accent on a paradoxically anti-traditional tradition, there are features both of form and content which make that work recognisably modern.'[6]

It can be argued that modernism as such was a dead-end, that mid- and late twentieth-century poetry, as exemplified in the work of Auden, Lowell, Larkin and Heaney, has more in common with the non-modernist modernity represented by Hardy and Yeats. But this is perhaps to take an English rather than an American view. On the western side of the Atlantic the continuing vitality of the Pound/Williams undermining of rational discourse to make way for more fluid kinds of imaginative relationship is more evident than it is on the eastern side; and it is given new emphasis by a genre of women's poetry which not only serves as the literary arm of feminism, but extends the range of language – and more specifically of perception as mediated through language – to include revolutionary ideas of gender. American women poets rather more than those from Britain and the Commonwealth use the formal licence encouraged by modernism to register a break with predominantly masculine criteria and assumptions. As with other continuers of the modernist tradition, however, this does not necessarily entail reproducing all the classically modernist characteristics. In general, women employ only those features which enable them to develop styles appropriate to their distinctively woman's experience and vision. And what tends to be more important in determining the character of particular women poets' work is their degree of commitment to specifically feminist causes as compared with the expression of more broadly feminine themes (which often have their counterparts in men's work, too).

Something similar might be said with regard to the homosexual and lesbian strains in post-modern poetry. New kinds of awareness of the self and the loosening of traditional patterns of relationship demand new modes of writing. For example, the curiously drifting syntax and unexpected confusion of persons and voices in the work of John Ashbery are explained by the poet himself in terms of his sense of a fluidity rather than fixity of personal identity: 'I guess I don't have a very strong sense of my own identity and I find it very easy to move from one person to another and this again helps to produce a kind of polyphony in my poetry.'[7] Some of the changes in the later work of Adrienne Rich can likewise be seen as the product of a new, and distinctively female, sense of being.

EROSION OF THE CENTRE

The re-shaping of poetry to express a new conception of identity, or with the purpose of trying to create that identity, accounts for another, increasingly important area within that vast range which constitutes twentieth-century poetry in English. This is the poetry of English-speaking – or perhaps one should say 'Anglophone' – writers who are embraced (sometimes reluctantly) within the United Kingdom, and of former members of the British Empire such as Canada, Australia, New Zealand and parts of the Caribbean. Strictly speaking, the USA should also be reckoned within this category, but the status of 'American' has long since become equal to, or even more important than, 'English' so that the same sense of a need to assert cultural along with political independence does not apply to its twentieth-century literature. Commonwealth countries, on the other hand, have more recent, as well as more ambivalent, linguistic problems; while Scottish, Irish and Welsh non-Gaelic literature presents problems which are different again. And just as significant are the regional diversities within 'English' English.

Deep and far-reaching aspects of change are evidenced, then, in all the varied manifestations of modern English poetry. 'The centre cannot hold' in yet another sense than that already discussed in connection with Yeats's 'The Second Coming'. Acute tensions develop between the established and forces which are at work to destabilise any established central authority. The deconstructionist tendencies of modern criticism further reflect this process. Acceptance of an integrated cultural hegemony is undermined by a radical scepticism which extends even to doubts about the very possibility of agreed, common foundations for the interpretation and valuation of literature. The reverse side of this coin, however, is a loosening of controls on experimentation, and a self-critical, potentially sobering, awareness of its own rejection of authority as itself subject to possibly unrecognised forces, which make this twentieth-century uncertainty also a source of creativity. When the field of poetry is surveyed as a whole, action is seen to be coupled with reaction; no one tendency ultimately prevails. If 'the price of freedom is eternal vigilance', that vigilance is what modern poetry incorporates in its at times bewildering multiplicity and multivalency. It is best read in all its mutually cancelling, but also mutually enhancing, diversity.

2

Modernism: Pound, Eliot, William Carlos Williams and Wallace Stevens

EZRA POUND (1885–1972) AND T. S. ELIOT (1888–1965)

The theme of modernism is, in Ezra Pound's phrase, to 'make it new'. Being 'modern' suggests being abreast of the times, aware of the twentieth century's technological change and its advances in knowledge which make superstition and ignorance relics of the past that are rapidly becoming outmoded. Yet, ironically, modernist poets such as Pound and T. S. Eliot 'make it new' by going back to the past – by insisting on the need to re-open those lines of communication which constitute tradition. Politically, too, they tend to celebrate authority and submission rather than democracy and the freedom of the individual. In their literary work they cultivate forms which are abrupt, discontinuous and rapidly shifting, as if to match the hasty, forward-moving pace of modern life, and their versification suggests impatience with the regularity and strict rhyme patterns of previous poetry. In addition, they are difficult and elusive, as if speaking an in-language known only to those who are the 'up to date' members of a self-consciously new *avant-garde*. And yet their feeling for the age which they thus reflect is one of disgust rather than approval; what they tend to see around them is pollution and decay, an urban environment which is dehumanised, if not inhuman, and a way of life which is morally corrupt: 'The burnt-out ends of smoky days' – to quote the early Eliot of 'Preludes'. To cap it all, the recondite material to which their allusive style esoterically refers often proves, when decoded, to be the very substance of the culturally burdened past from which, initially, they appear to be trying to break free.

A further paradox is to be found in the reaction against long narrative and/or discursive poems, which provided the monuments

11

of past literature (such as the *Iliad*, the *Odyssey*, the *Aeneid*, the *Divine Comedy*, *The Faerie Queene*, *Paradise Lost* and *The Prelude*) while continuing to use them extensively not only for allusion, but also for structural underpinning. In place of the long poem, favour is given to the short, intensive lyric which has hard, precise images and concentrates on the expression of concrete moments of feeling or perception. This was made quite consciously and deliberately the basis of the (admittedly short-lived) early twentieth-century movement to which Pound gave the name Imagism (or *Imagisme*). It is best illustrated by his own famous haiku-like poem 'In a Station of the Metro', where the terse language is nevertheless powerfully evocative. By its brevity and arrestingly abrupt *mise en scène* – its plunging unannounced and without explanation into a vivid moment of city experience – Pound's poem makes its challenge to prosiness and tedious argumentation by its very mode of presentation. But how could such moments be saved from the merely fragmentary and heterogeneous? The modernist vision also required its monuments, its more sustained explorations of its own peculiar response to the distinctively modern world, even if such monuments, by its own criteria, had to avoid the monumental.

In fact, both Pound and Eliot, and many modernists after them, wrote long, or comparatively long, poems which, though lyric in form, were epic in stature, and have indeed become 'monuments' of twentieth-century poetry. Pound's long (and at his death still unfinished) modern epic is his *Cantos*, which signify by their title both their relation to tradition and their song-like status as individual, lyrical effusions; and Eliot, by publishing *The Waste Land* complete with a critical apparatus of scholarly 'Notes' (although these do not appear to have been part of his original intention), gave his ultra-modernist poem the aura of a classical text and the trappings of academic respectability. Moreover, in its earlier, pre-publication version *The Waste Land* was a much longer poem than the one of a mere 433 lines which came out in 1922. Pound, to whom Eliot dedicated the poem as 'il miglior fabbro' (the better craftsman), was responsible for reducing it to the shape and dimensions by which we now know it. Some idea of what it was like before Pound took his scissors to it can be gleaned from Valerie Eliot's 1971 edition of *The Waste Land, a facsimile and transcript of the original drafts*. In this earlier form sudden, concretely realised moments of experience jostle with passages of curtailed narrative in a cinematic process of montage which elusively and tantalisingly seems to express the sensibilities of a whole, disillusioned generation, while also functioning as the private vision of an esoteric and highly sophisticated, individual consciousness. Other passages read like imitations, appropriate to our times, of eighteenth-century mock-heroic, cast in a verse that is sometimes juvenile, sometimes elegantly sly and ironic. The Poundian re-shaped version is much superior: scattering tradition into kaleidoscopically dispersed fragments, it contrives both to affirm an élitist criticism of modern decadence and to incorporate its essence in an iconoclastically modern form. But the sense of a lost, larger whole echoes in the poem like the 'aethereal rumours' of 'What the Thunder Said', which 'Revive for a moment a broken Coriolanus'.

Reviewers were initially baffled by *The Waste Land*. Some seriously questioned whether Eliot was perpetrating an elaborate hoax. Nothing so wilfully obscure and seemingly arbitrary had ever been offered to the public before under the revered guise of 'poetry'. Nevertheless, as George Watson has pointed out, the supposed unpopularity of the poem has been exaggerated. In a surprisingly short space of time it acquired for itself the apparently self-contradictory status of a classic of modernism; and it became the subject of repeated argument, analysis and, finally, learned explication. Eliot's 'Notes' led the way with their references, for example, to 'the incidental symbolism' which was 'suggested by Miss Jessie Weston's book on the Grail legend: From Ritual to Romance' and 'another work of anthropology' which 'has influenced our generation profoundly; I mean The Golden Bough.' Some commentaries, notably that of Grover Smith, virtually convert what is basically an Imagist anti-narrative poem into an elliptically condensed narrative poem with all the features of a full-blown mythological epic. Ironically, its fame has created for it a wider audience than the first reviewers would ever have conceived possible; and one whose demand for it to have a meaning has so fuelled a mass of interpretative comment that the mystery engendered by its first, disconcertingly disjunctive method has now been dissolved into a rationally comprehensible story.

As with certain present-day television programmes which begin with a strange juxtaposition of images which are subsequently explained as the plot unfolds – a technique paying unconscious tribute to the way an earlier phase of specialised, minority art has now entered the mainstream of popular culture – *The Waste Land* has become for most of its readers no more than a dramatic-cum-lyrical shorthand for an explicatory process which now unfolds its 'true' meaning. In this respect, of course, it suffers no more than much of Shakespeare's work and virtually all of the Bible; and history having done its work, it is perhaps futile to protest, as some critics do, that the poem has in consequence lost its essentially poetic nature. The modernist method provokes interpretation; and its somewhat perverse heightening of our consciousness of the present as an inheritor of a dying tradition makes scholarly attempts at artificial respiration all but inevitable.

Eliot's friend Conrad Aiken (1889–1973) claims to have seen certain passages of *The Waste Land* in existence as separate poems prior to their publication as elements of the 1922 version of the poem; and Eliot himself has undermined the notion that it is an organically integrated whole by describing it as 'a piece of rhythmical grumbling', and further suggesting that it could be described by the Dickensian sentence, 'He do the police in different voices.' The sense of 'different voices' is certainly what one gets when listening to the gramophone record of the poem read by Eliot, or, better still (in purely histrionic terms, that is), by the actor Robert Speight. Similarly, variations of tone, accent and seriousness remain a major part of the experience of reading the text to oneself in the silence of the study – not only where the punctuation specifically indicates that dialogue is taking place, as in 'A Game of Chess', but also in such changes as the shift from the elegiac opening of 'The Fire Sermon', with its eerie sense of late autumn leaves clinging to 'the wet bank' as if with desperate human fingers, to the episode of the typist and her 'young man carbuncular', which concludes with the ironic comment that when the modern woman 'stoops to folly' she merely settles her hair (Eliot's devastating phrase is 'with automatic hand') and nonchalantly 'puts a record on the gramophone'.

This latter example may seem a special case in that it depends on a parody of the song in Goldsmith's *The Vicar of Wakefield* which tells of a genuinely lovely woman's stooping to folly and finding no remedy for her lost virginity but suicide. The change of voice in Eliot's parody is an implied comment on a cultural change which exposes modern sexual behaviour to a damaging comparison with traditional moral attitudes. But such a technique of juxtaposition is one which is frequently used in *The Waste Land* – though not always to the detriment of the present. Echoes of Spenser and the Elizabethans, with the softly running River Thames as a refrain, suggest the contrast between a pre-industrial and a post-industrial, polluted London, but the political intrigues of Queen Elizabeth and her affairs with her courtiers, the Earl of Leicester in particular (also echoed in 'The Fire Sermon' at lines 279–82), may be regarded as on a par with, rather than superior to, the assignation of the typist. Their respective affairs are variations on a theme in a musical mode which includes past and present as varying tonal registers.

The point is, indeed, often made that *The Waste Land* is musical rather than discursive in form, i.e. it has neither a logical nor a temporally consecutive narrative, but consists of words, lines, paragraphs adjusted in relation to other words, lines and paragraphs, as sections of music are in a prelude or tone poem. But this analogy, though helpful in general terms, is only loosely appropriate. Despite the repetition and variation of themes which tend to occur in Eliot's poem (e.g. water, the desert, the questing hero who modulates into a Christ-like figure) there is no precise, symphonic structure to be found. Nor, notwithstanding references to *The Ring* and *Tristan und Isolde*, is there any very precise equivalent to the Wagnerian *leit-motiv*. The painterly metaphors of shifting perspective, spatial and colour relationship, and foreground/background adjustment might equally well apply – but with equal inexactness. The processes of the verbal art which is poetry may usefully be compared with those of other art-forms, but they none the less remain peculiarly linguistic. What Eliot does is to allow the inherent flexibility of the verbal medium to have full play, in conjunction with the syntactical and lexical ambiguity so ingeniously illustrated by William Empson in his well-known analysis of the opening lines of 'A Game of Chess'.[1] In this respect the 'making new' of modernism is part of Eliot's feeling for the freedom and expressiveness of language, but controlled and directed by his equally well developed feeling for traditional patterns and values as incorporated in the literature of the past.

The Waste Land was written in the years immediately following the First World War, and also at a time when Eliot himself was going through a personal crisis connected in part at least with the breakdown of his marriage to Vivien Haigh-Wood. 'These fragments I have shored against my ruins' (line 430) can thus be read as both a public and a private statement. Eliot himself, especially in his influential critical essay 'Tradition and the Individual Talent' (1919), insisted on the primacy of the public dimension – to the exclusion, in good art, of the private and personal. He argued that 'the more perfect the artist, the more completely separate in him will be the man who suffers and the mind which creates; the more perfectly will the mind digest and transmute the passions which are its material'. In part this can be attributed to the reaction against confessional poetry of the kind associated with the great Romantic poets (for example, Keats's 'Ode to a Nightingale' with its opening statement, 'My heart aches, and a drowsy numbness pains / My sense', or the somewhat self-pitying 'I fall upon the thorns of life! I bleed!' of Shelley's 'Ode to the West Wind'). The modernist wished to by-pass such explicit reference back to the self, in favour of a digesting and transmuting of emotion which would enable him to tap the deepest levels of the malaise of his time – to see 'the boredom and the horror' beneath the surface. Keats, one might retort, did this by making himself a sounding board for his time; the personal by virtue of the intensity with which it was recorded became universally representative. But this mode seemed to the early twentieth-century modernist to have deteriorated into merely sentimental imprecision. Eliot strove for something at once more restrained and exact, more 'scientific'. Hence his notorious reduction of the poet to a catalyst effecting, but not involved in, a kind of chemical reaction.

In spite, however, of this emphasis on impersonality, and the formidable apparatus of dramatic personae behind which the indi-vidually committed 'I' seems to disappear, Eliot's poetry retains a strongly personal flavour. And this becomes more apparent in the work after *The Waste Land*. In 'Marina' (1930), for example, although the first-person singular should perhaps be equated with Pericles, who loses and recovers his daughter in the Shakespeare play named after him, the note is more lyrical than dramatic. A strongly per-sonal sense of loss and regeneration throbs through the alternating rhetorics of a mist-clad, but hopeful, uncertainty and a hard, death-centred certainty; and the urgently wishful climax of 'The awakened, lips parted, the hope, the new ships' comes across as personal yearn-ing rather than detached dramatic monologue. The poem remains a characteristically modernist one in its allusiveness (including what Eliot himself calls a 'criss cross' between Shakespeare's play *Pericles* and Seneca's *Hercules Furens*[2]) and especially in its ambiguous, fractured syntax; but its impersonality, even more than that of *The Waste Land*, has become the movingly indirect means of voicing Eliot's own spiritual situation between the two worlds of a deca-dent, lethal, secular culture and a potential renewal offered by the Christian faith.

This is still more evident in the loose sequence of poems entitled *Ash Wednesday* (1930). These are 'confessional' in almost the strictly religious sense of a personal admission of guilt to a priest, made with the hope of absolution. The allusiveness here is heavily centred on the Bible, Dante and Cavalcanti (whose 'Perch' io non spero di tornar giammai' provides the repeated and varied motif, 'Because I do not hope to turn again'), and it is no longer part of the 'aethereal rumours' which in *The Waste Land* 'Revive for a moment a broken Coriolanus'. Here it tokens a religious tradition with which the 'I' of the poem seeks to merge himself – wishing, it is true, to extinguish his egocentric individuality ('As I am forgotten / And would be forgotten, so I would forget'), but with the hope of discovering a new self founded in submission to the will of God. The modernism here is a far cry from that of the self-consciously contemporary, urbanised earlier poems, but still to be felt in the disconcertingly abrupt shifting of syntax and images, and in a fragmentariness which – though it consists of fragments of prayer heard and partly repeated, as that of 'Marina' is derived from fog-shrouded things intermittently seen and heard – remains 'modernist' in its sudden, unexplained series of *mises-en-scène* and its mysterious, collage-like juxtapositions. *Ash Wednesday*, in fact, along with 'Marina', represents Eliot's purest poetry *qua* poetry, employing a distinctively modernist technique, though paradoxically almost entirely isolated from the pressures of a recognisably twentieth-century environment.

Eliot's last significant poetic work is *Four Quartets* – four separate but interrelated poems, the first of which, 'Burnt Norton', was published in 1936 (as part of *Collected Poems, 1909–1935*), followed by pamphlet editions of 'East Coker' (1940), 'The Dry Salvages' (1941) and 'Little Gidding' (1942). All four were printed together as *Four Quartets* in New York in 1943, and in London in 1944. Whether they constitute a unity is not quite so much a matter of debate as it is with *The Waste Land*. The 'musical' structure is somewhat more deliberately pursued. Each poem consists of five movements which, as Helen Gardner has shown, follow a similar pattern of: statement and counter-statement in section 1; more concentrated lyricism succeeded by a flatter, colloquial passage in section 2; a development towards reconciliation of the initial duality in section 3; a further passage of lyrical intensity in section 4; and, in section 5, a repeat of the double movement of section 2, but with the colloquial preceding the lyrical.[3] There are also interconnecting themes, such as a balancing of the affirmative and negative ways towards the fleeting glimpse of a Christian vision which each poem pursues, and images and symbols, such as fire and rose, water and air, which recur, with development and amplification, throughout the sequence. Words, however, do not lend themselves to the same kind of structuring as notes of music, and this modernist musicality remains suggestive rather than precise – a means of imaginative exploitation of contrast and association, repetition and tonal variation, rather than the precise imitation of sonata form.

It is even a little misleading, notwithstanding Eliot's title, to analyse these poems in musical terms, for to some extent they backtrack on the modernist developments which have led to the earlier poetry being considered on analogy with music. The *Quartets* are more rationally discursive than the earlier poems. In particular, the more prosaic parts – there is a deliberate alternation of colourfully lyric with prose-like passages – take on the conversational style of an academic lecture, or Eliot's own literary critical prose. For example, Section II of 'East Coker' follows a passage of tight, paradoxical octosyllabics, evoking a mysterious confusion of the seasons, with longer, looser lines which deliberately drop the temperature:

> Leaving one still with the intolerable wrestle
> With words and meanings.

And in Section V of 'Little Gidding' a similar reaction against the 'Metaphysical' lyric of Section IV produces a cool definition of the correct sentence which offers itself as a model for the poem as structured 'epitaph' in which every word has its proper, supportive relationship to the others, and the whole forms a 'complete consort dancing together'.

This does not, it is true, constitute a recantation of modernism. The drifting syntax (as in Section II of 'Burnt Norton', for example) and the disconcerting irruption of evocative images (as in Section I of 'The Dry Salvages': 'The salt is on the briar rose, / The fog is in the fir trees') continue to ruffle the discursive surface; but such features are now drawn into a relationship with more traditional discourse which suggests an at least tentative reconciliation of old and new. And as part of this reconciliation the urban dimension which made the early poetry seem so much a break with nineteenth-century pastoralism – though it may be said to be set in a musically contrapuntal dialogue with the seasonal passages of 'East Coker' II and 'Little Gidding' I, or the fisherman sestina of 'The Dry Salvages' II – is now sub-ordinated, syntactically and thematically, to the upward and down-ward trajectories which constitute the affirmative and negative rhythms of the *Quartets'* overall structure. This is seen clearly in 'East Coker' III, which begins with a resolutely prosaic plunge into the distinctively twentieth-century world of the City of London (though echoing the blindness of Milton's Samson), and then, through a triple epic simile evoking the changing of stage scenery, the Underground railway and the anaesthetics of the operating theatre, reaches the apparent hopelessness of 'wait without hope' and 'wait without love'; only, however, to pick up the subdued implication in 'wait' that there is, in fact, something to wait for ('But the faith and the love and the hope are all in the waiting') and point to the conversion of 'darkness' and 'stillness' into 'light' and 'dancing'. Hints of the child's garden vision of plenitude which had been evoked at the beginning of 'Burnt Norton' ('laughter in the garden, echoed ecstasy') then lead into a passage translated from St John of the Cross which makes it didactically explicit that deprivation, 'the way of dispossession', is also the way to spiritual enlightenment.

This forging of a connection between the contemporary and the past, of present-day secular emptiness with traditional religious mysticism, contrasts with the major technique in *The Waste Land* of ironic juxtaposition (though there is a minor, complementary theme in *The Waste Land* of 'fragments' being 'shored' against the poet's 'ruins' which is capable of being interpreted as an anticipation of what is done in *Four Quartets*). Similarly, there is a corresponding shift in the language of *Four Quartets* from Imagist disintegration to something which is much more in accord with traditional state-ment, argument and syntactical closure. As already suggested, this is not complete; the modernist fragmentariness continues, along with the modernist urban world. But commerce between the two, however tentative, is now affirmed. And at the same time Eliot, while subordinating individuality to faith and the Church, allows himself to be more explicitly personal than ever before. In one of the finest passages of the sequence – the Dantesque *terza rima* lines of 'Little Gidding' II, where, as dawn breaks after an all-night air raid on wartime London, he encounters 'a familiar compound ghost' – Eliot employs a simple directness of statement which, des-pite being put into the mouth of his interlocutor, amounts to a powerful and moving confession of private sinfulness, climaxing in 'the rending pain of re-enactment / Of all that you have done, and been'.

There is intensely personal feeling in these lines. But, again, private merges with public as, in words adapted, appropriately enough, from Johnson's *The Vanity of Human Wishes*, the individual experience is generalised: 'Then fools' approval stings, and honour stains.' The fire of personal torment blends with the fires of the blitz to become potentially a 'refining fire' (recalling that into which Arnaut Daniel flings himself in Dante's *Purgatorio*, quoted by Eliot towards the end of *The Waste Land*). This, in turn, takes up the fire motif which recurs throughout *Four Quartets*, but is especially the motif of 'Little Gidding', to modulate via the fire lyric of Section IV into the concluding mystic fire of the whole sequence in which 'the fire and the rose' are envisioned as becoming 'one'.

It is thus not too fanciful to see *Four Quartets* as Eliot's attempted reconciliation, not only of himself with the Anglican Church, but also of his own modernist crusade with the traditional elements which it paradoxically at once broke with and affirmed. The splintered discourse – which alienated and bewildered some of his original readers, while others welcomed it as a distinctive, and liberatingly appropriate, form for the twentieth century – remains, but as something which he subordinates to, and attempts to merge with, a more conventional language of religious orthodoxy. The result is a curious blend of the old and the new which, though it is no more a model for subsequent poets to imitate than *The Waste Land*, combines the two broadly divergent trends of modern English poetry.

WILLIAM CARLOS WILLIAMS (1883–1963)

With William Carlos Williams it is a different story. There are obscurities in his work; *Paterson*, in particular, is a long modernist poem to be set beside *The Waste Land* and Pound's *Cantos* as an allusive and elliptical work requiring careful reading and re-reading and a good deal of elucidatory commentary. But in general Williams is a much more accessible poet. He might even, without stretching the comparison too far, be regarded as a twentieth-century Wordsworth speaking to his fellow man (and, in Williams's case, emphatically his fellow woman also) of common human experience in the language commonly used by ordinary people. The other predecessor who inevitably comes to mind is Walt Whitman – like Whitman he is a democratic poet, and very much a poet of the American consciousness. He is well aware of the stance taken by his fellow American modernists, Eliot and Pound (and, indeed, he was a life-long friend of the latter), but he rejects their insistence on the need for the modern poet to recognise and situate himself in the European tradition. Though scarcely an 'isolationist' in the political sense, he is much more critical of the Old World and more eagerly intent on finding a voice appropriate to the New. And compared with Eliot, in particular, he is both less learnedly academic and less afflicted by a sense of the raw, uncultivated state of American culture. He is also less steeped in the New England consciousness of the ingrained sinfulness of man, and much less dependent on either a cultural or religious centre of authority. He responds instead to the spirit of the frontier, and to the openness and confidence in man's innate abilities and worth which make America seem a land of possibilities in contrast to the established rules and routine of Europe.

In an early poem, 'The Wanderer' (1914), crossing on the ferry from New Jersey to New York Williams finds himself posing the question, 'How shall I be a mirror to this modernity?' It is the actual American world around him which he is determined to reflect. He is a patriotic poet, but with a patriotism which defies conventional notions – no jingoistic waver of 'the star-spangled banner', but a compassionate observer of things as they are, including poverty and deprivation. Thus in one of several poems ironically entitled 'Pastoral' (1917) he contrasts his youthful ambition to 'make something' of himself with his willingness now to wander through humble back streets and even admire poverty-stricken houses which have ill-aligned roofs and junk-like 'yards' (in English usage 'gardens') in which chicken wire and ashes mingle with 'furniture gone wrong'.

'No one', Williams concludes, 'will / believe this / of vast import to the nation.' Which in the obvious sense is true, though for Williams it is a way of asserting the import of things that are unjustly neglected. Unlike T. S. Eliot, whose 'Preludes', for example, focus on similar details drawn from decaying urban life, Williams also finds something to admire in superficially ugly material. In this respect he has more in common with Thomas Hardy, who in the opening chapter of *The Return of the Native* suggests that 'haggard' Egdon Heath appeals 'to a subtler and scarcer instinct, to a more recently learnt emotion, than that which responds to the sort of beauty called charming and fair'. His newness and modernity involve a newness of vision.

However, Williams's 'visionary' poetry is the result, not of millennial transformation, but of defamiliarisation of the commonplace – though there are occasional pieces, like 'Overture to a Dance of Locomotives' (1921), which suggest a somewhat willed attempt, in the manner of the Italian Futurists and subsequent 'pylon' poets of the Thirties, to glorify modern technology. Well-known, and much anthologised, poems such as 'The Red Wheelbarrow' (1923) and 'This Is Just to Say' (1934) are examples of commonplace material – commonplace almost to the point of seeming trite – which is presented in such a way as to compel new attention. The distinction between 'prose' and 'poetry' is virtually eradicated, at least as far as subject-matter is concerned. Nothing is banal in itself, but only as it is seen, with or without awareness of its unique, independent existence: 'so much depends / upon / a red wheel / barrow'.

'Complete Destruction' (1921) illustrates the discovery of beauty in ugliness, and significance in the seemingly banal, particularly well. It records the destruction of a dead cat on 'an icy day' by burying it and then burning its box. Getting rid of a cat in such a way would seem to be no great matter; in this poem, however, it is not any cat, but '*the* cat', and it is, implicitly at least, precious to an intimate group designated as 'We'. The language accords it the dignity of a proper burial, and the burning of the box perhaps suggests a funeral pyre. There are other suggestions, too, of tradition – and, more particularly, human tradition – in the burial of the cat. The coldness of the weather, for example, hints at the use of the pathetic fallacy in pastoral elegy, which makes nature sympathise with human grief. The actual burning of the box effects a transition to the opposite condition of heat, with the slightest possible overtone of an act of purification by fire as fleas are driven from the box. In the final lines it is stated that those fleas which escaped death by 'earth' or 'fire' succumbed to 'the cold', and in this way three of the four elements are evoked and associated in the destruction of the cat. Thus, trivial as the poem's subject nominally is (and at no point does Williams make it sound pompous or pretentious), basic powers of nature seem to become involved: a commonplace act of common-sense cleansing seems to exemplify a profoundly traditional ritual.

This placing of the familiar in the foreground, but with overtones of something more radical and universal, is a cardinal feature of Williams's work: 'no ideas but in things' is a repeated slogan of his which sums up his inheritance from the Imagists and his insistence on the need to see the universal as inherent in the local and particular. His poetry requires its surface to be looked at, with a sense of wider significance implicit in it, and not, as in the symbolist tradition, to be read as a hieroglyph for transcendent meanings. Similarly important – especially so for the influence which it exerts on subsequent poetry – is the exact appearance of the poem on the printed page and the clues which this affords to its rhythmical structure. The enjambement in lines 4–5 of 'Complete Destruction' bridges the two stanzas, allowing both a separation of cat in stanza 1 from fleas in stanza 2, and a unification of them in one elemental process. In addition, though the movement and diction are those of ordinary speech, the formal arrangement heightens the two-beat rhythm and the circular structure, from cold to fire and back to cold.

In his later work Williams becomes even more deliberately experimental in his approach to enjambement, which he couples with unusual typography and minimal use of punctuation to create a controlled subversion of normal syntactical expectations. This aspect of Williams's poetry has been illuminatingly analysed by Stephen Cushman in his study of *William Carlos Williams and the Meanings of Measure*.[4] While sceptical of Williams's claim to have invented a new metric concept of the 'variable foot' (in practice, the freedoms he takes are not fundamentally different from those employed by the Jacobean dramatists or Gerard Manley Hopkins), Cushman reveals how effective Williams can be in liberating the possibilities of meaning by playing spatial arrangement off against speech units, lineation against syntax. There is a danger of the poetry becoming prose arbitrarily chopped up into lines of 'verse' – a danger which Williams does not always avoid; but when sensitively used the technique can be valuable as a way of defeating habit-formed responses and creating a fruitful ambivalence of meaning.

An example is the opening of 'Song' (from *Pictures from Brueghel*, 1962):

> you are forever April
> to me
> the eternally unready

forsythia a blond
straight-
legged girl

whom I myself
ignorant
as I was taught

to read the poems

(*Collected Poems*, II, 406)

In the context of lines 1–3 'the eternally unready' can be read either with reference back to the anonymous 'you' to whom the poem is addressed (the speaker's daughter?) or to 'me', i.e. the speaker himself. As one reads on to line 4, jumping the visual gap which separates the lines into stanzas, one makes a hasty re-adjustment to read 'unready' as a pre-modifier of 'forsythia', which in turn re-affirms the phrase as applicable to the girl – but without totally excluding its applicability to 'me', slightly absurd though that reading might seem. The remainder of stanza 2 is most likely a further extension of what the girl seems to be to the speaker, especially as it is more straightforwardly descriptive of her appearance; but, again, because of the lineation the possibility of its being a metaphor in apposition to 'forsythia' cannot be ignored. The two subordinate clauses which constitute lines 7–10 have the primary, or 'prose', sense of 'whom I myself, ignorant as I was, taught to read the poems' (but what poems? one wonders). Absence of punctuation, however, and the fact that separate lines are accorded to 'ignorant' and 'as I was taught', make it initially seem as if 'I was taught' is in the passive voice, and not until one has again jumped the stanza gap does the 'prose' meaning cancel that out.

None of this is clumsiness on Williams's part. The remainder of 'Song' gradually makes it apparent that the poem is an elegy for the lost forsythia-like girl ('a burst of frost / nipped / yellow flowers / in the spring / of / the year'), but also that the speaker was/is emotionally entangled with the girl to the point where his devotion to her almost seems to exceed normal bounds. The result is a degree of empathy which makes the flower an appropriate figure for both. It expresses love for the girl, but also hints at a self-critical awareness on the part of the speaker that his own attitude is immature. The girl, lost to him before her prime, remains 'forever

April' in his imagination, and so 'the eternally unready / forsythia'; but he himself also shares, at least subliminally, in that immaturity. If there is a tendency towards sentimentality or self-pity in the poem, the tendency is in this way also countered, if not entirely excluded. A complex of emotions is the more effectively communicated by virtue of the ambivalence built into the poem by its tactfully contrived structural and syntactical peculiarities.

Perhaps Williams's most successful poems are the short lyrics in which his seemingly bizarre lineation proves to be a highly effective means of achieving that defamiliarisation essential to modernism. He felt, however, that what he had to say was inadequately communicated by such poems, and that he needed the space and gravitas of the long poem to give his varied insights coherent expression. And yet, like other practitioners of the extended modernist poem, he could not accept traditional epic form. The result, in *Paterson*, is a four-Book poem (though a fifth was added in 1958, and fragments of a sixth also exist) which combines a narrative of 'loose juxtaposition', as Benjamin Sankey calls it,[5] with interpolated fragments of poetry and prose, somewhat uncertainly held together by a pattern of symbolism and *leit-motivs*. Like *The Waste Land* and *Ulysses* it is made distinctively of its age by being focused on the modern industrial and commercial city. But unlike Eliot's London, Williams's Paterson is not an 'unreal city'; it has the energy and strength of a personified male figure. Moreover, the counterbalancing female is not merely an exploited and polluted victim of the male, but, as is Joyce's Molly Bloom, a source of abundant fertility. Although Williams is a traditionalist in his treatment of the relation between male and female in terms of active and passive, this is subsumed within a symbolic relationship between the poet and his subject-matter which has its roots in the belief in the creative powers of the imagination held by Romantic writers such as Wordsworth and Coleridge, modified by Jung's notion of the interdependence of the male and female principles in the human psyche as such. Local and historical detail is likewise important: characters and events from Williams's own New Jersey anchor the poem in exact time and place, and the current of the River Passaic, above and below its Falls, provides a unifying metaphor for the flow of life itself.

However, Williams's poetry is unsympathetic to the integrative and culturally representative functions of epic. Both its fragmentary, Imagist origins and its anti-authoritarian bias are more appropriate to a poetry of Opposition rather than Government. The poet of *Paterson* mistrusts not only the past, but also his own influence in the present. Book Three, which takes place in 'The Library', is ultimately a rejection of literature conceived as a garnering of wisdom and tradition: 'all that is put down, once it escapes, may rot its way into a thousand minds, the corn become a black smut, and all libraries, of necessity, be burned to the ground as a consequence'. To this there is 'Only one answer: write carelessly so that nothing that is not green will survive' (Book Three, III, 129). The language of *Paterson* is accordingly spontaneous and fragmentary, kaleidoscopically changeable and multi-tonal, deliberately resistant to the harmony and comprehensiveness to which epic aspires. It is characteristic that even the planned structure, which was to carry the poem in four Books down the Passaic, over its Falls, and into the final sea of death, was subverted by the later but unfinished addition of further Books. It is poetry which by its nature is open-ended – an epic innately incompatible with the traditional inclusiveness and closure of epic.

WALLACE STEVENS (1879–1955)

Wallace Stevens is not so self-evidently modernist. He has some of the accepted features of modernism, particularly its aesthetic aloofness and unwillingness to make concessions to the common reader, resulting in almost intimidatory difficulty, but he is equally to be seen as belonging in the direct line of the English Romantics and the French Symbolists. Recent critics have also seen him as a precursor of post-modernism and as an influence on such poets as A. R. Ammons, Robert Duncan, Robert Kelly, John Berryman, John Ashbery, James Merrill and Michael Palmer, who, like him, seek 'to dramatize the mind in its speculative acts'.[6]

Stevens's debt to the Romantics and Symbolists is to be seen most clearly in his recurrent emphasis on the imagination as the means by which man engages with reality, but also as that which creates it for him. Its work is the creation of a world which is a 'supreme fiction' existing in the poem that embodies it. Just as the Coleridgeian imagination breaks down the appearances of things, resolving them into their original chaos, in order to re-create them with newness and unsullied freshness, so the poet in Stevens's 'Notes Toward a Supreme Fiction' must 'become an ignorant man again / And see the sun again with an ignorant eye' in order to create an 'invented world' which is simultaneously a poem that 'refreshes life'.

Paradoxically, however, the world so created seems to the uninitiated eye – like a modernist painting – a distortion rather than an imitation of 'things as they are'. In the Picasso-like poem 'The Man with the Blue Guitar', the poet is caught up in a slightly hostile dialogue with his audience: they complain that he does not 'play things as they are', he answers that 'Things as they are / Are changed upon the blue guitar', and they reply,

> But play, you must,
> A tune beyond us, yet ourselves.

In so far as the audience want a Wordsworthian heightening and enhancing of recognisable reality, this is perhaps where Stevens and the Romantics part company. He becomes more allied to the Symbolists, creating poetry which is not so much a renewed apprehension of the external world (even if in the interest of 'the mind of man') as an interior world of its own, with language that is connotative rather than denotative, conjuring up evocative associations, and with sounds and rhythms that aspire to the condition of music – as in 'The Idea of Order at Key West', where the imaginative principle (now feminine) 'was the single artificer of the world / In which she sang'.

Such an art releases the imagination not to indulge in 'art for art's sake' (though it has to be admitted that Stevens does have something in common with late ninteenth-century aestheticism), but to exercise its powers in a free play of activity which can be humorously bizarre, as in 'Bantams in Pine-Woods' ('Chieftain Iffucan of Azcan in caftan / Of tan with henna hackles, halt!'); or a verbal equivalent of a musical themes-and-variations, as in 'Thirteen Ways of Looking at a Blackbird'; or more quietly order-creating, as in 'Anecdote of the Jar'. In the latter poem the placing of a jar – itself a ceramic work of art – in 'the slovenly wilderness' of a Tennessee landscape endows that which was previously anonymous and insignificant with the significance and distinction of a work of art. The jar itself is very little characterised: it is not highly colourful, but 'gray and bare'; and if it seems to have a certain grace and dignity ('tall and of a port in air', where the curious word 'port' is more evocative than descriptive), that is after it has taken its 'dominion' in the landscape, and seems to derive from its ordering principle. The anecdote thus functions as a kind of allegory for the way art as such works: it is the mind entering into the landscape and giving it a mental reality without which it is, in effect, undifferentiated non-reality.

'Anecdote of the Jar' is thus a poem about poetry. This is also the theme of a large proportion of Stevens's work, and especially of his longer meditative poems such as 'The Idea of Order at Key West', 'The Man with the Blue Guitar', 'Notes toward a Supreme Ficton', 'Credences of Summer' and 'Owl's Clover'. Together with such longer pieces as 'Chocorua to its Neighbor' and 'Esthetique du Mal', these can be somewhat loosely termed 'philosophical/ discursive' poems, and to that extent may be related to the alternative discursive tradition of twentieth-century poetry in English (and largely British poetry) to be discussed in the following chapter. But the discursiveness is rarely a matter of strictly sequential discourse, and even less of argument, despite the not infrequent occurrence of passages of logical discrimination and refinement of meanings. Stevens himself declared that 'It is the *mundo* [world] of the imagination in which the imaginative man delights and not the gaunt world of reason;[7] and in 'Owl's Clover' he rejects with weariness 'the man that thinks' in favour of 'The man below' who uses his imagination and (with a palpable Keatsian echo) finds what he imagines to be true.[8]

Such statements place Stevens firmly in the modernist camp with its reaction against rational excess – that 'mental consciousness' which D. H. Lawrence believed to be overdeveloped in the Christian West at the expense of intuition and instinct, or 'blood consciousness'. There are moments, indeed, when Stevens sounds very like Lawrence, or the Stravinsky of *The Rite of Spring*, celebrating primitive consciousness and knowledge in the 'blood' as a redemptive power in contrast to the self-denying, spiritualised sacrifice of Christian religion:

> Supple and turbulent, a ring of men
> Shall chant in orgy on a summer morn
> Their boisterous devotion to the sun,
> Not as a god, but as a god might be,
> Naked among them, like a savage source.

> ('Sunday Morning')

Yet the note of primitive abandon is only incidental in Stevens. His reaction against 'the gaunt world of reason' is in the direction of a subtilising transcendence of reason rather than a rejection; it implies a modification of consciousness intended to make it responsive to refinements and nuances of awareness beyond those available to rational discourse, but none the less on the level of 'mental consciousness'.

This is the kind of awareness envisaged by Stevens in his manifesto (albeit one that eschews the stridencies of a manifesto as such) 'Of Modern Poetry'. His opening is a tentative definition of the modernity of the modern poem: 'The poem of the mind in the act of finding / What will suffice'. The subtext of 'finding / What will suffice' is that there is in the modern world a need to search for a ground of sufficiency which was not always felt in the past, for 'the scene was set' and the actor had only to echo what was in his script. This theatrical metaphor then provides Stevens with an instrument for discriminating between the situations in which the poets of the past and the present find themselves. The rational and religious framework which existed for the poet of the past has now been 'changed / To something else', but what the new something is is itself unknown to the poet of the present. In hermeneutic fashion he has to discover it as he feels his way forward, learning 'the speech of the place', facing the men and the women of the time, and thinking about war. A new stage has to be constructed, and the new poem has 'to be on that stage' like an actor rehearsing a part which is communicated to him from within his own mind, and which is heard by 'an invisible audience' with the sense that it, too, is listening to itself. Then, adding to the theatrical image his favourite image of the poet as guitar-playing musician, the actor becomes

> A metaphysician in the dark, twanging
> An instrument, twanging a wiry string that gives
> Sounds passing through sudden rightnesses, wholly
> Containing the mind, below which it cannot descend,
> Beyond which it has no will to rise.

There is no finality here, no arrived-at goal. What are caught (if 'caught' is the right word) are sounds *en passant*, 'passing through', which become surprising, unexpected (Stevens surely employs the archaic overtones of 'sudden'?) 'rightnesses', but still essentially of the mental consciousness – neither below, nor above it. It is an open question whether this describes what Stevens achieves in his own poetry or whether it merely projects what he feels modern poetry should be. But in the speculations of his poetry there is an open-endedness of discourse and a fluency of verbal technique which seem to point towards such an achievement. In the earlier verse, as Michael Davidson expresses it, 'His images are seldom tied to single objects or landscapes but tend to fracture, exfoliate, reform like the clouds that endlessly populate his poems.'[9] In the later, as Stevens himself expresses it in Section V of 'An Ordinary Evening in New Haven', 'The poem is the cry of its occasion.' The poem is not freighted with the past, but immerses itself in the process of the present to capture 'the reverberation / Of a windy night as it is' – the phrasing reminiscent of Eliot's in 'Rhapsody on a Windy Night', but modified to detach it from the moral colouring given to the city-scape in Eliot's poem. For Stevens the business of the poetry is to synthesise the windy night and the registering consciousness in its own verbal medium:

> The mobile and the immobile flickering
> In the area between is and was are leaves,
> Leaves burnished in autumnal burnished trees
>
> And leaves in whirlings in the gutters, whirlings
> Around and away, resembling the presence of thought,
> Resembling the presences of thoughts, as if,
>
> In the end, in the whole psychology, the self,
> The town, the weather, in a casual litter,
> Together, said words of the world are the life of the world.

The repetitions, with slight variations, the choice of restless words like 'flickering' and 'whirlings', the risks of bathos taken in a phrase like 'casual litter' and the play on 'words' and 'world' (again recalling Eliot, but with a difference) – all suggest language as a medium for the wavering variableness of consciousness. And this perhaps is Stevens's most characteristic achievement: the fashioning of a style adequate to his own modernist conception of the poem as 'the act of the mind'.

TWO VERSIONS OF MODERNISM

Modernism takes its departure from dissatisfaction with 'a worn-out poetical fashion'.[10] It seeks to make a conscious adjustment of the relationship between the old and the new. But modernist writers are not uniform in the way they make this adjustment. Broadly speaking, they fall into two different categories. Ezra Pound and T. S. Eliot 'make it new' by going back to a past in which they find a cultural unity and a sustaining faith which, for them, are cripplingly absent from the contemporary world. Through recondite allusiveness and an Imagist-inspired technique of juxtaposition and fragmentation their work suggests both the wholeness that has been lost and the condition of uncertainty and disconnectedness which such loss has inflicted on the present. Ironically, this brand of modernism, which seemed so revolutionary and iconoclastic in its day, has acquired for many late twentieth-century readers a somewhat reactionary air. It is seen as socially élitist, politically conservative and backward-looking in its religious thought. And there is evidence to support this: Pound, for example, allied himself with the Italian fascism of Mussolini, and Eliot declared himself (in 1928) as 'classicist in literature, royalist in politics, and anglo-catholic in religion'.[11] What matters more than such particular allegiances, however, is the kind of poetry that resulted; and this, though difficult and exacting, was more fluid and flexible than the word 'reactionary' might suggest. For example, the bridging of the gap between verse and prose by adopting more dramatic voices, and more freely colloquial diction and rhythms, helped to bring verse down off its authoritarian stilts. As Pound wrote in his partly self-mocking 'epitaph', 'E. P. Ode Pour L'Election de Son Sépulcre', instead of the effort 'to maintain "the sublime" / In the old sense' what the age demanded was

> an image
> Of its accelerated grimace,
> Something for the modern stage,
> Not, at any rate, an Attic grace.

If the voice in these lines is jeeringly conservative, it also has a significantly anti-conservative undertone, conveying a sense that old values and old postures cannot be restored. Moreover, if it is neither 'accelerated grimace' nor 'Attic grace' that the Pound/ Eliot variety of modernism has to offer, one must surely concede that a strangely new, barbaric beauty is created in *The Waste Land* (comparable to the dissonant raptures of Stravinsky's music in *The Rite of Spring*); and that in certain passages of the *Cantos* and Eliot's *Four Quartets*, the language does achieve that 'easy commerce of the old and the new' which marks a successful reconciliation of an ideal past and the real present.

William Carlos Williams and Wallace Stevens represent a more optimistic kind of modernism. They, too, break up accepted forms and at times expose themselves to the charge of wilful obscurity. But their trust in the free play of the mind and greater willingness to accept the sensuous pleasures of life contrast strongly with the scepticism of Eliot and Pound. Stevens, perhaps more than Williams, can be intellectually austere; and his dedication to the notion of poetry as a self-reflexive, autonomous whole can make him at times seem like a highly sophisticated, twentieth-century version of the aesthetic dandy. Nevertheless, his intelligence and wit, and the exuberance of his imagination, enable him to shrug off deference and servility to the past. For him 'words of the world are the life of the world'; they are man-made and create a worldliness which is hopeful and humane. Williams is less academic, more obviously Whitmanesque, democratic and self-consciously American. The obscurity he risks has less to do with recondite allusion or intellectual complexity than with the originality of his verse technique. His presentation of ordinary things in language that is disconcertingly different from the norm, both syntactically and in its seemingly bizarre lineation, is a strange experience for the reader. It compels a re-assessment of the commonplace and revaluation of what has become clichéd. As such, like the very different approach adopted in Stevens's poetry, it constitutes a playing on the modernist imagination's 'blue guitar' of a tune which is 'beyond us, yet ourselves', and one which gives a refreshingly novel view of 'things exactly as they are'.

3

An Alternative Tradition: Hardy, Housman, Frost, Kipling and Graves

THOMAS HARDY (1840–1928)

If Pound, Eliot, Williams and Stevens are names which immediately spring to mind when one thinks of early modern poetry, they are certainly not the only ones. Hardy, Housman, Frost, Kipling and Graves are equally prominent. The first quartet is American – though Eliot became a naturalised British citizen; the second English – with the exception of Frost (whose first volume of verse nevertheless was published in England). Though national consciousness probably has little to do with it (even where Kipling is concerned), the 'English' quartet differs from the American in being far less self-consciously modernist, more readily to be seen as continuing, rather than making a deliberately sharp break with, nineteenth-century practices. In particular, they are much more willing to retain the formally correct syntax that poetry had hitherto shared with prose, their verse is more likely to 'scan', and their allusiveness, when they employ it as a technique, is more likely to be self-explanatory – or at least not so essential to the overall meaning of the poem that annotation becomes indispensable to its understanding. To this extent they are easier than the poets of the previous chapter, with whom 'the fascination of what's difficult' (though that is a Yeatsian phrase) seems at times to become almost an obsession, and they hit the reader less frequently with a deliberately cultivated shock of the new.

None of this, however, should be taken as implying unquestioning conformity. Often enough the elements of nineteenth-century tradition which these poets sought to follow, and develop, were in themselves at odds with conventional expectations. Kipling, for example, is by no means so much the voice of the British Empire establishment as he is often assumed to be, nor is Hardy a euphonious and metrically smooth poet in the Tennysonian style of 'The Lady of Shalott'. Hardy, in fact, belongs to the tradition of Browning and Clough, in the sense both that his poetry is more often than not 'dramatic', i.e. he speaks through an adopted voice instead of committing himself to purely personal expression, and that his metre is often characterised by a studied irregularity. The latter, which he dubbed 'the Gothic art-principle' and associated with his training as an architect, was misunderstood by some of his critics, and occasioned the following self-defensive explanation in *The Life of Thomas Hardy*:

> In the reception of [*Wessex Poems*] and later volumes of Hardy's poems there was, he said, as regards form, the inevitable ascription to ignorance of what was really choice after full knowledge. That the author loved the art of concealing art was undiscerned. For instance, as to rhythm. Years earlier he had decided that too regular a beat was bad art. ... He knew that in architecture cunning irregularity is of enormous worth, and it is obvious that he carried on into his verse, perhaps in part unconsciously, the Gothic art-principle in which he had been trained – the principle of spontaneity, found in mouldings, tracery, and such like – resulting in the 'unforeseen' (as it has been called) character of his metres and stanzas, that of stress rather than of syllable, poetic texture rather than poetic veneer; the latter kind of thing, under the name of 'constructed ornament', being what he, in common with every Gothic student, had been taught to avoid as the plague. He shaped his poetry accordingly, introducing metrical pauses, and reversed beats; and found for his trouble that some particular line of a poem exemplifying this principle was greeted with a would-be jocular remark that such a line 'did not make for immortality'.[1]

Dennis Taylor has shown how these remarks connect with avant-garde Victorian prosodic theory as developed by Ruskin and Coventry Patmore, and continued by R. L. Stevenson and Robert Bridges.[2] Gerard Manley Hopkins's 'sprung rhythm' develops the implications of such theorising to a greater degree, and with his concentrated and highly innovative treatment of language produces something much more radically modern than Hardy. His roots, however, are in the same tradition.

If Eliot's work has become the prime example of modernism in poetry, Hardy's poetry has become the standard for that alternative tradition which is distinctively modern, but keeps its connection with rational discourse. This is the tradition which reaches forward, as Samuel Hynes has argued in his important essay, 'The Hardy Tradition in Modern English Poetry', through writers such as Robert Frost, Edward Thomas and Robert Graves to Philip Larkin.[3] It is marked by meticulous craftsmanship and close attention to the demands of paraphraseable sense. As with all good poetry, the resulting achievement is something which transcends the meaning that can be paraphrased, but the drive through carefully controlled syntax to a rounding out of rational statement is a vital part of poetry which belongs to this tradition. Larkin perhaps felt this when, as he records in his 1965 Introduction to *The North Ship*, he began reading 'the little blue *Chosen Poems of Thomas Hardy*', which was by his bedside:

> Hardy I knew as a novelist, but as regards his verse I shared Lytton Strachey's verdict that 'the gloom is not even relieved by a little elegance of diction'. This opinion did not last long; if I were asked to date its disappearance, I should guess it was the morning I first read 'Thoughts of Phena At News of Her Death'.

Strachey, in fact, was a little more perceptive than Larkin gives him credit for. Although he wrote disparagingly of the 'ugly and cumbrous expressions, clumsy metres, and flat, prosaic turns of speech' in Hardy's verse, he also recognised that by means of these supposed 'blemishes' Hardy 'brought the realism and sobriety of prose into the service of his poetry'[4] – the effect of which, as in the poetry of Browning, is to counter any effect of over-easy sentiment, and to compel instead a more thoughtful attention to structure and argument. With 'Thoughts of Phena' in particular, lyrical tenderness is kept under firm control (which is not to say that it is suppressed – on the contrary its emotional power is enhanced) by scrupulous attention to syntax and stanzaic form.

This structure is worth looking at in some detail:

> Not a line of her writing have I,
> Not a thread of her hair,
> No mark of her late time as dame in her dwelling, whereby
> I may picture her there;

And in vain do I urge my unsight
        To conceive my lost prize
At her close, whom I knew when her dreams were
    upbrimming with light,
        And with laughter her eyes.

    What scenes spread around her last days,
        Sad, shining, or dim?
Did her gifts and compassions enray and enarch her sweet ways
        With an aureate nimb?
    Or did life-light decline from her years,
        And mischances control
Her full day-star; unease, or regret, or forebodings, or fears
        Disennoble her soul?

    Thus I do but the phantom retain
        Of the maiden of yore
As my relic; yet haply the best of her – fined in my brain
        It may be the more
    That no line of her writing have I,
        Nor a thread of her hair,
No mark of her late time as dame in her dwelling, whereby
        I may picture her there.

The first stanza regretfully records the one-time lover's lack of any memento of his one-time love: 'Not a line of her writing have I'. The rise and fall of feeling is mirrored in the fluctuating line-lengths of the eight-lined stanza. These change from three feet, to two, to five, and back to two, in the first four lines; and then the same sequence is followed in the second four, with the ABAB CDCD rhymes emphasising the four-line division. At the same time the syntax is played off against this pattern: a series of negatives ('Not a line ...', 'Not a thread ...', 'No mark ...') climaxes in the fourth line with the lover's inability to 'picture' Phena, while the next line begins with the statement 'And in vain do I urge my unsight', which is expanded throughout the remaining three lines to come to rest on an idealised image of his love in the past, 'when her dreams were upbrimming with light, / And with laughter her eyes.' The second stanza poses three questions, the first two occupying two lines each, and the third four lines – varying the two-part division of the first stanza with a three-part division.

But even though question 1 opens up the possibility that Phena's last days may have been either happy or unhappy, question 2 elaborates the idea of happiness in the two lines which remain of the previous four-line division, while the next four lines via their distressfully cumulative syntax pile on the idea of unhappiness and mount finally to the striking neologism of '*Disennoble* her soul'. In the third stanza the two-part structure seems to be retained, but to be divided unequally into two lines plus the extra bit, 'As my relic', required to complete the statement that the lover retains only 'the phantom' of his love, and the much longer remainder which counters this by suggesting that 'the phantom' is nevertheless 'the best of her' because it lives unaided in his memory. Yet 'Gothic' irregularity is balanced by the re-assertion of regularity, in that the last four lines constitute a distinct unit in themselves, and are, in fact, almost word for word a repetition of the poem's opening lines. These lines also bring the poem full circle. In its end is its beginning. But the repetition is made with a significant difference: the contours of feeling have been carefully matched to the progress of the argument to convert deprivation into affirmation and gain.

Much else is 'Gothic' in this poem. Though the metre is basically anapaestic, it never sounds merely trippingly so. Its irregularities see to that; in a distinctively modern way they balance the accents of ordinary speech against the formal, dance-like movement of the metre. The adroitly directed enjambements similarly disguise, without breaking up, the pattern of the stanza, and are capable of creating (as they do, for example, in the double enjambement which completes stanza 2) an almost Metaphysical-style conjunction of opposites. The diction, too, contributes to this effect: plain, monosyllabic language rubs shoulders with the more latinate 'aureate nimb' and the compounds, 'life-light' and 'day-star'; while a scattering of neologisms, or at least archaic, or rare, forms – 'unsight', 'upbrimming', and the already mentioned 'Disennoble' – fall like discords in a piece of music, which, though distinctly jarring, are yet absorbed into the strange new harmony of the whole.

The combined result of these effects (which this analysis by no means exhausts) is to create a tone that is curiously elusive. The poem skates round sentimentality, keeping its tenderness, but grimly aware of change and decay. The sadness of missed opportunity which can now never recur, and the potential tragedy of promise destroyed, make themselves felt, and yet, as Larkin insists, do not warrant Strachey's 'gloom'. On the other hand, the consolation refined in the speaker's brain does not quite register as compensation for what is lost, and, like so much else in the poem, is only ('It may be ⋯') tentatively affirmed. And, close though the poem is to private confession, realism and the true voice of feeling, its artificiality – in the Elizabethan, non-derogatory sense – is subtly underlined by rhyme, structure, and even its very appearance on the printed page. In this sense it is relieved by considerably more than 'a little elegance of diction'. Such complexity, though entirely aloof from modernist 'difficulty' makes it just as much a modern poem as anything by Eliot or Stevens – just as much the product of a world in which emotional and intellectual orientation is uncertain, and in which the personal voice, though still introspectively trying to find itself, is projected on to a dramatically realised 'I' and a scrupulously shaped form.

Interaction between the past and the present adds yet a further dimension, and one very characteristic of Hardy. Many of the 'Poems of 1912–13', written after the death of his first wife, Emma (on 27 November 1912), are conceived in terms of this interaction. As in 'Thoughts of Phena', the death of a loved one transports the lover (uniquely, however, in these poems a widower of 72) back in time to the period of their courtship, re-creating the past, but always seeing it from the vantage of the present, and with the present reality incorporated in the poem as much as the distance-enchanted view which it gives of the past. 'After a Journey', 'Beeny Cliff', 'St Launce's Revisited', 'A Dream or No' and 'At Castle Boterel' relate to the actual journey which Hardy made in March 1913 to revisit the scenes of his courtship of Emma. The Cornish landscape 'seems to call out to [him] from forty years ago', and yet the speaker remains part of the present, no more than a 'thin ghost' who can only 'fraily follow' the beckoning of the idealised figure from the past. The tone may be plangently romantic, as it is at the opening of 'The Voice' (a poem written in the previous December), but the illusion of spring-time love regained is brittle. It is a projected figment of the imagination, subject to doubt even as it is evoked ('Can it be you ...?' 'Or is it only the breeze ...?'), and leaving the lover, in an often-praised transition from the at first urgently pressing rhythm to one that is designedly stumbling and 'faltering', with the need to face the blankness of a wintry present. And with still more complex interaction in 'At Castle Boterel' the recall of 'Myself and a girlish form benighted / In dry March weather' is made to alternate with the pilgrim lover's present-day journey as 'the drizzle bedrenches the waggonette'. Love is strongly affirmed against reason, and human values still more strongly against the 'primaeval' land-scape and 'Time's unflinching rigour' which 'In mindless rote, has ruled from sight / The substance now'. But the subtly noted effect of time on the speaker, and the 'shrinking, shrinking' of his loved one in the final stanza qualify the reader's overall response and keep him aware that the poem belongs unmoveably to the here and now of 'March 1913'.

Other poems of the sequence ('The Phantom Horsewoman', 'The Spell of the Rose', 'His Visitor', and – not strictly belonging to the sequence, but clearly related emotionally – 'Under the Waterfall') project the woman's rather than the lover's point of view, and further heighten the impression of his modernity. Although they do not explicitly deal with 'the woman question' as such, they locate the deep emotional responses of a particular woman in a sharply realised domestic setting. In 'His Visitor', for example, the speaker (again a ghostly version of the dead Emma) does not wish to return to haunt the house she once shared with her husband, since every-thing known and familiar to her has been changed. The recording of these details creates a poem in which feeling is attached to commonplace things, and yet, paradoxically, is more effective as poetry for doing so. The opposition between what is 'prosaic' and what is 'poetic' seems to be abolished; the two come together in a new, and more convincing, relationship.

The span of Hardy's vision is remarkable; he is equally effective in close-up and at long-range. His long epic drama *The Dynasts* clearly illustrates this, with its sweeping stage-directions (desig-nated 'cinematic' by John Wain) on the one hand, and its idiosyn-cratic mole's-eye view of the battlefield of Waterloo, on the other.[5] The equivalent among the lyric poems is to be found, for example, in the majestic remoteness of 'The Convergence of the Twain' and the democratic immediacy of 'An August Midnight'. Yet close-up and distance also interact with each other. The Titanic's predestined encounter with the iceberg which sinks her becomes an ironic 'consummation', the result of which, lying on the Atlantic oceanbed, is seen in weird specificity by 'sea-worm' and 'dim moon-eyed fishes'; and in 'An August Midnight' the concrete simplicity of 'A longlegs, a moth, and a dumbledore', which share the scene with the author himself composing the poem, challenge his sense of what humility means, and are credited impressively, yet not pompously, with knowing 'Earth-secrets that know not I'.

Continuity of form and discourse is no indication with Hardy of conventionality and predictability. He takes the reader as much by surprise as any modernist. The re-appraisal of what it is for a woman to be 'ruined', in the Victorian sense, humorously presented in 'The Ruined Maid', is now well known; the downright realism of a wife who wants a healthy, not a sickly child, in 'A Practical Woman', perhaps less so. 'Christmas' poems like 'The Oxen' and 'Christmas in the Elgin Room', a 'New Year' poem such as 'The Darkling Thrush', and the supposed self-criticism of 'In Tenebris II', are all examples of poems which play off, sometimes more, sometimes less subtly, against stock responses. The poise of 'In Tenebris II' especially is Hardy at his elusive best. This, like 'An August Midnight', is again an exploration of humility – seemingly that of the speaker accepting himself as the disgruntled odd man out in the progressive and optimistic late nineteenth century, but in fact turning his irony against the brash complacency of his time. The deceptively awkward and prosaically long, shambling lines are another variation on Hardy's Gothic style, springing a controlled ambush which makes the final 'Get him up and be gone as one shaped awry; he disturbs the order here' a reversal of the internalised judgement it ostensibly carries.

Finally, one other feature that makes Hardy distinctively modern is the concrete immediacy of his imagination and the incising of that quality in his language in a way that links him – though he was never one of their number – with the Imagists. For example, 'Overlooking the River Stour' is as exactly visual, and aural, as a poem by Pound, Hulme or H.D.:

> The swallows flew in the curves of an eight
>   Above the river-gleam
>   In the wet June's last beam:
> Like little crossbows animate
> The swallows flew in the curves of an eight
>   Above the river-gleam.

Where Hardy differs, however, is in the subordination of the natural world, no matter how vividly recorded, to the human – even when the human, as it is in this poem, is affirmed through negation. The last stanza regrets the preoccupation with the visual, at the expense of the human:

> And never I turned my head, alack,
>> While these things met my gaze
>> Through the pane's drop-drenched glaze,
> To see the more behind my back. ...
> O never I turned, but let, alack,
>> These less things hold my gaze!

The very faithfulness with which the details of the scene are recorded has the effect of intensifying their importance for the poetry – to *see* them so exactly, and translate them into such images, is implicitly to heighten the value placed on the imaginative process of defamiliarising the actual. When, therefore, such 'things' are downgraded in the last stanza, the effect is to endow the unspecified (and perhaps sinister, because unspecified) human concerns with still greater emotional intensity.

In addition, the repetitive, refrain-like structure of the poem foregrounds the change of attention to the absent human element in the last stanza. Whereas in each of the preceding stanzas the first two lines are exactly repeated as the last two, in the last stanza slight differences occur – heightening the emotional impact with a new 'O', hinting at culpability on the speaker's part through the auxiliary 'let', and above all, adding, in the last line, the telling qualification '*less*'. Thus Hardy combines Imagism with traditional form (the device he employs here is similar to that which enables Blake, in 'The Tyger', to gain such force by changing 'could' in the first stanza to 'dare' in the last). His combination of image and structure acts to give the images more than Imagist self-sufficiency, and also to imply a moral judgement which Pound, at least, wished to circumvent. Though highly lyrical – almost, it may be thought, pure lyric – 'Overlooking the River Stour' moves towards a discursive end. It may share with modernism a disturbing sense of irrational forces, perhaps welling up from the unconscious, which threaten to disrupt the vividly evoked scene, but actually the conscious mind is in control. It knows, at least retrospectively, what the source of the disturbance was, and it moves with its tacit argument towards self-criticism for neglect of the greater human and moral concern.

A. E. HOUSMAN (1859–1936)

Lyric temper combined with discursive control is also the hallmark of A. E. Housman's poetry. A distinguished classical scholar, whose academic reputation rested on his textual work on the Latin poets Manilius and Juvenal, his fame none the less is as the poet of *A Shropshire Lad* (1896) and *Last Poems* (1922). The form of these is mainly, but not exclusively, that of the ballad, rhyming ABAB, and overtones of the Scottish border ballads, with their arbitrary loves and acts of violence, are constantly felt, especially in *A Shropshire Lad*. But there is another, hidden theme in many of these poems, the theme of homosexuality (unmentionable in the Victorian climate in which Housman was brought up), which also links them with *The Ballad of Reading Gaol* by Oscar Wilde (1856–1900). As Philip Larkin wrote, he is 'the poet of unhappiness', and that unhappiness had to do with the death of his mother when he was scarcely twelve, and his love for his Oxford friend Moses Jackson:

> And his poems were its sole expression. … His sorrow required its own mythology, the haunting, half-realized legend of ploughing, enlisting, betrothals and betrayals and hangings, and always behind them summertime on Bredon, the wind on Wenlock Edge, and nettles blowing on graves.[6]

Housman has often been criticised for being too emotionally explicit, to the point of sentimentality; but the effect in his best poems can be just the opposite. A restrained and formally precise structure is made to reverberate in an indefinably haunting way by the subtle implications of what is superficially a mere gesture. 'The street sounds to the soldier's tread', poem number XXII of *A Shropshire Lad*, depends on a soldier's turning of his head ('A single redcoat turns his head. / He turns and looks at me.'). Nothing is said; the exchange between the two is concentrated wholly on that look; but what the poem is about is the meaning that look carries – cryptic, rhetorically vague, yet deeply disturbing as it is. The speaker of the poem may well be Housman himself, but as in many of the *Shropshire Lad* poems, there is an effect of distancing which, paradoxically, adds emotional depth. The mode of address to the soldier, 'My man' (though, of course, the speaker speaks only to himself, not directly to the addressee), is loaded with class implications – this is how a social superior might speak

to his social inferior, a soldier of the ranks. And the whole poem
functions on one level simply as the appropriate thoughts of a
gentleman who sees soldiers marching by on their way to war:
it is proper to wish them well, while recognising that they have
only this fleeting moment of communication in common. But,
without its ever being said (and to say it would be to destroy the
singular effect the poem has) there are hints of a much more
intimate relationship, and of a painfulness of loss which springs
from a very different kind of separation involving breaches of the
social and moral code far beyond what is formally acknowledged.
Yet the swing and lilt of the verse, its seemingly straightforward
directness, and its neat rhyming, all, as it were, observe convention
and propriety.

The 'romantic' element in Housman is similarly strong and yet
potentially deceptive. He looks like the poet of hallowed Words-
worthian landscape. Many of his best-known, and best-loved, lines
would suggest he is just such a poet of Nature:

> Loveliest of trees, the cherry now
> Is hung with bloom along the bough

> Oh see how thick the goldcup flowers
> Are lying in the field and lane

> In summertime on Bredon
> The bells they sound so clear

> Oh tarnish late on Wenlock Edge,
> Gold that I never see.

But he is neither a nature poet, nor truly a regional poet. Shropshire
was simply the horizon seen from Housman's native Worcestershire,
and recalled from his adult London as 'those blue remembered hills'
signifying 'the land of lost content'. The poetry quivers with his
own sense of isolation which makes him, as in number XII of *Last
Poems*, 'a stranger and afraid'.

The quintessentially Housman note is a sardonic one, which he
makes virtually the theme of *A Shropshire Lad* number LXII. This is
in satiric couplets rather than the more resonant ballad metre; and,
beginning as an address to a kind of shepherd-poet, Terence, it
stands as something like a poetic manifesto. For *The Poems of Terence
Hearsay* was originally the much less evocative title that Housman

chose for his 'Shropshire' poems. In this poem an unnamed friend
rebukes him for being so 'Moping melancholy mad', and asks him
to 'pipe a tune to dance to, lad'. But Terence replies that drink
would cheer them up better:

> And malt does more than Milton can
> To justify God's ways to man.
> Ale, man, ale's the stuff to drink
> For fellows whom it hurts to think.

And he elaborates a defence of his poetry which argues that it
has a function comparable to the gradual doses of arsenic which
Mithridates took to inoculate himself against poison. As B. J. Leggett
suggests, this 'mithridatic function' of Housman's own poetry
'requires that we experience a controlled amount of pain as defence
against the much greater pain inherent in the nature of the world
outside the poem'.[7] The poetry is not escapist, but fundamentally
realist – a means of coming to terms with that underlying 'unhap-
piness' which Larkin finds so emphatically there.

ROBERT FROST (1874–1963)

Robert Frost is another poet who, like Hardy and Housman, suf-
fered at one time from critical undervaluation. He seemed an old-
fashioned poet on whom the distinctively modern experience of
urban life had made little impact. The correctness and completeness
of his syntax likewise contributed to this impression. The sequence
of thought worked out through carefully articulated syntactical
structures that match the normal demands of prose argument is an
essential strategy of his verse; and the fact that it is usually backed
up by rhyme and a recognisably regular, if freely varied, metre
reinforces the sense of conventional conformity.

   Yet in certain respects Frost was a rebel. Two often-cited com-
ments by him on the nature of poetry illustrate the ambiguous
nature of his position. On the one hand, he speaks of poetry as
'a momentary stay against confusion'; on the other, he calls it
'a figure of the will braving alien entanglements'.[8] That is to say,
poetry both upholds order and willingly involves itself with con-
trary, even disruptive, forces. Frost is equally rational and anti-
rational, insisting that a paradoxical 'wildness of logic' distinguishes
the knowledge of the poet from that of the scholar. 'Both work from

knowledge', but 'Scholars get theirs with conscientious thoroughness along projected lines of logic; poets theirs cavalierly and as it happens in and out of books.'[9] Above all, when he began his poetic career (as Frank Lentricchia argues) Frost was a deliberate opponent of the then prevalent idea of lyric poetry as something concerned with an exclusively unironic, and undramatic, purity of feeling. He adopted a truculently 'masculine' voice, and, especially in his second volume, *North of Boston* (1914), cultivated 'a language absolutely unliterary, using only words *heard* used in running speech'.[10] Like Wordsworth, he strove for a language actually spoken by men – and, notwithstanding the aggressively masculine posture, by women also (for example, in 'A Servant to Servants' and 'Home Burial'). But he went still further than Wordsworth in imitating the vernacular, and extending the social range of his speakers. In sum, his poetic programme was a subversion of the conventional standards of early twentieth-century poetry (particularly in America) – 'a struggle carried out on behalf of a new lyric diction and therefore new (and low) lyric social materials (below even Wordsworth) for the purpose of re-engendering lyric for "masculinity," a word in Frost's and other poetic modernists' lexicons signifying not a literal opening of the lyric to actual male voices and subjects, but a symbolic shattering of a constrictive lyric decorum'.[11]

For all that, Frost's method is not by any means as violent as the word 'shattering' might suggest. Rather he works by a kind of pastoral stealth, a style characterised by Mordecai Marcus as 'rich in detail, determined to stay with the exact but down-to-earth word, and bent on avoiding exaggeration'. This style is also loaded with a kind of understatement that goes along with his 'sly discovery of significance in ordinary places and his shy manner of pointing it out'.[12] This is well illustrated by 'Mowing', from Frost's first book *A Boy's Will* (1913) – a volume which has still a rather Georgian sugariness in several of its poems, but to which 'Mowing' is a marked exception. The sound, made by the scythe's mowing, is no more than a 'whispering' (a word which occurs in four of the sonnet's fourteen lines), and speculation on what its subject might be includes the tentative 'Something, perhaps, about the lack of sound'. What it is not is more emphatically recorded than what it is. It is neither escapism nor part of a self-consciously 'poetic' fairy world:

> It was no dream of the gift of idle hours,
> Or easy gold at the hand of fay or elf.

The scythe gets on with the job in hand, eschewing imaginative elaboration:

> The fact is the sweetest dream that labour knows.
> My long scythe whispered and left the hay to make.

Though this is not quite the same thing as Frost's saying that *he* as poet eschews further imaginative implications. The scythe as instrument, and 'labour' as a generic abstraction, are limited to being themselves; the poetic 'I' who wields the scythe, and from whose will the 'labour' flows, shows a speculative awareness which, of course, is necessary to make the poem possible. Some interaction between consciousness and thing is a condition of poetic utterance; but respect for 'scythe' and 'labour', and a holding back from too easy poeticising of them, is necessary if that utterance is to be authentic.

The marked development in *North of Boston* and subsequent volumes is in the greater colloquialism already noticed and in the use of a mixture of speculation and dramatic narrative. This gives rise to some of Frost's best-known poems: 'Mending Wall', 'The Death of the Hired Man', 'After Apple-Picking', and (from *Mountain Interval*, 1916) 'The Road Not Taken', 'Birches', 'Out, Out –' and 'Snow'. The latter is the least successful because it allows too prosaic a scope to dialogue and narrative extension. The build-up is too long, and, when it finally comes, the dénouement too much of a let-down. By contrast, 'Out, Out –' may seem almost too restrained in its telling of the severing of a boy's hand by a mechanical saw, and especially in the curtness with which the boy's death and the reactions of the onlookers are communicated:

> No more to build on there. And they, since they
> Were not the one dead, turned to their affairs.

What saves this ending is partly that its seeming callousness has been prepared for by the hints conveyed earlier in the poem that the boy has been pushed a little too hard, or has been a little too eager ('big boy / Doing a man's work, though a child at heart'), and partly that the laconic style hints at feeling which does not wear its heart on its sleeve. Judgement on 'them' is there as an implicit ingredient of the poem (tacitly reinforced by the fact that the only relation mentioned is the boy's sister who calls to supper, and to whom the boy makes his pathetic plea, 'Don't let him cut my hand off – / The doctor, when he comes. Don't let him, sister!'); but it is not insisted on to the exclusion of a more sympathetic attitude towards the community 'they' belong to – a community which pauses for the tragedy, but is forced (by season? by economic pressures? by its sense of duty?) to turn to its affairs.

'After Apple-Picking' and 'The Road Not Taken', while retaining vestiges of the narrative form, lean more towards the lyrically meditative. Here one feels more strongly the pressure of that element in Frost's technique which caused him to say, 'I might be called a Synecdochist, for I prefer synecdoche in poetry – that figure of speech in which we use a part for the whole.' The details are sharply particularised, making the realism of the scene or mood evoked by the poem more intense, as when, in 'After Apple-Picking', the tired picker has the sensations of his work going on after he has finished it. His aching instep seems to keep the feel of the ladder rung, he still seems to feel the boughs swaying, and he continues to hear 'The rumbling sound / Of load on load of apples coming in.' But beyond the vivid re-creation of the moment there is for the reader a sense of its standing for something larger and more universal – perhaps the fulness of harvest itself, reaching proportions which make it seem excessively fruitful, perhaps the crowding of experience making life rich to the point of wearisomeness and so verging on the wish for death. To explicate in this way, however, is to distort the effect of the lines. The note of the ominous in the use of the word 'rumbling', for example, is achieved by its being inseparable from the actual sound it recalls while reverberating mysteriously with the suggestion of something vaster and more threatening. Frost goes on to lead his reader to the verge of more explicit meaning as he continues: 'I am overtired / Of the great harvest I myself desired', and points towards the coming on of sleep, only to withdraw, almost whimsically handing over explanation to the hitherto unmentioned 'woodchuck':

> Were he not gone,
> The woodchuck could say whether it's like his
> Long sleep, as I describe its coming on,
> Or just some human sleep.

The peculiarly Frostian magic is derived from that teetering on the brink. But it is a precarious balance, which he does not always maintain. The synecdochic concreteness may come coupled uneasily with moral or philosophical reflection which dissolves the lyric back into sententiousness. It is a moot point whether or not this happens with the celebrated 'Birches'. The boy's swinging of birch-trees, which takes him up but lets him down to earth again, as opposed to the ice-bent trees which never recover, is memorably described, but there is a slightly uncomfortable transition to moralising: 'Earth's the right place for love'; and the final nugget of wisdom, 'One could do worse than be a swinger of birches', understated though it is, makes the close of the poem a little too pat.

It could be argued that those poems, increasingly common in Frost's later work, where he is more directly committed to moral, political or philosophical comment, should be judged in different terms; that they are poems of statement or debate which stand or fall, not by their synecdochic poise, but by their pithiness, shrewdness or wit. Satirical girdings like 'An Importer' and 'No Holy Wars For Them' (from *Steeple Bush*, 1947) may be compared with D. H. Lawrence's *Pansies*, though they lack the paradoxically redeeming slackness of Lawrence which accords better with the short-lived, spur-of-the-moment irritation being expressed. The political poem 'The Gift Outright' (*A Witness Tree*, 1942), is more successful. It deploys traditional rhetoric in an interestingly modern way to express the paradox that the emergence of real American nationhood required control of a new land, coupled with submission to England as the colonial power, to give way to submission to the land itself, coupled with new-found political self-control:

> Something we were withholding made us weak
> Until we found out that it was ourselves
> We were withholding from our land of living,
> And forthwith found salvation in surrender.

In his essay on Frost W. H. Auden differentiates between 'Ariel' poetry, which produces poems beautiful and satisfying as works of art, and 'Prospero' poetry, which is valued for what it has to say about experience. Frost's poetry he assigns to the second category. It is the poetry of a fallen, and distinctively New England, world bred out of contact with a harsh, wintry nature that is also capable of 'a slow and theatrically beautiful fall'. Although dour and stoical, it is far from pessimistic; it reflects a nature which 'calls forth all man's powers and courage and makes a real man of him'.[13]

This is the message carried mainly in the later poetry, and for some readers rather too explicitly.[14] It is more acceptable, and more successful, when coupled with at least some of the features of Ariel poetry – especially so when Frost the Synecdochist combines with Frost the man of experience, as in such poems as 'Design' (1936) and 'The Most of It' (1942). In the latter, Frost seems to dramatise his own wish to articulate experience in explicit form, lamenting that the only voice he can wake from the universe is 'the mocking echo of his own', and crying out on life 'that what it wants / Is not its own love back in copy speech, / But counter-love, original response'. Of this, too, 'nothing ever came', he says, 'Unless' – and that conditional leaves it open to doubt whether what follows *is* such a response – 'Unless it was the embodiment that crashed / In the cliff's talus ...', taking the form of 'a great buck' wading through the water which

> landed pouring like a waterfall,
> And stumbled through the rocks with horny tread,
> And forced the underbush – and that was all.

According to Elizabeth Jennings (b. 1926) this is 'a passionate protest', and it 'ends on a grim and haunting note'.[15] But it could just as well be regarded as a natural epiphany, ending on a note of awe and wonder. Frost leaves one to make of it what one will – though always qualifying any suggestion by the subordinating 'Unless'. Although this would seem to be an example of 'synecdoche' which is capable of being generalised – and its context one that involves a search for 'response' which seems to encourage conscious formulation – Frost chooses to leave the reader with a resonant image rather than an explicit message. He neither affirms nor denies more precise meaning.

SOME OTHER AMERICANS

Other American poets of the earlier part of the twentieth century who cultivate a deliberately 'masculine' style include Carl Sandburg (1878–1967), Edgar Lee Masters (1868–1950), Edwin Arlington Robinson (1869–1935), Vachel Lindsay (1879–1931) and Robinson Jeffers (1887–1962). Sandburg, best known for presenting Chicago as 'Hog Butcher for the World', uses a deliberately coarsened, long-lined free verse to bring the vital, but seemingly rebarbative and unpoetic Middle West within the scope of poetry; while Lindsay, with the exaggerated tum-te-tum rhythms of 'The Congo' and, in 'Simon Legree', such broadly caricatured images as that of the devil eating a 'red ham bone' and drinking 'blood and burning turpentine', incorporates the negro spiritual into a bold and exciting variety of performance poetry.

Robinson is a subtler and more sensitive poet. 'Mr Flood's Party', for example, effectively blends sentiment with humour; and 'New England' – with its sardonic description of the north-eastern climate and its satiric treatment of Calvinism ('Passion is here a soilure of the wits') – has obvious affinities with the poetry of Frost. On the other hand, Jeffers' somewhat overstrained prophetic voice which celebrates the fierce energies of nature anticipates D. H. Lawrence and Ted Hughes. His theme is that man is essentially an animal, but one that has become too sophisticated. 'What are we,' he wonders, in 'Apology for Bad Dreams', to expect always to be fed and sheltered and to be left feeling 'intact, and self-controlled'? And he is the enemy of the anthropomorphic tendency which makes man erect himself as the measure of all life: in 'Carmel Point', for example, he suggests that we must 'unhumanize our views'; and in 'Birds and Fishes', that concepts such as justice and mercy are 'human dreams' which 'do not concern the birds nor the fish nor eternal God'.

RUDYARD KIPLING (1865–1936)

In England the 'masculine' equivalent of these American poets may, broadly speaking, be found in Rudyard Kipling – though some of the qualification that has to be made with regard to Frost has to be made with regard to him, too. Kipling's themes and his extrovert way of handling them, together with the immense popularity they brought him, give him the air of a man's man. His bold, swinging rhythms and his readiness to pronounce judgements which, super-ficially at least, endorse the accepted ideas of late nineteenth-century, imperialist Britain, seem to fit him as the spokesman of those 'stout upstanders' whose 'dust smokes around their career' in Hardy's 'In Tenebris II'. He does, it is true, represent several important aspects of his time – for example, the deliberate inculca-tion of duty to the British Empire, the cult of the 'White Man's burden', the code of the professional servant of the state, the celebration of military discipline, and the subordination of the individual to the simplified, lowest-common-denominator values of a group ('The game is more than the player of the game, / And the ship more than the crew'). But there is also room for the protest – albeit carefully circumscribed in the extent to which it is allowed to go – of the little man, or the obscure civil servant, against the blunders and self-seeking of his superiors; and he is capable of questioning the fundamental rightness of at least some of those assumptions which he is generally credited with bolstering uncritically.

Above all, Kipling's language, though seemingly traditional and conventional compared with that of Eliot, Pound or James Joyce, is realistically, and provocatively, based on the syntax and diction of uneducated, everyday speech. If his verse rhythms lack subtlety, that is more than compensated by the energy and vigour they draw from the ballad, the 'old fourteener', the street cry and the popular music hall song. The connection with popular music is especially relevant. As with the work of certain Elizabethan poets, such as Thomas Lodge and Thomas Campion, or (nearer to his own date) the lyrics of Gilbert and Sullivan opera, to be properly appreciated Kipling's verse often needs to be heard in performance to an actual, or at least implied, musical setting. The sentimental swing of 'Mandalay' and the very different rhythms of 'Boots' and 'Gentlemen-Rankers' (with its deliberately bizarre refrain, 'We're poor little lambs who've lost our way, / Baa! Baa! Baa!') have this in common, that they lose more than half their effect if read silently on the page instead of being sung, or chanted. And such hymn-like poems as 'Non Nobis Domine!' and 'Land of our Birth, we pledge to thee' ('The Children's Song' from *Puck of Pook's Hill*), which are movingly grave when sung, can seem merely banal when divorced from the musical settings which have made them so well-known.

Kipling had an excellent, if not particularly sensitive, ear. Although his attempt to capture the Glaswegian accent of his ship's engineer in 'McAndrew's Hymn' is not very convincing, the compulsive swing of the verse is successfully modified to take the pauses and emphases of actual speech; and his use of Cockney, which he knew much more intimately, for his soldier speakers in *Barrack-Room Ballads* produces a vindication of the vernacular which links him with the anti-poetic poets of America. His most 'modern' work is to be found in poems like 'Danny Deever', 'Tommy', '"Fuzzy-Wuzzy"', 'The Widow at Windsor' and, despite its tendency towards sentimentality, 'Gunga Din'. These are poems which get rid completely of the self-consciously poetic rhetoric and suburbanised nature themes which Pound so despised in later nineteenth- and early twentieth-century verse. They seem more dated than they are by virtue of their apparent acceptance of a code of stoic service which can too conveniently act as apology for a supposedly ordained system of social class. But the mimetic Cockneyism carries with it a sarcastic–realistic tone which sometimes undermines even where it seems to be propping up. In 'The Widow at Windsor' this is confined to the refrain, which in every fifth line takes a phrase from the preceding line and echoes it with slight distortion to suggest a counter-burden to that of the received imperial doctrine:

> There's 'er nick on the cavalry 'orses,
>   There's 'er mark on the medical stores –
> An' 'er troopers you'll find with a fair wind be'ind
>   That takes us to various wars.
>   (Poor beggars! – barbarious wars!)

In 'Tommy' it is much more explicit, contrasting the snobbery which segregates the common soldier from the respectable middle class, with the fawning praise lavished on him when he is needed to defend the established system:

> For it's Tommy this, an' Tommy that, an' 'Chuck
>   him out, the brute!'
> But it's 'Saviour of 'is country' when the guns begin
>   to shoot.

While nothing here suggests a radical criticism of the system which produces such hypocrisy (the implication is that right-minded imperialists will give credit where credit is due), and though the verse remains too easy-going for a really serious sense of disturbance to get through, the thinness of the cliché used when his detractors start belatedly to praise Tommy is foregrounded by the very way Tommy mimics it. The rhetoric which, in poems like 'Ave Imperatrix!' and 'Our Lady of the Snows', sounds unintentionally inflated is here exposed by contrast with a plainer, demotic speech. Such a strategy is even more effective than that employed in such deliberately critical poems as 'Recessional' and 'Mesopotamia'. 'Recessional', for example, attacks the hollowness of imperialist assumptions that might is right, and exhorts its readers to remain humble before the true, spiritual power of the 'Lord God of Hosts'. But other assumptions seem to go unquestioned (including that implicit in the notorious phrase, 'lesser breeds without the Law'), and the rather stilted language which Kipling finds appropriate for loftier themes such as this tends to blunt the edge of the very criticism which the poem is voicing. The vulgarisms of the 'barrack-room' poems, however, cut through the barriers erected by establishment rhetoric. Precisely by getting rid of the weightiness considered right for serious public poems – and even those meant to provoke more serious reflection about accepted public values – poems like 'Tommy' achieve a more modern effect of defamiliarisation.

ROBERT GRAVES (1895–1985)

Robert Graves is also a major contributor to the English discursive tradition. As it happens, he is intensely critical of Kipling – in the undiscriminating way of many anti-imperialist critics who can only see Kipling's establishment apologist side; but what he says about the 'unliterary or anti-literary' effect that true poetry must have in modern times could well be applied to Kipling:

> The trouble is rather that modern life is full of the stock feelings and situations with which traditional poetry has continuously fed popular sentiment; that most commonplaces of everyday speech are the detritus of past poems; so that the enlarged reading public must regard the poet who has an original experience to express as either unliterary or anti-literary.[16]

Graves, however, comes at the problem from the other end of the spectrum. Superficially, Kipling is populist, and Graves – as is implicit in this quotation – élitist. Along with Laura Riding (1901–91) he is an advocate of modernist 'difficulty', regarding poetry which makes its readers struggle to decipher it as a necessary stimulus to new apprehension. Yet he works within traditional forms and metric, and he is meticulous in observing the requirements of syntax and argument. Though he defends modernism, his own modernity is of a kind that makes him continuous with Hardy and Frost, and even Kipling.

This contradictoriness is a part of Graves's poetic nature, and built into his poetic credo. He is both rationalist and anti-rationalist, believer in the spiritual transcendency of love and in its inevitable physicality. And though he maintains that poetry is essentially a matter of inspiration, the unpredictable, undeserved gift of the White Goddess, he also treats it as a matter of careful craftsmanship painstakingly worked at by the conscious will. Again, though he exalts the White Goddess as a female deity whose authority derives from the powerful and irrational compulsions of an ancient, matriarchal society hostile to the now universally worshipped Apollo, god of a rationalist, patriarchal society, the Apollonian principles of order and restraint are as strongly present in his thought and work as the demonic inspiration of the White Goddess.

In common with many other twentieth-century poets Graves is hostile to the acquisitive materialism on which the civilisation of the western world is based (though in his case there are no political overtones to such a position), and he shares with D. H. Lawrence and Ted Hughes a deep sense of outrage at the suppression, or perversion, of primitive animal energies by that civilisation. In 'Rocky Acres', for example, the country of the poet's choice is 'harsh craggy mountain, moor ample and bare', where the savage buzzard is in the ascendant, scanning 'his wide parish with a sharp eye' and knowing no enervating compassion ('Tenderness and pity the heart will deny'). This is the 'first land that rose from Chaos and the Flood', a 'Stronghold for demigods', and (perhaps its strongest recommendation for Graves) 'Terror for fat burghers on far plains below'. Similarly, in 'Outlaws' the old gods, though 'tamed to silence', are sensed to be lurking still in ambuscade 'Where spider-like they trap their prey / With webs of shade'.

The image of the web is taken up again and developed in 'The Cool Web' as a metaphor for language which paradoxically articulates and emasculates the primitive powers. The inarticulacy of children, who are in immediate contact with these powers, is contrasted favourably with 'we' who 'have speech' only to 'chill', 'dull' and 'spell' them 'away'. Wound in by the 'cool web of language', we are diminished to a more cautious, enfeebled state: but that web is also our protection. Without it the immediacy of the children's vision would drive us mad. Again, there is more than a hint of affinity with Lawrence and Hughes, but the mode in which the theme is argued is distinctively Graves's own. If the Apollonian is that which, in Martin Seymour-Smith's summary, 'usurps the Muse, with the consequence that poetry gives way to rhetoric',[17] this poem is both the work of the indignant Muse and a construct of the usurping Apollo. It is an elaborately contrived piece of rhetoric, consisting of three carefully balanced four-line stanzas followed by one six-line stanza. The first four lines evoke the inspired 'dumbness' of children, focusing in turn (and foregrounded by anaphora) on the heat of day and the rose, and then the dreadfulness of dark and the soldiers. The next four lines, parallel but antithetical to the preceding ones, identify the 'speech' which cools all this down to commonplaceness; and the third four develop the cooling process till it reaches a witty anti-climax: 'We grow sea-green at last and coldly die / In brininess and volubility.' The final – somewhat longer – stanza recapitulates both the watery death associated with the cool web and (with the aid of anaphora once more) the violence of the children's four-fold vision, bringing the poem to the ironic conclusion that 'if we let out tongues lose self-possession' and face what we have been protected from, 'We shall go mad no doubt and die that way.' Again, this conclusion is as syntactically precise and complete in its articulation as all that has gone before, effecting a neatly controlled bathos that might have come out of eighteenth-century mock-heroic. The poem itself thus becomes a cool linguistic web carefully woven to catch the elusive fly of consciousness.

Clearly, the art of this poem could be interpreted as appropriate form demonstrating in its own linguistic being the debilitating rhetoric which is its theme. But the poem is the stronger, not the weaker, for its carefully fashioned structure. Nor is it by any means an exception to the rule of Graves's poetic output as a whole. The traditional resources of rhyme, rhetoric and scannable metre are as carefully employed by Graves as they are by predecessors such as Housman and Hardy, or will be by successors such as Auden and Larkin. With Graves, however, the tension between form and matter which is also common to each of these poets, takes on a special significance. He is defiant of convention, emphasising the need for exposure to the chaotic, and potentially destructive as well as creative, forces of the unconscious, while yet deliberately subjecting their expression to tight formal control. His poetry is thus born, not out of abandonment to the creative energies released (when she is gracious) by the White Goddess, but out of conflict between fairly evenly poised elements of both unreason and reason.

A poem like 'Flying Crooked' is another fine example of the peculiar tension thus generated. Its taut four-stressed rhyming couplets, with almost exclusively masculine rhymes, give it an epigrammatic quality, and these, coupled with the title and the seeming banality of the subject – a butterfly, but an un-exotic one, 'a cabbage-white', which in its 'honest idiocy' cannot master 'the art of flying straight' – suggest the mode of satire. Yet the suggestion of satire is conjured up only to be rejected. The butterfly possesses an enviably 'just sense of how not to fly'. Its fumbling, shambling, aerial gait is a paradoxically invaluable 'flying-crooked gift' which even the 'aerobatic swift' cannot emulate.

Graves, in fact, is often the bard of irrational near-absurdity like that of the cabbage-white, presented in a rationally and apparently satirical mode, but redeemed by its innate energy. Thus 'Down, Wanton, Down!' is a poem which is witty at the expense of the ridiculously irrepressible penis seen in mock-heroic fashion as a 'Poor Bombard-captain, sworn to reach / The ravelin and effect a breach', yet still capable of boasting itself 'a man of parts / To think fine and profess the arts?' Sex is the target here, but also the invigorating subject. Similarly, in 'Ulysses', where the famous hero is punningly 'much-tossed' and forever torn between variations on the faithful wife, Penelope, and the illicit mistress, Circe, the wanton libido is kept in place by humour and artistic control, but is also the energising power within the poem.

More disgusting aspects of sex lie behind poems such as 'The Succubus' and 'The Beast', and these, too, are authentic parts of Graves's experience. But the norm towards which he keeps returning is one in which excesses are only tolerated as inevitably incident to a flawed humanity. Moreover, the poems of disgust are counterbalanced by poems like 'Despite and Still' and 'Turn of the Moon' which suggest tenderness emerging out of strife. 'Turn of the Moon', in particular, beautifully evokes the unpredictable blessing which may still come from the imperious White Goddess (imaged as the Moon) when she changes to bringer of drought-curing rain. Graves evokes a night downpour which is 'Soft, steady, even' and does no harm, but sinks 'to the tap roots', leaving the drenched earth to exhale at dawn a 'long sigh scented with pure gratitude'. Such spontaneous rain, he says, is 'woman giving as she loves' – the White Goddess in a marvellously unforced, coming-on disposition.

In between is the witty, acerbic, though usually not ungenerous, Graves for whom humour is the saving grace – humour being 'one gift that helps men and women survive the stress of city life. If he keeps his sense of humour, too, a poet can go mad gracefully, swallow his disappointments in love gracefully, reject the Establishment gracefully, die gracefully, and cause no upheaval in society.'[18] This is Graves of 'The Persian Version' (and recognisably the same man as the author of the autobiographical *Goodbye To All That* and of the novels *I, Claudius* and *Claudius the God*). The implied standard is that of the classically educated English gentleman who is a traditionalist, an upholder of the middle way and – up to a point – a rather old-fashioned figure. But at the same time it is the work of a man who resolutely faces the vexatious contradictions of his own personality and accepts the unregenerate nature of the actual, contemporary world in which he has to live. Constantly aware of extravagance, extremism and irrationality in himself and his society, and equally aware of the limitations and inadequacies of reason to deal with all this, he remains an artist who brings rhetoric and reason to the expression and containment of the irrational. This is perhaps nowhere more explicitly spelt out than in the poem 'In Broken Images', which balances the two halves of his self against each other in a mutually critical, but also enhancing, dialectic. 'He', the rational self, 'quick, thinking in clear images', is balanced against the irrational self, which is 'slow' and does its thinking 'in broken images'; but the overconfidence of 'He' in the clarity of his images leads paradoxically to his becoming 'dull', whereas 'I become sharp, mistrusting my broken images.' Similarly, the rational self's assumptions about relevance and fact are poised against the irrational self's doubting both relevance and fact; and – notwithstanding the exact, seemingly rational, antithetic structure of the poem – the certainty of reason is gradually made to lose out to the quickening uncertainties of the irrational, till the upside-down non-conclusion is reached which leaves the rational 'in a new confusion of his understanding' and 'I', the irrational, 'in a new understanding of my confusion'.

Via its first-person spokesman this poem is, of course, weighted in favour of the 'broken images', the elusive relevance and the sensual immediacy of Graves's version of the modernist – though the conclusion is probably more optimistic than a more whole-hearted modernist would feel able to allow. Nevertheless, the rational third person, despite the derogatory 'dullness' attributed to his trust in clarity and relevance, stands as an effective counterbalance, if not equal, to the provocative 'I'. The very form of the poem with its crosscutting parallelisms tacitly affirms the value of rational structure. Although the speaker's images are broken, they do not accumulate in a disordered heap; nor are they seen as *Waste Land* fragments shored against his ruins. The victory is not simply handed to the irrational. Graves makes his poem out of the tensions between first person and third. If the confidence of reason is undermined to the extent that it generates 'a new confusion', and a new, presumably more sensitive and flexible, 'understanding' emerges from the self-confessed confusion of its opposite number, the newness that both attain is a product of their interaction. And it might even be argued that reason remains the master. It is his rationally balancing mode that determines the form of the poem, and his declarative manner that articulates what both third and first person experience.

MODERNIST AND NON-MODERNIST

This chapter has been based on the general premise that writers such as Hardy, Housman, Frost, Kipling and Graves can be seen as offering an alternative way of dealing with modern material to that of the more deliberately inconoclastic modern*ists*, Pound, Eliot, Williams and Stevens. The latter make a dramatic break with the time-honoured forms of poetry – its rhyming patterns, regularity of metre and syntax, and its rationally paraphraseable meaning; whereas the non-modernists tend to preserve these (though often with signficant modifications like those suggested by Hardy in his comments on the 'Gothic' style, and, in Graves's case, even while acting as a defender of modernism).

But the non-modernists are not therefore to be regarded as conventional conformists who merely repeat what has been done before. In many ways they are just as critical of the world in which they live; and often, in political terms, more to the left than modernists like Pound and Eliot. They can also be just as linguistically adventurous and technically innovative. Furthermore, they can be very different from each other in tone and subject-matter. To be non-modernist is to be neither indifferent to the modern, nor one of a herd. What the non-modernists do have in common, however, is their continued acceptance of the rationally discursive assumptions which underlie almost all previous poetry. And even in this respect it has to be conceded that a poet like Graves is somewhat ambivalent: he stands on the borderline between modernist and non-modernist – deeply in thrall to the unreason of the White

Goddess, but writing in the rational, structured manner of traditional poetry. As T. S. Eliot, doyen of the modernists, seems to be returning towards discursive methods in his later work, so Graves maintains those methods while seeming to become increasingly sceptical of reason.

Such crossing of borderlines is not infrequent. Although 'modernist' and 'non-modernist' are convenient labels, they should not be treated as rigidly separate categories. They point to major differences and significant orientations. But the poets whom one divides up in this way often have a foot in the opposite camp; and their successors among subsequent twentieth-century poets can likewise have affinities with either. Modernism, however (at least in its more extreme manifestations), has perhaps proved the less lasting of the two. If many later poets have acknowledged a debt to Eliot, for example, few have written quite like him, and none successfully. The influence of the non-modernists, if less spectacular, has been more benign. And, powerful as the upheaval of modernism has been, from the perspective of the end of the century it looks as if rhyme and reason have kept the field.

4

Private and Public:
Yeats and Lowell

IMPERSONALITY

The poem as a self-contained, independent work of art became one of the chief tenets of twentieth-century modernism. Emotional baring of the soul was rejected in favour of a posture of detachment and impersonality. According to T. S. Eliot in his influential essay 'Tradition and the Individual Talent' (1919): 'Poetry is not a turning loose of emotion, but an escape from emotion; it is not the expression of personality, but an escape from personality.' For the 'is' of this quotation, however, it might be more appropriate to substitute 'should be'. Eliot was not commenting objectively on a given state of affairs, but seeking to impose a doctrine favourable to his own agenda and that of the early modernists. Ezra Pound was doing the same, but with a franker acknowledgement of the manifesto-like nature of his assertion, when he claimed a year or two earlier that poetry in the twentieth century would be 'harder and saner' and 'as much like granite as it can be', adding, 'At least for myself, I want it so, austere, direct, free from emotional slither.'[1] What offended both Eliot and Pound was their sense that the poetry of the Romantics (and, more particularly, the Romantic tradition as developed by the Victorians) wore its heart too much on its sleeve, that it had become emotionally slack, and made the psychological state of the writer rather than the achieved substance of the poem too much the centre of attention.

Imagism was one strategy for getting round this state of affairs. The hard, sharp, *haiku*-like brevity of the Imagist poem focused attention on things outside the poet's mind (even if, ultimately, this 'objective' thinginess became a 'correlative' for an emotional condition) and seemed to preclude first-person statement. But the presence or absence of personal pronouns is not in itself a key to the impersonality which Eliot especially desired. 'The Love Song of J. Alfred Prufrock' begins with an unabashedly personal voice: 'Let us go then, you and I', and the body of the poem is full of personal lucubrations. As the title indicates, however, these are the sentiments of a named figure (and one whose name more than hints at his prissy, inhibited character). Like Browning, who had already set up a counter-current among the Victorians with his dramatic monologues that put words in invented characters' mouths, Eliot uses a device which does not commit him to what Prufrock is saying – which enables him, indeed, to mock at Prufrock, and yet does not simply set up Prufrock as a target of satire. If there is a streak of Eliot himself in Prufrock, it is not Eliot's own feelings which the poem luxuriates in. Prufrock is a persona with whom, to a degree, Eliot empathises, but of whom he can be simultaneously critical. Though creating him and contriving to put all that he says in a certain revealingly ironical light, Eliot speaks at the most only obliquely through Prufrock. In that sense the poem is personative rather than personal; its technique is such as to direct the reader's scrutiny on to the imagined character and the idiosyncratic language by which he is projected, and not (at least until a much later stage of analysis) onto the thoughts and feelings of Eliot himself.

As a device the persona encourages indirection and irony. If it is, as Eliot claims, an 'escape' from emotion and personality, it may also in a sense be said to be an evasion. At any rate, it has the potentiality of becoming a double-edged weapon, capable, as it seems to have been for the early Eliot, of cutting a way through to new resources of wit and energy, but also of severing the poet from commitment in a way that is ultimately debilitating. W. B. Yeats and Robert Lowell are two striking examples of this ambiguous relationship. Both create public personae from which in time they feel the need to escape, as much as Eliot feels the need to escape from the personal into the supposedly impersonal; but in each one the relationship between public and private is of a different nature and leads to quite different uses of the persona. Both are masters of the art of rhetoric, which as suggested by the definition, 'the art of persuasion', implies a definite engagement with the audience to which their poems are addressed, and yet both become more persuasive as they move towards a language which divests itself of the trappings of a certain kind of rhetoric. Both are also poets who, to a degree, become public figures in the sense of making their mark in the world of politics and social affairs, and who seek to incorporate that experience in poems which have a strongly personal, and even private, character.

W. B. YEATS (1865–1939)

The striking feature of Yeats's poetic career is the change it underwent *ca* 1914 with the publication of *Responsibilities*. That change, of which Yeats was highly conscious, is neatly encapsulated in his often-quoted poem 'A Coat', in which he seems to dismiss his earlier work as 'a coat / Covered with embroideries / Out of old mythologies'. This had set a style which 'fools' had imitated, and copied as if it were their own; but – in the curt, two-stressed lines which give the poem its abrupt, contemptuous energy – Yeats is prepared to fling away his proprietorial rights in this now out-moded 'coat', and walk 'naked'. This is Yeats deliberately making himself over as a distinctively *modern* poet. In place of the dreamy, symbolist style, and subject-matter frequently drawn from Celtic mythology, of his earlier volumes – including *The Wanderings of Oisin* and *Crossways* (1889), *The Rose* (1893), *The Wind among the Reeds* (1899), *In the Seven Woods* (1904) and *The Shadowy Waters* (1906) – he dedicates himself to a plainer, more earth-bound poetry. This is to become a poetry much closer in its diction and rhythms to ordinary speech, more taut and economical, and more arresting by virtue of its evident engagement with the social, philosophical and political controversies of his day. Titles such as 'The Song of the Happy Shepherd', 'To the Rose upon the Rood of Time' and 'The Song of Wandering Aengus' are replaced by those with more topical relevance such as 'To a Wealthy Man who promised a Second Subscription to the Dublin Municipal Gallery if it were proved the People wanted Pictures', 'Easter 1916' and 'A Meditation in Time of War'; and lines of lilting evocativeness such as those which open 'The White Birds' ('I would that we were, my beloved, white birds on the foam of the sea!') give way to the blunt immediacy found in 'The Balloon of the Mind', where the speaker tells his hands to bring down the wallowing 'balloon of the mind' and confine it to 'its narrow shed'.

And, towards the end of Yeats's career, come the still more vigorous directness of the 'Crazy Jane' poems, and the sheer bitterness of 'The Circus Animals' Desertion', which concludes with the declaration:

> Now that my ladder's gone,
> I must lie down where all the ladders start,
> In the foul rag-and-bone shop of the heart.

Yet the difference between the early and later Yeats can be exaggerated. His preoccupation with mythologies and fantasies is something which persists throughout his work, as do his love of rhetoric and, in particular, the sceptical detachment underlying his habitual use of the persona. For example, in *The Wanderings of Oisin* the theme is a recurrent one in the early poetry – the fascination exercised by the changeless world of 'faery' as opposed to the change and decay of the human world. But the poem takes the form of a dialogue between Oisin and St Patrick in which, though Oisin's Nietzschean energy seems more potent than the Christianity of 'lying clerics' who 'murder song / With barren words and flatteries of the weak', his experience of the inhuman faery world backhandedly endorses much of the Christian emphasis on human weakness. The three islands, emblematic of joy, fighting and forgetfulness, which, magically exempt from human ageing, Oisin visits with his faery love, Niamh, are all tinged with barrenness and futility; and the climax of his adventures, when, in the process of helping real, weak, human creatures, he himself slips from his horse and suddenly becomes his true age, reduces him to the same level as they. Although Oisin has the last word (he will join the Fenian heroes, 'be they in flames or at feast'), both Christian and pagan values are at best ambiguous.

In some versions of early poems Yeats uses various personae, including those of Michael Robartes, Hanrahan and Aedh,[2] to voice positions with which he may or may not agree; and these figures are similarly used elsewhere. In his work generally such recurrent figures as Helen of Troy, Maud Gonne and Crazy Jane are often, in effect, nodal points for values which he may seem to defend with passion, but which are at odds with each other. Even poems nominally spoken in his own voice do not necessarily carry his personal endorsement. It is thus virtually impossible to fix the essential Yeats. Poems are a trying out of different postures; and one of his favourite strategies in the later work (though it may be seen as a development of the spokesmen in *The Wanderings of Oisin*) is the use of dialectically opposed voices, either within the same poem, as with 'A Dialogue of Self and Soul' (*The Winding Stair and Other Poems*, 1933), or projected in paired poems such as 'Sailing to Byzantium' (*The Tower*, 1928) and 'Byzantium' (*The Winding Stair*).

For Yeats this became the principle of the 'mask' – a device formalising the dramatic adoption, without ultimate commitment, of various points of view, but also related to the antithetical system of 'gyres' by means of which he gave shape to his cyclic view of history. The spiral, or cone-like, movement of the gyre represents the development of a civilisation from its point of conception through a series of phases (corresponding to the twenty-eight days of the moon's cycle) to its widest expansion, which also becomes the start of its decay and supersession by another, and opposite civilisation. In the diagram by which this is represented the maximum expansion of the cone is pierced at its centre by the point of the antithetical cone, which here begins its own process of spiralling expansion and ultimate exhaustion. Each cone is locked within the other, and at each of its phases has its antithesis, or 'mask', within the other cone. The mask of one cone is thus in a Mr Hyde relationship to the Dr Jekyll of its counterpoint.

Whatever may have been the nature of Yeats's actual belief in this idiosyncratic system, poetically it was valuable in enabling him to release the contradictory energies which fuelled his rhetoric. He could write himself seemingly wholeheartedly into contradictory positions, and yet maintain an implicit sense of their relativity to each other. Byzantium, for example, in 'Sailing to Byzantium' represents the antithetical, cool, changeless world – the world of 'faery' in his earlier poetry of Celtic mythology now mutated into the deathless world of a highly stylised, hieratic form of religious art – with which the common world of change and decay is incompatible, but to which its denizens, especially when reaching the decrepitude of old age and no longer able to participate in the sensual pleasures of youth, long to be translated. The poem opens with that sense of antithetical incompatibility: 'That is no country for old men.' In the lines that follow the combination of youth, sexual energy and natural fecundity seems to be presented as a drug, an all-absorbing 'sensual music' which deadens the mind to the supreme achievements of the human race – the 'Monuments of unageing intellect' on which the stanza comes to rest in its final line. And yet, while being nominally rejected because of its association with an inevitable mortality, the youthful world reveals its attraction through the pulsating energy of the verse in which it is expressed. In the next stanzas, the poem moves on to evoke and celebrate the alternative world of intellect; but, again, there is a kind of in-built contradiction. Even as the poem bodies forth, with what should be a still more powerful appeal, the exotic magnificence of Byzantium – into which the aging speaker prays to be absorbed – it is accompanied by an antithetical subtext which all but breaks the surface in the last stanza. The climax of the speaker's urge towards Byzantium is the ironic image of himself as an artificial bird set upon the mythical 'golden bough' to sing merely in order to keep 'a drowsy Emperor awake'. Moreover, the subject-matter of his singing is 'what is past, or passing, or to come' – that is, the very world of 'nature', which as 'a dying animal' he wishes to escape from, is inevitably re-asserted at the supposed climax of his transformation. The poem is thus circular in structure, making a rhetorical affirmation which is dogged by its own antithesis.

Something similar can be felt in the companion poem, 'Byzantium'. This seems to assert 'the artifice of eternity' still more strongly; it seethes with contempt for 'all complexities of mire and blood'. But the transcendent power of the 'golden smithies' of the Byzantine Emperor is celebrated in language which evokes the ceaseless creativity of the phenomenal world with equal power:

> Those images that yet
> Fresh images beget,
> That dolphin-torn, that gong-tormented sea.

These closing words are perhaps the most resonant of all, in an intensely resonating poem. Without explicitly denying the rapturous rhetoric by means of which the poet seeks to leap imaginatively from the known world of change and decay to the changeless symbolic world of Byzantium, they keep that 'mask' in touch with its anti-mask. In so doing they also give the poem a human tension which redeems it from its own would-be inhuman theme.

Here lies a significant feature of Yeats's poetry. As Denis Donoghue says, he is a poet of 'power'.[3] In common with poets like D. H. Lawrence and Ted Hughes (and in marked contrast to Hardy), he has a Nietzschean tendency to exalt sheer, amoral energy for its own sake. This is an important element in the modernist reaction against a supposedly effete nineteenth-century, liberal civilisation. In his particular expression of it, however, Yeats is constrained, and enriched, by the pull of opposites. In 'The Second Coming', for example, he writes a prophetic poem about the end of an outworn Christian era, and the beginning of a new one, symbolised in the 'rough beast' now slouching 'towards Bethlehem to be born'. The birth of this beast is a parody of the birth of Jesus, and there is undeniably some relish for its terrible potency. As expressed, more crudely, in another 'Christmas' poem, 'The Magi', there is something which has not been satisfied by orthodox Christianity, and latter-day wise men actually *hope* to find a new access of power in 'the uncontrollable mystery on the bestial floor'. But in 'The Second Coming' the very rhetoric appropriate to enunciating such a theme of cyclic change also comes charged with anti-Nietzschean meanings which deplore anarchy, violence and the slaughter of innocence. The voice is that of a public orator, but (notwithstanding the fact that the poem is often quoted as if it were a traditionalist condemnation of revolutionary Terror or the Anti-Christ) one who is distinctly ambiguous both in what he advocates or condemns.

The extent of Yeats's personal adherence to a Nietzschean world-view is hard to assess, but what matters more is the way issues of power and authority are expressed in his poetry. To adapt a famous dictum of D. H. Lawrence's, one trusts the poetry rather than the artist. Even when Yeats seems to be making categorical statements his cultivation of a deliberately forceful rhetoric frequently leads to an overemphasis which suggests the trying out of extremes, or the venting of suppressed energies, rather than the balanced search for complex truth. And yet some of his finest poems are those which express sympathy for passionate commitment within a discursive mode implicitly sceptical of Nietzschean extravagance. Yeats's refashioning of his style from *Responsibilities* onwards is an act of criticism with practical consequences, giving him a wider range that encompasses both rhetorical vigour and the questioning common sense made more accessible through a language nearer to ordinary speech. These are also the poems in which he becomes more engaged with the events of his own time and place, benefiting, as is often suggested, from his close day-to-day involvement with the affairs of the Abbey Theatre in Dublin, and from having observed the influence of the Irish Nationalist cause, which he enthusiastically supported, on a number of close friends, including the woman he loved, Maud Gonne. They are poems in which he deals with public and political themes, but in a new style of private reflection; and in a style which gives his typical counterpoising of opposites a different, more realistic emphasis.

In 'Man and the Echo' (written in 1938, towards the very end of his life) Yeats looks back on the events of Easter 1916, when a group of Nationalists seized the Dublin Post Office in an attempt to assert Irish independence, and asks himself whether his own play about Ireland, *Cathleen ni Houlihan* (1902), was a contributory cause that sent out 'Certain men the English shot'. This is one among several questions put to himself by a man on his sickbed, never able to 'get the answers right'. 'Easter 1916' was the poem he wrote immediately after the rising, and its tone is quite different. It commemorates rebels transformed by their participation in a public cause from suburban nonentities into national heroes.

In 'Easter 1916' the casual, colloquial style comparatively new to Yeats at this point is used first to evoke the banality of the rebels' former lives, summed up in the repeated phrase 'polite meaningless words'. But at the end of the paragraph this gives way abruptly to the exclamatory and resonant:

> All changed, changed utterly:
> A terrible beauty is born.

These lines then constitute a new refrain, repeated at the end of the second paragraph and rounding off the poem at the end of the fourth; and to that extent they token a shift onto a more exalted plane where the rebels are transformed into patriots. Nevertheless, the language indicating what some of the rebels were like before their transformation can still be casual, even a touch satirical: 'That woman' (Con Markiewicz) had 'ignorant good-will', 'This other man' (John MacBride) was 'A drunken, vainglorious lout'. Such reminders of their unregenerate state do, of course, serve to heighten the aura of heroism which their sacrifice for the political cause has conferred upon them; but the effect of the less dignified language is also to maintain two perspectives which continue to interact in the poet's consciousness, giving the poem a dual quality of both public celebration and private reflection.

In the third paragraph a further dimension is introduced as the poem moves on to the level of natural symbolism:

> The horse that comes from the road,
> The rider, the birds that range
> From cloud to tumbling cloud,
> Minute by minute they change.

Through the next seven lines the sense of an unresting, but vital
mutability is heightened still further by the piling on of images of
natural activity, punctuated by the repeated phrase, 'minute by
minute'. The emphasis is again on 'change', but a different kind
from that evoked in the previous paragraphs. This is the ongoing
change of nature's essentially creative changeableness. And yet, in
the dialectic manner characteristic of Yeats, the climax of the para-
graph comes with a quite different line: 'The stone's in the midst
of all' – a line which sets the immutable, obstructive and inorganic
against the preceding accumulation of all that is fluently organic.

The stone's being placed 'in the midst' opens up the possibility
that it, too, may be regarded as part of the whole – a hard, resistant
phenomenon opposed to the organically flowing continuum around
it, but ultimately sharing in the same natural totality (and to that
extent offering a parallel to, and justification for, the political
change). Nevertheless, the reading suggested by its context is that
the stone represents inhumanly fixated emotion; and the speaker
goes so far as to make a specific equation between dedication to a
cause and petrifaction of the heart:

> Too long a sacrifice
> Can make a stone of the heart.

In the ensuing lines the poem returns to the level of political
discourse, with prosaic argument reverberating in the background
(England, which had promised to take up the question of independ-
ence again after the war, might still be trusted); but only to be
transcended once more as the poem moves back again to the level of
heroic commemoration and its final repetition of 'changed utterly'.

'Easter 1916' is thus a public and political poem in that it engages
immediately with a highly tense moment in Irish history, including
both the fervour felt by Nationalists passionately committed to what
is for them an overriding cause, and the more prosaic level of
day-to-day, suburban existence which that cause peremptorily inter-
rupts. But there is also a more private, subjective dimension,
in which the speaker stands back from the event, seeing it in the
ambivalent context of natural symbolism, where fervour has the
tragic overtones, simultaneously noble and perverse, of Sophocles'
Antigone. Language and imagery are correspondingly mobile, now
hieratic, now prosaic, now symbolic. If there is an argument, the
argument is not worked out; and yet the effect is not evasive.

It responds with imaginative sympathy to a situation in which both scepticism and commitment are evoked, but implicitly recognises the validity of different levels of response. Or, rather, it both affirms the validity of certain strong emotional responses and undermines them with an implicit awareness of their relativity.

This relativity becomes the central theme in one of Yeats's greatest poems, 'Among School Children'. Less celebratory, and more reflectively autobiographical, than 'Easter 1916', it represents Yeats's variably discursive mode at its best. The speaker, a self-styled 'sixty-year-old smiling public man', muses a shade ironically on his performance as a member of the Irish Senate visiting a progressive primary school. He is conscious of himself as a public figure, and by implication, too, as a writer whose present reflections are not made just for himself, but also for the benefit of his readers. Even the private is subtly conditioned by an audience. Old age (a theme also to the fore in other poems from the volume, *The Tower*, that includes 'Among School Children') lends him detachment, as well as a degree of disenchantment, which makes him conscious of the gap between intention and performance, belief and reality, in all human activities. This is generalised outwards from his own private experience, but weighted by the discourse which ranges widely over people, art and philosophy till it acquires an almost impersonal authority. The impulse, so powerful in the Byzantium poems, to fashion the soul as compensation for the decline of the body (but then found inadequate), is also present here. It is muted, however, and discounted by the anti-rhetorical element which, accepting that it is 'Better to smile on all that smile, and show / There is a comfortable kind of old scarecrow', can dismiss the systems of Plato, Aristotle and Pythagoras as 'Old clothes upon old sticks to scare a bird' – the scarecrow image reductive of himself thus becoming a means of saying that to set body against soul is itself a reductive process.

Nevertheless, the poem itself does not conclude reductively. It poses an alternative in which the imagination may transcend these divisions to express awareness of a complete, unified being, necessarily, and appropriately, in images of natural indivisibility:

> Labour is blossoming or dancing where
> The body is not bruised to pleasure soul,
> Nor beauty born out of its own despair,
> Nor blear-eyed wisdom out of midnight oil.

O chestnut tree, great rooted blossomer,
Are you the leaf, the blossom or the bole?
O body swayed to music, O brightening glance,
How can we know the dancer from the dance?

This is marvellous, and perhaps the very peak of Yeats's achievement. It is in a direct line from the organicism of the great Romantic poets, especially Wordsworth and Keats. But it is also distinctively modern in its development of a process of sceptical, discursive questioning. The sense of an indivisible wholeness of being is happily realised in the complementary images of the living tree and the dancer in the art of dancing, but so also is the analytically rational process which constructs them from their component parts – the tree from its individual parts, leaf, blossom and bole, and, still more tellingly, the dance-in-performance from its abstract, choreographical design and the performer who makes it a living reality. In particular, the final rhetorical question, 'How can we know the dancer from the dance?' functions as an emphatic way of saying that we cannot without murdering to dissect; and we are stirred emotionally by the ecstatic 'O's in the preceding lines to experience rather than analyse these images of wholeness. But the question also functions *as* a question, keeping us conscious that the whole is made of component parts – that there is, after all, a constructing verbal process that puts them together.

Awareness of this process also serves to link 'Among School Children' forward to the poems which were to appear in *Last Poems* (1939), where Yeats becomes conscious, more than ever before, of the work which he himself has created and of the part it plays in the history of art's relationship with reality. In 'Under Ben Bulben', for example, the purpose of art is seen as 'to define images of perfection, goals for our self-shaping'[4] – a theme taken up again, and more tersely expressed, in 'Long-legged Fly'. It is a high, exalted purpose. And yet in these poems elevated diction may suddenly find itself deflated by banality and vulgarity, as it is in 'News for the Delphic Oracle'. There a somewhat camped-up version of a Byzantine paradise (itself heavily indebted to certain famous paintings) is brought down to earth with a bump by a switch to language of deliberate bathos, including 'Foul goat-head' and the almost comical 'Belly, shoulder, bum'. The effect, however, is more complex than the word 'bathos' would suggest; it is more like that of discords in a piece of music which play off against the conventions of harmony while still working within them. The vulgarity is a sophisticatedly artistic form of intrusion which heightens awareness of the rules *qua* rules by daringly, and flagrantly, breaking them.

In yet another of *Last Poems*, however, 'The Circus Animals' Desertion', Yeats comes near to renouncing his art altogether. He gives a kind of 'retrospective' of his own past works, including *The Wanderings of Oisin* and *The Countess Kathleen*, but dismissively sums them up as 'circus animals' which 'were all on show'. What he regards as their merely worked-up artificiality is subverted by characterising their origins, in exaggeratedly low diction, as:

> Old kettles, old bottles, and a broken can,
> Old iron, old bones, old rags, that raving slut
> Who keeps the till.

And his conclusion is that he must go back to raw emotion – 'lie down where all the ladders start, / In the foul rag and bone shop of the heart'.

But the ultimate effect is not one, for all that, of mere dismissal. A truer connection is to be made with the mocking stance and debunking language of 'Among School Children', stanza 6, where the philosophies of Plato, Aristotle and Pythagoras are treated as 'Old clothes upon old sticks to scare a bird'. In neither poem are the things thus rubbished given serious dismissal. Rather the conjurer, or ring-master, suddenly decides to let the audience see the way the tricks are being played – in almost Brechtian fashion, to create his own 'alienation effect'. The passage of low diction is not just a way of bringing the poetry down to ordinary reality; in its own way, with its repeated 'old', its clattering alliteration, and its garish presentation of a barmaid (or whoever) as 'raving slut', it is as much a verbal artifice as the more splendid mythological material characterised as 'Those masterful images'. The antithetical Yeats is again at work, balancing one mask against another – the mythology-monger against the rag-and-bone man, and holding up his masks to public view as he fashions them. What the seeming return to rag-and-bone origins does in fact do is to put emphasis on the artist, or artificer, as such – the creator who does not mediate externally validated truths, but makes them, and decks them up in his study– forge, 'the foul rag and bone shop of the heart'.

ROBERT LOWELL (1917–77)

Lowell, like Yeats, remade himself in mid-career, the change for him coming dramatically with *Life Studies* (1959), after he had already established an imposing reputation with the earlier volumes, *Land of Unlikeness* (1944) and *Lord Weary's Castle* (1946). For Lowell the change was from a mythological, granitic massiveness (very different from the early Celtic faery world of Yeats) to something comparable to the colloquial immediacy of *Responsibilities* and *The Tower*, but more devastatingly personal and confessional.

Early Lowell is determinedly, even wilfully, modernist – consciously allied with the difficult, erudite, concentrated and allusive poetry of the Southern American 'Fugitive' writers centred on Robert Penn Warren (1905–88), Allen Tate (1899–1979) and Randall Jarrell (1914–65). These were academic poet-critics, admirers of Pound and Eliot, and practitioners of the analytical techniques of the so-called 'New Criticism' derived from I. A. Richards and Robert Graves. Their avowed intention was to load every rift with ore, creating a densely packed poetry that gave no quarter either to the lazy, ill-informed reader or to the commercial/industrial/consumerist values which they saw as the debased norm of twentieth-century America. Vivid, sensual immediacy combined with élitist cultural reference was the hallmark of their work, and abstraction and generalisation as much anathema to them as it was to the Imagists. Poetry – in the mode of the seventeenth-century poets, Donne, Herbert and Marvell as interpreted by Eliot in his celebrated essay 'The Metaphysical Poets' (1921) – was extolled as the expression of the simultaneously intellectual and passionate 'whole man'; and, in the words of Lowell's biographer, Ian Hamilton, it was 'at least as valid as scientific knowledge, and in certain ways more so, because it didn't abstract from experience'.[5] The accent was on poetry *as* poetry, with tight control of form and complete freedom from didacticism and log-rolling ideology.

The poetry Lowell wrote under the influence of this austere and intellectually exacting programme is ostentatiously disciplined, sharply physical and heavily freighted with learned allusion. Its most famous, but only partly successful, exemplar is 'The Quaker Graveyard in Nantucket', a poem influenced both by the learnedly Puritan Milton's *Lycidas* and, still more deeply, by Melville's *Moby Dick*.[6] Milton's dedication of *Lycidas* to his Cambridge contemporary Edward King is paralleled by Lowell's dedication to a kinsman,

Warren Winslow, drowned at sea in the Second World War, and there is a similar bursting of the bounds of elegy to write, not about the poet's grief for the dead, but about his own sense of isolation from the corrupt culture of his time. This is reinforced by reference to Melville's ambiguous hero, Captain Ahab, whose maniacal hunting down of the White Whale becomes a symbol of New England's Puritan obsession with denial of the flesh – and perhaps the relentless Puritan work-ethic on which America's current industrial power is based. The poem itself is full of a harsh verbal energy which, for example, enacts the desecration of the dead sailor caught in the drag-net of 'our North Atlantic Fleet' –

> Light
> Flashed from his matted head and marble feet,
> He grappled at the net
> With the coiled, hurdling muscles of his thighs

and yet seems to relish the violence it ostensibly deplores. This becomes still more marked in section 5, which vividly, and with great physical immediacy, presents the climax of the struggle between Ahab and the whale:

> The fat flukes arch and whack about its ears,
> The death-lance churns into the sanctuary, tears
> The gun-blue swingle, heaving like a flail,
> And hacks the coiling life out ...

The rhetoric here is biblical and prophetic, denouncing the sacrilege committed against the whale, but at the same time exulting in the power and ruthlessness of the hunters. Curiously, the next stanza, devoted to the shrine at Walsingham where Lowell's Roman Catholicism (as it was at the time – he lapsed some years later) pours soothing oil on the wild upheaval of the hunt, has a complementary ambiguity. The extra-temporal serenity of Our Lady almost denies her human significance: 'There's no comeliness / At all or charm in that expressionless / Face with its heavy eyelids.' In attempting to avoid devotional sentimentality, for the sake of unclichéd religious expression, Lowell cools the reader towards what should be a more benign vision. His final section, too, apostrophising the Atlantic as tomb of the unnamed sailor, and ending with an allusion to the biblical rainbow given to Noah as a sign that disaster would not overtake mankind again, cannot resist a touch of paradoxical wit which almost overturns the comfort offered: 'The Lord survives the rainbow of His will.' God is not mocked; although his creatures abuse the freedom he gives them, his beneficent will still triumphs. The syntax, however, puts the Lord in seeming opposition to his own rainbow. Lowell's modernist strategy (modernist, but learnt from the Metaphysicals) works by defamiliarising the happy ending obligatory for the Christian, but in so doing creates a brittle paradox which, like so much else in the poem, backfires on itself.

Nevertheless, what remains in the ear after a reading of 'The Quaker Graveyard in Nantucket' is the sound of a powerful orator. The poem asks to be declaimed. Perhaps the same could be said for another elegy, 'For the Union Dead'. But there are eighteen years between them, and in that time Lowell published the *Life Studies* poems which in effect retreated from public oratory to private confession. Their mark is left on 'For the Union Dead' explicitly in the way that poem approaches its honouring of Colonel Shaw and the negroes who fought under him in the Civil War by indirect reminiscence. The speaker looks at the now boarded-up South Boston Aquarium and remembers visiting it as a boy:

> Once my nose crawled like a snail on the glass;
> my hand tingled
> to burst the bubbles
> drifting from the noses of the cowed, compliant fish.

The rest of the poem, which is as politically public as 'The Quaker Graveyard' is religiously public, catches a more casual tone from those lines. The stanza is less formal and the rhetoric is reduced to subtler elements of assonance, consonance and half-rhyme. There is a movement between trivial and momentous which is mutually enhancing. The trivial (concretely realised) acquires resonance, and the momentous loses the inhuman distancing that attends on the monumental.

Though it could be said that this is a benefit from the changes wrought in *Life Studies*, it is in *Life Studies* itself that the virtues of the style, dubbed 'confessional' by M. L. Rosenthal, can be seen at their best. The source of these poems is, more emphatically than anything before, drawn from Lowell's own life, and the language is more open and direct. Their colloquial and dramatic elements can be related to the dramatic monologue, but, as Mark Rudman says, 'Browning, Eliot, and Pound [Lowell's predecessors in the form] impersonate, in varying degrees, other voices; Lowell infuses the force of his own personality and style into every line he writes.'[7] It is autobiographical to a degree that personal information, if not absolutely indispensable, is certainly a requirement for its understanding by most readers – as Lowell implicitly concedes by including the prose memoirs entitled '91 Revere Street' (the address of the house in Boston where he spent his childhood) as part of the text of the American edition of *Life Studies*.

This is also poetry which has a prominently psychological content – as can be seen not only in Lowell's own work, but in that of contemporaries such as John Berryman (1914–72), Delmore Schwartz (1913–66) and Theodore Roethke (1908–63), many of whom follow Lowell in making poetry out of their own psychiatric problems.[8] The revelations are often those which the poet might make in privacy to a close friend, or on the analyst's couch, and they sometimes have both the frankness and the extravagance of the mentally ill. As well as being potentially embarrassing to those who are involved in the private life of the poet, such poetry raises questions about its status. What is its value, other than that of private gossip or clinical case-book material? Is the often high-pitched personal anguish capable of being translated into something which the reader can perceive as a heightened statement about, or symbol of, themes central to the society from which it springs? Formally, too, the disturbed subject-matter tends to feed back into the style by which it is expressed. 'Confessional' poetry often imitates the fragmented stream-of-consciousness technique developed by the modernists, in an attempt to re-create the ramblings of a disordered mind; and while this makes for excitingly bizarre juxtapositions of material, it can, as Marjorie Perloff argues, also produce incoherency: 'The danger of the Lowell mode ... is that the poem too easily becomes self-indulgent confession on the one hand, or random description of objects on the other' – a danger exemplified in Perloff's opinion by the disconnected randomness of Berryman's 'The Hell Poem'.[9]

The best of *Life Studies*, however, manage to avoid this sense of incoherence. In 'My Last Afternoon with Uncle Devereux Winslow' the seemingly disconnected and the more widely significant are happily combined. The local and private details derived from

Lowell's own family background give the poem an air of dramatic immediacy. Following the title is a parenthesis equivalent to a stage direction: '1922: THE STONE PORCH OF MY GRANDFATHER'S SUMMER HOUSE'; and the poem opens with a snatch of dialogue – the five-year-old Lowell screaming to his parents, 'I won't go with you. I want to stay with Grandpa!' As the poem progresses other graphic details are added which give the sense of an authentic record of precise, quirkily individual reminiscences of private experience, including the '*Tockytock, tockytock*' sound of 'our Alpine, Edwardian cuckoo clock', Grandpa's making of his shandygaff 'by blending half and half / yeasty, wheezing homemade sarsaparilla with beer', and Great Aunt Sarah's demented practising of excerpts from *Samson and Delilah* 'on the keyboard of her dummy piano'. On this level the poem seems to exist as autobiographical documentary. But other bizarre images of decay – 'octagonal red tiles, / sweaty with a secret dank', 'Cinder, our Scottie puppy / paralyzed from gobbling toads' – mingle with the futility of Aunt Sarah's failure to appear at the concert hall on the day of her recital, and mount to the extended image of Uncle Devereux himself, elegant in his blue coat and white trousers, but dying from Hodgkin's disease at the age of twenty-nine. These, like the images of paralysis in James Joyce's *Dubliners*, evoke the wider sense of a moribund civilisation – a once distinguished family, as the Lowells were, running to seed, and with them the New England culture set perhaps irrevocably into decline.

The climax of *Life Studies* is its concluding poem, 'Skunk Hour'. This is still more explicitly concerned with the theme of decay. It starts with a wider, more generic sweep, and then narrows down from the general to the particular (though in sequence of composition the last four stanzas, focusing on the poet and the skunk, came first). The opening stanzas are detailed and precisely observed in the metonymic style characteristic of *Life Studies*, but offer what are almost allegorical figures of 'The season's ill' in the New England resort of Nautilus Island – the 'hermit heiress' who in her dotage 'buys up all / the eyesores facing her shore, / and lets them fall', the lost 'summer millionaire' (reminiscent of Eliot's 'ruined millionaire' in 'East Coker'), and the sardonically presented 'fairy / decorator' who, echoing the heiress, 'brightens his shop for fall'. Their symbolic animal is the fox, whose 'stain covers Blue Hill'. Comparably, the mother skunk who dominates the second half of the poem forages in a garbage pail, as if equally a denizen of this decaying world, and she and her brood also have 'red fire', in their 'moonstruck eyes'. But this is the redness of vitality, not of stain: the final image of her –

> She jabs her wedge-head in a cup
> of sour cream, drops her ostrich tail,
> and will not scare –

is one of defiance, finding life amidst the rubbish, not submission. In between, the poet, who voyeur-like drives his car up 'the hill's skull' to spy on courting couples, seems an extension of the town's decay, but aware of his own corruption – like Milton's Satan conscious that he himself is hell. Here the poem touches on Lowell's own private experience of mental illness ('My mind's not right'), but internal and external become fused. The whole poem has a psychological dimension, as if it were the rehearsing of a crazily precise nightmare for the benefit of an analyst. Equally, however, it has the air of sociological and cultural observation; each mirrors and interpenetrates the other.

Later Lowell leans increasingly towards the sociological, and also political. The casual, off-the-cuff style gets still nearer to prose and the detail nearer to reportage. But the underlying purpose remains to achieve the imaginative reverberation which differentiates poetry from prose. Whether this really succeeds, however, is debatable. The poetry tends to be arresting by fits and starts, but without quite achieving the balance between public and private which makes 'Skunk Hour' so satisfying a whole. What is virtually Lowell's own reflection on this problem occurs in a poem which he calls, significantly, 'Epilogue'. The problem he broods on there is how to combine factual accuracy, like that of the camera, with the poet's essentially subjective vision; and the style in which he tries to cope with it is that of the 'confessional' poem. Lowell becomes his own frankest (and harshest) critic, admitting that sometimes what he writes becomes a kind of photographic snapshot:

> lurid, rapid, garish, grouped,
> heightened from life,
> yet paralyzed by fact.

Such art is highly elusive – as elusive for Lowell as the desired reconciliation of transience and permanence was for Yeats; and 'Epilogue' ends like 'Among School Children' on a prayer for the spontaneity which might almost magically bring it about:

> Pray for the grace of accuracy
> Vermeer gave to the sun's illumination
> stealing like the tide across a map
> to his girl solid with yearning.

As a consummate painter of very private, domestic scenes the seventeenth-century Dutch painter Vermeer solved the problem confidently and serenely. Lowell's achievement is much more haphazard. Nevertheless, in breaking out of his own rhetorical shell to something more casual and self-questioning at the least, as he modestly claims, he manages to give each person in his verbal snapshots 'his living name'; but he also at the best gives glimpses of a more satisfying reconciliation between private and public.

CONCLUSION

Though very different poets, in subject-matter and style, Yeats and Lowell raise comparable questions about the relation of public to private experience. Both are highly rhetorical poets who address their audiences in grave, even at times hieratic, tones; and yet both react strongly against the grand style they so effectively practise in favour of a more down-to-earth speaking voice capable of being harshly colloquial and deliberately coarse.

For Lowell, getting off his stilts in this way is a necessary means for coming to terms with deeply disturbing, personal material. In the process he runs the risk of substituting a kind of note-book series of jottings which gets as far from true poetry in one direction as the almost mechanically armoured rhetoric of some of his earlier work does in the opposite direction. But in the best of *Life Studies* an autobiographical immediacy is successfully combined with symbolic suggestiveness to enable the private experience to take on general significance.

For Yeats the problem is the somewhat more difficult one of reconciling a personality fragmented into a variety of *personae*. Or, to put it another way, of establishing an equilibrium between the various dramatic embodiments of his 'masks' that will allow them their own, separate validities, and yet recognise their participation in an organically interrelated whole. The bulk of his work is an exploration of the multiplicity of stances which his sense of the complexity of experience compels him to adopt. This kaleidoscopic method also enables him to deal effectively with public, and especially Irish political, themes, with passion and commitment, while managing to avoid the kind of commitment that would become distortingly partisan. In the best of his poems (such as 'Easter 1916', 'The Second Coming', 'Sailing to Byzantium' and 'Among School Children') the voice of the public man addressing an audience is subtly counterpointed with that of the private person musing to himself, to produce a multidimensional poetry which satisfyingly balances its constituent voices.

5

Poetry of
Two World Wars

WILFRED OWEN (1893–1918)

In the unfinished Preface to what seems to have been intended as a volume of his war poems Wilfred Owen wrote:

> This book is not about heroes. English Poetry is not yet fit to speak of them.
> Nor is it about deeds, or lands, nor anything about glory, honour, might, majesty, dominion, or power, except War.
> Above all I am not concerned with Poetry.
> My subject is War, and the pity of War.
> The poetry is in the pity.

This is a personal statement rather than a poetic manifesto, and quite possibly does not contain Owen's final, considered judgement on his own work. But it is strikingly modern. The implicit reaction against the celebration of 'glory, honour, might, majesty, dominion, or power' voices a feeling which became widespread during the First World War among troops fighting on the western front (if not among civilian stay-at-homes), and the rejection of 'Poetry' with a capital 'P' reflects a sense of disillusionment and disgust with a rhetoric which seemed out of touch with the degrading realities of trench warfare.

What is probably the most frequently quoted of all Owen's poems, 'Dulce Et Decorum Est', details the horrors of a gas attack, and insists on the difference between that and the falsified image of war cultivated for the benefit of youth by an ignorant and unthinking patriotism:

> My friend, you would not tell with such high zest
> To children ardent for some desperate glory,

The old Lie: *Dulce et decorum est*
Pro patria mori.

The Latin phrase, meaning 'It is sweet and meet / decorous to die for one's country' (Owen's own translation), is taken from Horace's Odes III, ii, which formed part of the staple of a classically educated middle class; and the poem as a whole was dedicated ironically 'To a certain Poetess' – Jessie Pope, a writer of patriotic verse.[1] The poem is thus both an illustration of, and comment on, reality and illusion as reflected in the actual fighting conditions and propaganda of the First World War. Verbally, too, it is in conscious revolt against poetic conventions which gloss over unpleasant realities. The imagery of 'old beggars under sacks' and the graphic horror of

> the blood
> Come gargling from the froth-corrupted lungs,
> Obscene as cancer, bitter as the cud
> Of vile, incurable sores on innocent tongues

are also part shock-tactics, part determination to replace 'poetic' diction by a language adjusted to contemporary facts of a kind which leads elsewhere to Kiplingesque dialogue based on working-class rather than middle-class speech:

> I mind as 'ow the night afore that show
> Us five got talkin', – we was in the know.
> 'Over the top to-morrer; boys, we're for it.
> First wave we are, first ruddy wave; that's tore it!'

> > ('The Chances')

Censorship is still at work here – 'ruddy' is almost certainly semi-polite substitution for the universal military (and here more appropriately alliterative) 'f' word; but the overall impression is one that cuts through elegance to crude immediacy. 'The Chances' is modern, too, in that it is attributed to a persona. Owen does not speak in his own voice, but in that of the common soldier. Nevertheless, awareness of a significant difference in register is communicated through the speaker's ironic reference to being taken prisoner: 'An' one, to use the word of 'ypocrites, / 'Ad the misfortoon to be took be Fritz.' Hypocrisy in this context is middle-class and establishment, as it is more explicitly in 'Inspection', where the first-person 'I' is Owen, or at least his 'officer' self, and the demotic element comes from the sergeant's 'Old yer mouth' and 'I take 'is name, sir?' However, the levels of language are more complex in 'Inspection' in that the soldier who has come blood-stained on parade is not noticeably working-class in diction. The way he speaks allows him to seem the projection of another aspect of Owen's self – the one who can, as in 'Apologia pro Poemate Meo', see 'God through mud', while the official military clichés of 'confined to camp' and 'dirty on parade' seem the linguisitc automata against which the conclusion of the poem,

> But when we're duly white-washed, being dead,
> The race will bear Field-Marshal God's inspection

is set in ironically charged contrast. The routine military inspection is itself subjected to a linguistic inspection which questions unexamined assumptions.

Formally Owen looks more traditional. His metrics are English iambic and his verse rhymed, his most notable innovation being his use of pararhyme in which vowel-sounds change, but their enclosing consonants remain the same (e.g. 'escaped' / 'scooped', / 'groined' / 'groaned', 'Strange Meeting' lines 1–4). The hard, punching rhymes of 'The Chances' and 'Inspection' are suitable for the grim, sardonic mood in which they are cast; the more melancholy and visionary styles of 'Strange Meeting' and 'Miners' are appropriately matched with pararhyme. But in his use of traditional verse forms such as the sonnet (as in 'Anthem for Doomed Youth') or the Tennysonian *In Memoriam* stanza (as in 'Soldier's Dream') Owen is arguably more subtly original. For example, 'Anthem' is a sonnet in near-Shaksperean form; it varies the regular ABAB CDCD EFEF GG pattern by rhyming the third quatrain EFFE in the *In Memoriam* manner. This in itself underlines the change from major to minor key in the Petrarchan rather than Shakespearean division between octave and sestet, which corresponds with a change from an anti-rhetorical manipulation of rhetoric in lines 1–8, dealing with the front-line experience of soldiers, to the more sadly reserved grieving of their relatives and girl-friends in lines 9–14. There are echoes of Shakespeare and Keats, most notably in lines 6–7 where the 'mourning' of the 'shrill, demented choirs of wailing shells' recalls 'Then in a wailful choir the small gnats mourn' in 'To Autumn', itself an echo of 'Bare ruined choirs, where late the sweet birds sang' in Sonnet 73; but these are neither merely derivative, nor allusive in the modernist manner. They suggest a traditional music of mortality (highlighted by the 'Anthem' of the title), but converted Nietzsche-like into a 'musical dissonance' which is at once a language of protest against the mechanical mass-slaughter of modern warfare and a strangely new, powerful music of destruction peculiar to itself.[2]

Another dimension to the language of 'Anthem for Doomed Youth', to be found also in poems like 'Greater Love', 'At a Calvary near the Ancre', 'Strange Meeting' and, in more subdued form, 'The Send-Off' and 'Futility', is that of religion – more specifically, the Christian religion. As a former lay-preacher Owen had mixed, if not confused, feelings about the possibility of reconciling Christianity with warfare; in a much-quoted phrase he described himself as a 'conscientious objector with a very seared conscience'.[3] But setting aside his own, private reservations, one can see it as another aspect, and a representative one, of his modernity that conventional religious attitudes should come into conflict with the scepticism evinced, for example, in the work of Thomas Hardy. The religious rituals echoed in 'Anthem' are both poignant and sardonic, rubbing shoulders as they do with the insensate machinery of contemporary war, while the furtive dispatch of soldiers to the front in 'The Send-Off' gains much of its curiously restrained emotive power from the subdued suggestion that they are sacrifices to the unacknowledged guilt of those who remain safely at home. 'Futility', on the other hand, is more specifically Hardyesque in the sense it creates of a meaningless creation:

> – O what made fatuous sunbeams toil
> To break earth's sleep at all?

And 'Strange Meeting', with its echoes of Vergil or Dante's underworld combined with the strange, dreamlike meeting of enemy transformed into friend, converts the idea of Christian brotherhood into a visionary aspiration which is subversive of the religious orthodoxy on which war is predicated. In this sense Owen's poetry emerges as something more Christian than Christianity, but distinctively modern in its simultaneous revaluation of both message and context.

SIEGFRIED SASSOON (1886–1967), ISAAC ROSENBERG (1890–1918) AND EDWARD THOMAS (1878–1917)

Such poetry also exemplifies Owen's central position as First World War poet. It places him between Siegfried Sassoon on the one hand and Isaac Rosenberg on the other, and with a dimension that also connects him to Edward Thomas. The front-line immediacies of his poetry link him to both Sassoon and Rosenberg, but the link with Sassoon is mainly through protest at military incompetence and civilian complacency, seen respectively in 'The General' and 'Blighters' – the latter sharply juxtaposing music-hall patriotism with 'the riddled corpses round Bapaume'. The Owen of 'Strange Meeting' is suggested by the setting of 'The Rear-Guard', which opens with a soldier 'groping' along a tunnel by the light of a 'prying torch' and ends, as the soldier climbs back to daylight, with an Owen-like sense of 'Unloading hell behind him step by step'. But this is not really a visionary hell; it is much nearer the 'hell' of common speech. Sassoon's war-poetry voice, and what makes him sound distinctively modern, is that of the day-to-day man *speaking* to the reader projected as a sympathetic interlocutor who is freed, as he must suppose the speaker himself, of rhetorical illusions, but impatient with those who are not. And perhaps his finest poem, 'To Any Dead Officer', is a variation on that formula in which the speaker–poet converses with a dead brother-officer in the language, and taking for granted the attitudes, which come out of their shared officer-class past as it has now been modified by the reality of life in the trenches. Their God is like the Field Marshal of Owen's 'Inspection':

> Good-bye, old lad! Remember me to God,
>   And tell Him that our Poiticians swear
> They won't give in till Prussian Rule's been trod
>   Under the Heel of England ...

The remainder of this final stanza is moving by virtue of its underplayed, officer-class cheeriness; the language could be that of the public school or the London club, but the context gives it a new, elegiac power.

The social background implicit in 'To Any Dead Officer' is one of several features which mark its author off from Isaac Rosenberg. Born of Jewish parents who had emigrated from Russia to England,

Rosenberg was brought up in extreme poverty in the working-class East End of London. As a bright boy he was helped by well-to-do patrons to attend the Slade School of Art along with avant-garde artists like Victor Bomberg, Mark Gertler, Stanley Spencer, Paul Nash and C. R. W. Nevinson – many of whom became war artists who contributed as much visually to the re-shaping of war experience as the war poets themselves. But when he joined up he went as a private in a 'bantam' regiment, being neither tall enough nor physically strong enough for a regular unit. His point of view was that of the ranks, combined in almost bizarre fashion with that of a latter-day Blakean visionary. If realism is the mark of the anti-poetic side of Owen, determined to communicate things as they are in the degradation of modern warfare, the Rosenberg of 'Louse Hunting', 'Break of Day in the Trenches' and 'Dead Man's Dump' is every bit as realistic; but he echoes still more the visionary dimension of Owen, turning realism into surrealism. Men stripped naked to rid themselves of vermin fling themselves about in 'a demons' pantomime' and

> gargantuan hooked fingers
> Pluck in supreme flesh
> To smutch supreme littleness.

'Break of Day in the Trenches' juxtaposes the splendid bodies – 'fine limbs, haughty athletes' – of soldiers with the 'shrieking iron and flame' of artillery barrages which give them less chance of evading 'the whims of murder' than the 'queer sardonic rat' which jumps over the speaker's hand as he decorates himself with a poppy pulled from the parapet. The rat-like imagination is indifferently reductive, by-passing the tremendous difference war would officially make between English and German, spanning enormous contrasts, but ending with white dust on a red flower. And in 'Dead Man's Dump' both the horrific realism of Owen's 'Dulce et Decorum Est' and his religious element combine garishly to create a concentratedly contradictory epic of violence and compassion.

The connection between Owen and Edward Thomas is to be found in the elegiac tone shared by poems such as 'Miners' or 'Strange Meeting' and 'Lights Out' or 'As the Team's Head-Brass'. Although Thomas does not write directly about front-line experience, he glances at it from a deceptively pastoral setting which sets it in a similar kind of distancing perspective to that which Owen also achieves when he 'escapes' out of battle. In 'Lights Out', Thomas may seem more resigned, even, in Keatsian fashion, 'half in love with easeful Death'. The superficially comparable sense in 'Strange Meeting' of war-weary sleepers glad of death is countered in Owen by a neo-Romantic vision of a new society cleansed by suffering (the Wordsworthian echo in 'Even with truths that lie too deep for taint' seems to make that affinity with the Romantics conscious). But it is transcendence of self rather than mere resignation which gives 'Lights Out' its peculiarly elegiac tone. For Thomas to 'come to the borders of sleep' (likewise an alternative word for 'death') is to 'lose' both 'my way / And myself'. Although the only explicit hint that this is about war is in the title, the poem is suffused with a sense that war is an inevitable experience – an extension of the universal death-experience, which makes war not only an occasion for protest, but a necessary, dis-illusioning process.

Such a placing of war is open to the criticism which D. H. Lawrence aims at modern tragedy as he sees it exemplified in novels like *Anna Karenina*, *The Return of the Native* and *Jude the Obscure* – namely, that it treats essentially man-made evils as if they were inherent in a divine scheme of things: 'Anna, Eustacia, Tess or Sue – what was there in their position that was necessarily tragic? Necessarily painful it was, but they were not at war with God, only with Society'.[4] The 'war poet' as we have come to think of him thanks to the reputations acquired by Owen and Sassoon is a poet of protest against society: society is to blame for its ignorance or indifference, and the consequent implication is that therefore society can be, and ought to be, changed. But at the same time war is a recurrent expression of the destructive violence inherent in mankind which can only be come to terms with tragically – that is, by recognising and accepting it as part of the natural scheme of things. Owen differs markedly from Sassoon in adding this dimension to his poetry; he is both 'war poet' of protest and tragic poet who sees war as a manifestation of the evil inherent in the human being, hence the Aristotelian 'pity of war, the pity war distilled' complementing the terror evident in his more horrific front-line poems.

Edward Thomas's claim to tragic status rests not so much on poems such as 'Lights Out' and 'Rain', moving as both of these are, as on 'As the Team's Head Brass' and 'Old Man' (though it would be stretching the term to call the latter a war poem). Here Thomas both succumbs to, and resists, the destructive impulse. The immediate moment from which he takes his departure is very different from that of Owen. It is at home, not in France. But it is only deceptively Georgian in its seemingly very English, pastoral nostalgia. 'As the Team's Head Brass' looks out towards France from its very traditional at-home context of ploughing the field, and its dialogue of ploughman and poet against the rhythmic to-and-fro of the horses, their meaning sexually enhanced by the lovers' entering and leaving the neighbouring wood, incorporates both destruction and creation. The death of the ploughman's mate unites war and natural violence:

> The second day
> In France they killed him. It was back in March,
> The very night of the blizzard, too.

This is the blizzard which had felled the elm where the poet sits next to 'a woodpecker's round hole', and, if the ploughman's mate had not been killed, together they would have moved the tree. Now it must wait till the war is over. Woodpecker's hole, the wait, and the lovers in the background, all, however, imply continuity in spite of destruction; and, rather more distinctively modern in tone, the prosaically ironic way in which the poet anticipates his own fate at the hand of war –

> I could spare an arm. I shouldn't want to lose
> A leg. If I should lose my head, why, so,
> I should want nothing more. ...

combines the soldier's humour of sardonic understatement, implying a much deeper revulsion than its surface acknowledges, with a kind of equation between the limbs of his body and those of the tree. What Rosenberg does, in 'Dead Man's Dump', by positing Earth as a goddess waiting for war to deliver her victims to her, Thomas does, less garishly, in 'As the Team's Head Brass', by treating the slaughter of World War I as an aspect of the destruction and creation which goes on perpetually in the cycle of nature. Neither diminishes the destructiveness of war – though, clearly, the emphasis laid on it in 'Dead Man's Dump' is greater than in Thomas, but both give it another dimension as well. In Rosenberg's case this dimension is mythic, in Thomas's something less easy to define. His much more conversational manner deflates any suggestion of epic grandeur, without in any way resembling the antirhetorical rhetoric of Owen's 'Dulce Et Decorum Est', and yet still expresses a tragic vision based on the acceptance of contradictions woven into the fabric of life itself. The quietly groping movement of 'As the Team's Head Brass' is typical of Thomas, and also typical of his particular version of the modern, combining scepticism with affirmation. Its closing lines make no great statement, yet effectively hint at the creative/destructive ambivalence of the ploughing:

> The horses started and for the last time
> I watched the clods crumble and topple over
> After the ploughshare and the stumbling team.

POUND, ELIOT AND THE WAR

Thomas's affinities are with Hardy. The closing lines of 'As the Team's Head Brass' recall the last line of 'During Wind and Rain', 'Down their carved names the rain-drop ploughs', and its creative/destructive theme echoes that of Hardy's wartime poem (dated 1915) 'In Time of "The Breaking of Nations"'. Neither is self-consciously modernist. The same could be said for Owen, Sassoon, Graves, Blunden, Sorley, Gurney and a whole string of lesser World War I poets. But the modernists do also react to the war in their poetry, though in the main retrospectively. Pound's 'Hugh Selwyn Mauberley' (1920) refracts the war through the complex personality of its namesake, partly alter ego for Pound himself, partly dubious aesthete, who becomes most impassioned not about the suffering of those engaged in the war (though he speaks of 'Daring as never before, wastage as never before'), but the sterility of the values for which they were sacrificed –

> For an old bitch gone in the teeth,
> For a botched civilization.

And Eliot's *The Waste Land* is certainly a work which, as D. H. Lawrence said of his own *Women in Love*, 'actually does contain the results in one's soul of the war'.[5] Incidental characters point to war experience – for example, Lil's 'demobbed' (i.e. demobilised) husband and Stetson who, though he is said to have been with the poem's speaker in a naval battle of the Punic Wars, is also in effect an old comrade of World War I. But, as with Pound, it is the sense of waste and decay in a Europe exhausted by war which is its pervasive theme. The nightmare images, particularly of section V, 'What the Thunder Said', read like evocations of the desolate Flanders landscapes described and painted by wartime artists such as Paul Nash, Stanley Spencer and C. R. W. Nevinson,[6] and the moral and political bankruptcy which was an outcome of the war is echoed in the inverted vision of 'hooded hordes swarming / Over endless plains' and the collapsing syntax of 'Falling towers' juxtaposed haphazardly with a roll-call of European and Middle East cities.

DAVID JONES (1895–1974) AND *IN PARENTHESIS*

But it is David Jones's *In Parenthesis* which most fully adapts modernism to the expression of World War I experience. Although its subject is the war, and Jones draws on his own experience of fighting in the trenches with the Royal Welch Fusiliers (the same regiment as Sassoon's and Graves's), *In Parenthesis* was not begun till 1927/8 and was first published in 1937. In a sense it is a long poem, dealing with the embarcation of a platoon of troops to France, their first experience of trench warfare, and their virtual annihilation on the Somme in July 1916; but given its mixture of prose and free verse (the prose quantitatively greater than the verse) its claim to be considered as a 'poem' must depend on the unusualness of its language and an acceptance of the modernist position which would see nominally prose works like Joyce's *Ulysses* or Virginia Woolf's *To the Lighthouse* as essentially poetic. Even its character as 'war' literature is open to question. Elizabeth Ward argues that it stands apart from the work of Owen and Sassoon, and should be seen as a myth-making work in the tradition of Pound, Joyce and Eliot. In the disintegration of modern warfare it finds an equivalence to the psychic and cultural disintegration characteristic of the modern world in which the holistic, 'symbol-producing' capacity of primitive culture has been catastrophically lost.[7] Its intellectual environment is that of Freud and Jung, and, among artists, Picasso, Stravinsky and D. H. Lawrence; and its allusive method, encompassing frequent references to the Bible, Shakespeare (especially *Henry V*) Arthurian legends, Milton, Coleridge and, above all, the sixth-century Welsh epic *Y Gododdin*, which tells of a raid on the English-held Catraeth (Catterick), is markedly akin to that of Eliot's

The Waste Land in its juxtaposition of fragments from past and present warfare experience. The function of its hero, John Ball, like Eliot's Tiresias, is 'tenuous', and 'his presence transparently a linking device, his voice only one of many voices which sound throughout the poem'.[8]

Nevertheless, *In Parenthesis* can lay claim to the distinctiveness of war literature. In his Preface Jones explains his title by saying that it is something written 'in a kind of space between', the war itself being 'a parenthesis'. The 'space between' is that which the soldiers, enlisted for 'the Duration' and torn from their normal civilian context, have to inhabit and accommodate their minds to. Whether it is possible to do this is the underlying theme of the work. One answer is tentatively suggested at the beginning of Jones's Preface, where he distinguishes between the war as it was prior to July 1916 and what it became thereafter – 'a more relentless, mechanical affair' with 'wholesale slaughter' which 'knocked the bottom out of the intimate, continuing, domestic life of small contingents of men'. The strange language of the work, mixing the demotic speech of ordinary soldiers with military jargon, self-consciously rhetorical diction and syntax and also archaism appropriate to its remote, allusive content, both emphasises the disorienting horror of trench warfare and its links through tradition and discipline to what previous generations, from centuries back, had experienced. In unprecedented circumstances some kind of 'continuity' and 'domesticity' is still contrived. But the new warfare, tokened by the first shell to impinge on John Ball's consciousness (described in the last paragraph of Part 2) which comes out 'of the vortex, rifling the air . . . bright, brass-shod, Pandoran' opens a Pandora's box that can never be shut again. Weaponry itself undergoes radical transformation, and the personal rifle of the infantryman, the care of which is constantly insisted on by regimental tradition, is at the end abandoned by the wounded John Ball:

> It's a beautiful doll for us
> it's the Last Reputable Arm.
>   But leave it – under the oak,
> leave it for a Cook's tourist to the Devastated Areas and crawl
> as far as you can and wait for the bearers.

WORLD WAR II: KEITH DOUGLAS (1920–44), ALUN LEWIS (1915–44) AND ROY FULLER (1912–91)

In general the poetry of World War II is more circumscribed. It neither aspires to the mythopoeic largeness of David Jones, nor to the admonitory urgency of Wilfred Owen. This can be explained in a number of ways. The illusions and subsequent disillusionment which were the substance of so much World War I poetry created a legacy for World War II poets which made scepticism and realism their starting point, and the combatants, at least on the Allied side, felt that the need to counter fascism was a cause which could not be reduced to the terms of a merely spurious propaganda. (The poets of the Thirties had also played their part in enabling this to be seen and accepted as an un-illusioned necessity.) Nor was there the same separation of military from civilian experience. In many cases danger and suffering was as great at home as at the front; war was to that extent something much less 'in parenthesis'.

Among English soldier poets Keith Douglas, Alun Lewis and Sidney Keyes (1922–43) have become the best known names; but only Douglas is a combatant poet whose work is comparable with that of Owen, Sassoon, and Co. Even so, the 'pity of war' is hardly his theme. Douglas's poetry has a quality of harsh concentration (Edna Longley comments that '"every word must work for its keep"' is a dictum of his which 'is not nearly as well known as it should be'),[9] and, thanks in part to a persuasive introduction by Ted Hughes, it is a poetry which has come to be associated with the kind of unsentimental celebration of natural violence to be found in poems like Hughes's 'The Jaguar' and 'Hawk Roosting'.[10] Poems like 'How to Kill', 'Vergissmeinnicht' and 'Cairo Jag' lend some support to this view. The dead German soldier on whose skin

> the swart flies move;
> the dust upon the paper eye
> and the burst stomach like a cave
>
> ('Vergissmeinnicht')

or the corpses littering the desert among whom

> a man with no head
> has a packet of chocolate and a souvenir of Tripoli
>
> ('Cairo Jag')

taken in isolation seem images of violence observed with almost inhuman detachment. But the syntax which controls them, and the consequent relationship which they are given to the rest of the poem, compels a rather different kind of response. In 'Vergissmeinnicht' the dead body has to be related to the living soldier who three weeks earlier from behind the barrel of an anti-tank gun posed an equally dire threat for Douglas and his tank crew, and also to the lover whose girl-friend had written 'Forget me not' on her photograph 'in a copybook gothic script'. The poem tries to adjust these facets of reality to each other:

> For here the lover and killer are mingled
> who had one body and one heart.

Similarly, in 'Cairo Jag' the seedy, sensuous life of Cairo has to be seen in conjunction with the desert front-line which constitutes 'a new world' only 'a day's travelling' away, where

> the vegetation is of iron
> dead tanks, gun barrels split like celery.

This is war poetry enforcing a disquietingly new perspective on things, an initiation into the workings of an imagination which is not necessarily humane.

Douglas was killed in the Normandy invasion at the age of 24, Keyes even earlier, at the age of 20, in Tunisia. But there seems more than four years difference between them. The somewhat artificially 'literary' quality of Keyes's work is not challenged in the same way by a grim newness of perception. Much of his verse remains too gracefully elegiac, though there is a hint in 'War Poet' – for example, in the statement, 'I am the man who groped for words and found / An arrow in my hand' – that for him, too, intention and reality were becoming fruitfully at odds. Lewis (1915–44), on the other hand, was on the way to being an established writer prior to the war, and the war is a modifier rather than precipitator of his maturity. His imagination is civilian rather than military, and for him war is essentially an interruption of civilian life.

Lewis is a Welshman looking from the perspective of the enlisted man caught up in the 'parenthesis' of war, but with no inclination to give it the mythologised Welshness that David Jones does. His affinities are much more with Edward Thomas ('To Edward Thomas' speaks for itself and 'All Day It Has Rained' bears a strong resemblance to Thomas's 'Rain'). Thomas looks forward from England to the devastating prospect of war, Lewis from the phoney war of enlistment and embarcation back to the normality and domesticity of the Wales he is leaving, or has left, but with a similar sense that what is taking place is divorcement from a way of life that has both continuity and the possibility of development. Although such poetry is open to the charge of pastoral sentimentality, and Lewis indulges the lingering, dying-fall cadence which comes easily to that elegiac mood, it is balanced by a counterpoint of more realistic observation and probing question:

> In all the ways of going who can tell
> The real from the unjustified farewell?

The brittleness of this comments obliquely on the corrosive effect of war, adding a dimension more sinister than that of mere nostalgia.

The poems Lewis wrote in the last months of his life in India and Burma suggest the development of a different kind of response to a very different, non-Welsh landscape and society. 'The Mahratta Ghats', for example, opens with lines reminiscent of Eliot's waste land scenery:

> The valleys crack and burn, the exhausted plains
> Sink their black teeth into the horny veins
> Straggling the hills' red thighs ...

But, unlike Eliot, it is the relationship between land and people which absorbs Lewis's attention as he focuses on those who are forced to scratch a living from such unwelcoming soil. The compassionate element which enables him, despite being an officer, to articulate the ordinary conscript soldier's view of war is here pushing him towards sympathy with a peasantry seen as enslaved by, rather than living creatively close to, the land. A tacit comment on imperialism may also be involved with this: Lewis and his fellow-soldiers are brought into contact with these people only because they are there on the Indian sub-continent to defend the Empire, and in a string of questions both the motivation of the soldiers and the future of empire are cast in doubt.

Elsewhere (for example, in 'All Day It Has Rained' and 'After Dunkirk') Lewis reveals a scepticism about official propaganda and 'the loud celebrities / Exhorting us to slaughter' which is reminiscent of poets like Owen, Sassoon and Sorley, but this, if somewhat obscurely, hints at even more far-reaching doubts concerning the role of the country he is ostensibly fighting for. In a better, because more focused, poem, 'Burma Casualty', such loss of confidence manifests itself in the suffering of an Indian Army captain whose leg has to be amputated to save his life. The core of the poem is an exploration of the state of mind induced by the anaesthetic, from which the man returns 'Retching and blind with pain, and yet Alive'. The capitalisation of 'Alive' lends the word ironic effect. In the final section of the poem the captain thinks of his 'regiment too butchered to reform' and of his own venture into, and back from, the death which still holds so many of his comrades. That death is 'a beautiful singing sexless angel' which 'flatters and unsexes every man' – language which suggests its siren-like quality of seduction, and would seem to carry the implication that its deception must be resisted. Yet the alternative is curtly dismissed in the last two lines of the poem:

> And Life is only a crude, pigheaded churl
> Frowsy and starving, daring to suffer alone.

At one level this is simply an expression of post-operative trauma and the sense of guilt so many combatants feel when they survive a battle while their friends do not. But the reductive manner in which recovery is presented suggests a more radical failure of nerve. The amputee is isolated from what may be the only meaningful community he has known.

Another war poet, who survived the war and continued to write for a further 40 years, is Roy Fuller. At times Fuller sounds like an Auden *alter ego* – one who did not remove himself to America, but joined the Navy and served both in England and East Africa. In 'Autumn 1940' he places World War II in its Thirties context as a bringing home and actualisation of the conflicts which up to that point had occured only in Spain and China:

We see as inevitable and with relief
The smoke from shells like plump ghosts on the purple,
The bombers, black insect eggs, on the sky's broad leaf.

If this seems more ideological than anything to be found in Alun
Lewis, he none the less shares with Lewis a strong concern for men
caught up unwillingly in the 'inevitable'; and dialectic and formal
though his poetic structures are (again very much in the Auden
manner), he can write directly about the people, places and things
of wartime England in a way that justifies his later claim (in the
post-war 'Dedicatory Epistle' of *Epitaphs and Occasions*, 1949) that
the poet ought to go back to Wordsworth's verse 'meant for men'.
The poems written in East Africa (for example, 'The White Conscript
and the Black Conscript', 'The Tribes', and the longer narrative,
'Teba') continue this concern, but, like Lewis's Indian poems, become
less war poems as such than expressions of a new awareness opened
up by contact between warring Europe and tribal Africa.

Back in England again, war's effect on the civilians, as in 'During
a Bombardment by V-Weapons', puts military experience in
the background. Fragments of domestic life, such as 'Drippings
between the slates and ceiling' and 'the feet of a mouse', give an
unexpected perspective to the poem's title. These, 'at the ending of
a war', alarm the speaker more than 'the ridiculous detonations'
outside; and in the final stanza, addressed to the speaker's 'love',
yet another dimension is introduced: with her 'pallor' (caused by
anger, suffering, injury, illness?)

> Now all the permanent and real
> Furies are settling in upstairs.

By implication war is not only impermanent, but less real than the
presumably emotional turbulence of love.

An alternative reading of 'During a Bombardment ', guided by
the language of 'ridiculous detonations' and 'gently coughing cur-
tains' (and the perhaps inflated quality of 'Furies'), is to see it as
humorous. Fuller can be over-earnest, but in general his posture is
rational, his rhyme-schemes neat and his diction, increasingly so in
the later verse, capable of a deliberate flatness that makes for comic,
or at any rate serio-comic, effect. As a war poet he has something
in common with Henry Reed (1914–86) whose 'Naming of Parts'

(Part 1 of 'Lessons of the War') wittily juxtaposes the language of nature and the jargon of weapons training. Both Fuller and Reed manage to be funny and serious at the same time, adding a welcome difference of tone and truthfulness to the war poetry of World War II.

'BLOOD, DIRT AND SUCKED SUGAR STICK'

In what have now become a notorious couple of sentences W. B. Yeats wrote disparagingly of the war poetry of Wilfred Owen: 'He is all blood, dirt and sucked sugar stick (look at the selection in *Faber's Anthology* – he calls poets "bards", a girl a "maid" and talks about "Titanic wars"). There is every excuse for him but none for those who like him' (letter to Dorothy Wellesley, 21 December 1936). In his Introduction to *The Oxford Book of Modern Verse* (1936) Yeats also wrote generally of war poetry that 'passive suffering is not a theme for poetry. In all the great tragedies, tragedy is a joy to the man who dies; in Greece the tragic chorus danced.' On both scores it is now generally accepted that Yeats was grossly unfair; though Bernard Bergonzi is prepared to concede that the 'criticism of Owen's diction does point to the undeniable fact that his language was slower to develop than his sensibility, and wasn't always equal to Owen's demands on it'.[11] The reference to 'bards' and 'maid' seems to be an allusion to the heavily Keatsian 'From My Diary, July 1914', which is really before Owen became a war poet, and can therefore be discounted. 'Titanic wars', however, comes from 'Strange Meeting', probably written in 1918 along with the great poems of Owen's maturity. It is a phrase which does precisely what Yeats seems to want war poetry to do – 'titanic' helps to distance the poem from the immediate horrors of battle. The phrase, and the poem as a whole, belongs to that element in Owen's poetry which sees war in the perspective of tragedy and myth, transcending particular moments of suffering to evoke 'The pity of war, the pity war distilled'. And in this respect it has its counterpart in the work of other World War I poets such as Edward Thomas, Isaac Rosenberg and David Jones.

But the 'blood' and 'dirt' of war, its here-and-now ghastliness and violence, do also matter greatly in Owen's poetry, as in that of his front-line contemporaries. Likewise the sardonic protests of Siegfried Sassoon. These are part of the shock of the modern, which demands to be expressed unmitigatedly in all its unconventional, unorthodox reality; and, again Yeats (strangely for a poet who wrote as he did, particularly in *Last Poems*) missed the point with regard to diction, which in Owen, and in others, was shaken out of old 'poetic' moulds by the new urgency of what was felt: the 'damned spot' became 'blood', and that blood 'dirt'.

If the poetry of World War II reverberates with us less than that of World War I, it may be because the shock to sensibility was less unprecedented; sensibility itself had been conditioned by what the poets of the previous war had written, and by the notes of warning sounded by poets of the Thirties (to be discussed in the following chapter). That changed sensibility, however, is unmistakable in the poetry of Keith Douglas; and the democratic note it brought into the poetry of World War I poets is echoed and expanded in the work of Alun Lewis. Although, in Dryden's phrase, 'the second temple was not like the first', a range and variety was added which reflected something less exclusively of the military world – a war experience involving civilians as well as soldiers, and a soldiery still civilian in many of its values.

6

Auden and Co.

> I sit in one of the dives
> On Fifty-Second Street
> Uncertain and afraid
> As the clever hopes expire
> Of a low dishonest decade.

These are the lines which begin W. H. Auden's 'September 1, 1939' (a poem which its author virtually disowned in later life). The 'decade' in question is that of the 1930s; and the comments made on it, including its 'clever hopes' and its 'low dishonest' nature, suggest the character it acquired for a group of poets who themselves take their place in literary history, rightly or wrongly, from the work they did in the 1930s. Chief among them are Auden, Louis MacNeice, C. Day Lewis and Stephen Spender – mockingly clustered together by Roy Campbell as 'MacSpaunday', and by Auden himself as 'Daylewisaudenmacneicespender'.

The four did not share either a tight-knit philosophy or set of political opinions, though it is their generally left-wing outlook and opposition to fascism (particularly to the rise of Franco in Spain) which has stamped them as 'poets of the Thirties'. Day Lewis and Spender were the only ones to have affiliated themselves with communism, and that only for a while. Moreover, they diverged very sharply from each other after the 1930s, Auden, for example, becoming an American citizen and a Kierkegaardian Christian, MacNeice a classics lecturer, Day Lewis the British Poet Laureate (in 1968), and Spender co-editor of the anti-communist journal, *Encounter*. What connected them more lastingly was their social compassion and their interest in a witty, 'clever' and determinedly contemporary poetry of the twentieth-century urban-industrial environment. And in the cases of MacNeice, Day Lewis and Spender their enthusiasm for the extraordinary precocity of Auden, whom they first encountered as students at Oxford in the 1920s. Auden speaks for the Thirties character of their work when he writes, in 'Letter to Lord Byron' (1936):

> Tramlines and slagheaps, pieces of machinery,
> That was, and still is, my ideal scenery.

But as poets each of them had their own individual careers which embraced much wider material and more diverse styles.

W. H. AUDEN (1907–73)

Auden began in his 'teens as an admirer of Wordsworth, Hardy and Edward Thomas, but soon after going up to Oxford in 1925 he started to read T. S. Eliot. In the words of Edward Mendelson, 'Eliot served as a great liberator. Poetry, Auden learned, could be comic and grotesque. ... Using Eliot's exotic vocabulary as his model, Auden brought into his poems the science and psychology he learned in his father's library, while discarding the traditional poetic diction and poetic subjects favored by his mother.'[1] However, much as he admired *The Waste Land*, and much as his early poetry in particular suffered from the characteristic obscurity of modernist poetry, Auden remained in the English main stream of rational discourse and syntactical coherence. This continued to be so even when he left England for America in 1938; and his later work, written in the USA and subsequently in Italy and Austria, accentuates, if anything, his commitment to the discursive tradition.

It could be argued that the rediscovery of the Metaphysicals by Eliot influenced Auden more than it did Eliot himself. Auden's obscurity is not that of Symbolist music, Imagist discontinuity or self-consciously modernist allusion, but of concentration and ellipsis. Another important influence here is Gerard Manley Hopkins; the 'telegraphese' (omission of articles and merely connective words) in many of Auden's early poems is an attempt to achieve a powerfully compact language from which all superfluous elements have been ruthlessly pruned. The line of argument may thus be made more difficult to follow, but it is deliberately pursued. The reader must focus on the reasoning process which forms the structure, and to which all evocative or associative elements are strictly subordinated.

Even a seemingly lyrical love poem such as 'This Lunar Beauty' (1930) is a tough intellectual exercise which, to adapt Dryden's comment on Donne, perplexes the mind rather than entertains with the softnesses of love. The diction, though plain (unlike some of the eccentric and aureate poems of Auden's later years), is abstruse to the point of severity. It creates strange conjunctions in the modernist manner, which astonish and provoke, as in the opening lines, where 'lunar', in the phrase 'lunar beauty', and its predicate, 'Is complete and early', are as disconcerting to normal expectations as in any modernist poem. The next four lines,

> If beauty later
> Bear any feature
> It had a lover
> And is another,

are also disconcerting in their rhetorical patterning (including the ambiguous effect of the positioning of 'later', and the parallelism of 'had'/'is' with 'Has/Is' in the preceding lines), but especially by virtue of their elliptical syntax. A possible paraphrase might run thus: 'If beauty at some later time [or perhaps 'a later beauty'] were to bear any feature, it would be because it had a lover and in consequence has become something different.' However, other interpretations are possible, and for that very reason the lines remain teasingly mysterious. Yet as the poem develops it becomes clear enough that changeless 'lunar beauty' stands in antithesis to changeable 'daytime' beauty, which is capable of being haunted by 'ghosts' from the past, i.e. subject to, not exempt from, 'history'. This is the position reached in the second stanza. The third and last stanza reaches an ambivalent conclusion from this – namely, that while the aloofness of 'lunar beauty' will prohibit love from approaching it ('near' being used as a verb), it will also be protected from sorrow's 'endless look'.

The beauty celebrated in this poem may thus be compared to the arrested lovers in Keats's 'Ode on a Grecian Urn'; immunity from change and contact with normal, historically determined reality is both a plus and a minus. Auden, however, shades his argument with further uncertainty. Since the moon as governor of the tides is traditionally associated with change, it is odd to qualify the poem's changeless form of beauty as 'lunar'. Is the moon, then, being shifted from its Renaissance significance to a more Romantic one (the 'Queen-Moon', for example, of Keats's 'Ode to a Nightingale', 'Clustered around by all her starry Fays'); or is some pun on 'lunar/lunatic' being implied? How are 'complete' and 'early' to be construed? Positively, as 'fulfilled, balanced' and 'innocent, prior to the Fall'? (The original title, 'Pur', may have pointed towards this meaning of 'early'). Or negatively, as 'finished, closed off from experience' and 'immature'? The 'endless' in the last line of the poem is similarly uncertain, suggesting an eternity which might appropriately be connected with the timelessness of unhistorical 'lunar beauty', but syntactically part of the negatived construction which deprives the 'sweetness here' of love – as if to be deprived of sorrow, too, is equally a loss. As in the later love poem 'Lay your sleeping head, my love' (1940), the contradiction may conceivably be resolved by reference to the fallen condition of the human being; but what is noteworthy in the comparison between these two poems is the structural emphasis given to the word 'human' in the later one, where it both opens and concludes the poem in close conjunction with 'love', but its complete absence from 'This Lunar Beauty'. Humanity and 'lunar beauty' are, it seems, incompatible. There is as little reconciliation in view as in Marvell's 'The Definition of Love'. It is a cold, rather remote poem; a poem in which beauty and love are divided.

Division is a recurrent theme of Auden's earlier work, with the myth of the border exploited to suggest a dividing line between an unhealthy, corrupt condition of being, and one that is hopeful and life-affirming. Against a medieval quest landscape, brought up to date with images of twentieth-century industry in drastic decline, he sets a latter-day version of the questing knight who must try to cross into the new land, or, in Lawrentian fashion, die the hard and bitter death of the old self to be re-born into new life, since love 'Needs death, death of the grain, our death, / Death of the old gang' ('1929', IV, *Collected Shorter Poems, 1927–1957*, p. 39). The enemy, seen in Freudian terms, is the repressive ego which bottles up and perverts instinctual forces, or, in Marxist terms, an unjust society which blocks the creative energies of the people; and what is needed of the hero is the ability to 'look shining at / New styles of architecture, a change of heart'.[2] But decadence and despair are more strongly registered than hope, the most memorable lines – such as 'They gave the prizes to the ruined boys' ('Consider'), and 'That gap is the grave where the tall return' ('O where are you going?') – being suggestive of misjudgement and defeat. Although it is not explicitly

anti-fascist in theme, the paramilitary language and the sense of
sadistic menace make Auden's poetry of the 1930s sound at times
(and did so sound to many of his contemporaries) like a political
rallying cry against the rise of the dictators Franco (in Spain),
Mussolini (in Italy) and Hitler (in Germany). Indeed, he himself felt
the need to communicate to a wider audience than his intellectually
abstruse style could reach, and some of his most effective, if general-
ised, poems warning of the brutalising forces at work in the Europe
of the day are to be found in his adaptations of old ballad and saga
forms. The most successful of these is 'O what is that sound' (1932),
which one critic dubs 'a pastiche eighteenth-century ballad',[3] in
which overtly contemporary reference is eschewed in favour of
characters drawn from an archaic, semi-pastoral world of doctor,
parson, farmer and invading red-coat soldiers. However, the
glamorous distancing – for example:

> O what is that sound which so thrills the ear
>   Down in the valley drumming, drumming?

only gives the sinister reality which gradually penetrates this sur-
face a sharper edge; and the final stanza, seasoned with conscious
melodrama, mimes the storm-trooper violence of fascism the better
for its archaic disguise:

> O it's broken the lock and splintered the door,
>   O it's the gate where they're turning, turning;
> Their boots are heavy on the floor
>   And their eyes are burning.

Judging the tone and 'meaning' of an Auden poem is not usually
that easy. Seriousness is often undermined by a mocking posture,
creating a duality, to use Justin Replogle's terms, between Poet and
Antipoet – the former vatic and solemnly rhetorical, the latter pro-
saic and deflationary.[4] Sometimes these can be clearly distinguished,
but more often they alternate, or counteract each other, within the
same poem. The most characteristically Auden poem is of this
mixed kind, and joins forces with what the deconstructionist critic
John R. Boly terms the 'ludic' principle which 'covertly turns abso-
lutes into contingencies and certitudes into anxious decisions'.[5] This
makes for a poetry which, though it may sound authoritarian and
prescriptive – Auden the schoolmaster translating pedagogy into

verse – slyly deposes its own authority, opens up the possibilities of alternative (often contradictory) meanings, and ultimately, in the later post-war, Christian and Kierkegaardian poetry, flowers in a relaxed comic mode which allows conflicting attitudes and tones of voice to mingle playfully together.

An example from the earlier poetry, revealingly analysed by Boly, is 'The Wanderer'. With its Middle-English-derived first line, 'Doom is dark and deeper than any sea-dingle',[6] it suggests the banning of some rebel who refuses to submit to the ordinances of his tribe – an effect enhanced by the portentously suspended syntax of 'Upon what man it fall / In spring ... That he should leave his house, / No cloud-soft hand can hold him. ...' The 'sonorous doom' of the rhetoric is such that it 'confers upon its elect, the invincible bard, the power ... to silence potential dissidents'.[7] But against that would-be controlling music other notes sound which offer possibilities of a different meaning. For example, the supposed outcast 'waking sees / Bird-flocks nameless to him', with its hint of fresh, hitherto unknown life free to fly the bonds restraining the tribe; and the hearing 'through doorway voices / Of new men making another love' ambiguously suggests both forbidden practices (including, perhaps, homosexuality) and new, constructive experience.[8] Yet again, the wanderer's tired evening dream of home, with 'Waving from window, spread of welcome, / Kissing of wife under single sheet', can be either a dream of needlessly sacrificed domestic bliss, or a ludicrously phrased banality that saps his will. The final stanza, beginning 'Save him from hostile capture', seems to swing to a different version of the wanderer as daring adventurer on behalf of the tribe, or knight in quest of the holy grail; but the final lines, 'Bring joy, bring day of his returning, / Lucky with day approaching, with leaning dawn,' sound too much like the tired rhetoric of a wilfully up-beat ending. Exile or hero, another side to the wanderer's story always seems to be implicit. The poem demands a kind of poised Brechtian reading – detached rather than involved, critical rather than empathetic.

The absence of this poise is what is unsatisfactory about one of Auden's best-known poems, 'Spain 1937'. The poem has a highly rhetorical structure: its initial stanzas introduced by 'Yesterday' review the panoply of history, but insist that history is the outcome of choices made by the unidentified addressee (the English middle-class reader of Auden's generation? the reader in general?). Subsequent stanzas suggest the might-be of 'To-morrow', but conclude with the choice facing the addressee 'To-day'. The poem does not, however, debate the issues raised by the Spanish Civil War. As a so-called political poem it is curiously a-political, its treatment of the idea of historical necessity being mainly influenced by a wish to mock those who look for a *deus ex machina* to absolve them from choice:

> Intervene. O descend as a dove or
> A furious papa or a mild engineer, but descend.

And what, in the 1937 text, might have been regarded as a Marxist-style justification of killing, on the ground that it is an historically necessary means leading ultimately to the end of a fairer society:

> To-day the deliberate increase in the chances of death;
> The conscious acceptance of guilt in the necessary murder

was altered in the 1940 text (perhaps as a result of criticism from George Orwell) to the less politically marked 'conscious guilt in the fact of murder'. (This, incidentally, is one of a number of alterations, or suppressions, of earlier work in later printings which were to give the post-war Auden something of a reputation for Wordsworthian revisionism.[9])

The truth is that the Auden of the 1930s was never as committed politically as the legend suggests. Day Lewis and Spender were more sympathetic to Marxism than he, and Day Lewis in particular, in his critical work *A Hope for Poetry*, saw communism as the inevitable next step in the development of the arts. (Day Lewis, of course, like other liberals of the Thirties, later came to see communism as a repressive, not liberating, political movement.) Although Auden warned readers of the dehumanising influence of fascism, the beginnings of which he saw when he stayed in Berlin for a year after leaving Oxford, and although 'Spain 1937' was the outcome of a brief involvement in the Civil War in 1936–7 on the Republican side, his active political campaigning was limited; nor was his poetry explicitly left-wing. His leaving England for America in 1938, with his most frequent collaborator, Christopher Isherwood, and declining to return at the outbreak of the 1939–45 war, led to accusations of cowardice and desertion. His motives have never been completely explained,[10] but emigration to America, and subsequent years spent in southern Italy and Austria, were part of a developing change in his attitude towards England which was consistent with the anti-conformist, rather than politically disaffected, nature of his poetry of the thirties.

The simple equation, that betrayal of the political 'cause' also led to a loss of sharpness and originality in Auden's poetry, has its appeal. For some readers the later Auden (like the later Eliot) will always seem a let-down compared with the earlier. His devotion to Kierkegaard, and subsequent conversion to Christianity (though in some respects this was a return to the faith of his childhood), produced a different, more sophisticated, but also more relaxed poetry which, despite its extreme technical virtuosity, can seem too much of a mere apology for the unregenerate state of things as they are, instead of the disturbing diagnosis of social sickness which can be found in Auden's earlier poetry. The very tolerance in the tone of voice of the later Auden seems to discourage too critical a response; and, coupled as it is with an almost neo-Renaissance delight in sheer verbal skill – in particular, command of a high degree of syntactical ingenuity and willingness to ransack the dictionary for outlandishly far- fetched terms – this sophisticated pursuit of artifice seems to signal a new dilettantism. The conclusion to a poem like 'Lakes' (1955), 'Moraine, pot, oxbow, glint, sink, crater, piedmont, dimple …? / Just reeling off their names is ever so comfy', might even suggest that Auden is abandoning his former asperity for a slightly sentimental self-indulgence. But poems like 'In Praise of Limestone' (1948), 'The Shield of Achilles' (1952), and 'Horae Canonicae' (1955) suggest otherwise. Here Auden is both technical master and mature commentator: style and matter fuse inseparably.

'In Praise of Limestone' is later Auden at his very best. Written at the beginning of his stay in Italy (the reluctant conclusion to which is regretfully celebrated in 'Good-Bye to the Mezzogiorno'), it is a poem combining his liking for the yielding, water-penetrated character of both southern (Italian) and northern (Yorkshire) limestone landscapes, but fundamentally concerned with the easy-going nature of its essentially Italianate inhabitants. In a quiet, unassertive way it is also a homosexual poem, allowing Auden's imagination release from the more painful tensions of his non-conformist poems of the thirties:

> What could be more like Mother or a fitter background
>   For her son, for the nude young male who lounges
> Against a rock in the sunlight, displaying his dildo …?

To live in this landscape is to be at least partially re-immersed in the amniotic fluid. To severer minds this is a regressive life; to more sentimentally poetic ones a retreat into Arcadia. But, as in all good pastoral, awareness of the harsher reality of the outside world is incorporated within it, and placed in a certain critical perspective. The speaker acknowledges that 'The best and worst never stayed here long but sought / Immoderate soils' – 'granite wastes' for the saint, the plains of 'clays and gravels' for the militarist, and for 'the really reckless' (who, with typical ambivalence, may be seen by the reader as either heroic or crazed) a solitude 'that asks and promises nothing', but seems to offer a kind of existential freedom. Yet the implication is that all these step aside from the ongoing life of the here-and-now. Whether consciously or not, the later Auden joins hands with the later Lawrence – not the Lawrence whose ideas (rather than art) so strongly influenced his earlier work, but the Lawrence of *Birds, Beasts and Flowers*, and especially *Last Poems*, whose art rejects a transcendent idealism and prefers to celebrate the life of the flesh. However, his style is not that of Lawrence. Auden cleaves to the tradition of rational discourse, of Dryden-like debate in verse, developing a sophisticatedly moulded syntax which is quite different from that of Lawrence. Yet in the process of weaving his more self-consciously contrived phrases and clauses he still manages to embody the pleasures of sense, elevating them – even though they are deliberately less exaltedly elevated – above the ultimately life-denying objects to which history's tragic and epic personae dedicate themselves. The result is something religious (one remembers that Lawrence thought of himself as 'passionately religious'), and an appropriate subject for prayer in a completely non-otherworldly mode:

> Not to lose time, not to get caught,
> Not to be left behind, not, please! to resemble
> The beasts who repeat themselves, or a thing like water
> Or stone whose conduct can be predicted, these
> Are our Common Prayer.

The poem is rounded off, too, in a traditional mode; it ends neatly where it began, with the suggestion that when the speaker's imagination strives towards perfection in love or a vision of the after-life what he hears 'is the murmur / Of underground streams' and what he sees is 'a limestone landscape'. Which is perhaps just a shade too neat. But it is redeemed by the slight withdrawal implied in 'try to imagine' and its governing 'when'. The absoluteness of 'faultless love' and the grandeur of 'the life to come' are only tentative reachings-out. They are brought to earth in a sensual landscape that one is aware of through the senses, and which is thus reduced to an appropriately human scale. The true praise of limestone is that it is porous – fallible as ordinary human nature is, and with its charm inseparable from its fallibility.

LOUIS MACNEICE (1907–63)

Among the Thirties poets whose names are associated with Auden, Louis MacNeice stands out by virtue of his unclouded view of 1930s circumstances. He is very much a poet of the markedly contemporary social scene. Places where he has lived and worked, Belfast or Birmingham, come through in his poetry with clear, precise, novelistic detail: 'the streets run away between the proud glass of shops, / Cubical scent-bottles artificial legs arctic foxes and electric mops' ('Birmingham'); 'The brook ran yellow from the factory stinking of chlorine, / The yarn-mill called its funeral cry at noon' ('Carrickfergus'). And his metaphor is determinedly (in common with other Thirties poets sometimes over-determinedly) modern: 'The jaded calendar revolves, / Its nuts need oil, carbon chokes the valves …' ('An Eclogue for Christmas'); 'now the mind is / Back to the even tenor of the usual day / Skidding no longer across the uneasy camber / Of the nightmare way' (*Autumn Journal* IX). Topical politics are also caught up in the weave of the verse, as 'Hitler yells on the wireless' and trees are cut down on London's Primrose Hill to clear a space for anti-aircraft guns (*Autumn Journal* VII); and in 'Bagpipe Music' current intellectual, sociological and commercial fads, and references to the Herring Board and Government grants, combine with jazzy rhythms and the bored refrain 'It's no go the …' to evoke a raffish, jaded, cynically devil-may-care attitude typical of the morally bankrupt spirit of the times:

> It's no go the merrygoround, it's no go the rickshaw,
> All we want is a limousine and a ticket for the peepshow.

There is, of course, in 'Bagpipe Music' a deliberate element of exaggeration, an almost music-hall heartiness in sending up the speaker's posturing which allows the reader to enjoy the poem as an

amusing tour de force. The manner defuses what might otherwise
be its scornfully high-brow criticism; and in this it is representative
of MacNeice's position generally. While taking the stance of a social
critic he manages to avoid the self-righteous, and sometimes hector-
ing, tone that can creep into Auden's poetic rebukes to his contem-
poraries. Although, like Auden, he is insistent on the need to avoid
indulging in escapism (the recurrent theme of dreams in his earlier
work is invariably coupled with the need to wake up and accept
daylight reality), he identifies with the target of his criticism, sees
himself as belonging with 'the others' rather than being in a position
of superior enlightenment, and, in *Autumn Journal* II, can say
(unashamedly sharing their clichés as well):

> I must leave my bed and face the music.
> As all the others do with a grin
> Shake off sleep like a dog and hurry to desk or engine.

And his attitude is constructive: 'I must go out to-morrow as the
others do / And build the falling castle' – which, he adds, has not
actually fallen thanks 'to the human animal's endless courage'.

MacNeice's training as a classicist is also a help to him in this
respect. The modernist allusiveness which might well have been
expected from a writer with such a background, though it is to be
found in his poetry, is enlisted in the name of continuity rather than
contrast. He declines to romanticise 'The Glory that was Greece'.
Autumn Journal, IX, like a modern-dress production of the classics,
sometimes a little too slickly aligns the Greeks with contempor-
ary 'demagogues' and 'quacks', but significantly rounds off its
disenchanted view with the comment, 'and lastly / I think of the
slaves'. (Likewise, the earlier Ode, 'Tonight is so coarse', though con-
demning the 'celluloid abstractions' beloved of modern film-goers,
recognises the 'escape' they offer to modern slaves of 'the eight-hour
day or the wheel / Of work and bearing children'.) The Greeks,
'Conscious – long before Engels – of necessity', had 'plotted out
their life with truism and humour'. The poem records a subsequent
decline which leaves the speaker resignedly concluding that 'It was
all so unimaginably different / And all so long ago.' But that is a
strategy to foil facile analogies; the essential continuity is to be found
in the classical spirit of realistic, humane appreciation of reality.

Edward Lucie-Smith (b. 1933) comments that MacNeice's poetry
after the 1939–45 war went through a period of 'dismaying
flatulence', but then recovered to combine 'an underlying gravity

with the flippant, glittering surface which had delighted the readers of his early poetry'.[11] One could see this development as a return to what was always in fact there. What is different, however, is an emphasis on the private and personal not to be found even in such earlier autobiographical poems as 'Belfast' and 'Carrickfergus'. Poems such as 'Soap Suds', 'Star-Gazer' and 'The Habits' show a new interest in the vision of childhood – with little or nothing of the former emphasis on social awareness and the social conscience. 'Soap Suds', in particular, is on the Proustian theme of the search for lost time. The poem opens: 'This brand of soap has the same smell as once in the big / House he visited when he was eight', and it lays a trail of association which leads the anonymous third-person figure to reconstruct a long-lost scene of croquet-playing innocence. A slightly aseptic irony distances the scene, however: 'The day of course is fine.' The child holds the croquet mallet, but it is 'a grown-up voice' which cries 'Play!' Then, as if the child has no control, 'The mallet slowly swings', and a curiously sinister sequence follows:

> Then crack, a great gong booms from the dog-bark hall and
>   the ball
> Skims forward through the hoop and then through the next and
>   then
>
> Through hoops where no hoops were and each dissolves in
>   turn
> And the grass has grown head-high and an angry voice cries
>   Play!
> But the ball is lost and the mallet slipped long since from the hands
> Under the running tap that are not the hands of a child.

The world of Innocence is converted into that of Experience, but what MacNeice offers is not simply a latter-day variation on Blake, for his Innocence is structurally contained within Experience, subverting and questioning, if not denying, its truly innocent status. The variation is a variation on the escape theme which recurs so frequently in MacNeice's earlier poetry, and in spirit more akin to Hardy than Blake. Obliquely it hints that the childhood vision is itself an illusion, a looking backward to a supposedly paradisal state which never existed and which is only so constructed by the saddened adult mind. Escape is no more possible than it was in the earlier poetry, but the conclusion drawn has less implication for action. Perhaps none at all. It simply registers feeling, but with a new power of psychological reverberation. For better, for worse, it is a more purely lyrical poetry.

C. DAY LEWIS (1904–72)

The return to childhood themes in the post-war phase of his career is also a feature of the poetry of C. Day Lewis. As a 'Thirties' poet he is rather more the left-wing political enthusiast than Auden or MacNeice, and in his subsequent disillusionment he is rather more of a pessimist – or at least, like Hardy, who then becomes his acknowledged master, and to whom one of his best poems, 'Birthday Poem for Thomas Hardy' is addressed, a meliorist for whom a hard look at the worst is an absolute pre-condition of hopefulness. A poet of considerable technical gifts, Day Lewis has suffered perhaps from the fluency which enables him to write personal and propaganda lyrics, narratives and translations with equal facility – and perhaps, too, from the accessibility which made him a popular poet in his time and earned him the Poet Laureateship.

Somewhat dismissively, Robert Graves refers to the early Day Lewis as 'a simple-minded Red',[12] and Bernard Bergonzi quotes lines which Day Lewis wrote in 1938 praising the Soviet Union in uncritical terms;[13] but his poems of 1929–36 would be grossly underestimated if seen merely against such comments. The pastiche-Auden 'As one who wanders', with its conceit of a disused mine ('old workings') for a moribund society and its countervailing image of a train driven by 'current flashed from far-off dynamos', is naive in its politically confident conclusion:

> Train shall spring from tunnel to terminus,
> Out on to plain shall the pioneer plunge,
> Earth reveal what veins fed, what hill covered.
> Lovely the leap, explosion into light.

But poems like 'But Two there are' and 'Tempt me no more' show awareness at least of the personal cost involved in 'easing' a supposed 'saviour's birth'. Looking back at his own work Day Lewis comments ruefully on 'an over-enthusiastic, often perfunctory use of "modern" imagery';[14] but the recurrent balancing of natural, especially bird-related, and hard, steely images[15] suggests awareness of the difficulty of bringing traditionally pastoral and modern industrial values into creative relationship. Day Lewis is particularly successful in making this contrast by parody in such poems as 'Nearing again the legendary isle' and 'Come, live with me and be my love'. In the first of these 'Hunger and sweat have stripped' Odysseus' men 'to the bone' and the sirens have become chorus-girls 'past their prime' against whom there is 'No need to stop the ears'; and in the second Marlowe's shepherd is a Thirties docker inviting his love to the pleasures.

> Of peace and plenty, bed and board,
> That chance employment may afford.

Its political message is simple, but sardonically effective.

The childhood echoes explored in the later poems are concerned with the process of disillusionment. In 'O Dreams, O Destinations', seeing the morning mist which covers the valley, children itch to tear it away and 'unwrap / The flags, the roundabouts, the gala day'. Adults would restrain them,

> But they slip through our fingers like the source,
> Like mist, like time that has flagged out their course.

In a Wordsworthian descent into the light of common day adults learn to settle for 'the limited objective', lose 'The appetite for wholeness' and 'prize / Half-loaves, half-truths'. There is little doubt that this disenchantment is embraced by the poet himself. Paradoxically, however, it opens up new areas to him – a lower-toned, but more sensuously precise poetry of childhood itself in 'The Innocent', 'Passage from Childhood' and 'Cornet Solo', and, in 'Sex-Crime' and 'The Neurotic', a more inward response to society's shunned outsiders.

Like Auden (possibly even in some kind of competitive response to him) Day Lewis also becomes in his later work a more flexible and self-consciously expert craftsman and, in *An Italian Visit* (1953), for example, an easier talker in verse. Writing sometimes seems to go on for writing's sake, and the stance is more conservative and conventional. Yet in 'Sheepdog Trials in Hyde Park', the greater particularity of the later poetry, the new inwardness, and the self-consciousness combine to fashion a minor masterpiece. A neo-pastoral, though quite un-ironic poem, it is concerned nevertheless with the transfer of what belongs to 'hills, dales, bogs, walls, tracks' from country to city and from work to 'game'. Dogs control sheep, shepherd controls dogs, and the rhythm and syntax of the poem (foregrounded by the absence of rhyme) skilfully imitate these highly sophisticated controlling processes. A kind of mechanism is established, but just as the control, even of the shepherd, is 'never absolute', so the mechanism, despite the 'guided missiles' imagery, is never inorganic. The dogs

> follow each quirk and jink of
> The evasive sheep, play grandmother's-steps behind them,
> Freeze to the ground,

doing all this 'As if radar-controlled', but not mechanically. One can sense their moments of 'doubt' as well as 'mastery'; and 'Machines don't frolic when their job is done.'

Finally, the 'game', it is suggested, is 'A demonstration of intuitive wit / Kept natural by the saving grace of error', and as such, an analogy for the poet's own work. Although that might have been left to speak for itself, the coda is not unduly explicit. The poem does not become yet another poem about writing a poem, but rather a demonstration of the way spontaneity and order interact with heightened effect in the specialised circumstances both of a sheep-dog trial and of a poem. It reveals the peculiarly poetic insight that the honed skills of the later Day Lewis can achieve in a rare moment of thoughtful gamesmanship.

STEPHEN SPENDER (1909–96)

The earlier Spender is also a typical poet of the Thirties. A catalogue of his subjects would include such socio-political topics as: war ('Thoughts during an Air Raid', 'Two Armies', 'Fall of a City') and the threat of war ('Who live under the shadow of war'); the intrigue of politicians and diplomats ('Perhaps'); Nazi repression ('Van der Lubbe'); communism as the hope of the future ('oh young men oh young comrades'); left-wing cadres who 'were jokes to children' and 'had the pale unshaven stare of shuttered plants / Exposed to a too violent sun', but who are destined to become the new heroes of historical inevitability ('Exiles from Their Land, History Their Domicile'); the nature of heroism ('I Think Continually of Those Who Are Truly Great'); and poverty and deprivation ('Moving through the silent crowd'). And many of his images are likewise drawn from self-consciously 'modern' material: 'Where the praise may loop like an aeroplane' ('Variations on My Life'); 'Our bodies are the pig and molten metal' ('Exiles from Their Land'); 'Drink from here energy and only energy, / As from the electric charge of a battery' ('Not Palaces, An Era's Crown'); 'As clerks in whited banks / With bird-claw pens column virgin paper' ('Polar Exploration').

What distinguishes Spender, however, from those with whom he is usually grouped is a more rapt idealism, with corresponding exaltation of tone and mood, and a strong compassion for society's victims and losers – those men who (in 'Moving through the silent crowd')

> lounge at corners of the street
> And greet friends with a shrug of shoulder
> And turn their empty pockets out,
> The cynical gestures of the poor.

As a consequence, the earlier poetry has a warm, appealing quality which, though at times it can become vapidly effusive, is a welcome change from the more astringent, clinically sharp intelligence to be found in other members of Auden and Co. Yet Spender, too, is also an intellectual poet, with a marked introspective bent which gives much of his work an abstract air.

This becomes more apparent in the 1942 volume *Poems of Dedication*, where Spender relaxes the ideological commitment of previous volumes in favour of more private and personal subjects (as in Part One, 'Elegy for Margaret') and poetry of a philosophical complexity in which thought and verbal play are intertwined. In Part Three, 'Spiritual Explorations', the theme is human consciousness itself and the paradox of the human being who can entertain ideas of infinite time and space, but is bound within temporal and spatial limitations which make him a comic contradiction of himself:

> The Universe, the dead, humanity, fill
> Each world-wide generation with the sigh
> Which breathes the music of their will.
> Their sensitive, perceiving witness, I,
> See mirrored in my consciousness, the ill
> Chameleonic harlequin who'll die.

In the recent volume, *Dolphins* (1994), there are signs of further change. Several of these late offerings are modest, but, as in

'Dolphins' itself and 'Letter from an Ornithologist in Antarctica', cool, clear poems of reflection. What differentiates them from *Poems of Dedication* is a more marked sense of the need to connect lonely introspection and sociable warmth. This is most evident in 'Letter', where the ornithologist, though happy to pursue his search for baby petrels by himself in the cold antarctic night, is also grateful for the cable that connects him to his companions; and beyond that to have the reassuring sense

> that six hundred miles far north the tip
> Of Tierra del Fuego has some settlers
> (Four hundred further north there come real towns).

Autobiographical poems also link the simple immediacies of childhood with awareness of a fuller, more complex, and more dangerous, world beyond. In 'Worldsworth', for example, the speaker remembers his parents reading poetry as he lay in bed as a child and

> Rhythms I knew called Wordsworth
> Spreading through mountains, vales,
> To fill, I thought, the world.

These coalesce in his mind as '*Worldsworth*' and become, to him, 'a vow'.

In glaring contrast, however, *Dolphins* also has its poetry of raw, hideously un-idyllic moments, most notable in the shocking sequence of poems, 'Poètes Maudits' (based on the lives of Rimbaud and Verlaine), which form a reminder of the perversity and nastiness from which great art can nevertheless emerge.

Spender was once regarded as among the most exciting of the Thirties poets: Kenneth Allott found him, with the exception of Auden, 'the most interesting poet of his generation and the one who seems most capable of further development'.[16] If this prediction now looks too optimistic, the promise of development, especially in his latest work, was fulfilled, and Spender remains a poet of arresting vision.

POSTSCRIPT

Auden remains the major figure among this loosely associated group of four; and he is the one who has had most influence on more recent poets, especially in England. His versatility and astonishing craftsmanship have done much to sustain the tradition stemming from Hardy, Frost and Yeats; and his wit (both in the old sense of 'intellect' and the current one of 'humour'), his command of colloquial fluency, and his syntactical brilliance have ensured that the discursive element in that tradition has remained strong. He has also shown, as Philip Larkin was to do subsequently, that it is possible to be modern and popular.

If other members of the Thirties group have been overshadowed by him, the full span of their careers – and especially what they produced after 1939 – proves them to have distinctive talents of their own. Louis MacNeice's reputation, in particular, has grown steadily since his death; though his unusual combination of shrewdness, satire and lyricism always marked him off as the one least carried on the tide of fashion. By comparison with him Day Lewis and Spender seem to have worn less well, but both have attractive qualities which deserve recognition. Like the minor poets of the early seventeenth century who were happy to be 'sealed of the tribe of Ben Jonson', they are secured as worthy companions of Auden.

7

'Black Mountain', and the Poetry of D. H. Lawrence and Ted Hughes

PROJECTIVE VERSE

In the 1940s the American poet Charles Olson (1910–1970) became the rector of Black Mountain College, a liberal institution in the western part of the state of North Carolina. The College's aims included the development, both in theory and practice, of a free and informal (but not formless) style of poetry dubbed 'projective verse'. In his essay on this subject Olson deplores what he sees as 'the reaction now afoot [i.e. in 1950] to return verse to inherited forms of cadence and rime'; and, harking back to the work of Ezra Pound and William Carlos Williams, he argues for a more 'open verse' which will be responsive to the ebb and flow of emergent meaning. It will not be a verse of orderly shaping and monumental solidity, but a lithe, flexible and energetic verse capable of picking up intimations of the future rather than enshrining ideas and emotions of the past. Instead of accentual metre and rhyme Olson promotes a new technique in which syllables and lines are governed purely by the sensitivity of the poet's ear, and in which there is an instinctive appreciation of the relation between phrasing and breath comparable to that of a good actor or musical performer. (Although he makes no actual reference to the speaking of verse, Olson was a dramatist as well as a poet; and, still more to the point, he was also a trained musician.)

Olson also sees projective verse as part of a necessary corrective to the arrogance of modern man whose technology has substituted machinery and mechanical repetition for the supple rhythms of nature. Thus traditional metric is associated in his mind with assertion of the ego – 'that peculiar presumption by which western man has interposed himself between what he is as a creature ... and those other creations of nature which we may, with no derogation call objects'. Projective verse is to be free from this egotism. It springs from a proper understanding of man's relation to nature, which Olson defines as 'that force to which [man] owes his somewhat small existence', and instead of using 'artificial forms' it allows shapes to 'make their own way'. Nevertheless, although organic form and organic development are its preferred means, one modern mechanical invention is an asset to projective verse – the typewriter:

> It is the advantage of the typewriter that, due to its rigidity and its space precisions, it can, for a poet, indicate exactly the breath, the pauses, the suspensions even of syllables, the juxtapositions even of parts of phrases, which he intends. For the first time the poet has the stave and the bar a musician has had.

The setting-out of the poem on the page enables the projective poet to incorporate in his printed text a kind of notation, or stage-directions, for the reading and understanding of his poetry. Pound had already begun to do something like this in his *Cantos*, but Olson advocates a more systematic spatial programme which makes use not only of gaps marking caesuras within the line, but also indentations and visual stepping-stones, and adroitly controlled enjambements which make rhythmical use of 'that time to pass that it takes the eye – that hair of time suspended – to pick up the next line'. The visual element, always at least a subliminal influence in any form of printed verse, thus acquires a positively creative role in the new poetry, providing a notation for that internal discipline (for the aim is not mere licence) which is to replace the more rigidly external discipline of traditional rhyme and metre.

Like the Poundian modernist Olson is also against traditional syntax, asserting that 'the conventions which logic has forced on syntax must be broken open as quietly as must the too set feet of the old line'. The implications of this dictum are not spelt out, but projective practice suggests that what is meant is that the new poetry should be opened up to the paratactic looseness and fluidity of conversation, and the spasmodic, exclamatory nature of excited speech, to achieve a more spontaneous kind of emotional expression than the logic-dominated syntax of conventional verse allows. A more flexible use of tenses should also be cultivated: 'must they not' he asks, 'also be kicked around anew, in order that time, that other governing absolute, may be kept as must the space-tensions of a poem, immediate, contemporary to the acting-on-you of the poem?'[1]

D. H. LAWRENCE (1885–1930)

Projective verse, as conceived by Olson, thus refines on the initiatives of Pound and Williams, who in their turn continue the distinctively American freedom of the long, untrammelled, rambling lines of Whitman. Even more relevantly, however, he also echoes the comments made by D. H. Lawrence on the nature of verse when the latter is defending his own practice against the criticism of his early mentor, Edward Marsh. In an astute letter written to Marsh in November 1913 Lawrence argues that conventional scansion is inappropriate both to his own verse and to English poetry generally. Poetic rhythm, he says, is more 'a matter of movements in space than footsteps hitting the earth'; and he suggests that 'it is the hidden *emotional* pattern that makes poetry, not the obvious form'. Marsh scans (as most readers do) with an ear too mechanically habituated to the syllable and accent-counting of text-book metric. Something more fluid is required:

> It is the lapse of the feeling, something as indefinite as expression in the voice, carrying emotion. It doesn't depend on the ear, particularly, but on the sensitive soul. And the ear gets a habit, and becomes master, when the ebbing and lifting emotion should be master, and the ear the transmitter. If your ear has got stiff and a bit mechanical, *don't* blame my poetry.[2]

Although Lawrence is defending himself, he chooses to analyse lines from Ernest Dowson, perhaps to gain authority by showing that his principle also applies outside his own verse. But in so doing he also suggests that a trend is already apparent in English poetry towards greater freedom in versification, and therefore that the movement which he represents (and subsequently Olson and Hughes) has English as well as American origins. But it is the influence of Whitman which is decisive, as becomes evident with the publication of the very different kind of love poetry to be found in *Look! We Have Come Through!* (1917). Some of it is strident and rhetorically forced, but at its best it has precisely that fluently *carried* quality expressing what Olson regards as the proper relation between man's 'small existence' and the larger force of nature. In 'Not I, not I, but the wind that blows through me!' Lawrence rejects the egotistical will, and instead calls on the 'fine wind' which 'is blowing the new direction of time' to carry him along with its impersonal force. 'If only,' he exclaims with rapturous yearning, he can be sensitive enough and allow himself to be 'borrowed' by the wind, to be 'Driven by invisible blows', a revelation will come – 'The rock will split, we shall come at the wonder, we shall find the Hesperides.'

In what is, appropriately, the American edition of *New Poems* Lawrence writes a Preface (August 1919) that becomes more emphatically still a manifesto for intelligently conceived free verse, and a justification for the kind of verse he himself is now writing and will gather together in the highly innovative volume, *Birds, Beasts and Flowers* (1923). He expresses his admiration for past poetry, Keats and Shelley in particular, but sees that as essentially a matter of 'exquisite finality'. He looks, however, for a 'poetry of the present' – something more open-ended; not perfected, but shimmeringly unfinished, imitative of the fluctuations and transient immanence of the living organism:

> But there is another kind of poetry: the poetry of that which is at hand: the immediate present. In the immediate present there is no perfection, no consummation, nothing finished. The strands are all flying, quivering, intermingling into the web, the waters are shaking the moon.

The medium of such poetry is free verse, for 'in free verse we look for the insurgent naked throb of the instant moment'. But this does not confer a licence for slackness. Lawrence is scornful of 'free-versifiers' who merely break 'the lovely form of metrical verse' and 'dish up the fragments as a new substance, called *vers libre*'. Free verse, he claims, has its own nature, which is 'instantaneous like plasm'; and although 'externally applied law' would be death to it, it has its own inner discipline: 'The law must come new each time from within.' And he acknowledges his supreme debt to Whitman: 'The most superb mystery we have hardly recognised: the immediate, instant self. ... Poetry gave us the clue; free verse: Whitman. Now we know.'[3]

Such a poetry is also the complement to Lawrence's emphasis on life here-and-now as opposed to the life of the hereafter:

> For man, the vast marvel is to be alive. For man, as for flower and beast and bird, the supreme triumph is to be most vividly, most perfectly alive. Whatever the unborn and the dead may know, they cannot know the beauty, the marvel of being alive in the flesh.[4]

The reference to 'flower and beast and bird' may well be Lawrence Mozart-like alluding to his own work, for it is in *Birds, Beasts and Flowers* that he most fully realises his ideal of a poetry which has the immediacy and open-endedness of life itself. For example, the impressionism of the two bat poems ('Bat' and 'Man and Bat') dabs in by means of its fragmentary, exclamatory syntax and its casual, off-the-cuff commentary an authentically living sense of a creature which only reveals itself in odd, disconcerting images:

> Dark air-life looping
> Yet missing the pure loop ...
> A twitch, a twitter, an elastic shudder in flight
> And serrated wings against the sky,
> Like a glove, a black glove thrown up at the light,
> And falling back.

Likewise in the tortoise poems ('Baby Tortoise', 'Tortoise Shell', 'Tortoise Family Connections', 'Lui et Elle', 'Tortoise Gallantry' and 'Tortoise Shout') a sensitively controlled free verse reflects the unique, changeable being of tortoises, and combined with a humorous treatment of their sexuality (which also makes a wry, oblique comment on the erotic forces that drive human beings with or without their will) creates a quite unstuffy, open-ended poetry of the living moment. The tone is at times mock-heroic, at times tenderly sympathetic, and again sardonic or ruefully down-to-earth; the diction and syntax never far from that of unedited conversation, though capable of rhetorical excitement or exaggeration – an elusive, fluctuating language beautifully adapted to the representation of process.

Lawrence is not, however, simply the detached observer. The unself-conscious otherness of bat or tortoise alive in the immediacy of the present is mediated through the voice of a highly self-conscious commentator – the authorial 'I' of the poem. In 'Tortoise Shout' this voice, prompted by the 'last, / Strange, faint coition yell / Of the male tortoise at extremity', modulates into a series of memories which are intensely subjective, culminating in the remembered sound of

> The first wail of an infant,
> And my mother singing to herself,
> And the first tenor singing of the passionate throat of a
>   young collier, who has long since drunk himself to death.

These are not merely associations, but indications of the continuity which exists between the animal and the human worlds. Ultimately they lead to identification of the tortoise shout with the agony of Christ on the cross and the cry of the pagan god, Osiris, who is torn in pieces, but found and restored again by Isis:

> The same cry from the tortoise as from Christ, the
>   Osiris-cry of abandonment,
> That which is whole, torn asunder,
> That which is in part, finding its whole again throughout
>   the universe.

Consciousness breaks up the unity of the living moment, but in creating the immediacy of the experience and allowing it to reverberate along the memory the poem becomes a speech-act seeking to recover wholeness. This is the theme on which many of the finest poems in *Birds, Beasts and Flowers* play variations, and in pursuit of which Lawrence develops his own peculiar rhetoric of iteration. In 'Almond Blossom', for example, phrases constantly echoed, or repeated with slight variation, and strung along a syntactically loose free verse enact the organic development of blossom miraculously emerging from the iron-like deadness of the wintry almond tree and creating the paradox of 'the Cross sprouting its superb and fearless flowers!' This is nature defying the human consciousness (and orthodox Christianity as well) which splits the physical from the spiritual. The 'annunciation' is not a flying down from heaven, but a 'Strange storming up from the dense under-earth', maintaining sensual continuity with the soil, not renouncing its own substance, but growing out from that substance. And the growth of the poem from its own phrasal substance is an analogous realisation of that process.

The rhetoric of 'Almond Blossom' is thus an experiment in making language counter its own self-consciousness. In the tortoise poems, however, and still more in poems such as 'Snake' and 'Fish' the division inherent in consciousness becomes the focus of attention. 'Snake', in fact, has two languages: the iterative language of the unconscious (if that is not a contradiction in terms – more precisely, it is a language, as in 'Almond Blossom', paralleling organic process) and the more prosaic, casually deflated language of the sceptical mind, or, as the 'I' of the poem calls it, 'of my accursed human education'. The overlapping repetition of the first is associated with the snake, and is again emphatically of the earth, earthy:

> He lifted his head from his drinking, as cattle do,
> And looked at me vaguely, as drinking cattle do,
> And flickered his two-forked tongue from his lips, and
>   mused a moment,
> And stooped and drank a little more,
> Being earth-brown, earth-golden from the burning bowels
>   of the earth.

The second is associated with the voices which tell the poet to kill the snake and his picking up 'a clumsy log' to throw at the water-trough 'with a clatter'. That he does so is a token of the prescriptive power of consciousness, but, as he immediately recognises, also an admission of the opportunity thereby lost to welcome 'one of the lords / Of life'.

Looked at in this way, 'Snake' is a poem perhaps too neatly adorned with a moral. But like Coleridge's 'Ancient Mariner', to which its conclusion alludes ('And I thought of the albatross ...'), the dialogic nature of the poem is more impressive than its argument. The juxtaposition of the two languages balances mind against body, common-sense prose against evocative repetition, and to isolate the one from the other would be to lessen the poem's total value, which implies not so much the superiority of the one to the other, as their necessary interrelationship through the 'I' who narrates the poem. The free verse, with its open-ended variability and its absence of clinching rhyme, supports this.

In 'Fish' – at least until the second half, beginning 'I saw a water-serpent swim across the Anapo' – this open-endedness is still better achieved. Here, assisted by the wit that so enlivens the tortoise poems, Lawrence empathises with fish-life and yet keeps a cool, amused distance. He is fascinated by a different, unconscious, non-human mode of being and yet preoccupied with the distinctively human consciousness which he himself is exercising as he writes the poem. The common theme is sexuality, the aspect of human experience which relates the human being most closely to the animal, but which for the human being is also the focus of intense, non-animal self-consciousness. Fish sex, however, is neither animal nor reptile:

> No fingers, no hands and feet, no lips;
> No tender muzzles,
> No wistful bellies,
> No loins of desire,
> None.
>
> You and the naked element,
> Sway-wave.
> Curvetting bits of tin in the evening light.

The anaphora ('No ..., No ..., No ...') defines fish sex by its lack of the libido and sentiment which combine in the paradoxically animal-cum-self-conscious sexuality of the human being (the paradox heightened by language mingling distinctively human 'fingers' and 'hands' with distinctively animal 'muzzles' and projecting onto them the human self-awareness of 'tender' and 'wistful' sentiment). Oneness with the water – encapsulated in the above quotation in 'Sway-wave', and elsewhere in the poem communicated by marvellously supple free verse imitating its essentially aquatic being – makes the fish almost a mystic symbol of otherness and the lost paradise of wholeness; but instantly the 'bits of tin' image, at once visually arresting and tinged with a sense of the ludicrous (and very much fish as glimpsed by a human onlooker), deflates this potentially overblown effect. The poetry calls itself to order: whimsicality, longing for something that transcends human sexuality, self-mockery, imagistic vividness, verbal teasing – each of these can be momentarily indulged in, but is quickly corrected by the poetry's inherently lithe, uncommitted movement.

As in 'Snake', this movement derives from the interplay between conscious and unconscious. It does not, however, like 'Snake', take sides against itself – not, that is, until the poem shifts gear and becomes anecdote followed by reflection. In the earlier part Lawrence plays with modes of address, sometimes speaking to the fish in the second person, sometimes referring to it in the third. Now he forbids himself this freedom: 'I left off hailing him. / I had made a mistake, I didn't know him.' Anthropomorphosis is over-weening presumption. He speaks only to himself: the fish is beyond him, and its god is outside man's god.

This, however, is self-consciousness with a vengeance! It loses the multidimensional quality of the earlier part of the poem and becomes a poetry of conscious commentary on the limitations of human consciousness – still impressive, but less compelling by virtue of the contrast it creates with the more flexible poetry which precedes it.

The other high point in Lawrence's achievement as a poet is to be found in *Last Poems* (posthumously published in 1932). The most celebrated of these are 'The Ship of Death' and 'Bavarian Gentians'. Both poems exist in different versions; Lawrence may not have reached a definitive text for either poem. Some critics prefer the more sexually orientated version of 'Bavarian Gentians', which has Pluto piercing Persephone 'with his passion of the utter dark', to the 1932 printed version, which is more intensely rhetorical in its variations on the theme of 'dark-blue daze'; and similarly, accomplished as is the 1932 version of 'The Ship of Death', the more Vergilian version to be found in appendix III of the *Complete Poems*, and the trial versions to be found in such poems as 'All Souls' Day', 'Beware the Unhappy Dead!' and 'Song of Death' are at the least a valuable complement to it.[5] Taken together these different versions suggest a process of exploration and trying-out which suits the tentative mode in which Lawrence deals with the theme of approaching death: his exhortation is to 'build your ship of death', but that means the preparation of consciousness rather than a monument. On the one hand, the goal of the preparation is the 'lapsing / of this my soul into the plasm of peace'; on the other, it is a possibility of renewal, phrased tentatively as a question: 'But can it be that also it is procreation?' Yet in the end, 'Oh, nothing matters but the longest journey' – the essence of the poetry is in the imagined voyage rather than its conclusion.

Last Poems also shows Lawrence moving into a mythological mode which is new for him, but has little in common with myth as used by modernists such as Pound and Eliot. It is true that he harks back, as they do, to an earlier sensibility which is supposedly superior to that of the present, but his emphasis is on vitality rather than order, on *insouciance* – freedom from nagging anxiety and self-consciousness – rather than religious discipline. Thus in 'For the Heroes are Dipped in Scarlet' the desired prelapsarian state is pre-Platonic – Plato symbolising the debilitating fall into a consciousness that is limitingly intellectual:

> Before Plato told the great lie of ideals
> men slimly went like fishes, and didn't care.

The poem wishingly celebrates the return of such men, dipped all over in vermilion, the colour of life-blood – a new kind of warrior-heroes, dedicated to laughter and dancing. A relaxed, wavering free verse imitates their imagined carelessness, and is also capable, for example, in 'Red Geranium and Godly Mignonette', of modulating this laughter into a very attractively humane mode of satire on the ridiculous pretentiousness of a religion which has lost the saving grace of contact with 'sensual experience'. Lawrence here becomes a master of non-conformist satire (and incorporated in it is a good-humoured travesty of the Congregational Non-conformist religion in which he was brought up) which uses the classical technique of bathos in a totally unclassical way. The speaker mockingly conjures up – only to dismiss it as absurd – a preposterous picture of 'the Most High' (Lawrence's version of the biblical God of late nineteenth-century chapel-goers) 'cudgelling his mighty brains' and straining

> to think, among the moss and mud of lizards and mastodons
> to think out, in the abstract, when all was twilit green and
>   muddy:
> 'Now there shall be tum-tiddly-um, and tum-tiddly-um,
> hey-presto! scarlet geranium!'
> We know it couldn't be done.

Such verse also benefits from the inspired 'doggerel', as W. H. Auden calls it, of the frequently rhymed satires in *Pansies, More Pansies* and *Nettles*.[6] Lawrence's mockery can be scathing. It is rarely, however, an end in itself. 'Red Geranium and Godly Mignonette' subsequently modulates to a 'tremendous creative yearning' which the verse is able to reflect sympathetically, and becomes itself a religious poem (as most of the *Last Poems* are) growing out of the need for a new connection between religious awe and the distinctively human.

BLACK MOUNTAIN POETS: CHARLES OLSON, ROBERT DUNCAN (1919–88) AND ROBERT CREELEY (b. 1926)

As early as 1914 (though referring to his work as a novelist) Lawrence had asserted that he was primarily 'a passionately religious man'[7] – a claim which he made in spite of the shock he knew he was giving to the conventionally religious, which for him in his time and place meant the conventionally Christian. Throughout the rest of his work he continued a quarrel with Christianity (even, in *The Man Who Died*, daring to re-write the story of Christ as a saviour who rose from the dead to renewed physical life and sexual love), and sought for his kind of passionate religion in pre-Christian/pre-Platonic civilisations where (in Yeats's phrase) 'the body is not bruised to pleasure soul'. His ideal religion was one which integrated man with nature rather than divided him from it, and this meant one in which the self-conscious, abstracting intellect was by-passed in favour of a direct, affirmative union with natural forces.

Here, as in other respects, there is a strong connection between Lawrence and Olson's Black Mountain philosophy. In an unfinished essay, 'D. H. Lawrence and the High Temptation of the Mind', Olson imagines Christ being offered a fourth temptation by Satan – that of possessing 'all the understandings the mind is capable of'. He does not know whether Christ would have resisted that temptation also, but he is sure that Lawrence would: 'For Lawrence knew, as no metaphysician ever does, the discipline and health of form, organic form as distinguished from that false form which the arrangements of the intellect, in its false speed, offer.'[8] And as Lawrence looked to such pre-Christian forms of religion as that of the Incas, Olson looked to the Mayans, and also to the primitive culture of Pleistocene man understood, with the help of Frobenius, as a holistic condition in which man the craftsman was not isolated from his craft by self-consciousness, but engaged in a continuous process of doing and being.[9] His early poem 'The Kingfishers' (regarded by Olson himself as a valuable introduction to his work) is concerned with 'recovery of a pre-Greek orientation', and has the Mayan Indian civilisation as a crucial point of reference.[10] Its method (in line with the comments later included in the 'Projective Verse' essay) is anti-discursive – phrasal and, as a matter of principle, syntactically incomplete in an attempt to circumvent the in-built ordering and moulding of experience which for Olson is a characteristic of formal, grammatical discourse inimical to the unified sensibility he wishes to recover. Likewise in 'The Distances' the spontaneous, uncontainable nature of true love, echoed in the free-flowing projective verse, contrasts with the imperial designs of 'old Zeus' and 'young Augustus' and the obsessional love of a 'German inventor' for a Cuban girl which drives him to ghoulish measures for keeping her corpse in his bed. The purpose in each case is at once to exemplify and celebrate instinctual energies affirming themselves in unhampered (though not anarchical) freedom against the petrifying and distorting forces of intellect.

The same broad spectrum would include the work of fellow Black Mountain poets such as Robert Duncan and Robert Creeley, and those like Denise Levertov (b. 1922) and Paul Blackburn (1926–91) who came under Black Mountain influence. Within that spectrum, however, each has his or her own set of variations. Duncan – also deeply influenced by Blake and Whitman – develops a more conventional, but also more visionary, rhetoric, exemplified by the hermetic explorations of 'Apprehensions' and, in extreme form, by the persistent anaphora of 'A Sequence of Poems for H.D.'s Birthday', Section 3 ('Father adopted and Father of my soul, / Father of roots and races, Father of all, ...'), which attempts to reconcile the poetry of Christian devotion with the poetry of process. Creeley, on the other hand, is a tighter lyricist whose moralising, short-lined poems – disconcertingly enjambed in the manner of William Carlos Williams, and often bare of imagery – are the vehicles for a curiously anti-intellectual wit.

For example, in Creeley's 'Don't Sign Anything', although the narrative and syntax are more conventional than Olson's, the line breaks inhibit a reading in terms of the apparently simple prose meaning, and reinforce the warning given in the title. The poem opens with the casual juxtaposition of the speaker's riding his horse, as was his 'wont', and cows in a field. But immediately the implication of a Platonic harmony between rational rider and sensual horse is undermined by the fact that it is the horse which seems to take control as it chases the cows, and the expression of this in a sentence which, though grammatically as simple as it can be, is made strange by being fractured across three lines: 'The horse / chased // them' (with 'them' being still further broken from the rest of the sentence by the additional stanzaic division between it and 'chased'). The rider becomes merely an 'accompanist' in a new kind of music – and an 'uneasy' one at that. And then, in a disconcertingly arbitrary jump, the poem moves on to cite a Chinese proverb which states the seemingly otiose (yet not quite obvious) truth that lying in a field and falling asleep means that 'you will be found in a field // asleep'. The relationship between this and the rider's experience of having his horse run away with him is left for the reader to construe. It might, somewhat didactically, be a way of warning against the danger of losing control; but the relaxed, colloquial nature of the language and the disorientating effect of the curious line breaks seem to act against, rather than with, such a meaning. The 'wonted', habitual character of the rider's riding of his horse, and the taken-for-granted assumption that the horse is there for the rider's convenience, is made to give way to something less predictable, more open-ended.

New suggestions of meaning emerge – or seem, perhaps, about to emerge, but without quite having done so. Looking back over the poem, one realises that there are two words which constitute complete lines in themselves: 'chased' (line 4) and 'asleep' (the final line of the poem). Again, the active nature of 'chased', the verb of which 'horse' is the subject, and the passive nature of 'asleep', which is what the indeterminate 'you' will be found to be if he 'lies', could be construed didactically to reinforce the warning already suggested. But, at least equally, it is the vigour and purposiveness of the horse which stands out in the isolating of that word 'chased', and the not disagreeable passivity of 'you' which is emphasised in the final 'asleep'. The surface banality of the Chinese proverb is re-shaped (and Creeley's playing with lineation is an important means to this end) to allow different, and potentially richer, meanings to emerge. The ultimate effect is such that a potentially rather banal didacticism is subverted by the reader's being caught up in a counterpointing process which leaves 'chased' and 'asleep' – not-so-simple anecdote of rider and horse, and not-so-platitudinous Chinese proverb – in a wittily ambiguous, undetermined conjunction with each other.

DENISE LEVERTOV: 'A TREE TELLING OF ORPHEUS'

Levertov also responds to Olson's projective verse programme in an individual way, and produces at least one poem, 'A Tree Telling of Orpheus', which is a masterpiece of its kind. In an illuminating essay on this poem Marilyn Kallet demonstrates how the way it is positioned on the page, with Olsonian typographical intervals, indentations and the breaking and down-stepping of lines, brings out its expressive pauses and supple rhythmical effects.[11] The verse form is especially appropriate to Levertov's re-enactment of the tree's response to the music of Orpheus by receiving sounds into the very substance of its being:

> he spoke, and as no tree listens I listened, and language
>   came into my roots
>   out of the earth,
>   into my bark
>   out of the air,
>   into the pores of my greenest shoots
>   gently as dew.

The story of Orpheus' musical powers, which can stir even trees to follow him, is a well-known, and well-worn, part of ancient myth; but Levertov succeeds in giving it new life and new meaning. Via the personified voice of one of the trees (which we do not at first recognise for what it is) a whole new perspective on the process of feeling and knowing is created. It is something much more than the operation of the pathetic fallacy by which non-human being is endowed with the human capacity for perception and feeling, as in pastoral elegy, to intensify a sense of tragic pathos. The use of the first person encourages subjective identification with the imagined responses of the tree, but in the process adjustment has to be made to a mode of perception which is sensuously immediate rather than rationally discursive. Kallet touches on this when, in her commentary on the poem, she refers to an impression of 'rhythmical, sexual energy' and (notwithstanding the use of male gender words such as 'he' and 'brothers') of 'androgyny and wholeness'.[12] The effect of Orpheus on the tree is a stirring and arousing which, though it does have strong sexual overtones, is primarily a development of consciousness through immediate sensuous awareness. It is an imaginative re-creation of the process which both Lawrence and Olson wished to attribute to Mayan and other primitive cultures, treated by Levertov, however, as a metaphor for a holistic experience which is not irretrievably lost, but lastingly capable of revival:

> Perhaps he will not return.
>   But what we have lived
> comes back to us.
>   We see more.
>   We feel, as our rings increase,
>   something that lifts our branches, that stretched our furthest
>   leaf-tips
>   further.

TED HUGHES (b. 1930)

The latest inheritor of this particular tradition in modern poetry in English, and a powerful and influential voice in its further development, is Ted Hughes. His more recent volumes, from *Gaudete* (1977) onwards – including *Moortown Elegies* (1978), *Remains of Elmet* (1979), *River* (1983) and *Wolfwatching* (1989) – are deeply concerned with what Leonard M. Scigaj calls his 'biocentric vision': 'Reverence for the nurturing powers of organic Nature and respect for the intrinsic worth of all of Nature's creations.'[13] The earlier poems, though not inconsistent with these, are more assertive of the neglected energies of the natural, especially bird and animal, world – at times to the point of an aggressive violence which can seem brutally inhuman. There may, indeed, be some degree of ambivalence in such poems as 'The Jaguar', 'Hawk Roosting' and 'Pike', and in the near-masochism of 'The Martyrdom of Bishop Farrar' and 'Bayonet Charge'. As A. E. Dyson (a critic who is very sympathetic to, and admiring of, the earlier Hughes) comments: 'For Ted Hughes power and violence go together: his own dark gods are makers of the tiger, not the lamb. [The allusions here are to Hughes's evident affinities with both D. H. Lawrence and William Blake.] He is fascinated by violence of all kinds, in love and in hatred, in the jungle and the arena, in battle, murder and sudden death.' But, on the other hand, 'Violence, for him, is the occasion not for reflection, but for *being*; it is a guarantee of energy, of life, and most so, paradoxically, when it knows itself in moments of captivity, pain or death.'[14]

'Hawk Roosting' (from Hughes's second volume, *Lupercal*, 1960) illustrates this fascination with violence, but also the ambivalence that goes with it. The poem's voice is that of the hawk itself, essentially a predatory bird, moved entirely by its instinct to kill. In its solipsistic view of the world everything is created to facilitate its single-minded hunting:

> The convenience of the high trees!
> The air's buoyancy and the sun's ray
> Are of advantage to me;
> And the earth's face upward for my inspection.

Even in sleep it rehearses 'perfect kills'. It sees itself as the summation of all Creation, and as having an inalienable right to destroy: 'I kill where I please because it is all mine.' Rational processes are irrelevant: 'There is no sophistry in my body', and 'No arguments assert my right'. And in its own view it is immune from change:

> The sun is behind me.
> Nothing has changed since I began.
> My eye has permitted no change.
> I am going to keep things like this.

The effect of this is both magnificent and absurd. The undeviating, unqualified, purposeful immediacy of the hawk demands admiration; and this is clearly meant to contrast with the doubts, hesitations and queasy rationalisations characteristic of mere human beings. But there is also self-evident absurdity in the claim that the bird has arrested change (already in the previous volume, *The Hawk in the Rain* (1957), the hawk in the poem of that title had seemed immune from man's mud-clogged existence, but ended mixed with 'the mire of the land'). Furthermore, there is deep irony in the very fact that a reader reads the hawk's extravagant claims in a printed medium which is totally alien to a hawk, or any other bird or animal. Although the poem is presented as the hawk speaking, the hawk engages in speechless 'roosting'; and the language used, even when considered as a verbal realisation of the essence of hawkish instinct, is full of inappropriately abstract terms such as 'Creation', 'sophistry' and 'arguments' which presuppose the infinitely more complex, culturally determined consciousness of human beings for whom the artifice of language is a means of communication radically un-hawklike.

In another poem from *Lupercal*, 'Thrushes', Hughes evokes the instinctual energy of thrushes with an original exactness which commands still more admiration than the bird in 'Hawk Roosting'; and he then produces a metaphorical identification of worm-hunting thrush with 'Mozart's brain' and a blood-fixated shark which jolts the reader out of any possible complacency. What is admired (at least ostensibly) is an 'efficiency which / Strikes too streamlined for any doubt to pluck at it / Or obstruction deflect'. Mozart's genius is clearly meant to be seen as of this order. But man (i.e. ordinary, sub-Mozartian man) lacks this capacity for single-minded fusion of energy and purpose. He may strive for it, but only to be cast into a hellfire of distraction and self-doubt. On the other hand, the shark turns this fusion into confusion, hungering 'down the blood-smell even to a leak of its own / Side and devouring of itself' – like the fish in 'Pike' which are so fixated on predation that they are found 'One jammed past its gills down the other's gullet'. What formerly seemed pure admiration thus becomes ambiguously uncertain. Although the instinctual energies of the non-human, natural world contrast favourably with the diffidence and doubts of humanity, conscious human standards are still at work in the poetry. As in 'Hawk Roosting', the reader is again brought up against what is at least implicitly a radical difference between man and nature – with that difference underscored by the verbal medium itself.

In the next major phase of his development, initiated by the Crow poems (collected as *Crow: From the Life and Songs of the Crow*, 1970), Hughes chooses a mode which is once simpler and more extravagantly absurd than in his early poems. Crow is an even less romantic creature than the birds, animals or fish of *The Hawk in the Rain* or *Lupercal*, and the language is deliberately anti-poetic. As Hughes himself explains, in an interview with Ekbert Faas:

> The first idea of *Crow* was really an idea of style. In folktales the prince going on the adventure comes to the stable full of beautiful horses and he needs a horse for the next stage and the king's daughter advises him to take none of the beautiful horses that he'll be offered but to choose the dirty, scabby little foal. You see, I throw out the eagles and choose the Crow. The idea was originally just to write his songs, the songs that a Crow would sing. In other words, songs with no music whatsoever, in a super-simple and a super-ugly language which would in a way shed everything

except just what he wanted to say without any other consideration and that's the basis of the style of the whole thing.[15]

If Crow is a bird, he (or 'it' – the personal or impersonal pronouns seem equally applicable) entirely lacks the glamour, even the qualified glamour, of the earlier hawk. He is a mythical creature, related to folktale lore, but updated so that he takes on, as David Lodge suggests, the more distinctively twentieth-century characteristics of caricature and the comic-book cartoon.[16] At times he resembles the repulsive, yet vitally irrepressible skunk of Lowell's 'Skunk Hour' – notably at the end of 'Crow and the Birds' when, unlike the rest of the birds evoked in the poem, 'Crow spraddled head-down in the beach-garbage, guzzling a dropped ice-cream.' Driven by the crudest instinct of self-preservation, Crow is, from the Christian-romantic point of view, as resolutely ugly and self-centred as it is possible to be. In 'Crow's First Lesson' he cannot be taught the meaning of 'love'; in 'Lineage', which parodies the language of Genesis, the remorseless series, 'In the beginning was Scream / Who begat Blood / Who begat Eye', etc., ends with his begetting 'Never Never Never' and his

> Screaming for Blood
> Grubs, crusts
> Anything
>
> Trembling featherless elbows in the nest's filth.

But, as 'Examination at the Womb-door' suggests, this extreme negativity is also a means of survival. Crow's innate resistance to illusion enables him to 'pass' an initiation rite in which the power of death over everything else seems supreme; and again and again his crude, sardonic wit, as in 'Crow's Theology' and 'A Horrible Religious Error', armours him against the emotional relapse that comes from romantic enchantment collapsing into disenchantment. In the black comedy of 'The Battle of Osfrontalis' it is even suggested that he in some way survives the collapse of language as such:

> Words came with Life Insurance policies –
> Crow feigned dead.
> Words came with warrants to conscript him –
> Crow feigned mad.

In the end 'Words retreated ... Taking the whole world with them', but Crow merely yawned – 'long ago / He had picked that skull empty'. The value-carrying words (and *Crow* is steeped in mythical, biblical, scientific and literary allusion) are devalued, creating a crisis not only of belief, but of communication itself, which is central to the entire poetic effort which these poems represent. It is as if Hughes is trying to touch bottom in an empty sea that swamps him, and using Crow as a final talisman.

Yet Crow does not appear as an entirely dehumanised, conscienceless being. His capacity as impossibly Batman-like survivor in a comic-book, cartoon world is qualified in certain poems by seemingly alien touches of sensitivity. For example, 'A Disaster', with its post-nuclear vision of a word-blighted universe in which all that remains is 'a brittle desert / Dazzling with the bones of earth's people' (not for the first time echoing T. S. Eliot), ends with an unusually reflective Crow: 'Where Crow walked and mused'. And 'Crow's Nerve Fails' suggests a Crow who almost succumbs to guilt and remorse:

> Crow, feeling his brain slip,
> Finds his every feather the fossil of a murder.
>
> Who murdered all these?
> These living dead, that root in his nerves and his blood
> Till he is visibly black?

In additon, in such poems as 'How Water Began to Play' and 'Littleblood' (which, admittedly, seem tacked rather arbitrarily on to the main collection) a gentler, almost tender quality is discernible. The problem is how, if at all, these relate to the rest of *Crow*. It is tempting to see them as an equivalent of the re-emerging vessel at the end of D. H. Lawrence's 'The Ship of Death' – a hint of new, cleansed life following the self-destruct of the word-world known to Crow hitherto. But there is no apparent connective sequence, as there is in Lawrence's poem, to orientate the reader. A permutation in Crow is perhaps implied, but, if so, it is difficult to see what structure exists to support such change.

If *Crow* originally had a narrative structure (in performance Hughes seems to have given it a story of sorts), in its printed form it exists only as a collection of scenes and dramatic episodes. Contrastingly, the next long poem, *Gaudete*, seems Hughes's attempt to give his mythic material stronger narrative shape. It has a story which is summarised in the 'Argument': an Anglican clergyman, the Reverend Nicholas Lumb, is carried away into the spirit world, and his place is taken by a log animated in such a way that it is indistinguishable from Lumb himself. This 'Lumb' starts a new religion in which he is to father a new Messiah on one of the women of his parish. Their husbands hunt him down and kill him. The original Lumb appears in the West of Ireland 'composing hymns and psalms to a nameless female deity'. The method, however, is still that of virtually independent pieces, somewhat resembling the scenarios of a film-script – poetically intense, and often dramatically gripping, but violating narrative sequence in a way that creates a bewilderingly nightmarish effect.

The real strength of the work is in its combination of Hughes's characteristically physical poetry, merging human, animal and landscape, with anthropological material rendered in vividly expressionist terms. The dual climax, involving the ritual slaying of an innocent girl followed by Lumb's being hunted to death, is presented with revoltingly concrete immediacy, and yet makes its impact on a psycho-symbolic rather than realistic level. The underlying theme is that of the fractured psyche, releasing hideously destructive powers for which neither extant forms of myth and religion (in particular, twentieth-century Anglican Christianity) nor the re-enactment of primitive rituals in black magic form can provide an adequately channelling and controlling vehicle. The two Lumbs, as an epigraph taken from *Parzival* suggests, are 'the two sons of one man', constituting a divided being, a split between spirit and flesh, with the emphasis of the poem's narrative on the tearing apart which the flesh suffers as a result of this division. But the wholeness which would, implicitly, result from their union is no conventional harmony of body and soul. What it might be is hinted in the hyper-vitality of such passages in the lyrically inspired narrative as the following:

> A squirrel flees up through a beech, like a lashing rocket,
>   and rips into the outermost leaf-net with a crash.
> Voices recede, snatch back their words and meanings,
> Become bramble stem, leaf hollows, reticulation of twigs.

This is part of a rendering of Lumb's state of tormented consciousness as he tries to find some freedom for his will in the midst of

the nightmare conditioning which makes him play the doomed
part assigned to him in this garish tragedy. But it also contains
intimations (as in Hughes's earlier animal poetry) of a consciousness
undivided from the surging energies of nature, exemplified in the
squirrel, and in the 'voices' which merge with natural vegetation.
Although the total effect of *Gaudete* is of something violently, and
even obscenely, split, and the poem, it must be admitted, is more
a latter-day Gothic horror story than a successful psychic drama,
the sense of what has been violated is still to be glimpsed in such
revealing poetic moments.

In the later volumes Hughes has brought the human and non-
human more succesfully together. Drawing upon his farming
experience in poems like 'February 17th' and 'Sheep' (*Moortown*)
he combines the anti-poetic forcefulness of *Crow* with an unsen-
timental sympathy for animals which, after all, form part of a
commercial enterprise. In 'An October Salmon' (*The River*) the life-
cycle of the salmon is viewed from the perspective of its nearing
death, bedraggled and sordid (and entirely of the twentieth-century
in the prosaic noting of the 'bicycle wheels, car-tyres, bottles / And
sunk sheets of corrugated iron' which accompany him as he skulks
under the mill-wall), but 'epic', too – less for what is recalled of his
splendid past, 'the sea-going Aurora Borealis of his April power',
than for the present 'poise / That holds him so steady in his
wounds'. Intense feeling combines with cool recognition of the
natural inevitability of it all, to be accepted as part of 'the machinery
of heaven'.

HUMAN AND ANIMAL

In these poems Hughes recaptures something (if not all) of the
intense commitment to elemental animal life which made his early
poems such stunning achievements, but also adds a tragic dimen-
sion which makes them more deeply relevant to the modern world.
The past and the present of the October salmon are, in fact, much
like the past and present of Hughes's own work. On the one hand
there is natural energy rendered with an equivalent verbal energy
that is simultaneously realistic and unexpectedly bizarre:

> Body simply the armature of energy
> In that earliest sea-freedom, the savage amazement of life,

The salt mouthful of actual existence
With strength like light.

On the other, the acceptance of a 'chamber of horrors' which is 'also home'.

Like Lawrence, and to a lesser extent like Olson as well, Hughes strives in his work for a re-integration of the human and the animal – a re-integration in which animal violence and decay are unsentimentally accepted as an inevitable part of the natural whole. And again like them, he strives 'projectively' to make his verse a more appropriately flexible medium for this holistic vision.

Since this text was prepared Ted Hughes has also published *Birthday Letters* (London: Faber and Faber, 1998). This is a remarkable collection of poems concerning Hughes' relationship with Sylvia Hughes (Plath), ranging from their first meeting to her suicide. Because of the intense publicity surrounding their marriage and its breakdown, and the hostility to Hughes shown by some strongly feminist admirers of Sylvia Plath, its publication has excited much journalistic comment, focused mainly on the biographical aspects of the work. This is a legitimate interest; Hughes weaves reminiscences of Sylvia Plath and even quotations from her work into the sequence, and, taken as a whole, these poems help to balance the account of the two poets' relationship by giving Hughes' own side of a very controversial story. More importantly, however, the collection includes many fine poems which add significantly to the corpus of Hughes' work. Poems like 'Fingers', with its highly sensitive evocation of the 'winged life' of Sylvia Plath's expressive fingers as she played the piano or talked excitedly, and 'Daffodils', which has an almost Lawrentian quality of flower-feeling, and yet poignantly recalls Hardy in its concluding image of the lost scissors used for cutting the daffodils, are great love-poems in their own right. Other poems, such as 'Grand Canyon' and 'Karlsbad Caverns', based on incidents from a journey which Hughes and Plath took across America, are in a more familiar Hughesian style, but, again, deserve attention for what they show of his intrinsic, poetic powers.

8

Women's Poetry

ADRIENNE RICH (b. 1929)

The freedom and informality sought by Charles Olson implies a questioning of all established attitudes and cultural certainties. His projective verse is the expression of a rebelliousness which is not harnessed to a philosophical or political programme such as Marxism, for example, might require, but seeks to release the mind from the constrictions which it has inherited from the past and internalised so that they act as a self-policing sense of style. It is this aspect of his work which has also led to his influence on twentieth-century women writers who are vastly different from – and even in many respects actively hostile to – D. H. Lawrence and Ted Hughes.

Prominent among these is the contemporary American poet Adrienne Rich, who began her writing career with poetry that looked as rationally formal as that of the early Robert Lowell, but found in Olson a model which enabled her to produce an almost anti-intellectual style. As one sympathetic critic puts it:

> Like Olson, Adrienne Rich recoiled from the overemphasis upon intellect in poetry, including her own work. For her, this emphasis meant an adherence to the male principle as the source of light or consciousness. Turning toward the female principle – the nonrational or instinctual in the human psyche – and finding it a source of power, Rich increased her receptivity to projective verse.[1]

Implicit in this statement are a number of issues which relate to twentieth-century women writers generally, and especially the feminist critique of the male-centred type of rational discourse, or 'phallogocentrism', which constitutes the dominant mode of consciousness in the modern world. Oppression of women is equated with the intellectual processes which have served this dominance since they tend to exclude the possibility of finding validity in other modes of awareness; and, as a corollary, freeing oneself from such oppression becomes associated with the re-shaping of language to break down the logical inhibitors of other kinds of discourse. Here, however, the male/female opposition needs qualifying. A powerful element in twentieth-century modernist poetry, as indicated, for example, by Rich's response to the possibilities of projective verse (and already illustrated by the Levertov poem examined in the previous chapter), is itself subversive of traditional order and reason – though neither anti-intellectual nor anti-élitist. The underlying sense of a hardening of the linguistic arteries, and a complementary sense of the need to release freshness and a new complexity of meaning, which is at the root of the disconcerting innovations of modernism, is both precursor and ally of the shift desired. And, it may be added, the widespread critical effort to understand and justify such poetry modifies the expectations of readers, encouraging them to attend to paralogical as well as logical devices, so that the aim of women writers can be seen as going with, rather than against, the grain of such developments in modern poetry.

As Rich makes clear in her semi-autobiographical essay 'Blood, Bread, and Poetry: The Location of the Poet',[2] her own earliest encounter with poetry was confined to that 'written almost entirely by white Anglo-Saxon men' – a statement of fact which, however, is also a form of protest. The implication is that she was unwillingly (or perhaps at first, unknowingly) set within a cultural and linguistic mould determined by men which was unnatural, constricitng and even repressive to her as a person of potentially wider sympathies, and especially as a woman. Her development consists of a growing consciousness of the alien character of this particular inheritance, a rejection of the assumptions on which it is based, and an increasing identification with feminism, and ultimately (at least for herself) with lesbianism, as a way of realising the female individuality denied to her by her upbringing. Stylistically there is also the change referred to above by which she remakes herself as a female rather than pseudo-male poet – a change marked by a shift from formal, rhymed versification to a less assertive, more free-flowing free verse through which her true self can find expression. However, at least one of her models, as we have already seen, is that provided by a male poet, Charles Olson, who is likewise the inheritor of modernist developments by poets as different as William Carlos Williams and D. H. Lawrence. Without therefore denying the appropriateness of

Rich's stylistic changes to her changing perception of the true nature of her self, it is possible to see both as symptomatic of a much wider change in modern poetry resulting from the sense that important levels and kinds of feeling exist which demand the breaking up of old modes and the emergence of newer, more tentative ones.

Even that, however, is a simplification of what tends to be in practice a more complex relationship between masculine and feminine, old and new; as can be seen by comparing examples taken from Rich's own earlier and later poetry. 'Aunt Jennifer's Tigers' (1951) is a poem which is conventional in form, but unconventional in meaning. It consists of six pairs of rhyming couplets divided into three quatrains, with each couplet a self-contained unit of meaning and each line a fairly regular, end-stopped iambic pentameter. The subject of the poem is Aunt Jennifer's embroidery of a screen depicting 'Bright topaz' tigers in 'a world of green' and some unspecified men who are presumably hunting them. The poem's slightly archaic, Augustan style and structure seems appropriate to the antithesis on which it is built: the energy and fearlessness of the tigers in the first quatrain (A), as opposed to the terrified conformity of Aunt Jennifer in the second quatrain (B). That sequence is inverted, however, in the third quatrain, where in the first couplet the Aunt's death is wittily envisaged as simply a continuation of her dead–alive state (B), while in the second couplet the embroidered tigers 'go on prancing, proud and unafraid' (A).

In theme and structure the poem also echoes the famous 'Tyger' by the Romantic poet William Blake, further pointing up the antithesis between untamed energy and the asphyxiating conformity that Aunt Jennifer is subjected to. But Rich also has a particular emphasis of her own, seen, for example, in the symbolism of the 'ivory needle', which Aunt Jennifer hardly has the strength to pull through her fabric, and especially the wedding ring with its 'massive weight' sitting 'heavily upon Aunt Jennifer's hand'. Strictly speaking, i.e. as the poem chooses to put it, this ring is not even Aunt Jennifer's; it is 'Uncle's wedding band' – the 'band / hand' rhyme suggesting almost a state of bondage. The implication of such symbolism is that marriage is the cause of Aunt Jennifer's deadening blight, and more particularly marriage as the repressive institution shaped and controlled by man. The literary echoes now seem to relate to an entire criticism of socio-sexual conditions which operate as a tyranny (like the 'mind-forg'd manacles' of another Blake poem, 'London'), but given the particular modification that in Rich's poem that tyranny is associated with a male dominance accepted and internalised by Aunt Jennifer as a social norm. The only way she can deal with the suppressed energies inside her is by creating an artefact in which they become tigerish forces 'prancing, proud and unafraid', yet caught, ironically, in the static, conformist mode of traditionally domesticated female needlework. Form and meaning are thus interrelated: the poem's neat ringlike structure matches the socio-sexual structure that 'bands' Aunt Jennifer, while the tigers with which it begins and ends hint at the protest which it also contains. Via its precise formality the poem turns on itself, becoming a self-reflexive 'ring' which simultaneously imitates and criticises Aunt Jennifer's subjected condition.

One way, then, of interpreting 'Aunt Jennifer's Tigers' is to see it as an ironic poem which takes the rational formality attributed to 'phallogocentrism' and turns it inside out (though such an interpretation would have to concede that this could not be done unless the structure also contained the means of summoning up another vision from within). Even the early poetry of Rich is subversive of the methods it apparently adopts. But it is also to be expected that an alternative vision, questioning the validity of established masculine norms, should start to affect the form in which it is communicated and re-shape it to its own needs; and this is precisely what one finds in Rich's later work. A useful illustration is the poem called 'Solfeggietto' (from the 1989 volume, *Time's Power*). Like 'Aunt Jennifer's Tigers' this also criticises an inhibitory condition from within the system that generates it, but it does so in a more liberated style which corresponds to, and expresses, the creative release which is imagined and desired.

'Solfeggietto' is an autobiographical, retrospective poem, and to that extent more open, and 'confessional' even, than 'Aunt Jennifer's Tigers'. Its protagonists are mother and daughter, with the poet herself as the child, whose experiences she can re-create but also look back on from the vantage point of adulthood, and the mother a maternal figure presented in terms of both a child's and an adult's capacity for understanding. There is some degree of parallel in the symbolic structure of the two poems in that the traditionally feminine occupation of needlework provides the basic metaphor for 'Aunt Jennifer's Tigers', and in 'Solfeggietto' it is music, which is also marked as appropriately 'feminine' in the sense that piano-playing was a standard nineteenth-century female middle-class accomplishment , but which is here, despite the mother's attempts to teach it to her daugher, the object of rebellious rejection by the child. The music, however, is less satirically defined than Aunt Jennifer's screen and more ambiguous in its scope, ranging from Bach, Brahms and Mozart to the *One Hundred Best-Loved Songs* played by the mother on summer evenings in a rented holiday house. The mother–daughter relationship is ambiguous, too. For the mother music is something she has practised for hours in a 'life of prize-recitals' which she is encouraged to believe might lead to the serious achievement of concert performance, but comes, in fact, to little more than a music-teacher's teaching to 'boarding-school girls what won't be used'. For the child whom she also tries to teach, music is a tyranny. In infancy the piano seems

> a black cave
> with teeth of ebony and ivory,

and at a later stage something to which she is fastened in order to learn a 'keyboard world of black and white' from which she must extract a predetermined music of 'ruled and ruling staves'. What is potentially liberation and fulfilment for the mother is enslavement for the child, and their shared experience a cause of mutual frustration. What the mother tries to pass on is not 'magic' as far as her daughter is concerned: would-be togetherness is reduced to 'Side by side I see us locked.'

Mother and daughter are thus antithetical; but this is not the antithetical condition sharply delineated in 'Aunt Jennifer's Tigers'. The 'I' who speaks of seeing herself and her mother 'locked' is an older and wiser person than the rebellious child. This 'I' can see the ideology that lies behind their conflict. There is, for example, a brief mention of 'the Jewish father' who also 'teaches' (in his case books of the Old Testament), and this reinforces the sense that it is a fixed tradition, literally espoused by the mother and internalised in *her* teaching, that the daughter rebels against. The daughter wants a different mode of learning. The mother says 'she must learn to read by sight'; the daughter 'would rather learn by ear and heart'. But the language of the poem is alert and sensitive to both mind-sets, and to other potentialities that might have been realised. Its colloquially relaxed and rhythmically free-flowing verse, its visually spaced-out 'projective' breathing and its dissolving of times and scenes into one another, allow judgements to be made, but sympathies also to be kept alive. The poetry thus resists the simple, emotionally indulgent temptation to treat parents, the mother in particular, as embodiments of a repressive society seeking to produce clones of itself. The variable, flexible nature of the lines, and the reduction of punctuation to a minimum, keep intolerant certainty at bay, even though permitting such strong, forbidding, symbolic images as 'the ivory / and ebony teeth of the Steinway'; and in keeping with this the poem moves, not towards the full stop of an emphatic conclusion, but to a series of questions which the daughter asks of herself as well as her mother:

> I ask you, both of us
> – Did you think mine was a virtuoso's hand?
> Did I see power in yours?
> What was worth fighting for?   What did you want?
> What did I want from you?

Such open-endedness may not be entirely characteristic of Adrienne Rich. She is in many ways a decidedly militant writer. In her prose work especially she is a strongly committed advocate of the women's movement, and many of her best known poems seem the work of a deeply moved and angry opponent of patriarchal assumptions. Sympathetic critics such as Claire Keyes and Liz Yorke find elements in Rich's later work which suggest that, though still radically inimical to patriarchal values, she is developing a distinctively woman's voice which counters 'the argument and jargon that signifies the violence, competitiveness and combativeness of macho-modes of relating to the world' with a visionary poetry defining its goals 'in terms of caring for, rather than egocentrically dominating the world'.[3] However, the grim fire and fury of a poem such as 'The Ninth Symphony of Beethoven Understood at Last as a Sexual Message' (with a title that speaks its nature) or the sardonic 'Snapshots of a Daughter-in-Law', with its laconic contempt for masculine patronising –

> Sigh no more, ladies.
>   Time is male
> and in his cups drinks to the fair –

remain essential parts of Adrienne Rich's lasting achivement. She is the controversialist as well as the visionary, the wielder of sharp rhymes as well as the recorder of subtle, elusive rhythms; and not herself to be patronised or underestimated.

SYLVIA PLATH (1932–63)

Adrienne Rich might be seen as the inheritor and meeting point of two quite different kinds of twentieth-century women's poetry associated with her predecessors, Elizabeth Bishop and Sylvia Plath. Bishop will be discussed towards the end of this chapter; she represents the visionary tradition. Plath has moments of great visionary insight, also, and she is too diverse a poet to be easily summarised and classified. But nevertheless, in broad terms, she is the most striking example of the fiery, rebellious strain in women's poetry. If she is less politically committed than Rich, and less of an avowedly feminist poet, she is even more passionately driven by a vision of freedom and fulfilment which demands release from sexual stereotyping. Her early work is perhaps rather overcontrolled. The discipline which is sought for in elaborate metrical and rhyme structures has a tendency to become a straitjacket, and her use of assonance and alliteration can deteriorate into mere mannerism. In her later work, however, she combines this still highly self-conscious artistry with the looser, more dramatically immediate style of the 'confessional' poetry of Berryman and the mature Lowell to produce a poetry of fiercely articulated energy which is uniquely hers. 'Ariel', for example, is a vividly subjective impression of a precipitate horse ride in the early morning in which art and experience are fused into a strange linguistic intensity. The world that flashes by is so instilled with the rider's own heightened imaginative awareness that there is no cold, objective reality left. External nature becomes pure psychological sensation projected in a taut, yet seemingly unlicensed metre and a brilliantly controlled, but free-flowing sequence of echoing sounds and varied forms of rhyme, half-rhyme and internal rhyme:

> Nigger-eye
> Berries cast dark
> Hooks——
>
> Black sweet blood mouthfuls,
> Shadows,
> Something else

Hauls me through air——
Thighs, hair;
Flakes from my heels.

    This high-pitched, subjective intensity also catches up public and private, autobiographical material into itself – notoriously so in the controversial poems 'Daddy' and 'Lady Lazarus', where Plath makes use of her own psychological difficulties, deriving from the early death of her German-born father, exacerbated by the breakdown of her marriage to Ted Hughes, and mingles these with horrific material drawn from the Nazi concentration camps and Hitler's attempt to exterminate the Jews. In 'Daddy' identification with the fate of the Jews –

An engine, an engine
Chuffing me off like a Jew.
A Jew to Dachau, Auschwitz, Belsen.
I began to talk like a Jew.
I think I may well be a Jew.

and the savage irony of

Every woman adores a Fascist,
The boot in the face, the brute
Brute heart of a brute like you.

combine bizarrely with the language and rhythms of nursery-rhyme (especially 'There was an old woman who lived in a shoe') to create a sense of tragic outrage which borders on hysteria. Yet the total effect is not hysterical but cathartic. Private and public horrors, the experiences of victim and victimiser are fused in a paradoxically controlled outburst that purges the speaker's tormented consciousness.

    In 'Lady Lazarus' the manner is equally histrionic as the prima donna persona boasts of a 'theatrical / Comeback in broad day' from her act of attempted suicide; and the holocaust identification is again both electrifying and shockingly presumptuous as the speaker characterises her revived self as

A sort of walking miracle, my skin
Bright as a Nazi lampshade,
My right foot

> A paperweight
> My face a featureless, fine
> Jew linen.

Here the material lends itself to black comedy. With highly provocative wit death and resurrection are converted into a sensational pantomime in which this female version of the biblical Lazarus rises up again like a Demon Queen to challenge male hegemony, whether it takes the form of God or the Devil:

> Herr God, Herr Lucifer
> Beware
> Beware
>
> Out of the ash
> I rise with my red hair
> And I eat men like air.

These words are also closely akin to the conclusion of 'Stings', one of Plath's remarkable sequence of bee-keeping poems.[4] The speaker asserts that she has 'a self to recover', who is a queen-bee, and asks:

> Is she dead, is she sleeping?
> Where has she been,
> With her lion-red body, her wings of glass?
>
> Now she is flying
> More terrible than she ever was, red
> Scar in the sky, red comet
> Over the engine that killed her——
> The mausoleum, the wax house.

Both poems are inspired by reaction against a male dominance which is felt as a negative burden upon an active female selfhood. As in Adrienne Rich there is a Blakean sense of thwarted energy expressing itself in a dangerous violence which is all the greater for the repression it has suffered so long.

The bee-keeping poems, however, do more than protest. Their tragic anger is relieved by a comic vision. They draw upon a bee-society which is based on female rather than male dominance, and which has a creative basis. The fact that it is also associated with the destructive male imperialism of Napolean, whose symbol was likewise the bee, gives Plath the opportunity for some humorous mock-heroics. This is not immediately apparent in the first two poems of the sequence, 'The Bee Meeting' and 'The Arrival of the Bee Box'. There the initiation into bee-keeping is an ominous rite in which ordinary villagers are transformed by their bee-keeping attire into threateningly alien figures, and the poet is appalled by the sinister nature of what she has committed herself to:

> I put my eye to the grid.
> It is dark, dark,
> With the swarmy feeling of African hands
> Minute and shrunk for export,
> Black on black, angrily clambering.

But in 'The Swarm' (the poem which follows 'Stings') the tone changes. The bees are made to succumb to a bee-keeper who shoots with a childish 'Pom! Pom!' at the tree where they have swarmed, ludicrously bunched 'in their black ball, / A flying hedgehog, all prickles'. He compels them to enter his hive, and as they do so they make a sorry picture of Napoleonic Empire-style furnishings:

> The dumb, banded bodies
> Walking the plank draped with Mother France's upholstery
> Into a new mausoleum,
> An ivory palace, a crotch pine.

(The derogatory implications of 'mausoleum' and 'crotch' speak for themselves.) And in the last poem, 'Wintering', emphasis shifts from male to female, and the tone is more domestically matter-of-fact. The poet has her honey kept in the cellar 'Next to the last tenant's rancid jam'. As 'The cold sets in' the bees, barely kept alive (and not with nectar from the flowers, but with faintly ridiculous substitute Tate and Lyle syrup) are now 'all women', having got rid of the men – 'The blunt, clumsy stumblers, the boors'. Yet they manage to maintain, however low-key it may seem, some bulb-like life which holds out the hope of regeneration, tentatively expressed in a string of questions:

> Will the hive survive, will the gladiolas
> Succeed in banking their fires
> To enter another year?
> What will they taste of, the Christmas roses?

The final line is more positive: 'The bees are flying. They taste the spring.' What it conveys, however, is neither brash assurance, nor the angry, red flight of 'Stings' (and, for that matter, of 'Lady Lazarus'), but a laconic suggestion of the possibility of renewal.

ANNE SEXTON (1928–74)

Plath's name is also frequently associated with Anne Sexton. Both attended Lowell's creative writing classes; both committed suicide; and both used their mental struggles as material for their poetry. In the 1960s, with the publication of *To Bedlam and Part Way Back* (1960), *All My Pretty Ones* (1962) and *Live or Die* (1966) and as a result of her own highly dramatic poetry readings, Sexton was perhaps the better known of the two. However, Plath's posthumous reputation has almost eclipsed that of Sexton. Retrospectively, it seems that in poems such as 'The Abortion', 'Menstruation at Forty' and 'In Celebration of My Uterus' Sexton depends too much on the shock-effect of her subject-matter. Plath shocks, too, but more by the originality of her vision, and her almost 'Metaphysical' capacity to see connections between apparently disparate areas of experience. Where they come together most is in the exploitation of children's stories and nursery-rhyme techniques to effect a surprising re-focus of attention on the position of women. Sexton's most successful poems in this kind are her modern re-tellings of well-known fairy tales in her late volume, *Transformations* (1971). Here, though the voice is still one of protest (specifically, against the stereotyping of women by having them invariably placed in passive roles), it is less strident than in the earlier poems. As Carol Leventen suggests, there is a message: 'Sexton's protagonists are silenced, acted upon, and they acquiesce almost helplessly in continuing silence themselves.'[5] But it is via her stylistic 'transformation' of these vacuous Snow White heroines and the 'lived-happily-ever-afterwards' endings of their stories that the point is wittily, and entertainingly, made.

STEVIE SMITH (1902–71)

Among English women poets Stevie Smith, who died in the year when *Transformations* was published, is perhaps the one who most readily connects with the use of fairy tale by Plath and Sexton. Smith became an immensely popular poet after her death, but her lasting achievement is difficult to assess. Her work is a strange mixture of simplicity (or assumed simplicity) and literary sophistication (the constant echoing of Shakespeare, the Metaphysicals, Blake, Keats, Tennyson, Browning, Whitman and others can make her at times seem as allusive as the more academic modernists); and the alternation of nursery-rhyme lyricism with verse of an oddly prosaic, sometimes banal, nature can make her seem impossibly naive. Yet the total effect is disconcerting and disturbing. Poems like 'The Singing Cat', 'Avondale' and 'Le Singe Qui Swing' (the latter 'To the tune of Green-sleeves' and illustrated by one of Smith's own faut-naif drawings) sound like latter-day attempts to re-create the simple directness of Blake's *Songs of Innocence*. But a poem like 'The After-Thought', which begins with an echo of the fairy tale of Rapunzel being called upon by her lover to let down her hair, veers off in the very next line into the practical banality of his saying:

> And when I come up this time I will bring a rope ladder
>   with me
> And then we can both escape into the dark wood immediately.

The rest of the poem, with its reflections on Edgar Allan Poe and Indian fakirs, is still more disconcerting, while the off-beat conclusion:

> What is that darling? You cannot hear me?
> That's odd. I can hear you quite distinctly.

both deflates the initially romantic 'beautiful lover' and voices the reader's own sense of hearing and not hearing simultaneously.

Failure of communication in the context of apparently plain, uncomplicated language, and with deeply disturbing psychological undertones, is in fact a recurrent motif in Smith's work. It is the theme of her best-known poem, 'Not Waving But Drowning'. There is more to it than what 'must have been' the misfortune of a heart attack brought on by too cold water and the pathos of a drowning man's signal being misunderstood. The states of being 'dead' and 'dying' are curiously blurred ('still the dead one lay moaning'), as are the possible meanings of 'drowning' and the time when drowning takes place. The poem itself is a pessimistic cry for help from someone living an on-going death. Finally, Smith's accompanying drawing disconcertingly presents 'the dead man' as a woman (though with breasts almost non-existent and the lower part of her body hidden by water, as if to nullify gender). In the text all the third-person pronouns are masculine, and masculinity is heightened by the colloquial 'Poor chap, he always loved larking'; but the waif-like, almost de-sexed girl of the drawing compels a sudden re-thinking of the whole situation, and opens up the way to a quite different reading.

'Major Macroo' is more explicit. From its first stanza, with its ironic statement that 'Major Hawkaby Cole Macroo / Chose / very wisely / A patient Griselda of a wife with a heart of gold', to its final

> Such men as these, such selfish cruel men
> Hurting what most they love what most loves them,
> Never make a mistake when it comes to choosing a woman
> To cherish them and be neglected and not think it inhuman.

it is clearly attacking the exploitation of the loving, self-sacrificing woman. But the sense of conflict, for a woman, between the demands made on her, especially masculine ones, and her own innermost needs is more indirectly, and yet more compellingly, expressed in the ballad-like form of 'I Rode with my Darling ... '. The 'dark wood at night' refrain, evoking an attraction towards darkness, death and the unconscious which is endemic to Smith's poetry, has the inexplicable compulsion of the medieval ballad. Surrender to the compulsion is, if anything, more tragic than liberating – in the last stanza the speaker seems bereft not only of her lover, but of her own female relatives as well – and complicates the message while making it resonate more truthfully. It has the authentically disturbing note of Smith's poetry which so effectively disrupts her own apparent simplicities.

SOME RECENT WOMEN POETS: U. A. FANTHORPE (b. 1929), CAROL ANN DUFFY (b. 1955), FLEUR ADCOCK (b. 1934) AND AMY CLAMPITT (b. 1920)

More recent women poets such as U. A. Fanthorpe, Carol Ann Duffy and Fleur Adcock combine the sardonic humour of Smith with the colloquial shock-tactics of the Americans. But at the same time they are relaxingly willing just to entertain. Fanthorpe especially has a delightful gift for modern mock-heroic. The three stanzas of 'Not My Best Side' become three Browningesque dramatic mono-logues on Uccello's painting of St George and the Dragon, from the dragon's, the maid's, and the knight's points of view. Here the dark and sinister is debunked. The poem does not attempt to do justice to Uccello; but it amuses, and in doing so says things about the painting, and more particularly the situation of the maid, which compel the reader to a disconcertingly new look at it. Similarly, Fanthorpe's sequence 'Only here for the Bier', though hardly a poetic re-interpretation of Shakespeare on the level of Auden's *The Sea and the Mirror*, both entertains and defamiliarises. The writer comments: 'I wrote these four poems because I was interested to see how the masculine world of Shakespeare's tragedies would look from the woman's angle.' The result is not something anti-Shakespearean, but rather Shakespearean tragedy seen through the eyes of Shakespearean comedy and its anti-romantic heroines. (A plausible precursor is the story of Hero and Leander as told by Rosalind in *As You Like It*.) That these women are comically uncomfortable and uncomprehending (or mis-comprehending) in their tragic worlds deflates the masculine protagonists at least as much as the women themselves.

A not dissimilar kind of parodic verse is employed by Carol Ann Duffy in her presentation of women in *The World's Wife*. Here it is the partners of mythic or famous men who offer sardonic sidelights on the problems of their husbands, but, more complexly than is the case with Fanthorpe's women, Duffy's wives are both justifiably and also short-sightedly critical of the male world. Mrs Darwin is brief and to the point, but Mrs Midas, Mrs Lazarus, Mrs Tiresias and Queen Kong are less laconic. Mrs Midas, in particular, takes her time in unfolding the story of her husband's fatal touch that turns all to gold. She is a commonplace middle-class housewife, doing the cooking, and being a little wearily patronising towards her husband. The enormity of what has happened only breaks through to her gradually. Her first glimpse of Midas at the bottom of the garden plucking a pear, which 'sat in his palm like a light-bulb. On', merely makes her think to herself, 'Is he putting fairy lights in the tree?' When he sits down, however, 'He sat in that chair like a king on a burnished throne', the verbal echo of Enobarbus' description of Cleopatra both enhancing and diminishing the man; and his attempts to eat and drink begin to subvert daily routine alarmingly. Yet the inevitable disruption proceeds like a domestic row: 'I made him sit / on the other side of the room and keep his hands to himself ... Separate beds ... So he had to move out ...'. Only slowly, if at all, does the new, appalling reality penetrate Mrs Midas's consciousness, a characteristically feminine step towards this being her dream of bearing her husband a child with 'perfect ore limbs'. When she visits him in his isolation she finds him 'thin, / delirious; hearing, he said, the music of Pan / from the woods'. After his death, although she somewhat meanly reflects, 'What gets me now is not the idiocy or greed / but lack of thought for me. Pure selfishness', the final lines convey a less self-satisfied view:

> I think of him in certain lights, dawn, late afternoon,
> and once a bowl of apples stopped me dead. I miss most,
> even now, his hands, his warm hands on my skin, his touch.

The success of Duffy's poem depends not only on the ease with which she moulds her language to suit the half-perceptive, half-cliché-ridden mind of her female character, but also on her capacity to break into this comic level with moments of a more disturbing kind such as the bowl of apples that stop her dead. Her insight is less the result of animosity towards the male as exploiter than awareness of contradictory, yet mutually balancing, experiences (which are not, however, the same as the complementary roles of Victorian tradition leading to the paternalistically convenient separation of male and female spheres). 'Standing Female Nude', for example, is spoken from the point of view of an artist's model who works 'Six hours like this for a few francs'. Her monologue is not self-pitying; nor is it simply sociologically aware, despite the model's comment, on the artist and herself, that 'Both poor, we make our living how we can.' Nor, again, is it simply an exposure of the model's incapacity to understand something that 'they' call 'Art', though her final comment on the finished painting that 'It does not look like me' may seem to point in that direction; her judgements, straightforward enough to herself, are interestingly ambivalent for the reader – especially her comment that the artist 'possesses me on canvas as he dips the brush / repeatedly into the paint', *vis à vis* her slightly contemptuous remark, 'Little man, you've not the money for the arts I sell.' The painting, after all, may well be a form of sublimation of sex, and the painter's poverty something which makes him do on canvas what he cannot pay for in the flesh. The outcome is that both nominally disreputable characters gain the readers's understanding and respect. The poem does not invite a simple taking of sides.

Adcock's poetry is both humorous and tender; and often wryly self-critical. In 'For a Five-Year-Old' the speaker conveys both a mother's instinctive sense of the need to soften harsh realities for the sake of an innocent child and her admission to herself of behaving differently as an adult. But the poem disarmingly manages to reconcile the two: 'a kind of faith prevails ... that is how things are: I am your mother, / And we are kind to snails.' In the more astringent 'Advice to a Discarded Lover' this honesty (here both speaker and addressee are adults) is more direct, the element of cruelty heightened rather than mitigated. The poem opens with the disgusting image of a dead bird crawling with maggots, and the question, 'what do you feel – / More pity or more revulsion?' This becomes a metaphorical vehicle for a dead love affair, and the question a way of dealing with the maudlin reaction of a rejected lover whom the speaker dismisses with the words:

> If I were to touch you I should feel
> Against my fingers fat, moist worm-skin.
> Do not ask me for charity now:
> Go away until your bones are clean.

As a complement to these two poems, and a kind of bridge between them, in yet another poem, 'Grandma' (not, however, originally published in the same volume), the nastiness of physical decay at first excites revulsion, but is followed by self-critical relenting. The speaker recognises that what she finds loathsome in her dream of her grandmother's necrophiliac embrace is what she herself will become in due course:

> My blood too (Group A,
> Rhesus negative, derived exactly from hers)
> will suffer that deterioration

and she concludes therefore that she will

> apologise to my sons and their possible
> children for the gruesomeness: we do not mean it.

Relationships across the generations are recurrent themes in Adcock's poetry, giving it a breadth and variety which balance the sometimes seemingly cool tautness of her critical spirit. And in poems like 'Letter to Alistair Campbell', 'Settlers' and 'Going Back' these relationships are further supplemented by the toings and froings, both spatial and mental, between people who have left England for New Zealand, and (like Adcock herself) New Zealand for England. Difference and separateness are recurrent themes, but the underlying link is personal awarenss, usually of a distinctively female kind. In 'On the Border' (located in the tropics, probably in Africa) this takes the form of a woman's courage and individuality asserting itself in spite of deprivation and discomfort. The speaker is an English woman uprooted from her own environment, but able to write frankly, intimately, and with a delightfully humorous touch of vulgarity as well (even if only for the benefit of 'posterity') in a way that conveys her resilience of character:

> I don't care. I am standing here,
> posterity, on the face of the earth,
> letting the breeze blow up my nightdress,
> writing in English, as I do,
> in all this tropical non-silence.
> Now let me tell you about the elephants.

Although Amy Clampitt is older than this English trio (who are not, however, strictly speaking English, since Adcock was born in New Zealand, and Duffy in Scotland), her first books, *The Kingfisher* (1983) and *What the Light Was Like* (1985), were not published till she was in her sixties. She is American, but so interested in the English context that she might almost be called Anglo-American. Intertextual relationships with English poetry and echoes of particular English poems abound in her work. 'The Outer Bar', for example, echoes Hopkins's 'The Windhover': after a remarkable account of a seaward walk taken at low tide the speaker looks back and views the waves as

> chain-gang archangels that in their prismatic
> frenzy fall, gall and gash the daylight
> out there, all through the winter.

More extensively, one of the most interesting sequences in her second volume is on the life of John Keats ('Voyages: A Homage to John Keats'), and mingles English with American scenes and authors (notably Whitman and Hart Crane) to create a strangely modern counterpoint.

Like Fanthorpe and Duffy, Clampitt is also a humorous commentator on the modern woman's life. The mock-heroine of 'A New Life' – aptly named 'Autonomy' – is a second-stage women's liberationist who is 'moving up / in the corporate structure'. Having 'thrown over / the old laid-back lifestyle', she has taken to a business career that has her driving every day up and down the ironically labelled 'Freeway' from suburban home to Company's office. The jargon of business and the jargon of science mingle to suggest that the woman is on a rising curve to unprecedented freedom; but whether that is so, or whether the parody of marriage and motherhood entailed by her 'corporate' life is merely an 'apocalyptic freakout', is left in ambiguous balance at the end of the poem.

ELIZABETH BISHOP (1911–79)

So far this chapter has focused on women poets who deal with women's issues and women's experience, usually explicitly and often with passionately critical involvement. But the woman who stands at the fountain-head of twentieth-century women poets, Elizabeth Bishop, is less immediately recognisable as one of them. In the 68 years of her life she did not produce a very large quantity of verse (her *Complete Poems 1927–1979* occupies only one volume of less than 280 pages), but what she wrote is of a consistently high standard of excellence, and it has become increasingly admired for its deep humanity and formal perfection. In poems such as 'At the Fishhouses', 'The End of March', 'Crusoe in England', 'In the Waiting Room' and 'The Moose' she achieves a plainness and classic poise reminiscent of Wordsworth, though salted with a quite un-Wordsworthian wit. Yet her work, which has had a fruitful influence on succeeding American women poets, is firmly in the American tradition; and if it does not foreground gender in quite the manner of Rich or Plath, woman's experience and the woman's vantage point are none the less central to her vision of the world and her mode of expressing it.

This can be seen particularly clearly in the autobiographical poem 'In the Waiting Room'. Beginning as modestly as may be 'In Worcester, Massachusetts', where Bishop herself was born in 1911, and in a dentist's waiting room where her Aunt Consuelo has an

appointment, it swells, via the pages of the *National Geographic*
magazine read by the seven-year-old Elizabeth, to a cataclysmic
experience in which the 'bright / and too hot' waiting room

> was sliding
> beneath a big black wave,
> another, and another.

   The process is gradual and cumulative. Proleptically, the first
thing Elizabeth finds in the magazine is a group of photographs of
a volcano, first 'black, and full of ashes', then 'spilling over / in
rivulets of fire'. Other disturbing images follow, especially of babies
and black women:

> Babies with pointed heads
> wound round and round with string;
> black, naked women with necks
> wound round and round with wire
> like the necks of light bulbs.
> Their breasts were horrifying.

The heightened consciousness of the girl then makes her respond
to her aunt's cry of pain, there in the waiting room, as if it were
her own. Here-and-now and exotic far-and-away combine to make
her suddenly aware of her separate self ('you are an *I*, / you are
an *Elizabeth*'), but also of her involvement in a group ('you are one
of *them*'), which is shadowily present only as 'gray knees, / trousers
and skirts and boots / and different pairs of hands'. Reality and
unreality are so mixed that all sense of secure identity deserts her,
dissolving into impossible questions of 'Why', 'What' and 'How'.
The waiting room is swamped. Finally, however, she is back in it
and Worcester, Massachusetts, with the humdrum facts of 'night
and slush and cold'.
   One other feature is important – the date. This, too, is cumulative
in effect. It is first referred to, in connection with the yellow margins
of the magazine cover, simply as 'the date', then given as '*the*
National Geographic, / February, 1918', and finally, in connection
with the return to the waiting room and coupled with the statement
that 'The War was on', it is precisely specified as 'the fifth / of
February, 1918'. The cataclysm that is the War is left to speak for
itself, but yet is clearly enough the final volcanic upheaval in the

child's mind. Babies, 'those awful hanging breasts', the identification with her aunt, and her feeling herself as 'an *Elizabeth*' constitute a pre-puberty consciousness in the girl which is emotionally powerful enough to disturb the world's foundations, and is reflected in the actual shattering of civilisation's moulds which is going on across the Atlantic. (The pinpointing of the American Worcester, in Massachusetts, may also be a hint of the older Worcester, three thousand miles away in England.) What it means to be a particular female, and the shock of realising or resisting connections with other females, thus merges with a precipitating process that far transcends one little girl's private crisis, while yet being felt intensely as the consequence and culmination of that crisis.

Another poem which explores the female, and yet reverberates far beyond, is 'The Moose'. An even longer poem than 'In the Waiting Room', it develops even more slowly. The explicit subject is a bus journey from an up-country district to the city of Boston, but obliquely it is a story of dawning female awareness. The beginning is again modest, simple and domestic:

> From narrow provinces
> of fish and bread and tea,
> home of the long tides.

The world that the passengers are leaving behind in the evening light is coloured by their essentially home-based interests; and where gender is mentioned it is in the form of 'white hens' feathers' or 'a woman shakes a tablecloth / out after supper'. (A collie and a dog are also included, but these, too, *may* be female for later in the poem there is mention of 'the dog / tucked in her shawl'.) At the thirteenth leisurely stanza a woman boards the bus, 'brisk, freckled, elderly', and the talk that goes on is female gossip of such things as pensions, illness and death in childbirth.

Suddenly the (male) driver stops, and a moose stands there in the moonlight sniffing at the bus. At first the animal is referred to merely as 'it', but later it is given significantly female characteristics and associations:

> Towering, antlerless,
> high as a church,
> homely as a house
> (or, safe as houses).

At last a voice whispers '"Look! It's a she!"' The moose seems to
catch up all the homely, feminine implications of the preceding
journey, and now, embodying them in a form larger than life,
arouses 'this sweet / sensation of joy'.

The ending of the poem may appear somewhat anti-climactic.
The driver simply shifts gear, and, briefly, as the bus moves on

> the moose can be seen
> on the moonlit macadam;
> then there's a dim
> smell of moose, an acrid
> smell of gasoline.

Nevertheless, without any hint of portentousness or aggressiveness,
the moose has made a potent, even dominating impression as she
'looms' and stands there 'Towering'. A specifically 'man's voice'
seeks to reassure the passengers that she is '"Perfectly harmless"',
but the association with 'homely' and 'houses' renders that assur-
ance superfluous. Though 'big' and 'plain' and 'grand, otherworldly',
the moose is a visionary creature of a strange and comfortingly
non-heroic status, a startling visitor from another world, but one who
shows no interest in either startling or intimidating. And, curiously,
what the poem leaves its readers with at the end is the lingering
effect of two kinds of smell: one, the moose's, making its own
natural, unemphatic point, and the other, created by the male-
driven bus, an 'acrid / smell of gasoline'.

It is probably a mistake to underline the tacit gender differences
in 'The Moose' too strongly. The male presences are not treated
with hostility – though it may be that the would-be reassuring
'man's voice' is made to sound a shade patronising. The 'quiet
driver' of the bus is indeed on the moose's side; it is he who stops
and considerately switches off the light, and his comments, 'Curious
creatures ... Look at that, would you', if lacking any depth of
empathy, are tolerant, even sympathetic. It is the final gasoline smell
which seems to set the man-made against the benign feminine
emanation of the moose. That, however, is a possible flaw in an
otherwise faultless achievement. Even as a representation of the
mechanical *v.* the natural, it is slightly out of keeping with the
harmonising mood earlier in the poem which had so satisfyingly

blended the bus with late afternoon sun:

> through late afternoon
> a bus journeys west,
> the windshield flashing pink,
> pink glancing off of metal,
> brushing the dented flank
> of blue, beat-up enamel.

Taken as a whole, the poem suggests harmony rather than division; it is a revisionist anecdote of natural divinity which elevates, but without pretentiously exalting, the feminine principle; and, by the same token, if it is opposed to the masculine, it feels no need to disrupt its own serenity with harsh denunciations.

CONCLUSION

In a judicious and sympathetic essay Seamus Heaney praises Elizabeth Bishop's detachment and powerfully effective use of understatement:

> In an era of volubility, she seems to demonstrate that less is more. By her sense of proportion and awareness of tradition, she makes what is an entirely personal and contemporary style seem continuous with the canonical poetry of the past.[6]

These are valuable qualities, which have the merit of giving due emphasis to the continuity of women's poetry with that of the past, and reminding us that such poetry is valued above all for its personal, linguistic and visionary integrity – for being, in fact, poetry. Bishop's coolness and poise are deeply attractive. They should not, however, be mistaken for placidity. In the very different judgement of Patricia B. Wallace, delivered in an essay entitled 'The Wildness of Elizabeth Bishop', her very real capacity for coolness and calm should not be allowed to disguise the fact that her work can also be deeply disturbing:

> The respectful critical admiration currently surrounding Bishop's work lacks the brisk shock of surprise Emerson thrived

on. That admiration makes her seem tame, as 'perfectly harmless' as the moose of her poem. But Bishop resembles her moose in another, deeper way which belongs to wild poetry: it possesses the grand challenging power to stop us in our tracks. ... For all Bishop's control and restraint, immense and extravagant desires edge her language.[7]

Ultimately, however, these two different, critical evaluations are complementary rather than in conflict. They are corrective emphases to each other; and between them they make possible a properly balanced judgement of Bishop's essential achievement – an achievement which makes her an appropriate figure with which to round off this chapter. The qualities in her poetry which justify Wallace's use of epithets like 'wild', 'challenging', and even 'extravagant', anticipate those of her successors like Plath and Rich in whom these qualities are more immediately evident; and the more 'traditional' element found in her work by Heaney links with that, for example, of Stevie Smith (but she, too, has disturbing undertones). Viewed in this perspective Bishop may be regarded as an appropriate presiding genius for women's poetry in general, which passsionate as it often is in protest against a culture that has inhibited the very idea of female creativity in the arts, is equally committed to recovery from the divided consciousness such inhibition has caused. All the poets in this chapter (and others such as Margaret Atwood, Maya Angelou and Judith Wright not mentioned here, but discussed in other chapters), different as they are from each other, and admirably as they illustrate the strength and diversity of what women's creative powers can actually achieve, have a share in this double-edged vision. Each makes a contribution by discovering she is 'an *I*', 'an *Elizabeth*'.

9
Regional, National and Post-Colonial (I)

'WE ARE ALL REGIONALISTS NOW'

In a conference on the Literature of Region and Nation, held at Aberdeen in 1986, Seamus Heaney was able to say quite casually that 'we are all regionalists now'. His point is that in the latter part of the twentieth century there has been a decline (and, by and large, he regards it as a welcome decline) in the feeling that English literature has its centre in London and the south-east of England. Regionalism as a literary phenomenon in England began in the late eighteenth century in the work of Wordsworth, Crabbe and Clare, and it grew to great strength in the nineteenth century with the novels of the Brontë sisters and Thomas Hardy. But this was the regional mainly in tension with the metropolitan. Though Hardy wrote approvingly that 'A certain provincialism of feeling is invaluable. It is of the essence of individuality, and is largely made up of that crude enthusiasm without which no great thoughts are thought, no great deeds done,' it was in refutation of Matthew Arnold who maintained that the provincial spirit lacked 'the lucidity of a large and centrally placed intelligence ... it has not urbanity, the tone of the city, of the centre'.[1] It was Hardy's *Jude the Obscure* against Arnold's dreaming spires of Oxford. In the twentieth century, however, social, political and economic forces all conspired to make the 'centre' less self-confident. If London remained at the heart of publishing and reviewing, places like Liverpool, Manchester, Newcastle and Hull became much more the regional capitals of a still urban, but no longer London-based literary activity. Many of the best English poets came from the regions and maintained a non-metropolitan, or even anti-metropolitan, outlook, as do poets like Ted Hughes and Simon Armitage (b. 1963) today.

The other major de-centring influence has been, and is, nationalism. So much so that nowadays it is difficult to use phrases like

'English poetry' or 'the English novel' in other than a linguistic context. As in the title of this book which I am writing, the slightly awkward, slightly defensive re-phrasing 'poetry, or the novel, *in* English' has to be employed to make it clear that no assumptions about the existence of a uniform Englishness are being implied. Nor is the word 'British' any longer accepted as a neutral alternative. The Victorian 'North British', meaning 'Scottish' (once, but no longer, enshrined in the name of Edinburgh's leading hotel) is widely resented in present-day Scotland as both condescending and a means of glossing over the many differences in education, law, custom and culture which exist south and north of the Anglo-Scottish border. Moreover, Scottish literature is regarded by many, not as a regional variety of literature in English, but as literature in the 'mither tongue' of Scots; and in Scotland there is also literature in the undisputably distinct language of Gaelic. In Wales and Ireland important literatures in the Gaelic-based languages of Welsh and Irish likewise exist alongside the widespread use of English in the Anglo-Welsh and Anglo-Irish literary traditions.

More significantly still, English is the first language of many more speakers outside than within the British Isles. It is the language of the USA and Canada, of Australia and New Zealand, and, alongside the French-derived patois, of the Caribbean as well. It is one of the languages of South Africa, and it is still the most widely used second language in countries of the Commonwealth. Over and above that, thanks largely to the power and influence of the USA, it is the most commonly used language for international communication. All of which means that English, and the literature which is written in it, answers to the needs and experience of many more people than those who inhabit the British Isles. American English is, indeed, more important by far than English English, and it can at least be argued that in the twentieth century it is American poetry which is the dominant form of English poetry.

A chapter, therefore, devoted to 'Regional, National and Post-Colonial' poetry in English must reckon with the fact that English poetry in English is itself to some extent decentralised, on a par with the 'regional' and 'national' forms of poetry which its very title might seem to regard as tributaries of, or diversions from, the main stream. In reality the 'centre' cannot hold: 'we are all regional-ists now'. But this is gain rather than loss. The many competing forms of English, and the variety of contexts and cultures in which it is used, are a great enhancement of the richness and vitality of modern English poetry. Moreover, the movements towards regionality and nationality often counterpoise the diluting tendency, which can weaken English as a result of its increasingly international status. In place of a bland and generalised English based on the virtues suitable to a language of the universal market place these movements can offer sharply particularised, idiosyncratic styles which, though they may create difficulties (linguistic and otherwise) for outside readers, have unique energy and expressiveness.

HUGH MacDIARMID (1892–1978)

The risks and gains of such commitment are evident in the work of Christopher Murray Grieve, alias Hugh MacDiarmid. The most intensely and deliberately Scottish of all Scots poets, passionately committed to the cause of restoring Scotland to its pre-eighteenth-century status as an independent nation, MacDiarmid wrote in both Scots and English. His earliest work was written in a rather stilted form of English, but *ca.* 1925–34 he wrote in Scots – or, more strictly speaking, in Lallans, an artificial version of Scots which is augmented with words drawn from earlier Scots poetry and dictionaries of the Scottish tongue. The work of this period includes beautifully idiosyncratic lyrics such as 'The Watergaw', 'The Eemis Stane' and 'Empty Vessel'; his masterpiece, *A Drunk Man Looks at the Thistle*; and the Joycean *tour de force* 'Water Music' – a torrent of rare Scots words celebrating the three streams which meet at MacDiarmid's birthplace, Langholm, in Dumfriesshire. These are his purest, most quintessentially Scottish poems, and in the opinion of several critics, including the Highland poet Iain Crichton Smith, they remain his finest work.[2]

However, *A Drunk Man Looks at the Thistle* is the most ambitious, and also the most distinctively modernist poem of this group. As well as sharing the same linguistic originality as the lyrics, it is also a vehicle for MacDiarmid's encyclopaedic learning and his strangely volatile, cantankerous and contradictory personality. The drunk man's fuddled, moonlit night in a ditch becomes the occasion for a bewildering series of philosophical, political and sexual fantasies which he pursues with magnificently inconsistent abandon laced with sardonic banter and wit. Moderation is flagrantly eschewed. In uncompromising fashion the drunk man proclaims, 'I'll ha'e nae hauf-way hoose, but aye be whaur / Extremes meet.'[3]

His exaggerated postures are those of a romantic nationalist who sees himself as saviour of his dead-and-alive people:

> A Scottish poet maun assume
> The burden o' his people's doom,
> And dee to brak' their livin' tomb.

But they also express the down-to-earth disillusionment of one who recognises the thistle with its colourful, purple flower and prickly, shaggy stem as an apt emblem for 'The language that but sparely flooers [flowers] / And maistly gangs to weed'. The poem is a dialectic in which the many-sidedness of MacDiarmid can hold a fascinating quarrel with itself. Its extravagance is redeemed because it is offset by a canny realism that enables the poet to deflate his own excesses with a touch of sobering bathos, as he does at the end of the poem, where to cap his image of himself as an heroic, but unheeded, sufferer for his country's good the drunk man exclaims 'O I ha'e silence left', only to acknowledge what he knows will be the response of his wife: ' "And weel ye micht", / Sae Jean'll say, "eftir sic a nicht!" '[4]

Unexpectedly in view of the long campaign he had conducted on behalf of Scots and against English, and Englishness of all kinds, MacDiarmid returned to writing poems in English during the latter part of his career. In doing so, however, he was not making a recantation of the principles that underlay his previous work so much as moving towards a more international position and seeking, by means of what he called a 'language of fact', to adjust his poetry to the realities of a world of scientific materialism. This also accorded with his increasing emphasis on the politics of communism, to which he committed himself in characteristically unorthodox fashion.[5]

These later English poems are often long and tediously prosaic, forming a marked contrast with the concentratedly vivid lyrics of the militantly Scottish MacDiarmid. But there is at least one deeply impressive poem among them – the strange, meditative lines on a stony Shetland landscape (where MacDiarmid lived in the 1930s) entitled 'On a Raised Beach'. This poem, especially at its opening and close, has passages of such barbarously abstract language that Seamus Heaney is prompted to comment that 'In attempting a poetry of ideas MacDiarmid can write like a lunatic lexicographer.'[6] But elsewhere it has a plain, grave thoughtfulness reminiscent of

Wordsworth. Indeed, despite the modernist element in his previous work, MacDiarmid here seems to be renouncing his modernist sympathies when he alludes negatively to *The Waste Land* in the lines:

> This is no heap of broken images.
> Let men find the faith that builds mountains
> Before they seek the faith that moves them.

In Eliot's lines (*The Waste Land*, I, 20–4) the 'heap of broken images, where the sun beats' and 'the dry stone' that gives 'no sound of water' are symbolic of sterility and a decay of faith which undermines the civilisation built upon it. But for the MacDiarmid of 'On a Raised Beach' stone is the underlying, not undermining, permanence which guarantees a fundamentally reassuring vision of natural strength and vitality.

'On a Raised Beach' also reveals a preoccupation with depths of meaning beneath surface manifestations which is reminiscent of D. H. Lawrence's concern in his novel *The Rainbow*, with the 'pure single element of carbon' rather than its various particular forms such as 'diamond', 'coal' or 'soot'.[7] Stone becomes the embodiment of a similarly hidden creative source which permeates and unifies all natural phenomena, and the contemplation of it gives the poem (somewhat strangely, for a dialectical materialist such as MacDiarmid) an almost religious serenity:

> We must be humble. We are so easily baffled by appearance
> And do not realise that these stones are one with the stars.
> It makes no difference to them whether they are high or low,
> Mountain peak or ocean floor, palace, or pigsty.
> There are plenty of ruined buildings in the world but no
>   ruined stones.

If this seems inconsistent with the vivid particularisations that MacDiarmid achieves, in both image and language, in his earlier Scots poems, it can perhaps be put down to that cultivation of contradiction which he makes a virtue rather than a fault. But generality and particularity are not necessarily contradictory. The latter, as the Imagists in part perceived, is a necessary guarantee of the former, without which the general easily becomes vapid and meaningless. In this respect, 'On a Raised Beach' (which also, incidentally, tries to be particularised, if not very successfully, in its specifying, scientific jargon) can be regarded as an attempt to spell out the meaning of the universal which regionalists claim to be implicit in the local. It has a firm sense of place, and if MacDiarmid chooses to emphasise the underlying permanencies rather than the surface manifestations of stone, that does not preclude the kind of relationship between surface and deep structure which is implicit in the concept of regionalism.

Nationalism may also share these implications, and in his earlier Scots poems where the language foregrounds their Scottishness MacDiarmid may be said to be both regionalist and nationalist. But nationalism also has a political dimension which raises the sort of issues already discussed in Chapter 4 à propos Yeats's 'Easter 1916'. In the political area MacDiarmid is rather less successful. His specifically communist poems are ruthlessly international, and the political element in the nationalist poems is somewhat chimerical. If Yeats is the great nationalist poet of Ireland and MacDiarmid the pre-eminent poet of Scottish nationalism, there remains a significant difference in quality between their respective versions of nationalism and the poetry it produces.

SOME OTHER SCOTTISH POETS: G. S. FRASER (1915–80), ROBERT GARIOCH (1909–87), EDWIN MORGAN (b. 1920) AND TOM LEONARD (b. 1944)

It is perhaps a judgement of this kind on MacDiarmid's nationalism which leads the Scottish-born, but less militantly Scots poet, G. S. Fraser to write in a poem specifically addressed 'To Hugh MacDiarmid':

> What a race has is always crude and common,
>   And not the human or the personal;
> I would take sword up only for the human,
>   Not to revive the broken ghosts of Gael.

Fortunately, modern Scots poetry, including that which takes its cue from MacDiarmid, is not primarily occupied with attempts to revive either T. S. Eliot's 'broken Coriolanus' or 'the broken ghosts of Gael'. Although it frequently heeds MacDiarmid's imperative to look for its models to Dunbar and Henryson, not Burns and Scott (more for what the tourist industry had made of the latter than for what they were, in themselves), the focus is on contemporary Scotland, and especially its major cities where three-quarters of the population lives. Thus Fraser's poetry of exile, if sadly elegiac in tone as he looks back home from wartime service in Egypt and Eritrea, focuses on the streets and dance halls of Aberdeen; and Robert Garioch, following in both form and language the poetry of the eighteenth-century poets of Scotland, focuses on the post-war Edinburgh he knows, satirising its newly internationalised Festival in 'Embro to the Ploy', and, even when paying homage 'To Robert Fergusson', placing him in the context of present-day Edinburgh with its 'Greek pepperpat' statue of Burns and 'Sanct Andrew's Hous an' aa an' aa.

Glasgow, Scotland's largest and most working-class city, features prominently in the work of many poets, especially Edwin Morgan and Tom Leonard. Morgan is a highly eclectic poet, international as much as local, and one of the most original contributors to the 1960s genre of 'concrete poetry'. However, he has lived and worked all his life in Glasgow, which saturates his more traditional (but not conventional) verse. *Glasgow Sonnets* (1972), in particular, combines the pentameter and a strict sonnet rhyme-scheme (ABBA\ABBA CDCDCD) with colloquially run-on lines, evoking a city of slums and flyovers, shipbuilding and left-wing protest, which is rawly contemporary. Morgan is linguistically original, too; but it is Leonard who takes the 'phonetic urban dialect' of Glasgow and makes of it a regional poetic as disconcerting and difficult as MacDiarmid's nationalist Lallans. It is language primarily to be heard – and hearing it spoken by a native Glaswegian in many ways simplifies it; but the effect on the page is important, too. The speech is rendered phonetically, but without using the international phonetic symbols. As a result it *is*, with effort, accessible to the non-specialist reader, the effort itself being part of a defamiliarising process which compels fresh attention both to Glaswegian speech, and to Glaswegian life – not least its pawky humour, which is a fusion of its ways of feeling and speaking.

EDWIN MUIR (1887–1959)

Whether such language, thickly regional or densely nationalistic, can be used for other than powerfully poetic or fictional effects is something that the Scots themselves debate. Edwin Muir, whose childhood was spent in Orkney, but who also spent years of acute distress in Glasgow, came to the conclusion that standard English was the only viable medium for all a civilisation's interests, scientific and administrative as well as social and literary. Scots, it seemed to him, could not be the language of the whole man. It produced a divided consciousness:

> ... reduced to its simplest terms, this linguistic division means that Scotsmen feel in one language and think in another; that their emotions turn to the Scottish tongue, with all its associations of local sentiment, and their minds to a standard English which for them is almost bare of associations other than those of the classroom. If Henryson and Dunbar had written prose they would have written in the same language as they used for poetry, for their minds were still whole; but Burns never thought of doing so, nor did Scott, nor did Stevenson, nor has any Scottish writer since. In an organic literature poetry is always influencing prose, and prose poetry; and their interaction energizes them both. Scottish poetry exists in a vacuum; it neither acts on the rest of literature nor reacts to it; and consequently it has shrunk to the level of anonymous folk-song.[8]

This was written in 1936, before the twentieth-century 'Scottish Renaissance' had got fully under way (but after the best of MacDiarmid's Scots poetry had been published), and a later Muir might well have been less uncompromising. Modern poets writing in Scots, whether Lallans or demotic versions, have since gained confidence by each others' examples; and the political dimension has increased its importance. Thus Raymond Vettese writes:

> I hae a vision o Scotland set free
> and freedom and language tae me is ane.

But in the same context he expresses doubt: the matter has worried him for a long time, and he concedes even while writing in Scots that with regard to 'th' uprisin o Scots, och, I micht be wrang'.[9]

What is certain is that to write in Scots is not the only guarantee of authenticity, even for poets born and bred in Scotland and keen on Scottish political independence, as Muir's own example indicates. Though some of his early poems are in Scots, and owe much to the Scottish ballad tradition, his mature work is in standard English, including patriotic poems like 'Robert the Bruce' and 'Scotland 1941'. It is, however, perhaps significant that the latter finds the enemy that blights Scottish culture within it rather than south of the border. It takes the form of Calvinism and materialistic industrialisation:

> We watch our cities burning in their pit,
> To salve our souls grinding dull lucre out.

The Edenic world of Orkney is opposed to the fallen world of modern Glasgow, a condition of relatedness ('We were a tribe, a family, a people') to one in which the 'mummied housegods' are a Burns and a Scott, not as they truly were in themselves and their work, but as they have become in the tawdry symbolism of a culturally bankrupt Scotland – 'sham bards of a sham nation'.

There is, of course, a certain contradictoriness in Muir's position. He looks back to a wholeness which Scotland once enjoyed in the past, but sees the language of Scots, not as the means by which that wholeness might be restored, but as a limiting medium incapable of expressing the full range of a genuinely modern culture. The inspiration of his finest poems is to do with a sense of loss rather than hope for an integrated future. Thus the theme of 'The Journey Back' is an imaginary journey up the stream of 'kindred' in search of a lost, fruitful community centred on the warmth and surety of family life such as Muir's idealising imagination finds in his Orkney origins. But, as in T. S. Eliot's *The Waste Land*, the most memorable verse is that which evokes the contemporary condition of sterility and isolation, with imagery drawn from the soulless tenement blocks of the Scottish city:

> And now I'm locked inside
> The savage keep, the grim rectangular tower
> From which the fanatic neighbour-hater scowls;
> There all is emptiness and dirt and envy,
> Dry rubbish of a life in anguish guarded
> By mad and watchful eyes.

In at least two poems, however – 'The Labyrinth' and 'The Horses' – Muir seems to come to a more optimistic conclusion. 'The Labyrinth' is again based on a contrast between symbols of harmony and disintegration. The first paragraph's long opening sentence, chafed with parentheses and syntactical contortions, is a verbal equivalent of 'the maze', with its 'roads / That run through the noisy world, deceiving streets / That meet and part and meet', which is the divisive condition of modern life. By contrast, the second paragraph offers a vision of the gods who, from their position 'High in the sky above the untroubled sea', view the relatedness of all things, and speak a language – an 'eternal dialogue' – of 'peace' which contains the limited, human language within it as simply 'a chord deep in that dialogue'. In the third paragraph, the 'I' of the poem is returned to the maze, but now, thanks to the Platonic vision of the second paragraph, he can see it as mere illusion compared with 'the real world' of the gods, which once having touched he will know always. The poem plunges yet again into the horror of the maze, but now there is redemption from imprisonment:

> The maze, the wild-wood waste of falsehood, roads
> That run and run and never reach an end,
> Embowered in error – I'd be prisoned there
> But that my soul has birdwings to fly free.
> Oh these deceits are strong almost as life.
> Last night I dreamt I was in the labyrinth,
> And woke far on. I did not know the place.

However, despite this affirmation of the primacy of the Platonic 'real world', the power of 'these deceits' undoubtedly remains strong; and throughout the poem it is the poetry associated with them which bites deeper. Escape from the labyrinth seems more wish than fulfilment.

'The Horses' is more compelling in its presentation of a new reality supervening on the old. Instead of a somewhat hazy vision of the gods, it offers an almost Lawrentian symbol of horses which come 'drumming' out of the unknown and are awe-inspiring: 'We saw the heads / Like a wild wave charging and were afraid.' Also, instead of the labyrinth this poem offers as an image of the contemporary world a nightmare scenario of twentieth-century technology in post-nuclear collapse, made vivid by the haunting picture of a warship, 'heading north, / Dead bodies piled on the deck', and radios which no longer respond to the twiddling of nobs. In part, what makes the horses so effective is the collective sense of renunciation which precedes their coming. This is a poem of 'we', not 'I', and a 'we' set against a 'they' whose voice is the now dumb radios speaking the imperatives of a world which 'we' can no longer accept, nor wish to see renewed:

> But now if they should speak,
> If on a sudden they should speak again,
> If on the stroke of noon a voice should speak,
> We would not listen, we would not let it bring
> That old bad world that swallowed its children quick
> At one great gulp.

And the sense of community implied in this, with a defeated, yet potentially renewable, humane, communal will, is also what makes acceptable the conversion of the horses, when they come, from romantically mythical creatures, 'fabulous steeds set on an ancient shield / Or illustrations in a book of knights' that 'we' dare not go near, to domesticated beasts that freely pull ploughs and carry loads. These are powerful psychic as well as physical energies regenerated and re-oriented to creative, communal purposes.

The setting of 'The Horses' is easily enough recognised once again as Muir's Orkney, and the poem is in line with the Edenic theme which underlies so much of his writing. To that extent it is one more example of his neo-Wordsworthian vision drawn from recollections of early childhood. But it is moulded into a form which makes it more than usually compelling in its modernity, and which compels a deeper look into the interconnections between technology, community and primitive energies. It vindicates, too, the relevance for himself at least, and perhaps for a successor like George Mackay Brown (b. 1921), of his stance on English versus Scots. If Muir in general denies himself the advantages that can be derived from the sounds and speech-habits peculiar to Scots, in the best of his poems, and 'The Horses' in particular, he writes a language which reaches easily and naturally from the communal to the universal, and in so doing achieves a satisfying wholeness.

IAIN CRICHTON SMITH (b. 1928)

The language problem for the Highland poet Iain Crichton Smith is that he writes in English, but his native tongue is Gaelic. On his own view of himself he is not altogether at ease in either. He echoes the case made against Scots by Muir when he says that 'linguistically Gaelic may not have the resources to deal exactly and naturally with certain subjects, for example, technological ones'; but he feels doubts about being able to attain his 'full potential when writing in English'.[10] He has, in fact, achieved distinction in both languages, though it could be said of both him and Muir that there is a slightly unnatural purity about their English which sets them aside from the easy-going, even raffish, colloquialism found in a Pound or a Larkin.

The sense of a split, in style and in theme, continually makes itself felt in Crichton Smith's poetry. This is the burden of one of his finest sequences, 'Deer on the High Hills – A Meditation'. In section XIII, for example, he plays fancifully with language:

> Are rivers stories, and are plains their prose?
> Are fountains poetry? And are rainbows the
> wistful smiles upon a dying face?

But when, at the climax of the section, he poses similar questions about the central subject of his meditation, the deer, language seems to 'freeze' in the air:

> And you, the deer, who walk upon the peaks,
> are you a world away, a language distant?
> Such symbols freeze upon my desolate lips!

In the following section figurative language is totally rejected; things are only themselves, and 'The deer step out in isolated air'. The consequence for the poet, however, is a feeling of separation between his human world or 'colours' (which puns on the Elizabethan use of this word for rhetoric) and the serene and exalted, but essentially non-metaphorical, world of the remote deer. He feels a potentially lethal absence of connection, from which he prays to be delivered:

> This distance deadly! God or goddess throw me
> a rope to landscape, let that hill, so bare,
> blossom with grapes, the wine of Italy.
>
> The deer step out in isolated air.
> Forgive the distance, let the transient journey
> on delicate ice not tragical appear

for stars are starry and the rain is rainy,
the stone is stony, and the sun is sunny,
the deer step out in isolated air.

The deer are also a less bleak manifestation of the harsh Calvinist religion into which Crichton Smith, in common with many Scots men and women, was born. On its positive side this represented a purity of the will and the strength of a scrupulous conscience; but often, in Crichton Smith's experience, it seemed a 'scant religion' dragged 'at our heels, as iron chains' ('A Life', section 3). Yet his attitude is ambivalent, and, once again, symptomatic of the divided self which reveals itself so frequently in his work. 'The Law and the Grace' is an attempt to escape its intellectual and emotional tyranny; but in 'Old Woman' (one among many examples of the old woman figure which recurs again and again in Crichton Smith's poetry), although her 'set mouth' which 'forgives no-one, not even God's justice / perpetually drowning law with grace' powerfully symbolises the relentlessness of Calvinist belief in predestination and evil, the woman's endurance of her hard lot becomes itself a kind of saving grace. Crichton Smith's treatment of his native isle of Lewis is similarly ambivalent: its sparse scenery chimes in with its grim religion, but it also becomes a mental region of his poetry which stimulates more than it blights. As he expresses it in one of the prose poems of 'Eight Songs for a New Ceilidh', 'it was the fine bareness of Lewis that made the work of my mind like a loom full of the music of the miracles and greatness of our time'.

WELSH POETRY: DYLAN THOMAS (1914–53)

Though psychologically anchored in Lewis, Crichton Smith is in no way parochial. In this respect he belongs firmly to the Scottish tradition, which is as much international as it is regional or national. Welsh poets may make a similar claim. There the problem of the linguistic 'double man' is not perhaps so acute as it is for the Gaelic / English poet, since Welsh is a more widely spoken language and has had a stronger influence on the main stream of English poetry, in, for example, the work of Gerard Manley Hopkins and Wilfred Owen. Welsh poetry as such does not come within the scope of this survey; but there also exists an important body of Anglo-Welsh poetry which, unlike that of Scotland, is not split between Scots and 'English English'. If, for example, the stature of Dylan Thomas may be compared with that of Scotland's MacDiarmid, consideration of his poetry, distinctively Welsh though it is, does not become involved with a linguistic conflict such as that between Lallans and English. Dylan Thomas is a Welsh poet writing in English. The same may be said of Vernon Watkins (1906–67) or David Jones or Alun Lewis or R. S. Thomas. The case of R. S. Thomas is complicated by his dedication to Welsh nationalism and hostility to the cultural influence of England and the English language – themes which figure prominently in his poetry. However, he was not born into a Welsh-speaking family, nor did he learn Welsh till after training to be a priest; and though he has written prose in Welsh, his poetry is exclusively in English.

The Welshness of Dylan Thomas seems little affected by considerations of Welsh nationalism. It is a matter of style rather than language – a poetry steeped in alliteration, assonance, internal rhyme and half-rhyme, and technically very elaborate. Specific reference to Wales and Welsh places come almost exclusively in the later poems such as 'The Hunchback in the Park', 'Poem in October' and 'Fern Hill', from *Deaths and Entrances* (1946), and 'Over Sir John's Hill' and 'Poem on His Birthday', from *Collected Poems* (1952). An exception is 'After the Funeral', from *The Map of Love* (1939). All these are seen by Barbara Hardy, herself a native of Thomas's Swansea, as regional rather than national, praising 'a composite beloved landscape and seascape'.[11] They are allied with *Under Milk Wood* (first broadcast on 25 January 1954), which, though in dramatic form, is in effect a prose poem on Laugharne, South Wales, where Thomas lived in the latter part of his life.

These later poems are also more accessible than the earlier poems, in which Thomas's idiosyncratic style is seen at its most extreme. The basic method is, however, the same in both, and consists in the elaborately rhetorical packaging of a series of images bred from one another in a seemingly hectic, ungrammatical, yet dialectical, process. In Thomas's own words:

> I make one image – though 'make' is not the word; I let, perhaps, an image be 'made' emotionally in me and then apply to it what intellectual and critical forces I possess – let it breed another, let that image contradict the first, make, of the third image bred out of the other two together, a fourth contradictory image, and then let them all, within my imposed formal limits, conflict. Each image

holds within it the seed of its own destruction, and my dialectical method, as I understand it, is a constant building up and breaking down of the images that come out of the central seed.[12]

Add to this a penchant, especially marked in the earlier poems, for cutting across what are normally discrete verbal categories, and the result is such heady assertiveness as:

> A weather in the quarter of the veins
> Turns night to day; blood in their suns
> Lights up the living worm.
>
> ('A Process in the Weather of the
> Heart', from *18 Poems*, 1934)

Images drawn from the human body mingle with those from land, sea and the weather to create a deliberate confusion. Although this at first seems merely anarchic, it is ultimately recognised as a verbal equivalent of that inseparable intertwining of creation and destruction, the human and the natural, which is the poem's overall theme. Difficult as the poem seems, it is in fact a surprisingly new linguistic variation on the time-honoured theme of the interaction of life and death.

The justification for such poetry can be found in the Russian Formalists' concept of 'defamiliarisation', defined by Viktor Shklovsky as the technique of making forms difficult, increasing 'the difficulty and length of perception, because the process of perception is an aesthetic end in itself and must be prolonged'.[13] A characteristic device in Thomas's poetry is the use of travestied clichés: 'dead as nails' for 'hard as nails', 'hammer through daisies' for 'pushing up daisies', 'once below a time' for 'once upon a time', 'all the sun long' for 'all day long'. Stale linguistic units come re-charged with energy. Similarly, transferred epithets ('the whinnying green stable'), puns and word-play ('my prowed dove', 'the pitch was forking to the sun'), outrageous locutions ('And from the windy West came two-gunned Gabriel'), and mixed metaphors ('flesh was snipped to cross the lines / Of gallow crosses') throw words back into the melting pot from which they emerge with puzzlingly new interconnections demanding the kind of attention normally given only to a foreign language text. At worst such poetry is a gimmicky as a crossword puzzle; but at its best its difficulty for the reader becomes a stimulus to renewed perception and deeper aesthetic pleasure.

Overriding the rational demands of prose discourse Thomas creates a fresh poetic medium which answers immediately, in its own linguistic substance, to his sense of the fusion of man and nature; but with the corollary that it is in the text, and only the text, that the fusion is accomplished. His Welsh regional poetry, derived though it is from his own Swansea/Laugherne region, becomes essentially a linguistic reality. This is implicit in the early poem 'Especially When the October Wind'. In its beginning it points to an external, referential world as the poet walks on a Welsh beach with the October wind blowing through his hair. But already a transforming process can be seen at work as 'the October wind / With frosty fingers punishes my hair' and

> Caught by the crabbing sun I walk on fire
> And cast a shadow crab upon the land.

The crab-like pinching of the sun combines with the pun on 'catching a crab' and the verbal echo of the Miltonic Satan's 'walk on the burning marle' to produce the poet's 'shadow crab' – a crab-shaped shadow, perhaps, but more verbal than visual reality. Throughout the rest of the poem language itself becomes a recurrent metaphor, encompassing 'the syllabic blood', 'wordy shapes of women' and 'oaken voices', and reaching its climax in the final line: 'By the sea's side hear the dark-vowelled birds'.

Although the later poems are less self-conscious about their linguistic nature, and more willing to make concessions to their readers, the sense of region as verbal construct is at least as strong in them. 'Fern Hill' is the outstanding example. This is the poem in which the device of the transformed cliché is used most extensively, and to it is added the use of word-motifs which are repeated with variation like themes in a piece of music. 'Green' is one such motif. Beginning with the innocent 'happy as the grass was green' (stanza 1) and 'I was green and carefree' (first line of stanza 2), the word passes through the comparatively simple combination with 'golden' in 'green and golden I was huntsman and herdsman' (stanza 2) to the more startling locutions of 'fire green as grass' (stanza 3) and 'whinnying green stable' (stanza 4), to the repeated, but generalised, 'children green and golden' now following 'time' 'out of grace' (stanza 5), and finally (stanza 6) to the paradoxical conclusion:

> Oh as I was young and easy in the mercy of his means,
>   Time held me green and dying
> Though I sang in my chains like the sea.

The other key terms, 'grass', 'golden' and 'time' develop similar interconnections with each other as the poem progresses, and also with the farm animals, buildings and landscape which constitute the pastoral world of 'Fern Hill'. But those interconnections also become links between the child's world and the adult's, between innocence and experience, constituting a 'windfall' pastoral in which Time (from the very first line with its subtle tension between 'Now' and 'was') is simultaneously present and absent. Although on one level this is a verbal ambivalence preluding the loss of innocence baldly proclaimed in the sixth stanza: 'And wake to the farm forever fled from the childless land', the mutually qualifying nature of the verbal relationships in the poem is such that death and experience coexist with, rather than cancel out, life and inno-cence. Unlike the technically similar 'Over Sir John's Hill', it is not primarily elegiac (nor at all shot through, as the latter poem is, with the 'black cap' judgemental consciousness of Welsh Nonconformist religion). Hence the final 'green' paradox, and the distinction between the world created within the poem and the world outside. It is only within the verbal music which constitutes 'Fern Hill' that Time can be simultaneously merciful and tyrannical, giving the poet essentially something to sing about.

WELSH POETRY: R. S. THOMAS (b. 1913)

R. S. Thomas is very different. The paradisal landscape of childhood figures little in his image of Wales, while the political and cul-tural elements of Welsh nationalism, and, as might be expected of a clergyman, the religion of the Welsh church, are much more to the fore. Dylan Thomas's vocabulary is, of course, steeped in the Bible, and his visionary enthusiasm gives his poetry a kind of prophetic fervour, but both vocation and a much more serious engagement with difficult theological issues make the poetry of R. S. Thomas religious in a more precise sense. As a practising minister R. S. Thomas is committed to the Christian faith, and yet, as T. S. Eliot said of Tennyson, the strength of his belief is more evident in his doubt than in his faith. The picture of rural life and pastoral care presented in his 1952 radio play *The Minister* has more in common with the grim realism of Crabbe's *The Village* ('I paint the cot / As truth will paint it, and as bards will not') than with *Under Milk Wood*; and his spiritual agonies are more akin to those of Donne's 'Holy Sonnets' or Hopkins's 'terrible sonnets'. His own intellectual doubts as a man (despite his vocation) very much of the sceptical late twentieth century mingle with his acute awareness of the harsh conditions endured by his hill-farming parishioners to rob him of any possibility of blithe optimism. His theology is that of Kierkegaard, and his sermons those of a minister who feels (as in the poem 'Look', about two rain-soaked, disease-afflicted Welsh 'cronies') that

> We must dip belief
> Not in dew nor in the cool fountain
> Of beech buds, but in seas
> Of manure through which they squelch
> To the bleakness of their assignations.

The earlier work in particular is steeped in a Welshness that is determinedly truth-telling, but also militantly nationalist, with a streak of xenophobia reminiscent of MacDiarmid. This surfaces, not altogether to the benefit of the poetry as such, in sardonic poems like 'A Welshman to Any Tourist' and 'A Welsh Testament', and in those embittered lines of 'Reservoirs' which refer scathingly to 'the English / Scavenging among the remains / Of our culture'. But Thomas's more admirably Welsh poems are those which centre on characters drawn from his close knowledge of his parishioners – men (usually men) like the Iago Prytherch of 'A Peasant', who is 'Just an ordinary man of the bald Welsh hills, / Who pens a few sheep in a gap of cloud', and Walter Llywarch, who describes himself as 'Well goitred, round in the bum, / Sure prey of the slow virus / Bred in quarries of grey rain'. The language – a mixture of dourness and dry humour, suddenly shot through with laconic metaphor – lets the marriage of person and place speak arrestingly for itself. Conventional assumptions are knocked aside, but without the political bias of the more nationalist poems. The harshness, for example, in the portrait of Prytherch, deliberate in its emphasis on 'a half-witted grin' and 'spittled mirth', and the clothes 'sour with years of sweat / And animal contact', though intended to 'shock the refined', makes the civilised persona of the cleric-poet its target as much as non-Welsh outsiders. The R. S. Thomas of these poems is a self-critical, rather than self-righteous, Welshman, and the Wales he portrays is a place of distinctive landscape, culture and people, but rooted in a universal humanity.

In the more recent poems this reaching out towards universality is still more marked. Nationalism widens out to a concern with ecology and traditional culture, and Thomas's own twin vocation as poet-priest leads him to grapple with the interlocked problems of language and religion in an increasingly secular and materialistic world. In 'Postscript', for example, a more abstract, but still laconic and tautly controlled verse is focused on the possible decline of poetry itself in a world that seems more and more isolated from the gross physical restraints (which are, however, ultimately benign imperatives for an equally physical poetry) emphasised in the earlier work. Progress darkens poetry; and to the question as to whether there was 'oil / For the machine?' comes the gloomy answer that it consisted of 'The vinegar in the poets' cup'. The underlying note is one of tragedy rather than stoic endurance. What oils the machinery of an increasingly technological civilisation is achieved at the expense of the humane tradition on which poetry depends. There remains a parodic ghost of the human in the language which speaks (in the second stanza) of marching and 'Mouths opened', but (moving into the final stanza)

> Among the forests
> Of metal the one human
> Sound was the lament of
> The poets for deciduous language.

The transference of 'deciduous' from its normal association with trees to language both startles the reader into sharper awareness and heightens the tacit alliance between poetry and the organic. In addition, the metaphor of 'vinegar in the poets' cup' links poetry to Holy Communion and Christ on the Cross, creating a verbal chain from Thomas's religion of sin and redemption, to poetry, to nature's processes of decay and renewal. Poetry itself thus becomes a lament for the organic continuity which the mechanistic character of the modern world is destroying, and simultaneously a dirge murmured over its own threatened annihilation.

It is here that Thomas joins hands with Ted Hughes. A poem like 'Rough', for example, becomes his sardonic version of the ironic creation myths found in *Crow*. When Thomas's God looked at the predatory animal world he had created he found it 'perfect, a self-regulating machine / of blood and faeces'. Perfect, except that 'One thing was missing', which provides the cue for a bitterly sardonic version of the creation of man:

> he skimmed off a faint reflection of himself
> in sea-water; breathed into it,
> and set the red corpuscles whirling. It was not long
> before the creature had the eagle, the wolf and
> the jack-rabbit squealing for mercy.

However, the poem ends with a Christian note not found in Hughes: although God laughed with thunderous 'uncontrollable laughter', yet – curious as the redemptive phrase is – he had 'in his side like an incurred stitch, Jesus'. As with the 'deciduous' of 'Postscript', there is arresting oddity in the language. 'Stitch' suggests the pain in one's side that comes of excessive running, and its qualification by 'incurred' implies that it is an inevitable penalty like the 'incurring' of a debt. But also implicit is the stitching that repairs a tattered garment, and, as in the proverb 'A stitch in time saves nine', the remedy for potentially greater disaster. This ambiguity is resolved in the final word, 'Jesus', placed in apposition to 'stitch', for theologically Jesus is both the debtor and redeemer who takes on the sin incurred by man, along with the human form, and buys it back with his crucifixion.

If this in itself is quite un-Hughesian, the 'rough', trickster-like humour and physical nastiness, which is the dominant impression created by the poem, suggests no easy transition from despair to hope. Thomas remains deeply disturbed in his sense of the harsh mystery of life, and the texture of his poetry, that which makes him a poet rather than a thinker or preacher, is the gauge of his involvement with problems which admit no easy solution. Above all, he feels the compulsion to struggle with his inner doubts and yearnings – to test everything in that psychological arena on the beat of his pulse rather than (despite his vocation) taking his inherited faith on trust. As he asks himself at the end of 'Pilgrimages' (and it is typical that such a poem of self-probing should end with what is still a question):

> Was the pilgrimage
> I made to come to my own
> self, to learn that in times
> like these and for one like me
> God will never be plain and
> out there, but dark rather and
> inexplicable, as though he were in here?

IRISH POETRY

The pressure of commanding traditions countered by dark, disturbing uncertainties gives R. S. Thomas's poetry a Christian character, and a Welsh character, that paradoxically transcends its Welsh and Christian origins. Similar pressures, and a similarly paradoxical outcome, though they result in poetry of an unmistakably different quality, drive and shape the work of modern Irish poets – from Patrick Kavanagh (1904–67), John Hewitt (1907–87) and John Montague (b. 1929) to Thomas Kinsella (b. 1928), Michael Longley (b. 1939), Seamus Heaney (b. 1939), Derek Mahon (b. 1941), Tom Paulin (b. 1949) and Paul Muldoon (b. 1951).

There are many crosscurrents in the work of these Irish poets: impressions, on the one hand, of a peasant, provincial background with strong emphasis on family life and puritannical moral standards which are adhered to with steadfast confidence, and, on the other, exotic Celtic tales laced with a lyric sensibility; images of a wet, boggy lowland versus a bare, rugged, magnificent highland; religio/political tensions between Catholic/Nationalist and Protestant/Loyalist; and a sense of historical injustices which embrace sixteenth- and seventeenth-century wars of oppression, and nineteenth-century famine and emigrations to distant places such as America and Australia. In such a context there are strong pressures towards simplification and partisanship; but, as Edna Longley warns, these need to be resisted.[14] What is in reality a very tangled and involved social, cultural and political situation is matched in the poetry by a constant intercutting of 'borderlands' which produces an exciting and dazzling, but also bewildering and disconcerting, spectrum. At one end of this spectrum is the Crabbe-like renaissance of Irish rural realism in the work of Patrick Kavanagh, and at the other the often difficult sophistication of Thomas Kinsella and Paul Muldoon, whose poetry incorporates bizarre extremes. In 'Tao and Unfitness at Inistiogue on the River Nore', for example, Kinsella evokes a landscape haunted by outrages committed in the Anglo-Irish struggles:

> Black and Tan ghosts up there, at home
> on the Woodstock heights: an iron mouth
> scanning the Kilkenny road: the house
> gutted by the townspeople and burned to ruins ...

And in the punningly modernist, but also gangsterish pulp-fiction style of 'The More a Man Has the More a Man Wants' Muldoon makes the hero of Irish folk-lore a denizen of the contemporary Northern Ireland of motorway, Coca-Cola and skinheads. Between, and in touch with both extremes, is Seamus Heaney, acutely conscious of his multiple inheritance, and fast becoming the successor of Yeats as the representative modern Irish poet.

SEAMUS HEANEY

Heaney, an Irish poet writing in English, like R. S. Thomas, the Welsh poet also writing in English, is acutely conscious of the culture and national and religious issues which set him aside from the predominantly English culture of the British Isles. Ireland also has its own Irish-language tradition, as Wales has its equally potent Welsh-language tradition; and one strain in Irish poetry written in the English language, as Bernard O'Donoghue (himself an Irish poet) demonstrates in his important study of Seamus Heaney,[15] is the adapting of English to the phonological characteristics of Irish. But there is also an Anglo-Irish literature in its own right, exemplified above all in the poetry of Yeats, but stamped with a stronger stamp of the local and regional in the work of Kavanagh and Montague, which has a very special significance for Heaney.

Heaney has praised what he calls the 'artesian quality' of Kavanagh's work – its penetration to the 'hard buried life' of the Irish peasant-farmer, which lay 'beyond the feel of middle-class novelists and romantic nationalist poets'[16] – exemplified in the opening lines of 'The Great Hunger':

> Clay is the word and clay is the flesh
> Where the potato-gatherers like mechanized scarecrows move
> Along the side-fall of the hill – Maguire and his men.

Dominated by his mother and inhibited by a puritannical Catholicism, Maguire lives a life close to the soil, stirred by occasional outbursts of frustrated lust and longing. Other poems, such as 'A Christmas Childhood' and 'The Long Garden', are more Wordsworthian in their imaginative presentation of country life; but what is most characteristic of Kavanagh is the ability to give an epic quality to dourly local realism (consciously so in the poem 'Epic', which ends the evocation of a parochial dispute with an allusion to Homer: 'I made the Iliad from such / A local row'[17]) and to make lyrical poetry out of such seemingly un-poetic material as potatoes and 'barrels of blue potato-spray' ('Spraying the Potatoes') or a load of dung ('Art McCooey').

Heaney's first volume, *Death of a Naturalist* (1966), is very much in the Kavanagh vein – though improving on the master. Its opening poem, 'Digging', is a kind of manifesto, Kavanagh in style ('The cold smell of potato mould, the squelch and slap / Of soggy peat') and in theme (father and grandfather are local, turf-cutting heroes); and the title poem which follows is about the initiation of the filial poet into the sights, and still more the sounds, of the boggy land which is to become his parish and his world. The flax-dam 'festered' and

> Daily it sweltered in the punishing sun.
> Bubbles gargled delicately, bluebottles
> Wove a strong gauze of sound around the smell.

That 'strong gauze' is the swathing sound-music wrapped around nature again and again in Heaney's early verse, and the local heroes, and heroines (for mother and aunts are no less important than father and uncle) who live their lives in harmony with its symphonic echoes are the fitting (yet unsentimentalised and un-romanticised) inhabitants of this realistic Irish pastoral.

Yet 'Death of a Naturalist' ends threateningly. The frogspawn grow to bullfrogs, whose onomatopoeic 'slap and pop' become 'obscene threats', premonitory of a violence that terrifies the poet's boyhood self. The bullfrogs are imaged as 'Poised like mud grenades', and the boy feels that they were 'gathered there for vengeance'.

In 1966 the sectarian hatred and violence that was to plague Northern Ireland (where Heaney was born and then still lived) was yet to come, but is none the less foreshadowed in this military image and its ominous context of 'blunt heads', 'slime kings' and 'vengeance'. In *Wintering Out* (1972), and especially *North* (1975), 'the troubles' and the troubling of the poet by them are consciously focused in the poetry. Yet the immediacy of the violence and suffering, though disturbing the verbal texture of the poetry, is, in the best of these poems, distanced, as Owen distanced war in the best of his First World War poems. The feeling for the bog-like substance of Ireland so strong in the *Death of a Naturalist* poems carries over into Heaney's 'digging' into Irish history and legend, coupled with the deep reverberations aroused by his interest in the Iron Age bodies unearthed at this time from the Danish peat by Professor P. V. Glob. Through this ominously refracting lens Heaney saw the events of contemporary Northern Ireland in a tragic perspective which made them objects both of horror and pity, judgement and guilt. His own comments on his poem 'The Tollund Man', in his essay 'Feeling into Words', reveal how Glob's 'unforgettable photographs' of strangled or throat-cut victims of primitive fertility rituals 'blended in my mind with photographs of atrocities, past and present, in the long rites of Irish political and religious struggles'.[18] And in 'Punishment' the 'drowned / body in the bog' of an ancient adulteress blends with the shaven head and tarred body of a 1970s Irish girl 'guilty' of consorting with the English 'enemy'. The taut, short-lined verse suggests the disciplined effort being made to achieve distance and objectivity, while it is also shaken, in complex fashion, with feelings of condemnation and compassion, empathy with the victim and guilt for a kind of complicity (if only imaginary) in her death. Although he calls her 'poor scapegoat' and admits to almost loving her, he confesses – with a wry twist to the biblical phrase – that he 'would have cast ... / the stones of silence'; and he movingly exposes the ambivalence of his sympathies in the stark lines:

> I who have stood dumb
> when your betraying sisters,
> cauled in tar,
> wept by the railings,

who would connive
in civilized outrage
yet understand the exact
and tribal, intimate revenge.

In his more recent work, though Heaney continues to be a distinctively regional, as well as a nationally Irish and politically aware, contemporary Irish poet, there is a noticeable de-emphasising of this particular brand of commitment. The verse is less heavily charged with the accents of his 'guttural muse', and there is a trend towards a limpidity and impersonality which seem the work of language using the poet, rather than the poet using language. As O'Donoghue suggests, Heaney's art of poetry, in theory and in practice, comes closer to that in which 'Poetry is the direct, unwilled expression of the language itself, a "category of consciousness" which is nearly unconscious.'[19] There is perhaps some influence here from the kind of literary theory associated with Jacques Derrida and Umberto Eco which downgrades the importance of the author compared with that of the written text, though it is a position to which Heaney's humility and Keatsian respect for language itself leads him quite naturally. His instinctive preference for grammatically passive forms, for example, is a part of this general movement towards an unforced, non-aggressive listening for, rather than egotistical assertion of, meaning. So, likewise, is his increasing preference for metaphor which itself draws on the phenomena of language – foregrounded, for example, in 'Alphabets', the opening poem of *The Haw Lantern* (1987). Although this is on one level an autobiographical poem tracing Heaney's development, like so many modern scholarship boys, from the private, historical world of home via education to the timeless, international world of a cultured consciousness, the first-person 'I' is replaced by the detached, third-person 'he'. Maturity is marked by a change from a child's pictorial awareness of letters and numbers ('the forked stick that they call a Y ... A swan's neck and swan's back / make the 2 ...') to a more advanced sense of languages as such, and finally to a confident mastery of literature ('The globe has spun. He stands in a wooden O. / He alludes to Shakespeare'). However, the conclusion comes full circle; the adult glances back to his childhood when he had watched a plasterer writing the family name in the gable of the family house, but now from a distant perspective like that of an astronaut gazing back on 'The risen, aqueous, singular, lucent O' of the earth.

And in the final lines, which offer an alternative simile, two slight instances of the first person (one singular, one plural) are allowed to modify the impersonal style:

> Or like my own wide pre-reflective stare
> All agog at the plasterer on his ladder
> Skimming our gable and writing our name there
> With his trowel point, letter by strange letter.

This *is*, after all, a personal poem, but what is personal is the function of something larger, embedded in language itself (or languages, for Latin and Celtic as well as English are embraced in the poem): it is an overarching process which reaches its appropriate climax in '... letter by strange letter'. So for Heaney the poetic journey is away from digging in his Irish roots to a global consciousness which nevertheless keeps contact with its origins; and, this especially, which finds in the linguistic medium of poetry a kind of impersonal guiding power to which submission of the personal and parochial are required, but by which they are also sanctioned.

10

Regional, National and Post-Colonial (II)

AUSTRALIAN POETRY

In the opening chapter of *A History of Australian Literature* Ken Goodwin suggests that there are 'two major rival determinants' in the literature of Australia: the British written cultural tradition, which settlers brought with them to Australia, and the totally different environment of the new land, including the unwritten culture of its Aboriginal inhabitants. In addition, there is the fact that these settlers were, to begin with, mostly convicts – outcasts from the mother country, and often from backgrounds, Irish and Scottish, for example, which made them unsympathetic to established British values. Consequently, although there are many modern Australians who still 'emphasize commonality with and derivativeness from Britain', they 'exist alongside vociferous nationalists ... and those who reject both colonialism and nationalism in favour either of internationalism ... or of personal withdrawal and self-identification'.

These tensions between an 'Australian' and a 'British' (or, more widely, 'European') Australianism are inevitably reflected in the poetry. The self-consciously 'Australian' poet tends to be more democratic in both attitude and style than his English counterpart, and he is aware of a physical environment which is very different – of a sky which has different constellations, and of a land which is populated mainly on the coastal fringes, has a largely barren interior, and where the seasonal round is alien to that which is deeply embedded in the traditions of English poetry. April is not the Chaucerian spring-time of 'showres soote', nor summer (which belongs to January/February instead of July/August) Langland's season of the 'softe' sun, but of an altogether fiercer intensity. The theorists of the *Bulletin*, *Meanjin* and the Jindyworobak movement – including Adelaide poets such as Rex Ingamells (1913–55), Ian Mudie (1911–76) and Max Harris (b. 1921) – argued that these were essential characteristics of Australia and should be reflected in its poetry. Mudie speaks its manifesto in 'This Land':

> Give me a harsh land to wring music from,
> brown hills, and dust, with dead grass
> straw to my bricks.
>
> Give me words that are cutting-harsh
> as wattle-bird notes in dusty gums
> crying at noon.

On the opposite side poets such as A. D. Hope (b. 1907) and James McAuley (1917–76) stood for continuity with the English/European tradition; and Hope, in particular, directed his neo-Swiftian satire, 'Australia', against his native land, whose colours were 'drab green and desolate grey', and which he personified disparagingly, not as a young beauty, but as a fading, middle-aged woman:

> They call her a young country, but they lie:
> She is the last of lands, the emptiest,
> A woman beyond her change of life, a breast
> Still tender but within the womb is dry.

In the following lines Hope also castigates Australia as lacking 'songs, architecture, history' and the 'emotions and superstitions of younger lands'. This, of course, is satirical exaggeration, for there is already the history of exploration, transportation and settlement, the development of Australia's own institutions and political attitudes, and its involvement in the European wars of 1914–18 and 1939–45 – all of which are frequent reference points in its poetry. Moreover, there is a pre-history, unwritten, but being patiently assembled from the aural traditions which still survive, of Australia's indigenous population, the Aborigines, together with their 'songs' and 'emotions and superstitions' which amount to a peculiarly Australian religion of place. These generate in at least some white Australians a guilty sense of themselves not simply as victims of European colonialism, but as exploiters of the land's original black inhabitants; and this enters, too, into the poetry of the Jindyworobaks (a word composed of Aboriginal linguistic elements), and, more significantly, into the work of the two most important modern Australian poets, Judith Wright and Les Murray.

JUDITH WRIGHT (b. 1915)

In 'At Cooloolah' (from *The Two Fires*, 1955) Judith Wright is con-
scious of her own situation as 'a stranger, come of a conquering
people' needing to 'quiet a heart accused by its own fear'. Both
the bird life (a 'blue crane fishing in Cooloolah's twilight') and
the Aborigines ('Those dark-skinned people who once named
Cooloolah') are indigenous to Australia in a way that she is not, and
share a knowledge which challenges her own aggressive, European
inheritance:

> Those dark-skinned people who once named Cooloolah
> knew that no land is lost or won by wars,
> for earth is spirit: the invader's feet will tangle
> in nets there and his blood be thinned by fears.

Her poetry deals with the Australian landscape, its people, and the
interaction between the two. The sophisticated European is philo-
sophically minded (Wright is strongly influenced by Plato, for
example) and inherits a biblical and Christian culture; as a twentieth-
century writer she has the subjective awareness of one for whom
phenomena are essentially psychological projections. But her imag-
inative sympathy is with the Aborigine for whom 'earth is spirit',
and the complex interweaving of the two create a poetry of haunting
in which her mental world is subjected to a kind of conversion. Out
of this comes – to some extent against the grain of a mainly male-
dominated culture – a feminine poetry which finds in the landscape
repeated images of birth, death and rebirth, and in the drought and
fire which afflicts the Australian countryside Blakean symbols of
imaginative cleansing and creation.

Among her early poems the much-anthologised 'Bullocky' (from
The Moving Image, 1946) sets this haunting in a context that goes back
to English seventeenth-century Puritanism. The first four stanzas are
all in the past tense: the bullock team driver through his isolating
struggle with the weather and landscape of the Australian bush is said
to have entered 'a mad apocalyptic dream' in which he became 'old
Moses, and the slaves / his suffering and stubborn team'. Coloured
by his bible religion, at night his open-air became a temple where

> beneath
> the half-light pillars of the trees

he filled the steepled cone of night
with shouted prayers and prophecies.

The last two stanzas are in the present tense: the bullocky is dead,
the wagon-tracks grown over with grass, and the bush turned to
vineyards. But the cultivated land of the present is seen as continu-
ous with the wild religious energy that fed the religious enthusiast's
dreams, and the invocation which concludes the poem is a tribute
in similarly biblical terms to that continuity:

O vine, grow close upon that bone
and hold it with your rooted hand.
The prophet Moses feeds the grape,
and fruitful is the Promised Land.

Another early poem, 'Remittance Man', concerns a very different
kind of settler – the wastrel, 'spendthrift, disinherited and graceless',
who is packed off to remote Australia because he is an embarrass-
ment to his English relatives. This is narrated entirely in the past
tense, and ends with the English brother who inherits the remittance
man's estate feeling 'a vague pity' for his presumably wasted life.
But the body of the poem traces another sequence in which the
remittance man 'accepted his pittance with an easy air' and 'let
everything but life slip through his fingers'. The idleness which to
his relatives would have seemed dereliction of duty becomes a
significantly psychological as well as physical change of landscapes:

Blue blowing smoke of things from the noon fire,
red blowing dust of roads where the teams go slow,
sparse swinging shadow of trees no longer foreign
silted the memory of a greener climate.

That 'silted' is tellingly ambiguous. From the perspective of the
English back home it suggests an insidious clogging up of energy;
but in the context created for it by the rest of the poem it suggests
a more fertilising process, which (as the reference to 'the teams'
suggests) has a link with the religious fervour of 'Bullocky'. There
is ambiguity, too, in the lines that speak of the riots which led to
his exile, and his attitude to that exile. What to others would be
disgraceful escapades, 'the crazy tales', 'the blind-drunk sprees',
were things that 'suited his book'. His unsettled behaviour gave

way to a different settler style, at odds with the conformity required of him at home, but leading to a death in the Australian outback coloured with suggestions of something other than dissipation and waste:

> That harsh biblical country of the scapegoat
> closed its magnificence finally round his bones
> polished by diligent ants.

There is a hint here of influence from T. S. Eliot's *Ash Wednesday* ('And God said / Shall these bones live? ... And the bones sang chirping / With the burden of the grasshopper'); but it is a hint which acts in a different direction from Eliot's. *Ash Wednesday* is a poem in which Eliot seeks to accommodate himself to the rituals of Anglo-Catholicism, en route to the accommodation with English history and culture which is consummated in *Four Quartets*. 'Remittance Man' is the outcast from that history and culture en route to an alien 'magnificence' which, despite appearances to the contrary, links him to the visionary connotations of 'Bullocky' ('biblical' like Eliot's, but with the bible read in a very different, Protestant and Blakean, sense). Taken with 'Bullocky' its subject can be seen as the transformation (not rehabilitation) of the settlers who left England, some willingly, many unwillingly, from rejects and derivatives of Englishness to denizens of a landscape of 'trees no longer foreign', yet bringing a cultural baggage with them which they adapt to the needs of the totally new environment.

In subsequent work Judith Wright tries to preserve this continuity without being merely conservative. For example, the myth of spiritual renewal which is integrated in European literature and religion with the seasonal cycle of the northern hemisphere is adapted to the physical conditions of the southern hemisphere, but with an emphasis on forms of ugliness and drought which in the north would more likely be symbolic of permanent barrenness and sterility. In such poems as 'Phaius Orchid' and 'The Cicadas' (both from *The Gateway*, 1953) rebirth takes place from 'the brackish sand' and from a life 'crouched alone and dumb / in patient ugliness'. The sun which stirs the process, and towards which the renewed life reaches, is also, like the actual sun of the harsh Australian summer, an 'intolerable gold'. The break with tradition, while the continuity is still preserved, is again felt in a poem like 'Unknown Water', where a dialogue takes place in a time of drought between the poet and and old man who is 'part of my childhood'. The dialogue is, however, internalised; more properly speaking, it is between that part of the poet's self which knows, and sympathises with, what the old man knows, and that part of her self which cannot be understood by the old man. What they share is an understanding of the deep pathos of animal suffering in the conditions of drought – beautifully symbolised in the image of a mare whose milk is giving out, but will not leave her dying foal to look for water elsewhere. But what separates the poet is her search for the unknown:

>   I am not you,
> but you are part of me. Go easy with me, old man;
> I am helping to clear a track to unknown water.

She wishes to maintain continuity with that traditional part of herself which the old man represents, but she looks beyond that to a psychological climate that is without precedent.

The old man of 'Unknown Water' is also representative of a patriarchal society with which Wright is not violently at odds ('Bullocky', after all, shows great imaginative sympathy with it), but which again in her later work she feels she must go beyond. What she reaches towards has something in common with the poetry of Elizabeth Bishop – a feminine softening of the harsher contours of Australia's masculine world, combined with a feeling for landscape which emphasises patience rather than harshness and brashness. In 'Summer' (from *Phantom Dwelling*, 1985) what is apparently the landscape of a worked-out mining area is seen as reverting to the bush, and in so doing recovering its lost soul, engaging in 'a struggle to heal itself after many wounds'. What was once a scene of torn-up rocks that 'drank dark blood' and 'heard cries and the running of feet' now shelters wombats. Lichens, algae and spiders take over, and the symbol of this new/old world is the jenny-lizard digging the hard ground to lay her eggs, while keeping a wary eye for predator birds. Despite being part of 'a burned-out summer', these 'pearl-eggs' hint at a different, and better, quality of life which the poet seeks to identify with – though there remains an unavoidably separating consciousness, for she is compelled to live (in a phrase reminiscent of Robert Graves) 'through a web of language'.

In this poetry there is a quieter, more laconic note than before. The feminine insight embodied in the jenny-lizard is restrained and unassertive, 'wearing a wide grey smile'. More directly expressive of the human level, 'Smalltown Dance' finds this same quality in the domestic activity of two women performing the act of folding a sheet 'to a neat / compression fitting in the smallest space / a sheet can pack in on a cupboard shelf'. In one sense this is an elegiac poem about the limiting effects on women of their commitment to household routines: sheets tugging in the wind hint, as does a child's play among them, at 'unobstructed waiting green'; but 'women know the scale of possibility, / the limit of opportunity', and the poem ends with a resignation to that limitation:

> First pull those wallowing white dreamers down,
> spread arms: then close them. Fold
> those beckoning roads to some impossible world,
> put them away and close the cupboard door.

That last line has the cadence of a sigh. Yet there is also a countervailing freshness, like the freshness of clean sheets, within the poem, and a sense of orderliness ('you have to keep things orderly') which belongs not only to restraint, but also to the pervading image of the sheet-folding as 'an ancient dance'. The dance is performed by two women; the child of the second stanza is the poet herself as a girl; this 'smalltown dance' is entirely a female affair. And restrictive as it is, it does not (unlike the poetry of Anne Sexton or Sylvia Plath) seem to imply a repressive, man-made image to which women have to submit. Rather it suggests pleasure in the 'dance' combined with clearsighted realism (the key lines which open and close stanza 3 are: 'But women know the scale of possibility' and 'The household budget will not stretch to more') – a feminine vision balanced between the possible and the impossible.

LES MURRAY (b. 1938)

Les Murray is in many respects even more quintessentially Australian than Judith Wright; but he is also, paradoxically, more cosmopolitan and more fashionably post-modernist. He ranges over a wide variety of subject-matter, including meditations on the peculiar silence of the bush in 'Noonday Axeman', which talks about the attractions of the city (Sydney, in particular), yet exalts the countryside as the place where 'this silence' has been made 'human and familiar';

images, in 'The Sydney Highrise Variations', of the very different life characteristic of predominantly maritime, city-dwelling, late twentieth-century Australia; bizarre verbal play and self-consciously contemporary material in poems like 'Machine Portraits with Pendant Spaceman' and 'The Mouthless Image of God in the Hunter-Colo Mountains'; and, in 'Walking to the Cattle Place', 'The Buladelah-Taree Holiday Song Cycle' and 'The Idyll Wheel: Cycle of a Year at Bunyah, New South Wales', celebrations of the Australian rural idyll which are indebted to the European pastoral tradition, but re-make it in an entirely modern Australian fashion. The texture of the poetry is equally varied. For example, in 'The Dream of Wearing Shorts Forever', the slangy-colloquial manner of Australian speech is used for a humorous send-up of sartorial conventions. The 'cardinal points of costume' are divided into 'Robes, Tat, Rig and Scunge', with the humorous definition of 'scunge' providing the nearest visual equivalent to the unbuttoned attitudes and style of modern Australia:

> they are Scunge,
> ancient Bengal bloomers or moth-eaten hot pants
> worn with a former shirt,
> feet, beach sand, hair
> and a paucity of signals.

In 'The Buladelah-Taree Holiday Song Cycle' Murray uses a long-lined, 'cadential verse' based on the translation of an Aboriginal song-cycle to suggest a strange kind of continuity between modern picnickers in the Australian bush and a primitive people whose oral poetry blends repetition and catalogues of place names.[1] 'Walking to the Cattle Place' is a modernist poem of almost Joycean proportions, including allusion to such heterogeneous material as Greek myth, Hindu religion and down-to-earth cattle-farmer's lore, a section devoted entirely to cows' names set out like the pages of a concrete poem, and passages which sound like an Australian adaptation of the loose-limbed rhetoric of Walt Whitman.

To further complicate matters, Murray sees himself as an English-language poet whose verbal ancestry is Scots and Gaelic rather than English. 'Inverse Ballad' makes a bush-ballad narrative from the capture of one of Murray's ancestors by bushrangers (and it turns on the failure of his captors to recognise the Scots accent in his voice); the 'June' section of 'The Idyll Wheel' has an autobiographical paragraph which breaks into the language of Scots; and the fourth poem of 'Four Gaelic Poems' ('Elegy for Angus Macdonald of Cnoclinn') is a tribute to a lecturer at Sydney University who taught Gaelic. In the latter Murray writes that his forebears were High-landers, and then Borderers:

> – 'savages' once, now we are 'settlers'
> in the mouth of the deathless enemy –
> but I am seized of this future now.
> I am not European. Nor is my English.

If this is reminiscent of MacDiarmid, in practice Murray's English is in fact more English than MacDiarmid's Lallans; and, despite his rejection of the 'European', in much of his poetry he makes full use of the European inheritance. Indeed, to be Gaelic is only to lay claim to a variety of the European which can be distinguished from the Anglo-Saxon. What Murray seems to be after is a form of English which responds to the peculiarly Australian racial and linguistic mix, and which in the process relieves Australian writers and readers of the obligation to make the dreaded 'cultural cringe' to a London-based culture. The mission of his poetry is to give Australia a verbal reality making it capable of cultural independ-ence. In practice, however, this is achieved, not by severing all links with the English/European past, but establishing some commerce between here and there, now and then, in which the Australian present and the Australian setting constitute an equal rather than a subordinate arm. The (slightly willed) emphasis on a Scottish rather than English ancestry is mainly a help towards this end. And it has to take its place alongside the competing images of rural and metropolitan Australia, which also demand a balance between nineteenth- and twentieth-century Australia, inland bush and populous sea-board, the cycle of the year at Bunyah and the Sydney highrisers. Murray's own origins tilt him towards the glorification of the bushranger and the macho farmer (though fas-cinatingly counterbalanced by the cow-worshipping humour of 'Walking to the Cattle Place'), but the post-colonial city life and the post-modern culture, acutely aware of what is going on in Europe and America, of contemporary Australia is the educational process through which he has also come to his distinctively twentieth-century, Australian-English poetry. Together they form 'The C19–20' of Section 4 of 'The Sydney Highrise Variations', where the duality, appropriately enough to Australia's foreshortened history, is expressed in terms of the nineteenth and twentieth centuries – and even the exclusion of Dante and Cromwell is a reminder of an extra-Australian dimension which seems to be denied:

> The Nineteenth Century. The Twentieth Century.
> There were never any others. No centuries before these.
> Dante was not hailed in his time as an Authentic
> Fourteenth Century Voice. Nor did Cromwell thunder, *After all,*
> *in the bowels of Christ, this* is *the Seventeenth Century!*

> The two are one aircraft in the end, the C19–20,
> capacious with cargo. Some of it can save your life,
> some can prevent it.

NEW ZEALAND POETRY: ALLEN CURNOW (b. 1911)

New Zealand is similarly a country which for its European settlers has no centuries before the nineteenth and twentieth, though the consciousness of the pre-existence of Maori culture is, if anything, stronger than the Australian consciousness of Aboriginal culture. And in one poem at least, 'Landfall in Unknown Seas', Allen Curnow, the dominant figure among New Zealand poets, looks back to Tasman's discovery of the country in 1642. This, however, was written in 1942 (a '300th Anniversary' poem) in the midst of World War II, when New Zealand was anxiously aware of the possibility of invasion by the Japanese. In coolly detached verse it presents the discovery as experienced by Tasman and the business-like Dutch, but when it reaches the actual landfall the poem suddenly veers to the Maoris' point of view – and though the indigenous islanders' violent reaction is self-explanatory and sufficient to justify the poem's shift, the wartime reality of the time of the poem's composition broods ominously over it:

> Always to islanders danger
> Is what comes over the sea;
> Over the yellow sands and the clear
> Shallows, the dull filament
> Flickers, the blood of strangers:
> Death discovered the Sailor
> O in a flash, in a flat calm,

A clash of boats in the bay
And the day marred with murder.

Maori place-names and Maori words blend seemingly naturally into the language of Curnow and such poets as James Baxter and Hone Tuwhare (himself a Maori); but the pressure of a 'C19–20' inheritance, even for a Maori, creates problems of identity. Thus, writing an elegy for Ron Mason, a white European friend, Tuwhare finds himself in a 'confusing swirl' as a New Zealand/Maori/English poet. Mason has joined his 'literary ancestors'. But Tuwhare still has problems finding his own, lost as they are

in the confusing swirl, now thick now thin,
Victoriana-Missionary fog hiding legalized land-rape
and gentlemen thugs.

The guilty conscience felt by the Australian poet as the inheritor of settlers who were also dispossessors is equally felt by the New Zealand poet, but so also is the desire to make peace with the indigenous inhabitants and their landscape in the name of a new, national identity. Curnow, in particular, seeks for a fusion of the qualities associated with his Anglo-Scottish ancestry and his South Island environment that will be acceptable as a distinctively New Zealand whole, while not denying the tensions which are inescapably part of the New Zealand history. In 'A Raised Voice' the figure of his father – an Anglican clergyman, but also fourth-generation New Zealander – is a focus for these complex feelings. The poem begins autobiographically as a child's view of his father high above him in the pulpit delivering his Sunday sermon to the accompaniment of an 'alp-high / summer gale gusting to fifty miles'. The father, seemingly inflated to giant size,

stands twelve feet 'clothed in fine linen'
visibly white from the waist up, all

inferior parts masked

and the paternal gravity is heightened by the language of the church ritual. But there is a comic perspective too in the father's seeming, as he mounts the pulpit steps, to be 'cupped like an egg', and a hint of the sublime descending to the commonplace, if not the ridiculous, in that the voice which intones 'in the / name of the father and of the son / and of the holy ghost amen' is also 'a voice / that says Jess to my mother'. The dignity of the voice is again enhanced by the 'pale-coloured wood' of which the pulpit is made, but that, too, is undermined by questions about its nature. Is it, the poet wonders, made of *kahikatea*, easily wood-wormed, but 'ideal for butter-boxes', or tougher *kauri*? Both the woods' qualities and their Maori names suggest an alien influence, leading to a more sharply satirical gibe about 'the rape of the northern / bush' which almost breaks the child-reminiscence mode: and this is followed by another descent to commonplace detail (recalling the way Gordon Brown, the local grocer, adjusts an oil lamp) more appropriate to the childhood level, but provoking the adult poet to question the father/child 'certainty'. Then, as the sermon ends, everyone stands up, and there is a last disconcerting reference to the mother and her perfume, identified as '*vera violetta*', but thrown into uncertainty again by the final, contradictory 'That can't be it.'

For the most part this poem works by hints and implications rather than explicit statement, but the images of patriarchal grandeur and religious certainty are subtly undercut by a series of strangely heterogeneous influences – the unconsciously comic vision of the child, the oblique presence of the mother, the 'summer gale' from the Southern Alps, and the double 'rape' of nature and Maori rights. It is not difficult therefore to see it as an anti-imperialist poem. But so to label it is also to misrepresent it and distort it. The effect of the poem as such is more tentative, and its balance between admiration and scepticism much more delicate. In a similar way the poem 'An Evening Light', which again deals with child and father and includes Maori references to 'the Ngai-tahu / *kainga* and excavated *paa*', could be seen as a profound questioning of white male European rights in New Zealand. Such an interpretation does, in fact, gain support from Curnow's own note on the meanings of the Maori words, and his comment that 'The Ngai-tahu tribe ... occupied, and still claim, a great part of the South Island of New Zealand.'[2] But, again, the poem itself is much less emphatically single-minded. The cultural and political questionings are only elements in a more complex combination which is Curnow's exploration of the conflicting feelings involved in being a New Zealander – his development of a curiously unheroic nationalism.

Curnow, especially in his later work, is also something of an international modernist, in both technique and subject-matter. A spell in America during the post-war years brought him under the influence of the distinctly non-parochial regionalism of writers such as William Carlos Williams and Allen Tate; and his admiration for Wallace Stevens encouraged him to a combination of philosophical seriousness with verbal playfulness which, in some of his deliberately under-punctuated poems, makes him read more like a puzzle-setter than a poet. And the Pound–Eliot tradition of juxtaposing present and past, the familiar and the recondite, on a self-consciously European cultural scale is evident in the sequence of poems which make up *An Incorrigible Music* (1979). Here the 1478 Italian Pazzi conspiracy against members of the Medici family and the 1988 assassination of the Italian Prime Minister, Aldo Moro, by the Red Brigade are run loosely in parallel with a fishing expedition at Karekare 'on the steeply forested coast of the Tasman Sea, west of Auckland'.[3] Patrick Evans suggests that the connection is chiefly a matter of 'different sacrifices', of human beings and fish.[4] The fishing analogy is borne out by the use of refrains such as *'A big one! a big one!'* and *'And you're caught, mate, you're caught!'*, while the sacrificial principle is elaborated in 'Bring Your Own Victim', which extends the reference to Abraham and Isaac, Agamemnon and Iphigenia. Most striking, however, are the themes of guilt and the liberal conscience which recur through the sequence and climax in the letters Moro is permitted to write immediately before his death. To his wife he confesses:

> how incredible it is, this punishment
> for my mildness and moderation ... I have been wrong
> all my life, meaning well, of course ...

The plain, fragmented speech (contrasting with scenes elsewhere of histrionic violence), its fragmentation heightened by the near-prose run of the free verse, effectively singles out the crisis which this death represents for the well-meaning politician, and perhaps more deeply echoes the crisis of 'certainty' felt by the poet in his attempt to create a New Zealand nationalism which builds on its European ancestry, but is compromised by awareness of what it is supplanting in the natural world and in Maori culture. It is a low-key nationalism, tinged with tragedy.

CANADIAN POETRY: MARGARET ATWOOD (b. 1939)

Similar problems had already been experienced by writers in Canada. Thus Henry Kreisel, in an essay on 'The Prairie: A State of Mind' (1968), writes that 'The conquest of territory is by definition a violent process. In the Canadian west, as elsewhere on this continent, it involved the displacement of the indigenous population by often scandalous means, and then the taming of the land itself.'[5] As was to happen in Australia and New Zealand, this left behind a legacy of guilt, sometimes conscious and the subject of would-be expiation, but often subconscious and suppressed. Thus John Newlove, rejecting 'the romantic stories' told of the Indians, can acknowledge that they 'still ride the soil / in us, dry bones a part / of the dust in our eyes' ('The Pride', section 7), and A. M. Klein, in 'Indian Reservation: Caughnawaga', can write with sardonic sympathy of the tourist exhibition to which Indian culture has been reduced in twentieth-century Canada:

> Their past is sold in a shop: the beaded shoes,
> the sweetgrass basket, the curio Indian,
> burnt wood and gaudy cloth and inch-canoes –
> trophies and scalpings for a traveller's den.

But, more pervasively, Canadian poetry is haunted by a sense of violence committed, and desolation resulting, which registers in potent images and fantasies redolent of unexpurgated guilt. Dorothy Livesay (b. 1909), herself keenly aware that 'The many blinds we draw ... Can never quite obliterate ... The last, unsolved finality of night' ('Fire and Reason'), finds such an image in the description of a hunted bull moose's last stand against a pack of wolves in an epic poem by the earlier Canadian poet Archibald Lampman;[6] and in the 1970s Patrick Lane (b. 1939) records with cool, yet horrifying casualness the castration of a ram and the eating of its testicles, supposedly to make the ram's owner strong.

Such unblinking realism and coolly controlled disgust is the hallmark of Margaret Atwood, who perhaps more than any other has become the acknowledged representative of modern Canadian poetry. Her most frequently quoted lines are those which she uses as an epigraph to her volume *Power Politics* (1917), in which an unspecified 'you' is said to 'fit into me' like a fish hook into 'an open eye'. The curt minimalism is characteristic – as are the sadistic

coldness, and the posture of unidentified speaker towards uniden-
tified addressee. One critic notes the way that the personae in
Atwood's early poems are 'under siege and act as though they are
under siege'.[7] The 'I' is hostile to the 'you', in a defensive–aggres-
sive manner, but also suffering; and in the lines quoted, that double
quality is evident both in the sneer with which the cosiness in the
relationship is deflated and in the rawness of pain suggested by
'fish hook' in 'an open eye'.

What the lines also suggest is the pain associated with a sexual
relationship in which love is professed (presumably by a male
'you'), but rejected (by a female 'I') as a disguised form of cruelty.
As such they set the tone for the succeeding poems in *Power Politics*,
where again and again the reader seems to be eavesdropping on a
prolonged, acrimonious (and rather one-sided) lovers' quarrel, in
which 'you' is repeatedly accused of selfishness, self-ignorance,
heartlessness and male chauvinism generally, and in which 'love',
as in 'This is a mistake', is more like murder:

> Next time we commit
> love, we ought to
> choose in advance what to kill.

Here Atwood has clear connections with American women poets like
Sexton and Plath, and like theirs her work invites militantly feminist
interpretation; it is 'political' in that it seems to have an agenda
in which the 'power' wielded by a male establishment is scrutinised
and exposed as an all-encompassing culture inimical to the freedom
and development of women. For Atwood, however, feminism is one
facet of a situation of which the physical and political conditions of
post-colonial Canada are also facets. In *Survival*, a study of Canadian
literature, she singles out a 'sombre and negative' quality in her
predecessors' writings which betokens a literature 'still scarred and
misshapen by the state of mind that comes from a colonial relation-
ship'.[8] The man–woman relationship – at least as it is figured in the
early poetry – is another manifestation of this fundamentally imperial
relationship. Add the colonist's disorientation in face of a 'new world'
idealised as a land of opportunity, but experienced (by the persona of
Atwood's *The Journals of Susanna Moodie*) as 'vistas of desolation',
and one has the makings of a poetry that is simultaneously private
and public. In 'You did it' (from the *Power Politics* volume), for
example, the accused 'you' is equally valid as insensitive male lover

or modern Canadian citizen destroying the natural environment; and the exasperated question,

> When will you learn
> the flame and the wood/flesh
> it burns are whole and the same?

points, as the combined 'wood/flesh' implies, to a crisis which is simultaneously individual and representative.

The edgy, brittle quality of Atwood's poetry is the verbal enactment of her sense of a splintered consciousness. Though rarely obscure, her syntax is tortured and almost obsessively interrupted by parentheses, and she makes use of the sharp, ironic juxtapositions that earlier modernists learnt from seventeenth-century poetry as a means of at once arresting attention and forcing on the reader the imperative need to attempt some connection of the disconnected. Yet such poetry is not to be admired as an affirmation in itself. It constantly implies a want; and the personae who voice it are not in themselves admirable – they are defined by the language which they utter as embittered, unfulfilled, partial rather than whole, creatures. Which is neither to deny that there is much, if often peculiarly astringent, lyrical beauty in Atwood's poetry, nor to deny that her personae's critical feminism often hits its targets. Yet always brooding over the poetry is a sense of pain which comes from its necessary incompleteness.

This is stronger perhaps in the earlier than the later work, though it is still there. For example, in 'Aging Female Poet Reads Little Magazines' (*New Poems*, 1985–1986) the persona can look with a rather distanced sympathy at 'Amazingly young beautiful woman poets' who 'write poems like blood in a dead person / that comes out black, or at least deep / purple, like smashed grapes' – sympathy which derives from the recognition that 'Perhaps I was once one of them once.' Personal venom (and with it some of the vigour, too, of the earlier poems) seems to have been drained away. But the irony of the last two lines:

> If I were a man I would want to console them,
> and would not succeed.

reveals that this is not quite the case. Sympathy and a stab at the shortcomings of men virtually balance each other, revealing the persona of 'aging female poet' as itself a pose, or at most a posture which is being reached for rather than one that is achieved. Similarly with the conclusion to the last section of 'Galiano Coast: Four Entrances', where the subject is the Canadian landscape (though not so particularised that it could not be any wilderness landscape which also bears scars of the modern world's intrusion): the unconventional beauty of the scene is created in language which blends aspects of rock, wind, fish and human being into one synaesthetic whole:

> Sandrock the color of erosion,
> pushed by the wind
> into gills and clefts
> and heavy folds like snow melting
> or the crease of a doubled arm

The effect (it is claimed) is that 'A door is about to open / onto paradise', not in a magical other-world, but 'Onto a beach like this one, // exactly like it'. But the requirement of 'exactly like' to be properly met compels the speaker also to include other, discordant evidence, such as 'the red halfcrab eaten on the sand', the polluting 'rubber glove / gone white and blinded' and (particularly significant, linking as it does with the rest of the sequence addressed to an unspecified 'you' characterised by 'failed love and equivocation') 'the loss because you / can never truly be here'. The paradisal landscape is after all deeply flawed, and the attempt at a visionary acceptance which does not escape from, but seeks to come to terms with this, issues only in a verbal paradox:

> Can this be paradise, with so much loss
>
> in it?
>
>> Paradise
> is defined by loss.
>>> Is loss.
>
> Is.

The shrinking figure, heightened by its positioning on the page, offers a rhetorical conversion (with obvious Christian overtones) of loss into gain. It answers to the sadder and wiser poet's stance of maturity and compassion. But the sense of division between consciousness and landscape is, if anything, heightened, not eradicated.

'Is' stands for unqualified being – the collocation of fused landscape with the facts of nature red in tooth and claw, of man the polluter, and man the failed lover. 'Loss' is recognition, and judgement. It is only a verbal device which makes the one fade into the other. Yet the contriving of that device is itself the sign of a desire to escape from the impasse created by post-colonial resentment, whether sexual or political. As Atwood herself put it, in an interview with fellow-writer, Graeme Gibson:

> towards any object in the world you can take a positive or a negative attitude or, let us say, you can turn it into a positive or a negative symbol, and that goes for everything. You can see a tree as the embodiment of natural beauty or you can see it as something menacing that's going to get you, and that depends partly on your realistic position towards it; what you were doing with the tree, admiring it or cutting it down; but it's also a matter of your symbolic orientation towards everything. Now I'm not denying the reality, the existence of evil; some things are very hard to see in a positive light. Evil obviously exists in the world, right? But you have a choice of how you can see yourself in relation to that. And if you define yourself always as a harmless victim, there's nothing you can ever do about it. You can simply suffer.[9]

CARIBBEAN POETRY

The question of victimisation is of still more importance to the anglophone West Indian writer; and it is matched by a more complex interrelation between regionality, colonial dependence and independence, and mixed cultural influences. A recurrent frame of reference for the Caribbean is 'the middle passage', or the second side of the slave-trading triangle which links European ports to West Africa, where slave-traders took on their human cargo, West Africa to the West Indies and America, where the blacks were sold, and the New World back again to Europe. Many Caribbeans are the descendants of the unhappy victims of this triangular trade, their consciousness coloured by the knowledge of what their ancestors suffered as well as the subjected condition in which their parents lived, and their own sense of post-colonial domination lingering on in cultural and economic terms even in the days of political independence. Africa is a lost inheritance, but Europe an acquired one, which they enjoy in peculiarly ambiguous circumstances. The languages of the traders/conquerors – Spanish, Dutch, French, and especially English – have become their languages, while their culture has elements of both African and European, with the latter, however, enjoying a degree of social prestige and an internationally recognised dimension denied (until comparatively recently) the African. The language of the foreigner is likewise split into demotic varieties (patois, rap, etc.) which live a vigorous, informal life alongside the official tongues of administration and more formal culture.

The English-speaking Caribbean poet is thus a divided being, who shares something with those Scottish, Welsh and Irish poets who feel the tension between English and Gaelic cultures. But for the Caribbean that is not the end of the story. There is even greater complexity in that much of the modern population of the West Indies comes, not from Africa, but from India and South-East Asian countries which have their own pre-existing colonial relationships; and the English-speaking world which means still more in economic and social terms (and increasingly, too, in cultural terms) is that of the USA and Canada rather than Great Britain. The result is what Robert Hamner has called 'the global infusion of cultures within the Caribbean'[10] – a mélange of regional, national and post-colonial influences interacting more profusely than anywhere else in the modern literary scene.

In Abdur-Rahman Slade Hopkinson's (b. 1934) 'The Madwoman of Papine' a caricature is created of 'a pauper lunatic' who embodies both the wild, creative energy and the paradoxical burdensomeness of this complex Caribbean culture. In answering the question 'What of her history?' Hopkinson (his own history is that of a Guyanian, educated at the University of the West Indies, who became a Canadian citizen and converted to Islam) defines the climate in which the Caribbean poet operates:

> These are the latitudes of the ex-colonized,
> Of degradation still unmollified,
> imported managers, styles in art,
> second-hand subsistence of the spirit,
> the habit of waste,
> mayhem committed on the personality,
> and everywhere the wrecked or scuttled mind.

He ends the poem, however, with the madwoman's uttering of 'a kind of invocation', 'O / Rass Rass Rass / in the highest', which fuses degradation with religious rapture.[11] Though she is depicted as a victim, and her poverty and insanity are accepted realistically, the madwoman also has her potentiality for a kind of exaltation. In what looks like a pessimistic view of post-colonial deprivation and cultural derivativeness there is nevertheless a sense of human dignity and richness.

Other Caribbean poets such as Mervyn Morris (b. 1937), Edward Kamau Brathwaite (b. 1930) and Cyril and David Dabydeen (b. 1945 and 1955 respectively) similarly combine this truth to reality with a democratic indomitableness of spirit. Brathwaite's 'Horse Weebles' portrays another West Indian woman scraping together a poverty-stricken living with uncomplaining stoicism which, because of the dramatically caught lilting rhythms and native diction, neither sentimentalises, nor excuses, her plight. And, more baldly, David Dabydeen's 'Slave Song' – in his own words, 'an exploration of the erotic energies of the colonial experience'[12] – re-creates through the vigour of its West Indian dialect the irrepressible surge of defiance in the consciousness of the oppressed. In short, jerky lines the speaker cries: let the masters do what they can, 'Tie me haan up. / Juk out me eye',[13] put the slave's collar round his neck, set the dog on him – but for all that:

> yu caan stap me cack floodin in de goldmine
> Caan stap me cack splashin in de sunshine![14]

DEREK WALCOTT (b. 1930) AND *OMEROS*

Dabydeen's theme, however, is simple compared with that of Derek Walcott, the West Indian laureate who is both celebrator of his people and sophisticated Nobel Prize winner with a place among such international modernists as James Joyce and T. S. Eliot. Already it is becoming a commonplace of Walcott criticism to emphasise his divided loyalties, those strains in his work which 'reveal a poetic mind in conflict, a man who once described himself as "a kind of split writer" with one tradition inside him "going one way, and another going another" … he is "divided to the vein"'.[15] This, of course, is to highlight the disruptive effects of such a multicultural inheritance, justifiably so, as it is the aspect which is foremost in some of Walcott's most celebrated, and powerful, poems – intertextual poems like 'The Castaway' and 'Goats and Monkeys' which reveal the tortured self-consciousness of the educated West Indian reflected in the mirror of such English masterpieces as *Robinson Crusoe* and *Othello*. But there is a counterbalancing, and possibly even more important, integrative tendency in his work, which he speaks of in his Nobel lecture. A recurrent image in this lecture is that of a vase, broken, but lovingly restored; and Walcott characterises 'Antillean [or West Indian] art' as the 'restoration of our shattered histories, or shards of vocabulary, or archipelago becoming a synonym for pieces broken off from the original continent'.[16] Despite the bitterness generated by the suffering of the Caribbean at the hands of its European powers-that-were, a sense of possible wholeness (again with European antecedents) inspires a more creative effort. Another image in the lecture is that of an ideal Caribbean city which 'would be so racially various that the cultures of the world – the Asiatic, the Mediterranean, the European, the African – would be represented in it, its human variety more exciting than Joyce's Dublin', and which would be 'how Athens may have been before it became a cultural echo'.[17] Both images are revealing; and together they constitute an artistic complex that Walcott tries to realise in his longest and most important poetic enterprise to date, his epic poem *Omeros*.

Walcott has played down the epic nature of *Omeros*; and his critic and fellow West Indian poet John Figueroa (b. 1920) states categorically that '*Omeros* is not an epic, and it hardly touches on the gods.'[18] Yet *Omeros*, as its very title implies, is firmly in the European literary tradition. The central figures, Helen, Achille, Hector and Philoctete, all have Homeric names, and, even though this reflects an ironic tradition of the naming of West Indian slaves, there is some degree of conscious parallel between them and their Greek forebears. There are also broadly epic parallels in the narrative with the *Iliad* and the *Odyssey* (again, notwithstanding Walcott's denial of having read Homer all through). The correspondences are not exact: for example, in *Omeros* Walcott's Achille does not kill his Hector, and his Philoctete, though suffering from a suppurating wound caused by a rusty anchor, is not an archer whose bow is essential to any epic victory. Walcott's Helen, though in some sense a latter-day, democratised Helen of Troy, is also symbolic of the West Indies island of St Lucia (where the poet was born); and if she does launch a thousand ships, these are ships of the British and French navies, to which neither

Achille nor Hector belongs. But the tradition is not abandoned. Homer, and in places Vergil and Milton as well, remain a significant source and standard of comparison for Walcott.

Yet his characters are non-heroes, deliberately *un*heroic men and women of the Caribbean, their lives and landscapes realistic reflections of those 'peasantry' and 'fishermen' who are one with their environment in that (to quote Walcott's Nobel lecture again) 'they are trees who sweat' and, like the bark of those trees, 'filmed with salt'.[19] In part the relationship to traditional epic is deliberately antithetical, as signified, for example, by Walcott's variation on the Vergilian 'arma virumque cano',[20] which he places almost at the end of his poem instead of at the beginning:

> I sang of quiet Achille, Afolabe's son,
> who never ascended in an elevator,
> who had no passport, since the horizon needs none,
>
> never begged nor borrowed, was nobody's waiter
> ...
>   I sang the only slaughter
> that brought him delight, and that from necessity –
> of fish, sang the channels of his back in the sun.
>
> I sang our wide country, the Caribbean sea.

'Quiet' is a studiously non-epic epithet, but depending for its effect on the reader's recognition that this is so; and the jokey negativing of 'elevator', 'passport' and serving as a waiter, besides distinguishing Achille from the European and American tourists whose picture-postcard version of the Caribbean *Omeros* is designed to counteract, punningly rejects the elevated high style associated with traditional epic.

Antithesis nevertheless depends on its foregoing thesis, and in this sense *Omeros* also depends on its antecedents. Its very remodelling of epic is in a European tradition which, from Milton, to Wordsworth, Eliot and Joyce, continually adapts epic to contemporary circumstances and needs.[21] Eliot's adaptation of a kaleidoscope of heroic overtones to the post-war London of the 1920s – his singing ' "Jug Jug" to dirty ears' – preludes the dissonant music Walcott plays so skillfully; and Joyce's *Ulysses* places an advertising-agent hero in a sordid modern city freighted with comic-epic parallels which provide ample precedent for the complex elevation and de-elevation which goes on in the text of *Omeros*. More profoundly, through the relationship of his artistic *alter ego*, Stephen Dedalus, and Leopold Bloom, Joyce adapts Homer's theme of home-coming to a search for fatherhood, and a returning to roots in a deracinated, internationalised cultural situation, which pave the way for Walcott's own treatment of the father–son theme in *Omeros*, and his own inner conflict between local piety and international allegiances. Joyce is the modern artist he particularly admires, and, appropriately, he is given an appearance in *Omeros*, Chapter XXXIX, as a 'cane-twirling flaneur' whose Anna Livia is acknowledged as the 'Muse of our age's Omeros, undimmed Master / and true tenor of the place!' Like Joyce, Walcott is a nationalist who will accept no nationalistic parochialism. He celebrates the poor and illiterate, or semi-literate, while refusing to deny himself the vast range of literate, and literary, possibilities that his thorough absorption in European culture makes available to him.

Walcott's special contribution to the on-going process of epic modification derives from his cultural situation. In a 1993 interview for British television he speaks of his wish to make *Omeros* an expression of his love for St Lucia and its people, and of his original intention to write in the native patois. Some lines of dialogue remain in patois, but the narrative, the 'voice' of Omeros, and most of what his characters say, is in a lightly inflected version of received standard English. He acknowledges that writing in patois, despite the existence of a native West Indian tradition to support it, had for him become an artificial exercise. Though English is a 'foreign' language, it is the medium he is accustomed to – which he feels to be his as much as it is an Englishman's or an American's. The cultural situation is thus post-colonial, but with a post-colonialism which admits of no simple rejection of, or resentment towards, alien domination.

Which is not to deny the presence of an important vein of anti-colonial sentiment in *Omeros*. There is much to do with the evils of colonisation and slavery – in North America as well as the West Indies. Achille's variation on the standard epic episode of a visit to the underworld is a dream of walking under the Atlantic back to his ancestral home in West Africa, which includes witnessing the slave-trader's raid which snatched his forebears from their family and tribe to become the human property of European settlers in the Caribbean. However painful as such material is, it does not narrow the poet's sympathies to the victims of oppression only. Within the poem there are also representatives of the settlers, in the form of the English ex-soldier Major Plunkett, and his Irish wife Maud, who are neither pilloried nor caricatured. They have their case, too, and St Lucia is almost as much (or as little) theirs as it is Achille's or Hector's. Walcott can stand back and see that neither black nor white have centuries of rooted existence in the island, and yet they are deep 'lovers' of 'Helen'. The point of Achille's underworld is to confirm this. His origins, as well as the Plunketts', are overseas; and, although the ancestors of the Plunketts have been the exploiters of his ancestors – and a racial situation has resulted which still conditions present-day links between black and white – the Major and his wife still share some sort of community with the Helen who once served them as a maid, and her lovers. More importantly, the European culture of which they are products (if middle-brow ones, like Joyce's Leopold and Molly) is as much a cherished part of the narrator's mental world as his Creole inheritance. Through Walcott/Omeros the poem is established as multicultural rather than simply regional.

A further level of complexity is created by the relation of such a writer of English to the English fountainhead on which he draws. An important episode which explores this occurs in Chapter XXXVIII, where the narrator becomes a tourist visiting London. His sense that the cultural monuments surrounding him make implicit demands, to which all users of English must conform, leads to an ironic questioning of the capital's supremacy:

Who decrees a great epoch? The meridian of Greenwhich.
Who doles out our zeal, and in which way lies our
hope? In the cobbles of sinister Shoreditch,

in the widening rings of Big Ben's iron flower,
in the barges chained like our islands to the Thames.
Where is the alchemical corn and the light it yields?

Where, in which stones of the Abbey, are incised our names?
Who defines our delight? St Martin-in-the-Fields.
After every Michaelmas, its piercing soprano steeple

defines our delight. Within whose palatable vault
will echo the Saints' litany of our island people?
St Paul's salt shaker, when we are worth their salt.

The element of bathos here is in the tradition of eighteenth-century English satire, with the 'salt shaker' image of Wren's cathedral of St Paul's as its ludicrous climax. A touch of Marxist-style deconstruction reminds the reader that all this is the iron flowering of a trade relationship which (in a manner reminiscent of Conrad's parallel in *Heart of Darkness* between the River Congo and the Thames) forms a watery chain of exploitation between London and the economically dependent British colonies. Similarly, the 'delight' defined by St Martin-in-the-Fields may be the consequence of a cultural dominance which tutors the eye to see beauty in that particular set of Western-oriented proportions (themselves, of course, derived from Greece). And yet the delight is real; it is something to live up to until, notwithstanding the mockery, one becomes 'worth their salt'. The pun, and the deflating 'salt shaker' image for the imposing presence of St Paul's, may undermine London's credibility as cultural capital of the Empire, but the ambivalence of the language still allows for the validity of a complex city functioning as a true centre of excellence which transcends national and imperial values.

Omeros, then, is more than an anti-colonial protest, or a celebration of the unheroic virtues of the inhabitants of the West Indies – though it includes both. It is a poem in which Walcott, like Joyce in *Ulysses*, modifies the epic to find room for both satire and sympathetic comedy rather than an exclusively elevated tone. His central figure becomes neither an Homeric Achilles, nor a Miltonic Adam, nor even his own Greek-named descendants of slaves, but the anthropomorphised island of St Lucia set in a context which opens her to the widest possible range of influences. The omnipresent sea and the soaring sea-swift are symbols for that openness. The poem begins with a canoe being fashioned to sail on the sea, and it ends with the sea 'still going on'. The sea-swift is a Ulyssean bird travelling immense distances, whose wings perpetually make the sign of the cross; and the sea itself traces its waves on the shores of the island in a lacey foam which is the recurrent focus of the narrator's attention. It is through this openness to the sea that the island overcomes its own potential insularity, and, analogically, through his sea-like openness to influences that Walcott overcomes the limiting possibilities of his chosen material. If he shares the post-colonial critique of imperialism, and the post-modern scepticism of accepted values, he nevertheless remains the willing inheritor of a tradition which is flexible enough, and responsive enough to change, for him to write within it without traducing his own origins. The epic has a long history of change from country to country, and century to century; *Omeros* is a late twentieth-century addition to that history in which Walcott finds, rather than loses, his peculiarly West Indian self.

LANGSTON HUGHES, MAYA ANGELOU AND AFRO-AMERICAN POETRY

Pre-eminent as he is among Caribbeans, Walcott is also much influenced by North America. By profession he is a teacher at Boston University, and he is deeply interested, as *Omeros* reveals, in parallels between the experiences of Afro-Americans and Caribbeans. And it is through the literature of Afro-Americans that many modern readers first encounter the post-colonial experience – in, for example, the work of men such as Countee Cullen (1903–46), Langston Hughes (1902–67) and Amiri [LeRoi Jones] Baraka (b. 1934), and of women poets such as Gwendolyn Brooks (b. 1917), Sonia Sanchez (b. 1934) and Maya Angelou (b. 1928). Although these poets have affinities with the form and style of white poets such as Olson and the 'beat' poet Allen Ginsberg, with their characteristically loose-limbed, freely enjambed lines, the major source for their verse is the distinctively black idiom of jazz and 'Blues' music, and their themes are often those of protest against the social and cultural injustices suffered by the black people of America.

Langston Hughes is the master of the 'Blues' style. In poems like 'Minnie Sings Her Blues', 'Fortune Teller Blues', 'Listen Here Blues' and 'The Weary Blues' the 'Blues' form, with its easy, casual rhythms and simple repetition, achieves a lyricism which is deceptively plain, even naive. Beneath the surface, however, runs a current of insecurity and loss welling up from a centuries-old history of racial suffering and abuse. In other poems, 'Brass Spittoons', for example, this current takes a more specifically sociological form. Although the spittoon-cleaner is condescendingly called 'boy', he is an adult male whose dirty, ill-paid menial labour has to provide 'shoes for the baby', 'House rent' and 'Gin on Saturday, / Church on Sunday' – all of which are mixed up in his melancholy 'Blues' consciousness 'with dimes and / dollars and clean spittoons'. His biblical chapel religion (an important aspect of the black culture from which he comes) can give imaginative transformation to his filthy work:

> A bright bowl of brass is beautiful to the Lord
> Bright polished brass like the cymbals
> Of King David's dancers,
> Like the wine cups of Solomon.

But the reality of his situation is sardonically re-affirmed by the recurrent cry of 'Hey, boy!' and the final peremptory 'Come 'ere, boy!'

For the black poet (male or female), racial prejudice is an inescapable context. In 'The Ballad of Rudolph Reed' Gwendolyn Brooks uses the traditional form of the ballad to suggest the primitive force of this prejudice brought to bear on a black man who attempts to find a decent home for himself and his family 'in a street of bitter white'. The curious epithet 'oaken' ('Rudolph Reed was oaken. / His wife was oaken too.') echoes like a refrain to evoke the pathos of his simple aspirations, until he is provoked by stone-throwing to turn on his white tormentors. He then becomes a thing to be exterminated and referred to reductively as 'Nigger':

> By the time he had hurt his fourth white man
> Rudolph Reed was dead.
> His neighbors gathered and kicked his corpse.
> 'Nigger – ' his neighbors said.

On the other hand, in Baraka's free-verse poem 'It's Nation Time' – a poem from what the editor of *The LeRoi Jones/Amiri Baraka Reader* dubs his more extremist 'Black nationalist Period (1965–1974)' – the word 'niggers', repeated no less than sixteen times, becomes a political battle-cry deliberately adopted in defiance of its racially abusive associations to evoke an imagined future of regenerated and united black brothers:

> all niggers negroes must change up
> come together in unity unify
> for nation time
> it's nation time ...

'Black' is likewise used in defiance of its conventionally poetic associations with evil as a positive epithet for divinities drawn from Christianity, Hinduism, Mohammedanism and Egyptian and

Nigerian religions. Explosive onomatopoeia, 'Boom / Booom / BOOOM ⋯' (a parody perhaps of Vachel Lindsay's much-anthologised 'Congo'), and a form of punning stretching of words, 'It's nation time eye ime / it's nation ti eye ime', combine with this strange, multi-religious ecstasy to convert blackness – with implicit rejection of its history as the badge of oppression and suffering – into a transcendent, energising force and symbol of a pride in nationhood sanctifed by self-belief.

These two different images of black men and women form the antitheses on which much Afro-American poetry is hinged. One can see this particularly clearly in the poetry of Maya Angelou. In her own life she has moved from conditions of abject exploitation and abuse to public recognition and honour, culminating in her being commissioned to write and read her poem 'On the Pulse of Morning', at the inauguration of President Clinton's first term of office in 1993. Suffering and joy, both private and public, are present in equal measure in her work, mingled, however, with a sharply critical, and often humorous, intelligence. For example, in 'When I Think About Myself' the sixty-year-old speaker (recalling the 'boy' of Hughes's 'Brass Spittoons') comments wryly that 'The child I works for calls me girl / I say "Yes ma'am" for working's sake', but the refrain combats self-pity with laughter: 'I laugh until my stomach ache, / When I think about myself.' In 'The Calling of Names', a political satire on the insulting modes of address used for black people in America, a degree of astringency, more effective than indignant denunciation, is achieved by the ironic imitation of a prejudiced commentator's voice; and in the more overtly protest-poem 'Riot: 60s', the voices both of black rioters and white police-men are presented in taut, demotic lines that speak for themselves by sardonic juxtaposition.

Angelou is also a love poet and a feminist poet. Indeed, the black political writer and the women's writer cannot easily be separated. When she writes a poem of erotic appreciation like 'To a Man' ('My man is / Black Golden Amber / Changing'), beneath the sensuous, lyrical immediacy there is an undertone of assertiveness embracing both a rejection of women's passivity and an assertion of black as beautiful. Likewise, there is an implicit affirmation of black against white, reminiscent of Blake's revaluation of traditional values in *The Marriage of Heaven and Hell*, in the oppositions on which 'The Mothering Blackness' and 'Africa' are built, and these surface again in the more sociological contrasts between black inner city streets and white suburbs in 'Through the Inner City to the Suburbs'. In the longer, more dithyrambic, Whitman-like poem 'Our Grandmothers', the sufferings of the hunted female slave in the pre-emancipation past are seen as continuous with those of the present-day black woman, whether 'In the Welfare line, / reduced to the pity of handouts' or 'In the choir loft, / holding God in her throat'. Christianity teaches passive suffering, but Angelou's religion, connected though it is to the chapel-going experience of black people, involves the militant demand for a decent way of life here and now, not (as in 'Preacher, Don't Send Me') an after-life of

> some big ghetto
> in the sky
> where rats eat cats
> of the leopard type
> and Sunday brunch
> is grits and tripe.

And likewise in 'Artful Pose' she rejects the 'quiet path' of a smoothly-flowing, elegiac poetry, which is sung *sweetly*, in favour of a rough, stumbling, defiant verse which may be loaded with the unpleasant material of betrayal in love and 'hateful wrath', but is written – and the word suggests both haste and vitality – *quickly*.

Both kinds of music none the less constitute the music of Afro-American poetry. In Writing 'Artful Pose' (from her 1975 volume, *Oh Pray My Wings Are Gonna Fit Me Well*) Angelou may or may not have had in mind Hughes's 'The Weary Blues' (1925), in which the speaker (or, more appropriately, singer) says, 'I heard a Negro play' in Harlem, and the haunting music produced by the poem itself is a verbal counterpart to the rhythm and cadence of the blues:

> He did a lazy sway ...
> He did a lazy sway ...
> To the tune o' those Weary Blues.
> With his ebony hands on each ivory key
> He made that poor piano moan with melody.

The difference in date between the Angelou poem and the Hughes poem marks a difference in cultural and political status, with the civil rights protests of the 1960s marking a significant watershed in between. Yet Angelou is in the same line as Hughes; and the melancholy of the 'Blues' and the militancy of the post-60s black poetry are complementary to each other. Both disturb, and in disturbing shake, American poetry into new, authentic forms. But in addition, as a Hughes poem of 1949, 'Theme for English B', suggests, what disturbs the acceptedly 'American' can also be seen as an opportunity for creative interaction between two forms of the American, thus widening the American tradition itself. Given the task of going home and writing a page, '*And let that page come out of you – / Then, it will be true – '*, the speaker in 'Theme for English B' doubts if it is that simple. Nevertheless, he goes ahead, writing a poem which is both a record of his own tastes and experiences and an address to his instructor. The outcome is a paradoxical assertion of separateness and sameness, culminating in a, perhaps reluctant, recognition of common Americanness:

> You are white –
> yet a part of me, as I am a part of you.
> That's American.
> Sometimes perhaps you don't want to be a part of me.
> Nor do I often want to be a part of you.
> But we are, that's true!
> I guess you learn from me –
> although you're older – and white –
> and somewhat more free.

Black nationalism may not accept this. Its message may be that the stain of prejudice is too deep to be eradicated, and a return to exclusively African origins is imperative. But the work of Hughes and Angelou suggests the possibility of a fruitful adaptation, which may enrich not only the American tradition, but ultimately the capacities of twentieth-century poetry in English as a whole

REGIONAL, NATIONAL AND POST-COLONIAL: CONCLUSION

Poetry especially is an art in which learning is mutual, and interdependence a well-documented condition. The regional, national and post-colonial aspects of English poetry in the latter half of the twentieth century give added emphasis to this. Old-established literatures like those of Scotland, Wales and Ireland find opportunities in the decline of the London-based 'centre' to reassert themselves with greater vigour, while the emerging literatures of countries such as Australia, New Zealand and the Caribbean gain strength from the very process of finding a voice for themselves which is not merely derivative. Nor is the situation always as simple as this. Many 'colonials' are also at times involved in the ambiguous experience of being themselves dominant powers which have inhibited other, indigenous cultures, thus seeing themselves reflected in a peculiarly distorting mirror. Yet this, too, can be fruitful, not merely guilt-inducing, as the relationship between what is imported from England – or, increasingly, America, since America has now become the more potent shaper and mediator of English influences – and what they find in the countries of their adoption becomes itself a new source of creative energy.

However, to speak in terms of people, whose relationships may be seen either as exploitative or as mutually helpful, is to shift attention from what is still more important for poetry, namely the state and possibilities for development of the English language itself. When this becomes the focus, the complex proliferation dealt with in this and the preceding chapter can be seen as nothing but gain. If the internationalising of bureaucratic English as the world's new *lingua franca* is potentially debilitating for poetry, new phonic, lexical and rhythmical resources are opened up as it is moulded to the different needs of non-English English speakers and writers. Indeed, it may be argued that by undergoing such a process of de-*central*ising, English, and more particularly poetry in English, has received – and, it is to be hoped, will continue to receive – a very welcome injection of new life.

11

Experiment and Tradition: Concrete Poetry, John Ashbery and Philip Larkin

THE CLIMATE FOR EXPERIMENT

Consciousness of the arbitrary nature of language, its essential conventionality (in the sense not of conformity, but of operating in accordance with tacitly agreed codes which have no naturally inherent laws) has become a major feature of twentieth-century poetry. It is almost, one is tempted to say, *the* defining feature of the modern, were it not that *post*-modern poetry is still more marked by it than classical modernism of the Pound–Eliot–Williams upheaval. By freeing poetry from the demands of consecutive syntax and claiming as its own the modern cinematic technique of juxtaposing images for primarily emotional/dramatic effect, modernism opened the way to further experiments in the breaking down of accepted assumptions governing verbal expression. Once the standard of 'correct', transparent English, whether spoken or, still more significantly, printed, was breached, it became possible to question the conventions of presentation which educated writers and readers had come to take as inviolable rules, and which are still treated as such in the language of scientific, journalistic and critical discourse. It became possible for transgression, or non-observance, of the rules to function on a positively sophisticated, rather than vulgarly negative, level – though this, of course, also presupposes general familiarity and conformity with them, since the abnormal effects of dispensing with them, or operating them in unfamiliar ways, depends on the existence of a strong feeling for them as the linguistic norm. An experimental poetry thus came into being which turned on its own consciousness of itself as an arbitrary construct of signs and symbols, in tension with an established linguistic practice seeing itself as the right and proper way of doing things.

e. e. cummings (1894–1962)

One of the most self-consciously 'experimental' of twentieth-century poets is the American, e. e. cummings. The printing of his name without capitals is indicative of one of his innovations: the purposively irregular use of punctuation. Much modern poetry is very lightly punctuated, allowing a fluidity and open-endedness of construction which goes naturally with the rhythmical freedoms cultivated by poets like Williams and Olson. In contrast, cummings punctuates heavily, but in a disconcertingly original way. His mouse poem, 'here's a little mouse)and', has a closing bracket towards the end of its first line, but no opening bracket – as if to suggest that the beginning is not a beginning as such, but the interruption of some on-going process which the catching sight of a mouse itself interrupts. The frightened darting of the mouse, and the perceiver's nervous uncertainty as to whether he has seen it or not, are enacted in verbs such as 'jerks' and 'frisks', but still more tellingly in the odd punctuation which fractures the normal run of the syntax (and even words themselves) into unexpected units, uses capitals and commas only for its own peculiar emphases, and inserts question marks and parentheses for essentially dramatic effect:

> jerks Here &, here,
> gr(oo)ving the room's Silence)this like
> a littlest
> poem a
> (with wee ears and see?
>
> tail frisks)
>
>   (gonE)

The abnormal 'E' of '(gonE)', which cannnot be heard when the poem is spoken, any more than the enclosing brackets, is dramatic, but purely visual. It is part of a linguistic construct peculiar to the printed page. On the other hand, a poem like 'ygUDuh' is a sound poem – a dialect poem, based on a phonetic rendering of New York Bronx, comparable with Tom Leonard's bizarre transcriptions of

Glasgow-talk. Here the absence of pointing highlights the way the work of punctuating is done instead by the line breaks, and capitals are simply a replacement for conventional italics:

> ygUDuh
>
> > ydoan
> > yunnuhstan
> >
> > ydoan o
> > yunnuhstan dem
> > yguduh ged
> >
> > yunnuhstan dem doidee
> > yguduh ged riduh
> > ydoan o nudn
>
> LISN bud LISN

The poem opens with: 'ygUDuh'. This is a phonetic rendering of 'You got to', and the capitals 'UD' represent the speaker's urgent emphasis on 'got' (= 'really must'). As the poem gropes its clumsy way forward, there is constant repetition, especially of 'yunnuhstan' (= 'you understand' – and, by implication, though no use is actually made of the question mark, it is equivalent to 'Do you understand?') which serves, in effect, to emphasise not so much the supposed listener's failure to understand what is being said as the speaker's own uncomprehending stupidity and crude, racial prejudice. When he finally manages to formulate his version of the ugly phrase 'little yellow bastards', it comes out in the weirdly crippled form of 'lid yelluh bas / tuds'; and his final, triumphant claim – that he and his like, as superior beings, are going to bring civilisation to these inferior creatures – emerges as a grossly self-parodying piece of illiteracy: 'weer goin / duhSIVILEYEzum'.

Without the aid of speech this poem may seem virtually unintelligible. Spoken, however, it is much easier to understand: it becomes a fairly straightforward satire on the prejudice of a narrow-minded illiterate who yet thinks himself capable of bringing 'civilisation' to a supposedly inferior race.[1] But spoken it is also a much less good poem. The effort required to fight one's way through the bewilderingly clustered consonants is part of the process of defamiliarisation which makes the satire effective – an effort which is curiously at odds with the verbal tricks (anaphora, alliteration, assonance internal rhyme, half-rhyme, ambiguous word-play) foregounded, and in several instances created, by the visual layout. Ultimately, and contrary to normal standards, sound and sense are subordinate to visual impression.

CONCRETE POETRY

Although not all of cummings' poems are so dependent on their visual effect as these two – for example, '(of Ever-Ever Land i speak' is a modern ballad of the W. H. Auden kind which would be equally effective if presented in conventional typography – he is primarily a poet whose work is designed to be seen, and it is his exploitation of the letters-on-the-page dimension that makes him both amusing and seriously innovative. This is in keeping with his equally strong interest in the visual arts. If his experiments suggest affinities with those philosophers and critics of the twentieth century who emphasise the essentially arbitrary nature of language, there are equally strong affinities with the painterly poems, or verbal graphics, of the so-called 'concrete poetry' movement. Here, too, the visual tends to be the most important dimension, and the influence of contemporary artists is evident both in specific dedications (such as Ian Hamilton Finlay's 'Homage to Malevich' and 'To the painter, Juan Gris') and in the shapes formed by the printed works, which in many instances seem to use letters and punctuation marks as an equivalent of the artist's draughtsmanship and palette.

It is sometimes said that the graphic nature of concrete poetry gives it a particular relevance to an age of cinema and television rather than aural communication, and that its attempt to combine the customarily separate arts of poetry and painting (or sculpture) is characteristic of the 'trendy' 1960s and 1970s when all barriers were being thrown down, and 'multimedia' and 'interdisciplinary studies' were the fashionable cry. It is true that the term 'poesia concreta' was first used in the 1950s,[2] but in its use of the visual element it has predecessors in, for example, George Herbert's 'Easter Wings', Lewis Carroll's mouse-tail poem in *Alice in Wonderland*, and the unusual verbal arrangements of Mallarmé's *Un Coup de Dés* and Apollinaire's *Calligrammes*. The distinctive quality of 'concrete' is that it uses the visual as a structural principle based on spatial rather than temporal relationships. In its purest forms it is generated from vertical and horizontal placings that must be *seen* to be perceived, and it virtually divorces itself from traditional syntactical relationships. It makes frequent use of juxtapositions and repetitions, but in a manner akin to the distribution of masses and contrasts or gradations of colour in a painting. More loosely defined, however, concrete poetry can be understood as a form which develops and enhances the incipiently visual element inherent in many rhetorical devices.[3] In practice there is a spectrum from the purely structural and/or pictorial to the more verbally witty, and 'poets' (if that is the appropriate term) range themselves variously along it. What they all have in common, however, is an experimental enlivening of language by the use of a visual dimension which surprises the reader/viewer into a new awareness.

Concrete poetry also lays claim to being an international movement. Because much of its work is composed from a strictly limited verbal palette, and its emphasis on shape rather than sound creates a placard-like effect, it is able to transcend the regional and national divisions associated with the use of a spoken language. Thus Eugen Gomringer's 'silence', with its block of repetitions of the word round a central gap which eloquently speaks 'silence' by its absence, works equally well in German or English; and his generative poem translated as 'grow, flow, show, blow', where words beget words by a kind of spatial syntax that spreads in all directions, creates an effect readily comprehensible in any language (at least if it uses the Roman alphabet).

Two Scottish poets, Ian Hamilton Finlay (b. 1925) and Edwin Morgan, make an interesting comparison. Finlay is more inclined towards painting and sculpture, Morgan to literature; they are thus at opposite ends of the spectrum of concrete poetry. But neither moves off that spectrum. Finlay's best known poem is 'au pair girl', which repeats the phrase continuously, but is cut out in the shape of a pear – the result being an amusing (though, admittedly, one-off) visual pun. Slightly more complex are 'Ajar' and 'Acrobats'. In the former a columnar arrangement of the letters of 'ajar' creates the simultaneous effect of a door seen edge on, and of a *jarring* disruption of the word into its component letters; and the leaving of v-shaped gaps in the column also suggests a door ajar as seen from above. 'Acrobats', as Finlay himself explains, is a kinetic poem: 'Isolated, single letters are pattern but letters joined in words (as these are) are direction. Those in the "acrobats" poem are both, behaving like the real circus acrobats who are now individual units, now – springing together – diagonals and towers.'[4] Such a comment is not, however, definitive. Just as important would be the recognition that the diagonals which give shape to the poem consist of 'acrobats' standing on their own heads by virtue of a visual equivalent of the rhetorical device of antimetabole (i.e. repetition of words in reverse order, here applied to letters: 'acrobatstaborca'). The poem is not conveying a message, but playing with the verbal-cum-visual nature of letters – releasing them from their fixed condition as one particular word, which we read without thinking of its components, into a creative flux of unfixed possibilities.[5]

Morgan (as already shown in Chapter 9, a regular as well as a 'concrete' poet) makes an interesting comment on the relationship between the visual and verbal in this kind of poetry:

> I became interested in concrete poetry as a means of producing economically and arrestingly certain effects which would not otherwise be possible. These effects I still consider to be within the realm of poetry, though the use made of graphic space, and the exaggeration of such visual or sonic gestalts as exist in embryo in all poems, are clearly beginning to draw the poem over into other areas – painting, sculpture, advertising, music. In my own work I don't feel that the boundary into these other areas is crossed, because I have a strong sense of solidarity with words as parts of a semantically charged flux, and in so far as I isolate or distort them I do this in obedience to imaginative commands which come through the medium of language and are not disruptive of it.[6]

If this has a slightly defensive sound to it, suggesting that Morgan may feel the need to defend concrete poetry against critics who see it as inimical to that complex relation between syntax and semantics which feeds traditional poetry, his own practice seems quite free from such anxiety. In his 'pomander' poem, for example, he happily combines an almost Hopkinsian enjoyment of the imaginative possibilities of alliteration and assonance with a freedom which seems purely associative and yet operates syntactically within a visual 'pomander' framework akin to that of Finlay's 'au pair' pear-shape. And it contains within it its own justification for what it is doing: opening up a verbal pomander to release a flood of joyful affirmations which constitute an 'open hymn and pompom band and panda hamper'. It is a quintessential poem of the 1960s, delighting in the shedding of inhibitions in the name of renewed vitality and using an appropriately open-ended form for that end, while submitting easily to the constraints of a typically concrete-poetry visual stanza-shape.

Morgan's use of concrete poetry embraces humour, wit and satire; it is a delightful extension of the possibilities of traditional poetry into an arrestingly novel area, including light-hearted poems such as the computerised Christmas card, 'jollymerry / hollyberry / jollyberry', and the decoding parody, 'Unscrambling the waves at Goonhilly'; the elegant 'French Persian Cats having a Ball', which takes the punning series, 'chat / shah / cha cha / ha ha', and creates from it an amusing combination of phonic and visual effects to suggest a kind of feline ballet; and the serious political poem 'starryveldt', protesting against South African apartheid.

Unusually, Morgan also combines visual and narrative in his extraordinary anteater poem, 'Orgy'. This poem imposes on itself the strict requirement that it be contained within a square of 24 × 24 letters, all of which compose syllabic variations on the word 'anteater', except for lines 17 and 21 which are a series of asterisks. The result is a dazzling, op-art effect of visual congestion in which the repetition of 'a n t' acts out the orgiastic excitement, satiation and exhaustion of an anteater confronted with a seemingly inexhaustible feast of ants. But the poem also moves through time, telling a highly dramatic story of an anteater's bulimia which begins in frantic speed ('c a n t e r c a n t e r c a n t e r c a n t e r') and ends in ecstatic stasis ('n o c a n t e r n o c a n t e r n o c a n t e r'). It is a remarkable achievement, seeming to triumph over the perceived limitations of concrete poetry by creating, simultaneously, the spatial effect of a modernist abstract painting and the sequential effect of poetry and drama.

'Orgy', however, is the exception which proves the rule. The limitations of concrete poetry remain, and it may be for this reason that it is a form which has largely died out since the 1960s. Morgan has produced a 1988 volume, *Themes on a Variation*, which contains concrete poems (gathered together under the title 'Newspoems'), but these belong to the period 1965–71 and are, it must be admitted, slighter and less interesting than the more traditional forms used in the rest of the volume. The lack of modulation and complex mutation made possible by the syntactical richness of traditional forms ('Orgy' notwithstanding) has proved fatal to its further development, with the consequence that it has all but fallen into disuse.

Something of the visual dimension perhaps remains in the emphasis given to the arrangement of lines on the printed page in, for example, Robert Kroetsch's *Seed Catalogue* or Adrienne Rich's 'Children Playing Checkers at the Edge of the Forest'; but this could be attributed to the continuing influence of the rhythmical experiments of Pound and the Black Mountain poets rather than to the pictorial sense of concrete poets. (An interesting exception is Farquharson Cairns's 'BarcOde', which creates a leaning-tower-of-Pisa effect from the bar codes used in modern commercial packaging.)

JOHN ASHBERY (b. 1927)

Modernism, and subsequently post-modernism, in literature has found a useful ally in moden painting; and there is an obvious working relationship between the verbal and the visual in concrete poetry. John Ashbery, whom Dennis Brown cites as 'arguably the clearest case of a "postmodernist" poet', likewise has a strong interest in painting; as a member of the New York School, along with Frank O'Hara (1926–66) and James Schuyler (1923–91) he enjoyed close contact with contemporary American abstract paint- ers, particularly William de Kooning. But his poetry translates its painterly influences into very different terms from those of the concrete poets.

In an interview Ashbery goes so far as to say, 'I have perhaps been more influenced by modern painting and music than by poetry.'[7] Both of these sister art forms, however, work in media which do not, like language, have referential meaning built in to them. The painter's palette or the musician's sounds can be used in an entirely abstract way; the poet's words inevitably connect, no matter how tenuously, with everyday usage – they cannot be totally disinfected of the common reader's expectation of meaning. Like- wise words make their impact sequentially; they are heard, or read, one after another (though, as we have seen, concrete poetry tries to devise methods to overcome this). They cannot share the simultan- eous presence which colours and shapes have in the visual arts; nor, despite the fact that music, too, is inevitably sequential, can they occupy, as instruments or voices in a quartet do, the same temporal space without impairing their effectiveness as communi- cation.[8] Time is likewise of the essence in syntax, the means by which words establish their relation to each other, and syntax with its fundamental dependence on a pattern of subject–verb–predicate is an ordering principle of cause and effect.

Ashbery's interest in the other arts, and painting especially, is to do with a loss of confidence in this articulated coherence which the verbal medium demands as a condition of its being. One of his central themes, in David Shapiro's words, is 'the breakdown of causality in the nineteenth-century sense. His discontinuities tend to throw us most clearly into the middle of the century of the Uncertainty Principle, one in which the poet and scientist expunge false *copulas* for a truer style.'[9] Perhaps Shapiro's 'truer' somewhat begs the question, but Ashbery's syntax, with its Jamesian complexities somehow divorced from the Jamesian overall syntactical control, can be seen as a means towards the elusive end of getting behind the rational structures on which formally correct language is based in order to reach a level of consciousness which has not yet been tidied up by the inveterately organising mind. To this extent it may be called 'neo-Dadaist'.[10] But it is not Dadaist in the sense of discarding entirely the rational principle and relying instead on arbitrary, chance arrangements of language as a gesture of rebellion against the established order of society. Ashbery's is a more subtle subversion of rational discourse, working through an apparent acceptance of its principles, which raises the normal expectations of meaning only to defeat them. Nor is the versification and patterning of rhyme as loose and undisciplined as might be expected if there were a total abandonment of rational structures. On the contrary his forms are often highly exacting and tightly controlled, as, for example, in his use of the complicated sestina form in 'The Painter' and 'Farm Implements and Rutabagas in a Landscape', and the demandingly sustained anaphora (carried to quite deliberate excess) in 'He'. Order is employed to undermine order, replacing its semblance of certainty with a studied incoherence which foregrounds that semblance *as* semblance.

The curious kind of rhetoric which results from such a programme is illustrated by one of Ashbery's earlier poems, 'The Tennis Court Oath' (1962):

> What had you been thinking about
> the face studiously bloodied
> heaven blotted region
> I go on loving you like water but
> there is a terrible breath in the way all of this

You were not elected president, yet won the race
All the way through fog and drizzle
When you read it was sincere the coasts
stammered with unintentional villages the
horse strains fatigued I guess ... the calls ...
I worry

Much of this is recognisably modernist in technique: the discon-
certing plunge *in medias res*, with an unidentified addressee; the
fractured syntax; the vividly particularised metaphor coupled with
a surprisingly displaced epithet ('the coasts / stammered with unin-
tentional villages'); the defamiliarising comparison ('I go on loving
you like water'); and alliterated word-play ('studiously bloodied /
heaven blotted').[11] The jumpy montage is also modernist – indeed,
in itself, almost chiché-modernist. But what is more distinctive of
Ashbery is the air of reasonableness which is cultivated in the face
of unreason. The 'but' that ends line 4, for example, and is fore-
gounded by its position, does not introduce quite the expected
opposition to the first half of the coordinate sentence. What sort of
counterbalance to 'loving like water' is the existence of 'a terrible
breath'? And is there a verb missing after 'all of this', and, if so, what
kind could it possibly be? The dropping of the convention that each
line starts with a capital letter and the virtual absence of punctuation
are well-established features of modernism, justified perhaps by the
possibility of fruitful ambiguities which they open up, and the fact
that they force the reader into more active construction of the sense;
but why the occasional comma and the use of capitals for 'What',
'You', 'All' and 'When'? If the latter indicate the beginning of new
sentences, is 'All the way through fog and drizzle' an unfinished
sentence, for some reason not accorded the dots which follow
'I guess' and 'the calls'? And as an impressionistic detail, to what
does it attach? Likewise, why do 'the coasts' and 'the / horse' *not*
begin with a capital 'T'? And why should the lineation so bizarrely
separate 'horse' from 'the', its (paradoxically indefinite) definite
article?

If this were a passage from a play by the dramatist Tom Stoppard
(b. 1937) – for example, part of the bizarre opening of *Travesties* –
the seemingly arbitrary and wayward would in the end be given a
rational explanation; but Ashbery is not teasing in that particular
way. There is no rational key which unlocks his puzzle-door. The
meaning, if it exists, is situated somewhere between or behind the

component parts, and not in their suppressed links. One would even be tempted to say that the meaning is in the lack of meaning, were it not that the parts, by and large, seem meaningful enough. The parts are there, but not as parts of a greater organic whole.

Shapiro's placing of this subversion of reason within a context of 'breakdown' suggests that Ashbery's work is a continuation of what Eliot was doing in *The Waste Land*. But there is a significant difference of posture. Eliot, harking back to a lost age of faith, sounds an essentially conservative note of regret; Ashbery, on the contrary, welcomes his disintegration. He has more in common with the modern deconstructionist who seeks to undermine apparently clear, unified structures in order to make way for greater self-criticism and more pluralist values. In this respect the use of parody and cliché in his later work can be seen as part of an overall strategy of irony meant to deflate the modern reader's unthinking adherence to received values – such as those, for example, embodied in America's Declaration of Independence, a line from which ('We hold these truths to be self-evident') provides the starting point for the poem aptly named 'Decoy' (from the 1970 volume, *The Double Dream of Spring*).[12]

However, the implication here that the poetry forwards some kind of political programme is misleading. Ideally, what such poetry does is to enhance the alertness of the reader. A quotation might be excerpted from a particular poem, but the status of the quotation is ambiguous. It is perhaps no more than a feature in the cultural environment in which the mind exists, but without commitment or conviction. As 'Houseboat Days' somewhat elusively expresses it:

> The mind
> Is so hospitable, taking in everything
> Like boarders, and you don't see until
> It's all over how little there was to learn
> Once the stench of knowledge has dissipated, and the
>   trouvailles
> Of every one of the senses fallen back.

The possibilities of meaning here are various. Is this Ashbery himself hinting that a flexible mind is desirable? Or merely some other character, or aspect of his complex self, pontificating? Is the second half of the statement a deliberate deflation of the first? In relation to the whimsical word-play of the lines which immediately precede it in the poem – 'again / You walk five feet along the shore, and you duck / As a common heresy sweeps over' – bathos would seem to be what it is all about; and the subsequent lines,

> To praise this, blame that,
> Leads one subtly away from the beginning, where
> We must stay, in motion

seem to confirm that moral judgements are beside the point. But with such a shifting voice the disclaimer seems to have no more authority than the claim. Speakers are imaginable, but unidentifiable. The result is a tricksy poetry that lives from line to line, declining to argue a case through to its conclusion, or wear the badge of commitment. The poetry, in fact, appropriate to holiday in a houseboat, which offers a place to be in, but is only provisionally moored on an essentially unstable river. Yet to maintain some kind of poise in such uncertainty is what the poetry itself tries to do, and in so doing it is, at its best, a liberating experience.

PHILIP LARKIN (1922–85)

With all its sophistication, charm and wit, Ashbery's poetry is subversive of discourse. Although it continually suggests normal discursive development, it tends to veer away towards uncertainty and associational drift. In this, and in other respects, too, it contrasts sharply with the poetry of Philip Larkin. For Larkin the poets who mattered were those like Yeats, Auden, and above all Hardy, who maintained the discursive tradition. In an interview for the *Paris Review*, when asked the question 'Do you feel you belong to any particular tradition in English letters?' he replied:

I seem to remember George Fraser saying that poetry was either 'veeshion' – he was Scotch – or 'moaral deescourse', and I was the second, and the first was better. A well-known publisher asked me how one punctuated poetry, and looked flabbergasted when I said, The same as prose. By which I mean that I write, or wrote, as everyone did till the mad lads started, using words and syntax in the normal way to describe recognizable experiences as memorably as possible. That doesn't seem to me a tradition. The other stuff, the mad stuff, is more an aberration.[13]

Although this denies 'tradition', it is at least traditional in the sense that it deplores flagrant departures from prose sense and prose syntax, of the kind practised by so many American modernists; and it is clearly opposed to the experimental punctuation of e. e. cummings. The slightly unfair mockery of G. S. Fraser sidesteps the issue of whether he considers himself a poet of 'vision' or 'moral discourse', but the context may be taken as implying that he accepts the second, without either agreeing that it is inferior or conceding that his own poetry excludes vision. His position seems to be that verse and prose share the same processes of argument and debate, and that the same 'rules' of syntax and punctuation apply to each. To this extent it is a declaration for the traditional, and against the experimental.

In his *Oxford Book of Twentieth-Century English Verse* Larkin also declined to include poems 'requiring a glossary for their full understanding', which, on the face of it, suggests an equal dislike for the obscurity generated by modernist allusiveness. In the above interview, however, he states that this simply explained why he had not included dialect poems – adding for the benefit of his interviewer: 'We have poets who write in pretty dense Lallans. Nothing to do with obscurity in the sense you mean.'[14] But obscurity does seem to be a feature of modernism that Larkin dislikes, and (as the interviewer reminds him) there are strong words against it in the Introduction to *All What Jazz*, where he associates it with lack of concern for communication and an undue appetite for experiment:

> All I am saying is that the term 'modern', when applied to art, has a more than chronological meaning: it denotes a quality of irresponsibility peculiar to this century, known sometimes as modernism, and once I had classified modern jazz under this heading I knew where I was. I am sure there are books in which the genesis of modernism is set out in full. My own theory is that it is related to an imbalance between the two tensions from which art springs: these are the tension between the artist and his material, and between the artist and his audience, and that in the last seventy-five years or so the second of these has slackened or even perished. In consequence the artist has become over-concerned with his material (hence an age of technical experiment), and, in isolation, has busied himself with the two principal themes of modernism, mystification and outrage.[15]

And among illustrations of inappropriate experiment Larkin includes what looks very much like a mocking reference to concrete poetry: 'He [the modernist] has written poems resembling the kind of pictures typists make with their machines during the coffee break ...'.

Some of these comments should be taken with a pinch of salt. As his letters reveal, Larkin did not necessarily commit himself seriously to his off-the-cuff remarks; often they belong to the same category as the 'Books are a load of crap' in 'A Study of Reading Habits' – which is not the verdict of the Librarian of Hull University Library, but of a persona whose reading was never more than pulp fiction, and who doesn't 'read much now'. They do, however, square with the work in which Larkin *is* serious, to the extent that they reveal deep suspicion of experiment and modes of writing which seek freedom of expression by rejecting disciplined craftsmanship. This seriousness often includes an explicit upholding of tradition and conservative opinions, as in the satirical 'Naturally the Foundation will Bear Your Expenses' and the part-satirical, part-nostalgic 'Show Saturday'; but it is in 'Church Going', 'An Arundel Tomb', 'The Whitsun Weddings', 'Ambulances', 'The Building' and 'The Old Fools' (to name a half-dozen of the poems on which his permanent reputation is likely to rest) that his more deeply rooted conservatism is to be found. These are poems in which Larkin is both serious and self-critical – or, rather, in which seriousness is achieved as a result of a kind of imaginative journeying which carries him down from the level of off-the-cuff response and satirical mockery to a deeper, underlying awareness. And they are also the poems in which Larkin's craftsmanship is the most fastidious; in which he presses himself most keenly, like the legendary song-bird against the thorn, up against the discipline imposed by taxing verse-forms and intricate rhetorical structures, which have to conform to the 'rules' of normal syntax and yet be consonant with the rhythms and lexis of ordinary speech. His art is the traditional *ars celare artem* (the art to hide art), deployed in a naturalistic-seeming manner which, as the stylistic reconciling of past and present, matches the realistic immedicay of his 1950s/1960s surface and the temperamental conservatism of his nature.

This movement from surface to greater depth is clearly visible in 'The Whitsun Weddings'. It begins with the beginning of a railway journey from a northern town (not named, but obviously Hull) to London. Initially the atmosphere is one of relaxed escape from work, reflected in a strictly contemporary, and slightly sardonic, pastoral that mixes farms and 'short-shadowed cattle' with 'Canals with flotatings of industrical froth' and 'acres of dismantled cars'. At first the 'I' of the poem pays little attention to the people who board the train at its frequent stops, but gradually they penetrate his consciousness as newly-married couples being seen off on their honeymoons by friends and relatives whom he presents in a still more sardonic–satirical light than the semi-industrialised land-scape. The first time he notices them they are merely 'grinning and pomaded', girls dressed in 'parodies of fashion'. They start to arouse his interest, however, so that 'Struck, I leant / More promptly out next time, more curiously', and, though he still sees the fathers as having 'seamy foreheads' and the mothers as 'loud and fat', the girls, still vulgarly got up, begin to seem marked off 'unreally from the rest'. The sense of 'departing' deepens; from being mere butts of farce the wedding-guests start to become people with their own feelings, however banal. And the women – again, it is especially the women, as the poem itself seems to modulate from a masculine boorishness to a feminine conventionality that is nevertheless more serious –

> The women shared
> The secret like a happy funeral;
> While girls, gripping their handbags tighter, stared
> At a religious wounding.

The tone of these lines is still ambiguous: they could be sympathetic to the women's emotions or satirically portentous. The latter mood continues perhaps into the settling of hats and the cliché colloquial-ism of '*I nearly died*' in the penultimate stanza. But as the train nears its destination the poem becomes more thoughtful. The couples may not be aware of their temporary sharing of a significant experience with the other couples ('none / Thought of the others they would never meet / Or how their lives would all contain this hour'), but the persona's saying this – negative comment as it is – becomes for the reader an oblique form of affirmation, the equivalent of a musical modulation into a minor key. Mockery falls away from the final lines, and Larkin even risks a kind of moral sententiousness, heightened, by his Shakespearean image of shot arrows, to a gravity unimaginable in the opening stanza (despite the echo of the initial griminess of Hull in the 'walls of blackened moss' as the train approaches London). The 'frail / Travelling coincidence' is nearly finished,

> and what it held
> Stood ready to be loosed with all the power
> That being changed can give. We slowed again,
> And as the tightened brakes took hold, there swelled
> A sense of falling, like an arrow-shower
> Sent out of sight, somewhere becoming rain.[16]

G. S. Fraser's division between 'vision' and 'discourse' which Larkin seems to have resented is transcended in these lines. The poem has moved through its gradually deepening responsiveness combined with discursive thoughtfulness to a point where it makes a metaphorical leap into the visionary unknown. What is also worth noting is the way Larkin's control of his verse structure contributes to this momentum and change. The ten-line stanza rhymes ABABCDECDE and is composed of iambic pentameters, except for the short second line, the effect of which is to create a kind of studied stumbling before the rest of the stanza gets into its stride. Colloquial rhythms and run-on lines also resist the orderly structure, but for the first twenty lines the stanza is none the less a firmly containing sense-unit. From stanzas 3 to 7, however, run-on occurs between stanzas, slightly disrupting the expectation that the sense will be completed within the unit, and thus heightening the reader's attention in accordance with the increased taking of 'notice' that is required. But between stanza 7 and the final stanza the now established run-on pattern is again interrupted with an emphatic stop foregrounded by a colon after 'postal districts packed like squares of wheat'. This seeming arrest is nevertheless overcome when the last stanza starts with a 'There' ('There we were aimed'), which firmly links the train, its occupants and the verse to the destination, i.e. London, named in those closing lines of stanza 7 (and heightened, incidentally, by a metaphor which raises the tension in anticipation of the greater metaphor yet to come). The sharp caesura after 'aimed' is followed by run-on lines, onomatopoeia and closely packed stressed syllables (echoing the rattling points-crossing as the train nears the terminus) to come to another marked caesura, 'That being changed can give', which again arrests attention. 'We slowed again' retards the momentum, and the next line beautifully captures the ceasing of motion: 'And as the tightened

brakes took hold'. The syntax, however, is significant. 'And as ... '
puts the stopping into a subordinate clause, to be followed by a
different momentum associated with the verb of the main clause,
'swelled', poised at the end of the line for its run-on leap to the
paradoxical 'A sense of falling'. Finally, the metaphorical 'arrow-
shower' is again run-on to 'Sent out of sight' (yet creating a carefully
balanced effect as noun / verb contrasts with the previous verb /
noun) to end up converting that paradoxical 'sense of falling' into
a fall of (implicitly fertility-generating) 'rain'.

A similar marriage of deepening imaginative awareness, stanzaic
structure and syntactical flexibility is to be found in most of the
'serious' Larkin poems. It is a combination which he handles with
exceptional skill. But in the context of English poetry it is also
profoundly traditional, running, for example, through the work of
such varied predecessors as Donne, Keats, Hardy and Auden. The
poem becomes a means of burrowing into experience, but one in
which the tension between form and content is essential to the
progress that is made. This is seen particularly clearly in poems like
'The Building', 'The Old Fools' and 'Aubade' where Larkin faces his
own, now notorious, fear of decay and death. In 'The Old Fools' it is
the short last lines of the twelve-line stanzas which particularly
sharpen the poem's growing awareness of decay – a home-truth
which ultimately 'We shall find out'. In 'Aubade' it is the deflating,
Donne-like rhyming: 'Being brave / Lets no one off the grave.' And,
most potently of all, in 'The Building' it is the discipline of a form
which is affirmed even as it is tested and strained against which
pushes the poem further and further into compulsively painful areas.
Here Larkin's run-on lines and stanzaic overflows are reinforced by
a complex interplay between seven-line stanza-form and eight-line
rhyme-scheme (ABCBDCAD) to create an orderly disturbance of
order which increasingly confronts the reader with the unpleasant
reality of the building/hospital's *raison d'être*. Moreover, the pursuing
of the stanza/rhyme-scheme disjunction throughout the poem's
sixty-four lines results in a seemingly odd, left-over final line which
has a peculiarly poignant effect. The meaning of 'the building'
crystallises as 'a struggle to transcend / The thought of dying', but
the pathos-laden truth is that the struggle is unavailing,

> though crowds each evening try

With wasteful, weak, propitiatory flowers.

A COUNTERBALANCING OF TENSIONS

Larkin exploits the sequential nature of traditional syntax, driving through to an emotionally powerful climax. The poem unfolds with gathering momentum as it is read: it exists in time, rather than the space of the concrete poem; and, though it may wander and digress, it must, unlike the poetry of Ashbery, complete its controlled structure. The ultimate reward is a cumulative effect which enables the final line of 'The Building' to come loaded with the force of the gathering process of revelation which has preceded it. Such poetry is like music in that it accepts the necessity of note following note, word following word, in patterns of intricately varied order – and strikingly contrasted disorder, too (though classical music, or, in Larkin's particular case, jazz of the classic period prior to Charlie Parker, rather than modernist atonal music is the appropriate parallel). Ashbery, and, in different fashion, cummings and Finlay, experiment in subverting syntax and moving poetry in the direction of painting – and the concrete poets, especially, towards a spatial condition of everything-seen-at-once.

Of course, if a linguistic everything is heard at once, it tends to lose its basic relation to speech and risks becoming a meaningless cacophony. To this extent the traditional, discursive mode of Larkin is in keeping with the nature of language itself. A visual poetry, it may be said, is almost a contradiction in terms. And yet in the context of words as published on the printed page – which, notwithstanding poetry readings and recordings and the concept of 'performance poetry' as practised by poets such as Adrian Henri (b. 1932) and Roger McGough (b. 1937), is the context in which most twentieth-century readers still encounter poetry – the visual effect is inescapable. And, further paradox, the more poetry obeys the 'rules' of traditional verse the more it takes on an orderly visual appearance, so that the odes of Keats or Larkin tend to take pleasing shape on the printed page.

The sharpness of contrast between 'experimental' and 'traditional' should not, therefore, be taken to exclude all possibilities of rapprochement between them. As already suggested, there is at least a seemingly discursive basis to the anti-discursive poetry of Ashbery; and, balancing traditional poetry's tendency to give visual enhancement in print, there are narrative elements in the work of cummings and the concrete poetry of Edwin Morgan which imply a dependence on temporal sequence. Each is still within hailing distance of the other.

More importantly still, there is always a symbiotic relationship between experiment and tradition in that experiment is meaningless except as a reaction against what is felt to be the sterile order of tradition, while the urge to maintain traditional methods of ordering, through the building of structures and the preservation of discursive sequence (usually aided and abetted by conventions of spelling, punctuation and 'correct' grammar and syntax), answers a deeply felt need to ward off the corruption and attrition of meaning. Both imply a subtle counterbalancing of tensions, and the complementary existence of their opposites as sounding-boards against which their own practices vibrate. In this sense they are mutually dependent. And it is from such mutual dependence that they also derive their claim to a meaningful modernity. For it is their reaction to what they find potentially moribund in the contemporary state of the language, and not only the fact of their existence in the same time, place and society, which makes them either 'modern' or 'modernist'. Their joint enemy is the decline into an ordinariness which is deadeningly undifferentiated; and it is by the degree to which they counter that potentially inert condition that they earn their right to be considered as products of their time which are fully alert and alive. Their differences are signs of vigour; along with the other emphases which this book has tried to suggest, including the developing riches of twentieth-century women's poetry and the new-found energy of regional, national and postcolonial writing, they point to a variety which is both welcome and appropriate to a period of such profound and varied change as the twentieth century.

Notes

1 Introduction

1. Quoted by Russell Miller, 'Oh! What an Unlovely War', *Sunday Times*, 30 June 1996, section 3, p. 9.
2. Fredric Jameson, '*Ulysses* in History', in *James Joyce and Modern Literature*, ed. W. J. McCormack and Alistair Stead (London: Routledge, 1982); reprinted in *A Practical Reader in Contemporary Literary Theory*, ed. Peter Brooker and Peter Widdowson (Englewood Cliffs: Prentice-Hall, 1996; Hemel Hempstead: Harvester Wheatsheaf, 1996) p. 312.
3. Jonathan Culler, *Saussure* (Glasgow: Fontana/Collins, 1976) p. 23.
4. Roland Barthes, *Image–Music–Text*, trans. Stephen Heath, reprinted in *Twentieth-Century Literary Theory*, ed. K. M. Newton (London and Basingstoke: Macmillan, 1988) p. 157.
5. Ibid., p. 157.
6. The reader interested in further development of this theme is referred both to what is said in Chapter 3 and to my essay 'Hardy Among the Moderns' (from which these words are taken) in *A Spacious Vision*, ed. Phillip V. Mallett and Ronald P. Draper (Penzance, Cornwall: The Patten Press, 1994) pp. 89–101.
7. Comment by Ashbery in an interview. See *The Craft of Poetry: Interviews from 'The New York Quarterly'* (New York: Doubleday, 1974) p. 123.

2 Modernism: Pound, Eliot, William Carlos Williams and Wallace Stevens

1. William Empson, 'A Game of Chess', *Seven Types of Ambiguity* (London: Chatto & Windus, 1930; Harmondsworth: Penguin, 1973) pp. 100–1.
2. Cited by B. C. Southam, *A Student's Guide to the Selected Poems of T. S. Eliot* (London: Faber and Faber, 1968) p. 125.
3. See Helen Gardner, '*Four Quartets*: A Commentary', in B. Rajan (ed.), *T. S. Eliot: A Study of His Writings by Several Hands* (London: Dennis Dobson, 1947) pp. 57–77.
4. Stephen Cushman, *William Carlos Williams and the Meanings of Measure* (New Haven and London: Yale University Press, 1985).
5. Benjamin Sankey, *A Companion to Williams's* Paterson (Berkeley and London: University of California Press, 1971) p. 15.
6. Michael Davidson, 'Notes beyond the *Notes*: Wallace Stevens and Contemporary Poetics', in Albert Gelpi (ed.), *Wallace Stevens: The Poetics of Modernism* (Cambridge: Cambridge University Press, 1985) p. 145.
7. Wallace Stevens, *The Necessary Angel*, quoted by Gelpi, op. cit., p. 7.
8. Quoted by Frank Kermode, in *Wallace Stevens* (Edinburgh: Oliver and Boyd, 1960) p. 66.

9. Davidson, in Gelpi, op. cit., p. 149.
10. T. S. Eliot, 'East Coker' II, 19.
11. T. S. Eliot, Preface to *For Lancelot Andrewes*, quoted by John Hayward (ed.), *T. S. Eliot: Selected Prose* (Harmondsworth: Penguin, 1953) p. 11.

3 An Alternative Tradition: Hardy, Housman, Frost, Kipling and Graves

1. Thomas Hardy in *The Life of Thomas Hardy, 1840–1928* (Basingstoke and London: Macmillan, 1962) pp. 300–1. This 'biography' was published under the name of Hardy's second wife Florence Emily Hardy, but is now widely recognised to have been effectively Hardy's own work.
2. See Dennis Taylor, *Hardy's Metres and Victorian Prosody* (Oxford: Oxford University Press, 1988) pp. 27–48. Taylor also shows how the critical tradition extends into the twentieth century via an essay on 'Free Verse and the Parthenon' (1919) by Ramsay Traquair – an essay which Hardy probably knew.
3. Norman Page (ed.), *Thomas Hardy: The Writer and His Background* (London: Bell & Hyman, 1980) pp. 173–91.
4. Lytton Strachey, Review of Hardy's *Satires of Circumstance* in *New Statesman*, 19 December 1914; reprinted in James Gibson and Trevor Johnson (eds), *Thomas Hardy: Poems* (Casebook) (Basingstoke and London: Macmillan, 1979) p. 63.
5. See Introduction to the Papermac Edition of *The Dynasts*, ed. John Wain (London: Macmillan, 1965) pp. xi–xiii; and 'Chorus of the Years', Part Third, Act VI, Scene viii, p. 483.
6. Philip Larkin, *Required Writing* (London: Faber and Faber, 1983) p. 264.
7. B. J. Leggett, *The Poetic Art of A. E. Housman* (Lincoln, Nebraska, and London: University of Nebraska Press, 1978) p. 143.
8. Quoted by Mordecai Marcus, *The Poems of Robert Frost: An Explication* (Boston: G. K. Hall, 1991) p. 13.
9. 'The Figure a Poem Makes', in James Scully (ed.), *Modern Poets on Modern Poetry* (London: Fontana, 1966; reprinted 1973) p. 56.
10. Quoted from Frost's letters by Frank Lentricchia, 'The Resentments of Robert Frost', *American Literature*, vol. 62, no. 2 (June 1990) p. 183.
11. Frank Lentricchia, ibid., p. 185.
12. Marcus, op. cit., p. 15.
13. W. H. Auden, *The Dyer's Hand* (London: Faber and Faber, 1963) pp. 345 and 348.
14. Geoffrey Moore, for example, finds it too 'generalised'; and he also finds the earlier poetry a better vehicle for the experiential message. The later work is 'lacking in the bucolic wisdom and the self-contained justness of the earlier poems' (*The Penguin Book of Modern American Verse* (Harmondsworth: Penguin, 1954) p. 52).
15. Elizabeth Jennings, *Frost* (Edinburgh: Oliver and Boyd, 1964) p. 57.
16. Robert Graves, *The Common Asphodel* (London: Hamish Hamilton, 1949) pp. 98–9.
17. Martin Seymour-Smith, *Robert Graves* (Harlow: Longman, for the British Council, 1956; revised edition, 1970) p. 15.

18. Graves, quoted by D. N. G. Carter, *Robert Graves: The Lasting Poetic Achievement* (Basingstoke and London: Macmillan, 1989) p. 85.

4   Private and Public: Yeats and Lowell

1. Ezra Pound, 'A Retrospect' (1917), in *Literary Essays of Ezra Pound*, edited by T. S. Eliot (London: Faber and Faber, 1954; reprinted 1974) p. 12.
2. Cf. Yeats's own comment on these figures: 'I have used them in this book more as principles of the mind than as actual personages.' Quoted by Daniel Albright (ed.), *W. B. Yeats: The Poems* (London: J. M. Dent, 1990) p. 452.
3. Denis Donoghue, *Yeats* (London: Fontana/Collins, 1971) p. 16.
4. Albright, op. cit., p. 808.
5. Ian Hamilton, *Robert Lowell* (London: Faber and Faber, 1983) p. 85.
6. Eliot's 'The Dry Salvages' (the third of *Four Quartets*), published only two years before, and making use of the same New England shorescape, is also a possible influence.
7. Mark Rudman, *Robert Lowell: An Introduction to the Poetry* (New York: Columbia University Press, 1983) p. 47.
8. W. D. Snodgrass (b. 1926) also belongs to this group (though, strictly speaking, he is leader rather than follower, as Lowell acknowledges); and so do Anne Sexton and Sylvia Plath, whose work, however, is reserved for consideration in Chapter 8.
9. See Marjorie G. Perloff, *The Poetic Art of Robert Lowell* (Ithaca and London: Cornell University Press, 1973) pp. 175–9.

5   Poetry of Two World Wars

1. See Dominic Hibberd (ed.), *Wilfred Owen: War Poems and Others* (London: Chatto and Windus, 1973) p. 120.
2. *The Birth of Tragedy: Basic Writings of Nietzsche*, trans. Walter Kaufman (New York: Knopf, 1968) p. 141.
3. Quoted in Hibberd, op. cit., p. 37.
4. D. H. Lawrence, 'Study of Thomas Hardy', *Phoenix*, ed. Edward D. McDonald (London: Heinemann, 1936) p. 420.
5. Letter to Waldo Frank, 27 July 1917.
6. Cf. Paul Nash's letter of November 1917 describing 'the most frightful nightmare of a country more conceived by Dante or Poe than by nature', quoted by D. S. R. Welland, *Wilfred Owen* (London: Chatto & Windus, 1960) p. 30.
7. Elizabeth Ward, *David Jones: Mythmaker* (Manchester: Manchester University Press, 1983) pp. 80–3 and 117.
8. Ibid., p. 88.
9. Edna Longley, '"Shit or Bust": The Importance of Keith Douglas', *Poetry in the Wars* (Newcastle: Bloodaxe, 1986) p. 111. ('Shit or bust you are' is a comment reportedly made to Douglas by his batman.)
10. An exception to the view that Douglas is a precursor to Hughes is to be found in Donald Davie's 'Remembering the Desert', *Under*

Briggflatts (Manchester: Carcanet, 1989). Davie sees Douglas as a Byronic poet who does not want to be 'all author', but values the man of action as much as the poet.

11. Bernard Bergonzi, *Heroes' Twilight: A Study of the Literature of the Great War* (London and Basingstoke: Macmillan , 1965; reprinted 1980) p. 125.

6   Auden and Co.

1. Edward Mendelson, *Early Auden* (London and Boston: Faber and Faber, 1981) pp. 28–9.
2. Poem xxiii, in *Poems, 1927–1931* (*The English Auden: Poems, Essays, and Dramatic Writings, 1927–1939*, ed. Edward Mendelson (London: Faber and Faber, 1981) pp. 28–9).
3. Humphrey Carpenter, *W. H. Auden: A Biography* (London: George Allen & Unwin, 1981) p. 153. If it is eighteenth-century ballad, it also, of course, owes something to Romantic adaptations of the form, particularly the truncated fourth line of Keats's 'La belle dame sans merci'.
4. See Justin Replogle, *Auden's Poetry* (London: Methuen, 1969) pp. 91f.
5. John R. Boly, *Reading Auden: The Returns of Caliban* (Ithaca and London: Cornell University Press, 1991) p. 49.
6. John Fuller (*A Reader's Guide to W. H. Auden* (London: Thames and Hudson, 1970, p. 48) comments on the likeness of the poem to the Old English poem 'The Wanderer', but notes that 'The first line is actually taken from a Middle English homily, *Sawles Warde*: "Ha βeoδ se wise Þat ha witen alle godes reades, his runes ant his domes Þe derne beoδ ant deopre Þen ani sea dingle" ("they are so wise that they know all God's counsels, his mysteries and his judgments, which are secret and deeper than any sea dingle").'
7. Boly, op. cit., p. 101.
8. Boly writes of those who dare to go beyond the 'feral fires', which summons up a possible allusion to D. H. Lawrence's *The Rainbow*, Chapter 15, where Ursula Brangwen has a vision of dangerous animals in the darkness beyond the camp-fire light of science and knowledge: '… and some, having given up their vanity of the light, having died in their own conceit, saw the gleam in the eyes of the wolf and the hyaena, that it was the flash of the sword of angels, flashing at the door to come in'. On the other hand, 'new men making another love' echoes the very different situation in T. S. Eliot's 'Journey of the Magi', where the speaker, one of the Magi, concludes his account of the disturbing experience of his journey to see the (unnamed) Christ-child with the comment, 'I should be glad of another death.'
9. Other revisions include 'We must love one another and die' (from the original '*or* die'), and omissions of several stanzas from 'Spain 1937' and of three stanzas from Section III of 'In Memory of W. B. Yeats'.
10. See Carpenter, op. cit., pp. 242–6.
11. Edward Lucie-Smith (ed.), *British Poetry since 1945* (Harmondsworth: Penguin, 1970; revised edition, 1985) p. 65.

12. Robert Graves and Alan Hodge, *The Long Week-End* (London: Faber and Faber, 1941) p. 300.
13. Bernard Bergonzi, *The Myth of Modernism and Twentieth Century Literature* (Brighton: Harvester, 1986) p. 128.
14. Preface to *Selected Poems* (Harmondsworth: Penguin, 1951) p. 11.
15. Cf. the title of the early volume *From Feathers to Iron* (1931).
16. Kenneth Allott (ed.), *The Penguin Book of Contemporary Verse* (Harmondsworth: Penguin, 1950) p. 184.

7 'Black Mountain', and the Poetry of D. H. Lawrence and Ted Hughes

1. Charles Olson, 'Projective Verse', *Poetry New York*, No. 3 (1950); reprinted in James Scully (ed.), *Modern Poets on Modern Poetry* (London: Fontana/Collins, 1966) pp. 271–82.
2. *The Letters of D. H. Lawrence*, ed. George J. Zytaruk and James T. Boulton (Cambridge: Cambridge University Press, 1981) pp. 103–4.
3. *The Complete Poems of D. H. Lawrence*, ed. Vivian de Sola Pinto and Warren Roberts (London: Heinemann, 1964) vol. 1, pp. 181–6.
4. D. H. Lawrence, *Apocalypse* (Hamburg: The Albatross Verlag, 1932) pp. 219–30. (*Apocalypse* was written shortly before Lawrence's death in 1930, and first posthumously published in 1931.)
5. See *Complete Poems*, vol. 2, pp. 697 and 963 (for 'Bavarian Gentians') and pp. 716–20, 720–1, 722–3, 723–4 and 964–7 (for 'The Ship of Death').
6. W. H. Auden, *The Dyer's Hand* (London: Faber and Faber, 1963) pp. 277–95.
7. Letter to Edward Garnett, 22 April 1914.
8. Charles Olson, *D. H. Lawrence and the High Temptation of the Mind* (Santa Barbara, Cal.: Black Sparrow Press, 1980) p. 4.
9. See George Hutchinson, 'The Pleistocene in the Projective: Some of Olson's Origins', *American Literature*, vol. 54 (1982) pp. 81–96.
10. Thomas F. Merrill, *The Poetry of Charles Olson* (London and Toronto: University of Delaware Press, 1982) p. 68.
11. Marilyn Kallett, 'Moistening Our Roots with Music: Creative Power in Denise Levertov's "A Tree Telling of Orpheus"', *Twentieth Century Literature: Denise Levertov Issue*, vol. 38, part 3 (Fall 1992) pp. 305–23.
12. Ibid., p. 316.
13. Leonard M. Scigaj, 'Ted Hughes and Ecology: A Biocentric Vision', in Keith Sagar (ed.), *The Challenge of Ted Hughes* (Basingstoke and London: Macmillan, 1994) p. 179.
14. A. E. Dyson, review of *Hawk in the Rain* (and other volumes of poetry), *Critical Quarterly*, vol. 1, no. 3 (Autumn 1959) pp. 20–6.
15. Ted Hughes, in Ekbert Faas, *Ted Hughes: The Unaccommodated Universe* (Santa Barbara, Cal.: Black Sparrow Press, 1980) p. 208.
16. David Lodge, '"Crow" and the Cartoons', *Critical Quarterly*, vol. 13, no. 1 (Spring 1971) pp. 37–42 and 68. Lodge relates *Crow* specifically to the

cartoon 'in its harsher, post-Disney phase', which 'is one in which animals and birds, drawn in such a way as to caricature both their species and certain human types, are involved in knockabout comic situations in which there is a strong element of sado-masochistic fantasy'.

8 Women's Poetry

1. Claire Keyes, *The Aesthetics of Power* (Atlanta, Georgia: University of Georgia Press, 1986) p. 112.
2. Dated 1984 and printed in the volume *Blood, Bread and Poetry: Selected Prose, 1979–1985* (New York: W. W. Norton, 1986; reprinted London: Virago Press, 1987).
3. Liz Yorke, *Impertinent Voices* (London: Routledge, 1991) p. 139.
4. In Hughes's edition of Plath's *Collected Poems* (London: Faber and Faber, 1981) 'Lady Lazarus' is dated 23–29 October 1962 and 'Stings' 6 October 1962. The other poems in the bee sequence are: 'The Bee Meeting' (3 October); 'The Arrival of the Bee Box' (4 October); 'The Swarm' (7 October); and 'Wintering' (9 October). 'The Beekeeper's Daughter' (1959), though also a bee-keeping poem, does not form part of this sequence.
5. Carol Leventen, *'Transformations*'s Silencings', in Linda Wagner-Martin (ed.), *Critical Essays on Anne Sexton* (Boston: G. K. Hall, 1989) p. 136.
6. Seamus Heaney, 'Counting to a Hundred: On Elizabeth Bishop', *The Redress of Poetry* (London: Faber and Faber, 1995; paperback 1996) p. 182.
7. Patricia B. Wallace, 'The Wildness of Elizabeth Bishop', *Sewanee Review*, vol. xciii (1995) p. 95.

9 Regional, National and Post-Colonial (I)

1. Thomas Hardy in *The Life of Thomas Hardy*, and Matthew Arnold in 'The Literary Influence of Academies'. See Robin Gilmour, 'Regional and Provincial in Victorian Literature', in R. P. Draper (ed.), *The Literature of Region and Nation* (London and Basingstoke: Macmillan, 1989) pp. 51–60.
2. See the essays on MacDiarmid in Iain Crichton Smith, *Towards the Human* (Edinburgh: Macdonald, 1986); and, in particular, 'The Golden Lyric: The Poetry of Hugh MacDiarmid'.
3. 'I'll have no half-way house, but always be where / Extremes meet.'
4. '"And well you might", / So Jean will say, "after such a night!"'
5. Though a socialist from youth, MacDiarmid only joined the Communist Party after expulsion from the Scottish National Party in 1933. In 1938 he was expelled from the Communist Party, but re-joined in 1956 when many other intellectuals left in disgust at the invasion of Hungary.
6. Seamus Heaney, *Preoccupations: Selected Prose, 1968–1978* (London: Faber and Faber, 1980; reprinted 1984) p. 197.

7. 'You mustn't look in my novel for the old stable *ego* of the character. There is another *ego*, according to whose action the individual is unrecognisable, and passes through, as it were, allotropic states which it needs a deeper sense than any we've been used to exercise, to discover are states of the same single radically unchanged element. (Like as diamond and coal are the same pure single element of carbon. The ordinary novel would trace the history of the diamond – but I say, "Diamond, what! This is carbon." And my diamond might be coal or soot, and my theme is carbon.)' D. H. Lawrence, letter to Edward Garnett, 5 June 1914. Cf. also Lawrence's poem 'Fidelity', which is particularly close to MacDiarmid in its juxtaposition of flowers and rock:

> And man and woman are like earth, that brings forth flowers
> in summer, and love, but underneath is rock.
> Older than flowers, older than ferns, older than foraminiferae
> older than plasm altogether is the soul of man underneath.

(*Complete Poems*, vol. 1, p. 477)

8. Edwin Muir, *Scott and Scotland* (1936). Quoted by Douglas Dunn in his Introduction to *The Faber Book of Twentieth-Century Scottish Poetry* (London: Faber and Faber, 1992) p. xxxiii.
9. *The Faber Book of Twentieth-Century Scottish Poetry*, pp. 361–2.
10. Iain Crichton Smith, 'The Double Man', in Draper (ed.), *The Literature of Region and Nation*, p. 138.
11. Barbara Hardy, 'Region and Nation: R. S. Thomas and Dylan Thomas', in Draper (ed.), *The Literature of Region and Nation*, p. 100.
12. In Henry Treece, *Dylan Thomas: Dog Among the Fairies*, quoted by R. B. Kershaw, *Dylan Thomas: The Poet and His Critics* (Chicago: American Library Association, 1976) p. 194.
13. Viktor Shklovsky, 'Art as Technique', quoted by Raman Selden, *A Reader's Guide to Contemporary Literary Theory* (Brighton: Harvester, 1985) p. 10.
14. See Edna Longley's article 'Northern Irish Poetry: Literature of Region(s) or Nation(s)?', in James A. Davies and Glyn Pursglove (eds), *Writing Region and Nation*, special number of *The Swansea Review*, University of Wales, Swansea, 1994, pp. 63–83.
15. Bernard O'Donoghue, *Seamus Heaney and the Language of Poetry* (Hemel Hempstead, Herts: Harvester Wheatsheaf, 1994).
16. Seamus Heaney, 'From Monaghan to the Grand Canal', *Preoccupations*, p. 116.
17. Cf. Patrick Kavanagh's essay on 'The Parish and the Universe' with its claims for the 'parochial' as against the 'provincial': 'The provincial has no mind of his own. ... The parochial mentality on the other hand is never in any doubt about the social and artistic validity of his parish.'
18. Heaney, *Preoccupations*, pp. 57–9.
19. O'Donoghue, op. cit., p. 145. O'Donoghue is here paraphrasing what Heaney writes in his critical work *The Government of the Tongue*

(London: Faber and Faber, 1988); and the words in double inverted commas are those which he quotes from Heaney himself.

10   Regional, National and Post-Colonial (II)

1. I am specifically indebted here, as I am generally in my treatment of Murray's work, to the essay by Bruce Clunies Ross on 'Les Murray and the Poetry of Australia', in Draper (ed.), *The Literature of Region and Nation*, pp. 206–18.

2. Allen Curnow, *Selected Poems 1940–1989* (London: Penguin Books, 1990) p. 204.

3. Ibid., p. 198. Curnow adds a comment on the pronunciation of Karekare ('rather like English "carry-carry"'), and suggests that 'a native (or instructed) Maori speaker might give the vowels different values, more like Italian' – a hint perhaps that his taste for serious word-play led Curnow to make a connection between the fates of Moro and the Maori.

4. Patrick Evans, *The Penguin History of New Zealand Literature* (Auckland: Penguin, 1990) p. 235.

5. Henry Kreisel, in *Contexts of Canadian Criticism*, ed. Eli Mandel (Chicago: University of Chicago Press, 1971) p. 261.

6. Dorothy Livesay, 'The Documentary Poem: A Canadian Genre' (1961). The Lampman poem is 'At the Long Sault'.

7. Dennis Cooley, 'Nearer by Far: The Upset "I" in Margaret Atwood's Poetry', in *Margaret Atwood: Writing and Subjectivity*, ed. Colin Nicholson (Basingstoke and London: Macmillan, 1994) p. 72.

8. Quoted by George Woodcock, 'Margaret Atwood: Poet as Novelist', in *Critical Essays on Margaret Atwood*, ed. Judith McCombs (Boston, Mass.: G. K. Hall, 1988) p. 98.

9. Margaret Atwood in *Margaret Atwood: Conversations*, ed. Earl G. Ingersoll (London: Virago Press, 1992) p. 14. Cf. also the interview with Joyce Carol Oates, p. 73, where specific reference is made to Canadian attitudes to the USA, and allied to groups such as women, blacks and Québecois.

10. Robert D. Hamner, *Derek Walcott* (Boston: Twayne, 1981; revised edition, 1993) p. 143.

11. Paula Burnett explains that 'rass' is a Caribbean swear-word, but that in the language of Rastafarians 'Ras' is 'the appellation of holiness' (see *The Penguin Book of Caribbean Verse in English*, ed. Paula Burnett, London: Penguin Books, 1986, p. 420).

12. Quoted in Burnett, op. cit., p. 430.

13. 'Tie my hands up. / Poke out my eye.'

14. 'But you can't stop my cock [penis] flooding in the gold mine / Can't stop my cock splashing in the sunshine!'

15. Clement H. Wyke, '"Divided to the Vein": Patterns of Tormented Ambivalence in Walcott's *The Fortunate Traveller*', in *Postcolonial Literatures*, ed. Michael Parker and Roger Starkey (Basingstoke and London: Macmillan, 1995) p. 211. The phrase 'divided to the vein'

comes from 'A Far Cry from Africa' (in the volume *In a Green Night*, 1962).

16. Derek Walcott, *The Antilles: Fragments of Epic Memory* (New York: Farrar, Straus and Giroux, 1993; London: Faber and Faber, 1993) p. 9. The Antilles is the name of the string of Caribbean islands of which the (formerly) British West Indies are a part.

17. Ibid., p. 16.

18. Article by John Figueroa in *The Art of Derek Walcott*, ed. Stewart Brown (Bridgend, Mid Glamorgan: Seren Books, 1991) p. 211.

19. Walcott, *The Antilles*, p. 28.

20. 'Arms and the man I sing', alluding to Aeneas, hero of Vergil's *Aeneid* and mythical founder of the Roman dynasty. This becomes a standard epic formula, echoed in countless European epics, including Milton's *Paradise Lost*, which begins with the resonant lines: 'Of man's first disobedience, and the fruit / Of that forbidden tree ... Sing, Heavenly Muse.'

21. For a fuller discussion of epic adaptation and change see *The Epic: Developments in Criticism*, ed. R. P. Draper (London and Basingstoke: Macmillan, 1990).

11   Experiment and Tradition

1. A rather wooden paraphrase of this poem in Received Standard English would go something like this:

    You've *got* to ...

    > You don't
    > (you understand?) –
    >
    > you don't owe
    > (you understand?) those –
    > you've got to get –
    >
    > (you understand?) those dirty –
    > you've got to get rid of –
    > you don't owe nothing –

    Listen, buddy, *listen*:

    > those
    > God-
    > damned,
    >
    > little, yellow, bas-
    > tards – we're going

    to *civilize* them.

2. Edwin Morgan dates its use to 1955 in an article by the Brazilian poet Augusto de Campos, and an exhibition in São Paulo held in November of that year. See Edwin Morgan, 'Into the Constellation: Some thoughts

on the origin and nature of concrete poetry', *akros*, vol. 6, no. 8 (March 1972) pp. 3–18.

3. For the development of this argument see my article on 'Concrete Poetry' in *New Literary History*, II, no. 2 (Winter 1971) pp. 329–40.

4. Finlay's comment on the poem as reproduced in *Concrete Poetry: An International Anthology*, ed. Stephen Bann (London: London Magazine Editions, 1967).

5. The 'play' element is emphasised by a further sentence in Finlay's own comment: 'Properly, the poem should be constructed of cut-out letters, to occupy not a page but an entire wall above a children's playground.'

6. Note contributed by Morgan to the catalogue of the ICA exhibition, *Between Poetry and Painting* (London: ICA, 1965).

7. Quoted by Leslie Wolf, 'The Brushstroke's Integrity: The Poetry of John Ashbery and the Art of Painting', in David Lehman (ed.), *Beyond Amazement: New Essays on John Ashbery* (Ithaca, New York and London: Cornell University Press, 1980) p. 237.

8. Compare another remark made by Ashbery in an interview: 'Polyphony and polytonality are privileges which I envy composers for having' (Lehman, op. cit., pp. 111–12).

9. David Shapiro, *John Ashbery: An Introduction to the Poetry* (New York: Columbia University Press, 1979) p. 23.

10. Ibid., p. 30.

11. For a more elaborate account of Ashbery's rhetoric see Douglas Crase, 'The Prophetic Ashbery', in Lehman, op. cit., pp. 45–50.

12. See Keith Cohen's 'Ashbery's Dismantling of Bourgeois Discourse', in Lehman, op. cit., pp. 128–48. Despite its too blatantly Marxist line, Cohen's analysis of 'Decoy' provides a convincing example of the way Ashbery's poetry undermines received standards, not by head-on, didactic attack, but by a more humorous subversion of the tradition of discourse on which they are based.

13. Philip Larkin, *Required Writing* (London: Faber and Faber, 1983) pp. 74–5.

14. Op. cit., p. 72.

15. Op. cit., p. 293.

16. The image is 'Shakespearean' in two ways. It echoes but, of course, also transmutes Hamlet's words to Laertes:

> Let my disclaiming from a purpos'd evil
> Free me so far in your most generous thoughts
> That I have shot my arrow o'er the house
> And hurt my brother.

(Hamlet, V. ii. 233–6)

And, on Larkin's own evidence, it is prompted by the representation of the English archery at the Battle of Agincourt in Laurence Olivier's film of *Henry V* (see Andrew Motion, *Philip Larkin*, London: Faber and Faber, 1993, p. 288).

Select Bibliography

INDIVIDUAL POETS
PRIMARY TEXTS; SELECT BIOGRAPHY; CRITICISM

Adcock, Fleur (b. 1934)
Selected Poems (London: Oxford University Press, 1983; paperback 1991).
The Incident Book (Oxford: Oxford University Press, 1986).
Meeting the Comet (Newcastle: Bloodaxe, 1988).
Time Zones (Oxford: Oxford University Press, 1991).

Angelou, Maya (b. 1928)
The Complete Collected Poems (New York: Random House, 1994; London: Virago, 1994).

Armitage, Simon (b. 1963)
Zoom (Newcastle: Bloodaxe, 1989).
Xanadu (Newcastle: Bloodaxe, 1992).
Kid (London: Faber and Faber, 1992).
Book of Matches (London: Faber and Faber, 1993).

Ashbery, John (b. 1927)
Selected Poems (New York: Viking Penguin Inc., 1985; Manchester: Carcanet Press, 1986); paperback edition (London: Paladin, 1987) adds 'These Lacustrine Cities' and ' "America is a Fun Country ..." '.
April Galleons (New York, 1987; Manchester: Carcanet, 1987; London: Paladin/Grafton, 1988).
Flow Chart (Manchester: Carcanet, 1991).
Hotel Lautreamont (New York, 1992; Manchester, 1992).
And The Stars Were Shining (Manchester: Carcanet, 1994).
Can You Hear, Bird (Manchester: Carcanet, 1996).

Hoeppner, Edward Howarth, *Echoes and Moving Fields: Structure and Subjectivity in the Poetry of W. S. Merwin and John Ashbery* (Lewisburg, PA: Bucknell University Press, 1994).
Lehman, David (ed.), *Beyond Amazement: New Esssays on John Ashbery* (Ithaca and London: Cornell University Press, 1980).
Shapiro, David, *John Ashbery: An Introduction to the Poetry* (New York: Columbia University Press, 1979).
Shoptaw, John, *On the Outside Looking Out: John Ashbery's Poetry* (Cambridge, MA: Harvard University Press, 1994).

Atwood, Margaret (b. 1939)
Poems, 1965–1975 (Toronto: Oxford University Press, 1976; New York: Houghton Mifflin, 1976; London: Virago Press (Introduction by Margaret Atwood), 1991).

Poems, 1976–1986 (New York: Houghton Mifflin, 1987; London: Virago Press, 1992).

Davidson, Arnold E., and Cathy N. (eds), *The Art of Margaret Atwood: Essays in Criticism* (Toronto: Anansi, 1981).
Grace, Sherrill, *Violent Duality* (Montreal: Vehicule Press, 1980).
Howells, Coral Ann, *Margaret Atwood* (London and Basingstoke: Macmillan, 1996). (Novels mainly.)
McCombs, Judith (ed.), *Critical Essays on Margaret Atwood* (Boston: G. K. Hall, 1988).
Nicholson, Colin (ed.), *Margaret Atwood: Writing and Subjectivity: New Critical Eassys* (London and Basingstoke: Macmillan, 1994; New York: St Martin's Press, 1994).
Rosenberg, Jerome, *Margaret Atwood* (Boston: Twayne, 1984).
Van Spanckeren, Kathryn, and Castro, Jan Garden (eds), *Margaret Atwood: Vision and Forms* (Carbondale: Southern Illinois University Press, 1988).

Auden, Wystan Hugh (1907–73)

Collected Shorter Poems, 1930–1944 (London: Faber & Faber, 1950).
Collected Shorter Poems, 1927–1957 (London: Faber & Faber, 1966; New York: Random House, 1967).
Collected Longer Poems (London: Faber & Faber, 1968; New York: Random House, 1969).
Collected Poems, ed. Edward Mendelson (London: Faber & Faber, 1976; New York: Random House, 1976; revised edition, 1991).
The English Auden: Poems, Essays, and Dramatic Writings, 1927–1939, ed. Edward Mendelson (London: Faber & Faber, 1977; New York: Random House, 1978). (Includes 'September 1, 1939' and earlier versions of poems revised in *Collected Poems*).
Plays and Other Dramatic Writings, 1928–1938; Libretti (2 vols), ed. Edward Mendelson (Princeton: Princeton University Press, 1988 and 1993). (First volumes of new complete edition of Auden's works.)
The Dyer's Hand and Other Essays (London: Faber and Faber, 1963). (Essays by Auden on a variety of themes.)

Bloomfield, B. C., and Mendelson, Edward, *W. H. Auden: A Bibliography, 1924–1969* (Charlottesville, VA: University Press of Virginia, 1972).
Carpenter, Humphrey, *W. H. Auden: A Biography* (London: George Allen & Unwin, 1981; revised paperback edition, 1983).

Bahlke, George W. (ed.), *Critical Essays on W. H. Auden* (New York: G. K. Hall, 1991). (Extracts from various commentators, including Randall Jarrell, Richard Hoggart, Edward Mendelson, Cleanth Brooks, Igor Stravinsky and Stephen Spender.)
Beach, Joseph Warren, *The Making of the Auden Canon* (Minneapolis: University of Minnesota Press, 1957).
Boly, John R., *Reading Auden: The Returns of Caliban* (Ithaca and London: Cornell University Press, 1991).

Fuller, John, *A Reader's Guide to W. H. Auden* (London: Thames & Hudson, 1970; New York: Farrar, Straus & Giroux, 1970).
——, *Pleasing Ma: The Poetry of W. H. Auden* (Kenneth Allott Lecture), Liverpool Classical Monthly, Liverpool, 1995.
Haffenden, John (ed.), *W. H. Auden: The Critical Heritage* (London: Routledge and Kegan Paul, 1983). (Collection of reviews of Auden's work, 1930–74.)
Hecht, Anthony, *The Hidden Law: The Poetry of W. H. Auden* (Cambridge, MA, and London: Harvard University Press, 1993).
Hynes, Samuel, *The Auden Generation* (London: Bodley Head, 1976; New York, 1977).
Mendelson, Edward, *Early Auden* (London and Boston: Faber & Faber, 1981).
Replogle, Justin, *Auden's Poetry* (University of Washington Press, 1969; London: Methuen, 1969).
Rodway, Allan, *A Preface to Auden* (London: Longman, 1984).
Smith, Stan, *W. H. Auden* (Oxford and New York: Blackwell, 1985).
Whitehead, John, *A Commentary on the Poetry of W. H. Auden, C. Day Lewis and Stephen Spender* (Lewiston, New York: The Edwin Mellen Press; Queenston, Ontario; Lampeter, Wales, 1992).

Baraka, Amiri [LeRoi Jones] (b. 1934)

Selected Poetry (New York, 1979).
The LeRoi Jones/Amiri Baraka Reader, ed. W. J. Harris and A. Baraka (New York: Thunder's Mouth Press, 1991).

Baxter, James K. (1926–72)

Collected Poems, ed. J. E. Weir (Wellington and New York: Oxford University Press and Price Milburn, 1979).

Mckay, Frank, *The Life of James K. Baxter* (Auckland and Oxford: Oxford University Press, 1990).
Oliver, W. H., *James K. Baxter: A Portrait* (Auckland: Godwit Press, 1983).

Doyle, Charles, *James K. Baxter* (Boston, 1976).
O'Sullivan, V. G., *James K. Baxter* (Wellington and New York: Oxford University Press, 1976).
Weir, J. E., *The Poetry of James K. Baxter* (Wellington, 1970).

Berryman, John (1914–72)

The Dream Songs (New York: Farrar, Straus & Giroux, 1969; London: Faber and Faber, 1990).
Selected Poems, 1938–1968 (London: Faber and Faber, 1972).
Collected Poems, 1937–1971, ed. Charles Thornbury (New York, 1989; London, 1990).
The Freedom of the Poet (Criticism and short stories) (New York: Farrar, Straus & Giroux, 1976).

Haffenden, John, *The Life of John Berryman* (London and Boston: Routledge & Kegan Paul, 1982).

Mariani, Paul, *Dream Song: The Life of John Berryman* (New York: Morrow, 1990).

Connaroe, Joel, *John Berryman: An Introduction to the Poetry* (New York: Columbia University Press, 1977).
Haffenden, John, *John Berryman: A Critical Commentary* (London and Basingstoke: Macmillan, 1980; New York, 1980).
Kelly, Richard J., and Lathrop, Alan (eds), *Recovering Berryman: Essays on a Poet* (Ann Arbor: University of Michigan Press, 1993).
Matterson, Stephen, *Berryman and Lowell: The Art of Losing* (Totowa, NJ: Barnes & Noble, 1988).

Betjeman, Sir John (1906–84)
Summoned by Bells (London: John Murray, 1960).
Collected Poems (London: John Murray, 1958, 1962, 1979).
The Best of Betjeman, ed. John Guest (London: John Murray, 1978; Harmondsworth: Penguin Books, 1996).

Hillier, Bevis, *Young Betjeman* (London: Cardinal, 1988).

Blamires, Harry, *John Betjeman: Selected Poems* (Harlow: Longman, 1992).
Larkin, Philip, 'The Blending of Betjeman', in *Required Writing* (London: Faber and Faber, 1983) pp. 129–33.

Bishop, Elizabeth (1911–79)
Complete Poems, 1927–1979 (New York: Farrar, Straus & Giroux, 1983; London: Chatto & Windus, 1983).
Collected Prose, ed. Robert Giroux (short stories and other writings) (New York: Farrar, Straus & Giroux, 1984; London: Chatto & Windus, 1994).

Dareski, Carole Kiler, *Elizabeth Bishop: The Restraints of Language* (New York and Oxford: Oxford University Press, 1993).
Dodd, Elizabeth Caroline, *The Veiled Mirror and the Woman Poet: H.D., Louise Bogan, Elizabeth Bishop and Louise Gluck* (Columbia and London: University of Missouri Press, 1992).
Goldensohn, Lorrie, *Elizabeth Bishop: The Biography of a Poetry* (New York and Oxford: Columbia University Press, 1992).
Heaney, Seamus, 'The Government of the Tongue', in *The Government of the Tongue* (London: Faber and Faber, 1988).
Heaney Seamus, 'Counting to a Hundred: On Elizabeth Bishop', *The Redress of Poetry* (London: Faber and Faber, 1995; paperback 1996).
Lombardi, Marilyn May, *The Body and the Song: Elizabeth Bishop's Poetics* (Carbondale: Southern Illinois University Press, 1995).
McCabe, Susan, *Elizabeth Bishop: Her Poetics of Loss* (University Park, PA: Pennsylvania State University Press, 1994).
Miller, Brett, *Elizabeth Bishop: Life and the Memory of It* (Berkeley and London: University of California Press, 1993).

Rotella, Guy L., *Reading and Writing Nature: The Poetry of Robert Frost, Wallace Stevens, Marianne Moore and Elizabeth Bishop* (Boston: Northeastern University Press, 1991).

Blunden, Edmund (1896–1974)
Selected Poems, ed. Robyn Marsack (Manchester: Carcanet, 1982).
Undertones of War (autobiography) (London: Cobden-Sanderson, 1928, revised edition, 1930; Harmondsworth: Penguin, 1937, reprinted 1982).

Webb, Barry, *Edmund Blunden: A Biography* (New Haven and London: Yale University Press, 1990).

Mallon, Thomas, *Edmund Blunden* (Boston: Twayne, 1983).
Thorpe, Michael, *The Poetry of Edmund Blunden* (Wateringbury, Kent, 1971).

Bly, Robert (b. 1926)
Selected Poems (New York, 1986).

Nelson, Howard, *Robert Bly: An Introduction to the Poetry* (New York: Columbia University Press, 1984).

Bowering, George (b. 1935)
Selected Poems: Particular Accidents, ed. Robin Blaser (Vancouver and Los Angeles: Talonbooks, 1980).

Brathwaite, Edward Kamau (b. 1930)
Other Exiles (London: Oxford University Press, 1975).
Mother Poem (London: Oxford University Press, 1977).
Middle Passages (Newcastle: Bloodaxe, 1992).

Brooke, Rupert (1887–1915)
Collected Poems, ed. Edward March (London: Sidgwick & Jackson, 1918); with Introduction by Gavin Ewart (London: Papermac, 1992).
The Works of Rupert Brooke (Ware: Wordsworth, 1994).
Letters of Rupert Brooke, ed. Geoffrey Keynes (London: Faber and Faber, 1968).

Hassall, Christopher, *Rupert Brooke* (London: Faber and Faber, 1964).
Lehmann, John, *Rupert Brooke: His Life and His Legend* (London and New York: Quartet Books, 1981).

Brooks, Gwendolyn (b. 1917)
Selected Poems (New York: Harper & Row, 1963).

Brown, George Mackay (b. 1921)
Selected Poems, 1954–1983 (London: John Murray, 1991).
Following a Lark (London: Murray, 1996).

Bold, Alan, *George Mackay Brown* (Edinburgh: Oliver & Boyd, 1978).

Bruce, George (b. 1909)
Selected Poems (Edinburgh: Oliver and Boyd, 1947).
Collected Poems (Edinburgh: Edinburgh University Press, 1971).
Perspectives: Poems 1970–1986 (Aberdeen: Aberdeen University Press, 1987).

Alexander J. H., ' "Make Marble the Moment": The Poetry of George Bruce', in David Hewitt (ed.), *Northern Visions* (East Linton, East Lothian: Tuckwell Press, 1995) pp. 82–98.

Bunting, Basil (1900–85)
Complete Poems, ed. Richard Caddel (Oxford: Oxford University Press, 1994).

Forde, Victoria, *The Poetry of Basil Bunting* (Newcastle: Bloodaxe, 1991).
Makin, Peter, *Bunting: The Shaping of His Verse* (Oxford: Oxford University Press, 1992).

Carson, Ciaran (b. 1948)
The New Estate and Other Poems (Oldcastle, Co. Meath: Gallery Press, 1988).
Belfast Confetti (Oldcastle, Co. Meath: Gallery Press, 1989; reprinted Newcastle: Bloodaxe, 1990).
Letters from the Alphabet (Oldcastle, Co. Meath: Gallery Press, 1995).

Causley, Charles (b. 1917)
Collected Poems (London and Basingstoke: Macmillan, 1975).
Collected Poems (London and Basingstoke: Macmillan, 1992).
Collected Poems 1951–1997 (London and Basingstoke: Macmillan, 1997).

Clampitt, Amy (b. 1920)
The Kingfisher (London: Faber and Faber, 1983).
What the Light Was Like (London: Faber and Faber, 1985).
Archaic Figure (London: Faber and Faber, 1989).
The Collected Poems (London: Faber & Faber, 1998).

Crane, Hart (1899–1932)
Collected Poems, ed. Waldo Frank (New York: Liveright, 1933).
Collected Poems and Selected Letters and Prose, ed. Brom Weber (New York: Liveright, 1966). Reprinted as *Complete Poems*, ed. Brom Weber (Newcastle: Bloodaxe Books, 1984).
Poems, ed. Marc Simon (Introduction by John Unterecker) (New York: Liveright, 1986).
Letters of Hart Crane, 1916–1932, ed. Brom Weber (New York: Hermitage House, 1952; Berkeley: University of California Press, 1965).
Letters of Hart Crane and His Family, ed. Thomas S. W. Lewis (New York: Columbia University Press, 1974).

Horton, Philip, *Hart Crane: The Life of an American Poet* (New York: W. W. Norton, 1937).
Unterecker, John, *Voyager: A Life of Hart Crane* (New York: Farrar, Straus & Giroux, 1969).

Weber, Brom, *Hart Crane: A Biographical and Critical Study* (New York: Bodley, 1948).

Berthoff, Warner, *Hart Crane: A Re-Introduction* (Minneapolis: University of Minnesota Press, 1989).
Bloom, Harold (ed.), *Hart Crane: Modern Criitical Views* (New York: Chelsea House, 1986).
Brunner, Edward, *Splendid Failure: Hart Crane and the Making of 'The Bridge'* (Urbana: University of Illinois Press, 1985).
Combs, Robert, *Vision of the Voyage: Hart Crane and the Psychology of Romanticism* (Memphis: Memphis State University Press, 1978).
Hazo, Samuel, *Hart Crane: An Introduction and Interpretation* (New York: Barnes and Noble, 1963).
Paul, Sherman, *Hart's Bridge* (Urbana: University of Illinois Press, 1972).
Spears, Monroe K., *Hart Crane* (St Paul: University of Minnesota Press, 1965).
Trochtenberg, Alan (ed.), *Hart Crane: A Collection of Critical Essays* (Englewood Cliffs, NJ: Prentice-Hall, 1982).

Creeley, Robert (b. 1926)

Collected Poems 1945–1975 (Berkeley: University of California Press, 1982).
Selected Poems 1945–1990 (Berkeley: University of California Press, 1991; London: Boyars, 1991).

Edelberg, Cynthia Dubin, *Robert Creeley's Poetry: A Critical Introduction* (Albuquerque: University of New Mexico Press, 1978).

Cullen, Countee (1903–46)

My Soul's High Song: The Collected Writings of Countee Cullen, Voice of the Harlem Renaissance, ed. Gerald Early (New York and London: Anchor, 1991).

cummings, e. e. [edward estlin] (1884–1962)

Complete Poems, 1904–1962, ed. George James Firmage (New York and London: Liveright, 1991; revised edition, 1994).
Selected Poems, ed. Richard S. Kennedy (New York: Liveright, 1994).

Friedman, Norman, *e. e. cummings: The Art of His Poetry* (Baltimore and London, 1960).
Kennedy, Richard S., *e.e. cummings Revisited* (New York: Twayne, 1994).
Rotella, Guy (ed.), *Critical Essays on e. e. cummings* (Boston: G. K. Hall, 1984).

Curnow, Allen (b. 1911)

Selected Poems, 1940–1989 (New York: Penguin Books, Viking, 1990; London and Auckland: Penguin Books, 1990).
Early Days Yet: New and Collected Poems, 1941–1997 (Manchester: Carcanet, 1997).
New and Collected Poems, 1941–1995 (Manchester: Carcanet, 1997).
Look Back Harder: Critical Writings, 1935–1984 (Auckland: Auckland University Press, 1987).

Evans, Patrick, *The Penguin History of New Zealand Literature* (Auckland: Penguin Books, 1990).

Dabydeen, Cyril (b. 1945)
Distances (Vancouver: Fiddlehead, 1977).
Goatsong (Ottawa: Mosaic, 1977).
Stoning the Wind (Toronto: TSAR, 1994).

Dabydeen, David (b. 1955)
Slave Song (Mundelsrup, Denmark: Dangaroo Press, 1984).
Coolie Odyssey (London: Hansib, 1988).
Turner: New and Selected Poems (London: Cape, 1994).

D'Aguiar, Fred (b. 1960)
Mama Dot (London: Chatto & Windus, 1985).
Airy Hall (London: Chatto & Windus, 1989).
The Longest Memory (London: Chatto & Windus, 1994).

Daryush, Elizabeth (1887–1977)
Collected Poems (Introduction by Donald Davie) (Manchester: Carcanet, 1976).
Selected Poems (Manchester: Carcanet, 1985).

Davie, Donald (1922–95)
Collected Poems (Manchester: Carcanet, 1990).
Poems and Melodramas (Manchester: Carcanet, 1996).
Purity of Diction in English Verse (criticism) (London, 1952; New York, 1953).
These the Companions: Recollections (autobiography) (Cambridge: Cambridge University Press, 1982).
Articulate Energy (criticism) (London: Routledge & Kegan Paul, 1955; New York: Harcourt, Brace, 1958).
Ezra Pound: Poet as Sculptor (criticism) (New York, 1964; London, 1965).
Thomas Hardy and British Poetry (criticism) (London: Routledge & Kegan Paul, 1973).
Studies in Ezra Pound (Manchester: Carcanet, 1991).
New Oxford Book of Christian Verse (editor) (Oxford and New York: Oxford University Press, 1981).

Bergonzi, Bernard, *The Myth of Modernism and Twentieth Century Literature* (Chapters 5 and 11) (Brighton: Harvester, 1986).
Dekker, George (ed.), *Donald Davie and the Responsibilities of Literature* (Manchester: Carcanet, 1983).

Day Lewis, Cecil (1904–72)
Poems, ed. Ian Parsons (London: Cape, 1977).
Collected Poems, ed. Jill Balcon (Stanford, CA: Stanford University Press, 1982; London: Sinclair-Stevenson, 1992).
Selected Poems (Harmondsworth: Penguin, 1951).
The Buried Day (autobiography) (London: Chatto & Windus, 1960).

A Hope for Poetry (criticism) (Oxford: Blackwell, 1934).
The Poetic Image (criticism) (London: Cape, 1947).

Doolittle, Hilda ['H.D.'] (1886–1961)
Collected Poems, 1912–1944, ed. Louis L. Martz (New York, 1983; Manchester: Carcanet, 1984).
Selected Poems, ed. Louis L. Martz (Manchester: Carcanet, 1989).

Dodd, Elizabeth Caroline: *see under* **Bishop, Elizabeth**.
Friedman, Susan, S., and DuPlessis, Rachel B. (eds), *Signets: Reading H.D.* (Madison: University of Wisconsin Press, 1990).
Guest, Barbara, *Herself Defined: The Poet H.D. and her World* (Garden City, NY: Doubleday, 1984).

Douglas, Keith (1920–44)
Complete Poems, ed. Desmond Graham (Oxford: Oxford University Press, 1987).

Graham, Desmond, *Keith Douglas, 1920–1944* (Oxford: Oxford University Press, 1974).

Davie, Donald, 'Remembering the Western Desert', in *Under Briggflatts* (Manchester: Carcanet, 1989).
Hughes, Ted, 'The Poetry of Keith Douglas', *Critical Quarterly*, vol. 5, no. 1 (Spring 1963) pp. 43–8.
Longley, Edna, '"Shit or Bust": The Importance of Keith Douglas', in *Poetry in the Wars* (Newcastle: Bloodaxe Books, 1986).

Duncan, Robert (b. 1919)
Selected Poems (San Fransisco: City Light Books, 1959).
Roots and Branches (New York: New Directions, 1964).
Derivations: Selected Poems, 1950–1956 (London: Fulcrum, 1968).

Dunn, Douglas (b. 1942)
Selected Poems, 1964–1983 (London: Faber and Faber, 1986).
New and Selected Poems, 1966–1988 (New York, 1989).
Elegies (London: Faber and Faber, 1985).
Northlight (London: Faber and Faber, 1988).
Dante's Drum-Kit (London: Faber and Faber, 1993).
The Faber Book of Twentieth-Century Scottish Poetry (editor) (London: Faber and Faber, 1992).

Eberhart, Richard (b. 1904)
Collected Poems, 1930–1986 (New York and Oxford: Oxford University Press, 1986).

Engel, Bernard F., *Richard Eberhart* (Boston: Twayne, 1971).
Mills, R. E., *Richard Eberhart* (Minneapolis: University of Minnesota Press, 1966).
Roache, Joel, *Richard Eberhart* (New York, 1971).

Eliot, Thomas Stearns (1888–1965)
Collected Poems, 1909–1962 (London and New York: Faber and Faber, 1963).
Collected Plays (London: Faber and Faber, 1962).
Complete Poems and Plays (London: Faber and Faber, 1969).
The Waste Land, a facsimile and transcript of the original drafts, ed. Valerie Eliot (London: Faber and Faber, 1971).
Old Possum's Book of Practical Cats (London: Faber and Faber, 1939).
Inventions of the March Hare: Poems, 1909–1917, ed. Christopher Ricks (London: Faber and Faber, 1996).
Selected Essays (criticism) (London: Faber and Faber, 1932).
Selected Prose, ed. John Hayward (criticism) (Harmondsworth: Penguin Books, 1953).
Selected Prose of T. S. Eliot, ed. Frank Kermode (criticism) (London: Faber and Faber, 1975).
Letters, ed. Valerie Eliot (London: Faber and Faber, 1988).

Ackroyd, Peter, *T. S. Eliot* (London, 1984).
Gordon, Lyndall, *Eliot's Early Years* (Oxford and New York: Oxford University Press, 1977).
——, *Eliot's New Life* (Oxford and New York: Oxford University Press, 1988).

Bergonzi, Bernard, *T. S. Eliot: 'Four Quartets'* (Casebook Series) (London and Basingstoke: Macmillan, 1969).
Blamires, Harry, *Word Unheard: A Guide through T. S. Eliot's 'Four Quartets'* (London: Methuen, 1969).
Bloom, Harold (ed.), *T. S. Eliot* (Modern Critical Views series) (New York: Chelsea House, 1985).
Cookson, Lynda, and Loughrey, Brian (eds), *Critical Essays on 'The Waste Land'* (Harlow: Longman, 1989).
Cox, C. B., and Hinchliffe, Arnold P. (eds), *T. S. Eliot: 'The Waste Land'* (Casebook Series) (London and Basingstoke: Macmillan, 1968).
Frye, Northrop, *T. S. Eliot* (Edinburgh: Oliver and Boyd, 1963).
Gardner, Helen, *The Art of T. S. Eliot* (London: Cresset Press and Dutton, 1949; revised edition, 1965).
——, *The Composition of 'Four Quartets'* (London: Faber and Faber, 1978).
Grant, M. (ed.), *T. S. Eliot: The Critical Heritage* (2 vols) (London: Routledge & Kegan Paul, 1982).
Kenner, Hugh, *The Invisible Poet: T. S. Eliot* (London: W. H. Allen, 1960).
Matthiessen, F. O., *The Achievement of T. S. Eliot* (Oxford: Oxford University Press, 1935).
Moody, A. D., *T. S. Eliot: Poet* (Cambridge: Cambridge University Press, 1980).
——, *The Cambridge Companion to T. S. Eliot* (Cambridge: Cambridge University Press, 1994).
Rajan, B. (ed.), *T. S. Eliot: A Study of His Writings by Several Hands* (London: Dennis Dobson, 1947).
Ricks, Christopher, *T. S. Eliot and Prejudice* (Berkeley: University of California Press, 1988; London: Faber and Faber, 1988).

Scofield, Martin, *T. S. Eliot: The Poems* (Cambridge: Cambridge University Press, 1988).

Smith, Grover Cleveland, *T. S. Eliot's Poetry and Plays: A Study in Sources and Meaning* (Chicago: University of Chicago Press, 1956).

Sharpe, Tony, *T. S. Eliot: A Literary Life* (London and Basingstoke: Macmillan, 1991).

Southam, B. C., *A Student's Guide to the 'Selected Poems' of T. S. Eliot* (from 'Prufrock to the 'Ariel' poems). (London: Faber and Faber, 1968).

Tamplin, Ronald, *A Preface to T. S. Eliot* (London: Longman, 1987)

Wilks, A. J., *A Critical Commentary on T. S. Eliot: 'The Waste Land'* (London and Basingstoke: Macmillan, 1971).

Empson, William (1906–84)

Collected Poems (New York: Harcourt Brace, 1949; London: Chatto & Windus, 1955).

The Royal Beasts and Other Works, ed. John Haffenden (London: Chatto & Windus, 1986).

Seven Types of Ambiguity (criticism) (London: Chatto & Windus, 1930).

Some Versions of Pastoral (criticism) (London: Chatto & Windus, 1935).

The Structure of Complex Words (criticism) (London: Chatto & Windus, 1951).

Constable, J. (ed.), *Critical Essays on William Empson* (Aldershot: Scolar Press, 1993).

Gardner, Philip and Avril, *The God Approached: A Commentary on the Poems of William Empson* (London: Chatto & Windus, 1978).

Gill, Roma (ed.), *William Empson: The Man and His Work* (London: Routledge & Kegan Paul, 1974).

Enright, Dennis Joseph (b. 1920)

Collected Poems (Oxford and New York: Oxford University Press, 1987).

Ewart, Gavin (b. 1916)

The Collected Ewart, 1933–1980 (London: Hutchinson, 1980).

Selected Poems, 1933–93 (London: Hutchinson, 1996).

Fanthorpe, Ursula Askham (b. 1929)

Selected Poems (Liskeard, Cornwall: Peterloo Poets, 1986; Harmondsworth: Penguin Books, 1986).

A Watching Brief (Liskeard, Cornwall: Peterloo Poets, 1987).

Neck-Verse (Liskeard, Cornwall: Peterloo Poets, 1992).

Figueroa, John Joseph Maria (b. 1920)

The Chace: A Collection of Poems, 1941–1989 (Leeds: Peepal Tree, 1992).

An Anthology of African and Caribbean Writing in English (Portsmouth: Heinemann, 1982).

Finlay, Ian Hamilton (b. 1925)

The Dancers Inherit the Party (Ventura, USA and Worcester: Migrant Press, 1959).

Canal Stripes Series (Edinburgh: Wild Hawthorn Press, 1964).

Glasgow Beasts, An a Burd (Edinburgh: Wild Hawthorn Press, 1960; Edinburgh: Polygon, 1996).
Telegrams from my Windmill (Edinburgh: Wild Hawthorn Press, 1964).
Open Stripe Series (Edinburgh: Wild Hawthorn Press, 1965).
[See also the examples of Finlay's work in the various anthologies listed under 'Anthologies: Concrete Poetry'.]

Abroux, Yves, *Ian Hamilton Finlay: A Visual Primer* (1985).
Murray, Graeme (ed.), *Ian Hamilton Finlay and The Wild Hawthorn Press, 1958–1991* (Edinburgh: Graeme Murray, 1991).

Flint, Frank Stuart (1885–1960)
In the Net of the Stars (London: Elkin Matthews, 1909).
Otherworld: Cadences (London: Poetry Bookshop, 1915).

Fraser, George Sutherland (1915–80)
Poems of G. S. Fraser, ed. Ian Fletcher and John Lucas (Leicester: Leicester University Press, 1981).
The Modern Writer and His World (criticism) (London: Derek Verschoyle, 1953; revised 1963).
Vision and Rhetoric (criticism) (London: Faber and Faber, 1959).
Metre, Rhyme and Free Verse (criticism) (London: Methuen, 1970).
Essays on Twentieth Century Poets (criticism) (London: Faber and Faber, 1977).
A Stranger and Afraid (autobiography) (Manchester: Carcanet, 1983).

Bernard Bergonzi, 'Poets of the 1940s', in *The Myth of Modernism and Twentieth Century Literature* (Brighton: Harvester, 1986) pp. 129–42.
Draper, R. P., 'G. S. Fraser: The Poetry of Exile', in David Hewitt (ed.), *Northern Visions* (East Linton, East Lothian: Tuckwell Press, 1995) pp. 99–109.

Frost, Robert (1874–1963)
The Complete Poems of Robert Frost (London: Jonathan Cape, 1951).
Selected Poems (selected by Frost; Introduction by C. Day Lewis) (Harmondsworth: Penguin Books, 1955).
The Poetry of Robert Frost, ed. Edward Connery Latham (New York and London, 1969).
Selected Letters of Robert Frost, ed. Lawrence Thompson (New York, 1965).

Meyers, Jeffrey, *Robert Frost: A Biography* (London: Constable, 1996).
Pritchard, William H., *Frost: A Literary Life Reconsidered* (New York, 1984; London, 1985).
Thompson, Lawrence, and Winnick, R. H., *Robert Frost: A Biography* (3 vols) (New York, 1970–7; single-volume edition, 1981).

Brower, Reuben Arthur, *The Poetry of Robert Frost: Constellations of Intention* (Oxford: Oxford University Press, 1963).
Jennings, Elizabeth, *Robert Frost* (Edinburgh: Oliver and Boyd, 1964).
Marcus, Mordecai, *The Poems of Robert Frost: An Explication* (Boston: G. K. Hall, 1991).

Poirier, Richard, *Robert Frost: The Work of Knowing* (New York: Oxford University Press, 1977).
Rotella, Guy: *see under* **Bishop, Elizabeth**.

Fuller, John (b. 1937)
Selected Poems, 1954 to 1982 (London: Faber and Faber, 1985).

Fuller, Roy (1912–91)
New and Collected Poems, 1934–84 (London: Secker & Warburg, 1985).
Last Poems, ed. John Fuller (London: Sinclair-Stevenson, 1993).

Garioch, Robert Sutherland (1909–87)
Collected Poems (Loanhead, Scotland: Macdonald, 1977; Manchester: Carcanet, 1980).
Complete Poetical Works, ed. Robin Fulton (Edinburgh: Macdonald (for the Saltire Society), 1983).

Ginsberg, Allen (b. 1926)
Collected Poems, 1947–1980 (New York: Harper and Row, 1984).

Miles, Barry, *Allen Ginsberg: A Biography* (London: Viking, 1989; Harmondsworth: Penguin, 1990).

Hyde, Lewis (ed.), *On the Poetry of Allen Ginsberg* (Ann Arbor: University of Michigan Press, 1984).

Graham, William Sydney (1918–86)
Collected Poems, 1942–1977 (London: Faber and Faber, 1979).

Graves, Robert (1895–1985)
Complete Poems (3 vols), ed. Beryl Graves and Dunstan Ward (Manchester: Carcanet, 1995–).
Poems, 1914–27 (London, 1927).
Poems, 1938–1945 (London: Cassell, 1946).
Robert Graves: Poems Selected by Himself (Harmondsworth: Penguin Books, 1957).
Collected Poems, 1975 (London: Cassell, 1975).
Selected Poems, ed. Paul O'Prey (Harmondsworth: Penguin Books, 1986).
A Survey of Modernist Poetry, with Laura Riding (criticism) (London: Heinemann, 1927; reprinted, New York: Haskell House, 1969).
The White Goddess (prose) (London and New York, 1948; revised editions, 1952, 1961); ed. Grevel Lindop (Manchester: Carcanet, 1996).
The Common Asphodel (criticism) (London: Hamish Hamilton, 1949).
The Crowning Privilege (criticism) (London: Cassell, 1955).
Oxford Addresses on Poetry (criticism) (London: Cassell, 1962).
Collected Writings on Poetry, ed. Paul O'Prey (Manchester: Carcanet, 1995).
Goodbye To All That (autobiography) (London: Cassell, 1929; revised edition, 1957; Harmondsworth: Penguin Books, 1960).

Carter, D. N. G., *Robert Graves: The Lasting Poetic Achievement* (London and Basingstoke: Macmillan, 1989).
Day, Douglas, *Swifter than Reason: The Poetry and Criticism of Robert Graves* (Chapel Hill: University of North Carolina Press, 1963).
Kirkham, Michael, *The Poetry of Robert Graves* (London: Athlone Press, University of London, 1969).
Seymour-Smith, Martin, *Robert Graves* (Harlow: Longman (for the British Council), 1956; revised edition, 1970).
——, *Robert Graves: His Life and Work* (London and New York: Abacus, Sphere Books, 1983).

Gunn, Thom (b. 1929)
Collected Poems (London: Faber and Faber, 1993).

Dyson, A. E. (ed.), *Three Contemporary Poets: Thom Gunn, Ted Hughes and R. S. Thomas* (Casebook) (London and Basingstoke: Macmillan, 1990).

Gurney, Ivor (1890–1937)
Collected Poems, ed. P. J. Kavanagh (Oxford: Oxford University Press, 1982).
Selected Poems, ed. P. J. Kavanagh (Oxford: Oxford University Press, 1990).
Best Poems and the Book of Five Makings, ed. R. K. R. Thornton and George Walter (Ashington: Mid Northumberland Arts Group, and Manchester: Carcanet, 1995).

Hurd, Michael, *The Ordeal of Ivor Gurney* (Oxford: Oxford University Press, 1978).

Hardy, Thomas (1840–1928)
Complete Poems: Variorum Edition, ed. James Gibson (London and Basingstoke: Macmillan, 1978; New York: Macmillan Publishing Co., 1979).
Complete Poetical Works, ed. Samuel Hynes (3 vols) (Oxford and New York: Oxford University Press, 1982–5).
Thomas Hardy: A Selection, ed. Samuel Hynes (Oxford: Oxford University Press, 1984; World's Classics, 1996).
Selected Poems, ed. David Wright (Harmondsworth: Penguin Books, 1978).
Letters (7 vols), ed. Richard Little Purdy and Michael Millgate (Oxford and New York: Oxford University Press, 1978–88).
Personal Writings: Prefaces, Literary Opinions, Reminiscences (prose), ed. Harold Orel (Lawrence: University of Kansas Press, 1966; London: Macmillan, 1967).

Hardy, Florence Emily, *The Early Life of Thomas Hardy, 1840–1891* (London and New York: Macmillan, 1928).
——, *The Later Years of Thomas Hardy, 1892–1928* (London and New York: Macmillan, 1933).

(These two volumes were reissued in one volume as *The Life of Thomas Hardy, 1840–1928* (London: Macmillan, 1962; New York: St Martin's Press, 1962). They were both written in effect by Hardy himself, as explained in the revised edition, edited by Michael Millgate: *The Life and Work of Thomas Hardy*, London and Basingstoke: Macmillan, 1985.)

Gittings, Robert, *The Young Thomas Hardy* (London: Heinemann, 1975; Boston: Little Brown, 1975; revised edition, Harmondsworth: Penguin Books, 1978).

——, *The Older Hardy* (London: Heineman, 1978; revised edition, Harmondsworth: Penguin Books, 1980).

Millgate, Michael, *Thomas Hardy: A Biography* (Oxford: Oxford University Press, 1982; New York: Random House, 1982).

Seymour-Smith, Martin, *Hardy* (London: Bloomsbury, 1994).

Brooks, Jean, *Thomas Hardy: The Poetic Structure* (London: Paul Elek, 1971).

Clements, Patricia, and Grindle, Juliet (eds), *The Poetry of Thomas Hardy* (London: Vision Press, 1980).

Cox, R. G. (ed.), *Thomas Hardy: The Critical Heritage* (London: Routledge & Kegan Paul, 1970).

Davie, Donald, *Thomas Hardy and British Poetry* (New York: Oxford University Press, 1972; London: Routledge & Kegan Paul, 1973).

Gibson, James, and Johnson, Trevor (eds), *Thomas Hardy: Poems* (Casebook) (London and Basingstoke: Macmillan, 1979).

Hynes, Samuel, *The Pattern of Hardy's Poetry* (Chapel Hill: University of North Carolina Press, 1961; London: Oxford University Press, 1961).

Johnson, Trevor, *Thomas Hardy* (London: Evans Brothers, 1968).

Marsden, Kenneth, *The Poems of Thomas Hardy* (London: Athlone Press, 1969; New York: Oxford University Press, 1969).

Paulin, Tom, *Thomas Hardy: The Poetry of Perception* (London and Basingstoke: Macmillan, 1975.)

Taylor, Dennis, *Hardy's Poetry, 1860–1928* (London and Basingstoke: Macmillan, 1981; Columbia University Press, 1981).

——, *Hardy's Metres and Victorian Prosody* (Oxford and New York: Oxford University Press, 1988).

Heaney, Seamus (b. 1939)

Death of a Naturalist (London: Faber and Faber, 1966).

Door into the Dark (London: Faber and Faber, 1969).

Wintering Out (London: Faber and Faber, 1972).

North (London: Faber and Faber, 1975).

Field Work (London: Faber and Faber, 1978).

Station Island (London: Faber and Faber, 1984).

The Haw Lantern (London: Faber and Faber, 1987).

Seeing Things (London: Faber and Faber, 1991).

The Spirit Level (London: Faber and Faber, 1996).

New Selected Poems, 1966–1987 (London: Faber and Faber, 1987).

The Cure At Troy (play) (London: Faber and Faber, 1990).

Preoccupations: Selected Prose, 1966–1978 (London: Faber and Faber, 1980).

The Government of the Tongue (criticism) (London: Faber and Faber, 1988).

The Redress of Poetry (criticism) (London: Faber and Faber, 1995).

Andrews, Elmer, *The Poetry of Seamus Heaney: All the Realms of Whisper.* (London and Basingstoke: Macmillan, 1988)

Bloom, Harold (ed.), *Seamus Heaney: Modern Critical Views* (New York: Chelsea House, 1986).

Buttel, Robert, *Seamus Heaney* (Lewisburg, PA: Bucknell University Press, 1975).

Corcoran, Neil, *Seamus Heaney* (London: Faber and Faber, 1986).

Curtis, Tony (ed.), *The Art of Seamus Heaney* (Bridgend: Poetry Wales, 1982; reprinted 1985, 1994).

Hart, Henry, *Seamus Heaney: Poet of Contrary Progressions* (New York: Syracuse University Press, 1992).

Morrison, Blake, *Seamus Heaney* (London: Methuen, 1982).

O'Donoghue, Bernard, *Seamus Heaney and the Language of Poetry* (Hemel Hempstead: Harvester Wheatsheaf, 1994).

Henri, Adrian (b. 1932)

Collected Poems, 1967–85 (London: Allison & Busby, 1986; reprinted 1993).

Hewitt, John (1907–87)

Collected Poems, ed. Frank Ormsby (Belfast: Blackstaff, 1991).

Dawe, Gerald, and Longley, Edna (eds), *Across a Roaring Hill: The Protestant Imagination in Modern Ireland: Essays in Honour of John Hewitt* (Belfast: Blackstaff, 1985).

Heaney, Seamus, 'The Poetry of John Hewitt', in *Preoccupations* (London: Faber and Faber, 1980).

Hill, Geoffrey (b. 1932)

Collected Poems (Harmondsworth and New York: Penguin Books, 1985).

Robinson, Peter (ed.), *Geoffrey Hill: Essays on His Work* (Milton Keynes, 1985).

Sherry, Vincent, *The Uncommon Tongue: The Poetry and Criticism of Geoffrey Hill* (Ann Arbor: University of Michigan Press, 1987).

Hope, Alec Derwent (b. 1907)

Collected Poems, 1930–1970 (London: Angus & Robertson, 1972).

Selected Poems, ed. Ruth Morse (Manchester: Carcanet, 1986).

Kramer, Leonie, *A. D. Hope* (Melbourne, 1979).

Hopkinson, Abdur-Rahman Slade [Clement Alan Slade Hopkinson] (b. 1934)

The Four, and Other Poems (Bridgetown, Barbados, 1955).

The Madwoman of Papine (Georgetown, Guyana, 1976).

The Friend (Georgetown, Guyana, 1976).

Housman, Alfred Edward (1859–1936)

Collected Poems and Selected Prose, ed. Christopher Ricks (London: Allen Lane, 1988).

Selected Writings, ed. Alan Holden (Manchester: Carcanet, 1997).

Graves, Richard Perceval, *A. E. Housman: The Scholar Poet* (London: Routledge & Kegan Paul, 1979).

Page, Norman, *A. E. Housman: A Critical Biography* (Basingstoke and London: Macmillan, 1983).

Bayley, John, *Housman's Poems* (Oxford: Oxford University Press, 1992).
Leggett, B. J., *Housman's Land of Lost Content: A Critical Study of 'A Shropshire Lad'* (Knoxville: University of Tennessee Press, 1970).
——, *The Poetic Art of A. E. Housman: Theory and Practice* (University of Nebraska Press, 1978).
Ricks, Christopher (ed.), *A. E. Housman: A Collection of Critical Essays* (Englewood Cliffs, NJ: Prentice-Hall, 1968).

Hughes, Langston (1902–67)
The Collected Poems of Langston Hughes, ed. Arnold Ranpersad and David Roessel (New York: A. A. Knopf, 1994).
The Big Sea (autobiography) (New York and London: A. A. Knopf, 1940).
I Wonder As I Wander: An Autobiographical Journey (New York: Hill and Wang, 1964).

Appiah, Antony, *Langston Hughes: Critical Perspectives Past and Present* (Amistad: Amistad Literary Series, 1993).

Hughes, Ted (b. 1930)
The Hawk in the Rain (London: Faber and Faber, 1957; New York: Harper, 1957).
Lupercal (London: Faber and Faber, 1960; New York: Harper, 1960).
Wodwo (London: Faber and Faber, 1967; New York: Harper & Row, 1967).
Crow (London and New York: Faber and Faber, 1970; 2nd (extended) edition, 1973).
Season Songs (New York: Viking, 1975; London: Faber and Faber, 1976).
Gaudete (London: Faber and Faber, 1977; New York: Harper & Row, 1977).
Cave Birds (London: Faber and Faber, 1978; New York: Viking, 1979).
Remains of Elmet (London: Faber and Faber, 1979; New York: Harper & Row, 1979).
Moortown (London: Faber and Faber, 1979; New York: Harper & Row, 1980).
River (Faber and Faber/James and James, 1983; New York: Harper & Row, 1984).
Wolfwatching (London: Faber and Faber, 1989; New York: Farrar, Straus & Giroux, 1991).
Birthday Letters (London: Faber & Faber, 1998).
Selected Poems, 1957–1981 (London: Faber and Faber, 1982; New York: Harper & Row, 1982).
Shakespeare and the Goddess of Being (criticism) (London: Faber and Faber, 1992).

Dyson, A. E. (ed.) *see under* **Gunn, Thom**.
Faas, Ekbert, *Ted Hughes: The Unaccommodated Universe, with Selected Writings by Ted Hughes and Two Interviews* (Santa Barbara, CA: Black Sparrow Press, 1980).
Gifford, Terry, and Roberts, Neil, *Ted Hughes: A Critical Study* (London: Faber and Faber, 1981).

Hirschberg, Stuart, *Myth in the Poetry of Ted Hughes* (Dublin: Wolfhound Press, 1981).

Robinson, Craig, *Ted Hughes as Shepherd of Being* (London and Basingstoke: Macmillan, 1989; New York: St Martin's Press, 1989).

Sagar, Keith, *The Art of Ted Hughes* (Cambridge: Cambridge University Press, 1978).

—— (ed.), *The Achievement of Ted Hughes* (Manchester: Manchester University Press, 1983; Athens, GA: University of Georgia Press, 1983).

—— (ed.), *The Challenge of Ted Hughes* (Basingstoke and London: Macmillan, 1994; New York: St Martin's Press, 1994).

Scigaj, Leonard M., *The Poetry of Ted Hughes: Form and Imagination* (Iowa City: University of Iowa Press, 1986).

——, *Ted Hughes* (Boston: Twayne, 1991).

Jarrell, Randall (1914–65)
Complete Poems (New York: Farrar, Straus & Giroux, 1969).
Selected Poems, ed. William H. Pritchard (New York: Farrar, Straus & Giroux, 1990).

Pritchard, William H., *Randall Jarrell: A Literary Life* (New York, 1990).

Jeffers, Robinson (1887–1962)
Collected Poetry, ed. Tim Hunt (Stanford, CA: Stanford University Press, 1988).
Selected Poems, ed. Colin Falck (Manchester: Carcanet, 1987).

Jennings, Elizabeth (b. 1926)
Collected Poems, 1953–1985 (Manchester: Carcanet, 1986).
Times and Seasons (Manchester: Carcanet, 1992).
In the Meantime (Manchester: Carcanet, 1996).

Jones, David (1895–1974)
In Parenthesis (London: Faber and Faber, 1937; paperback edition, with Introduction by T. S. Eliot, 1963).
The Anathemata (London: Faber and Faber, 1952).
The Sleeping Lord and Other Fragments (London: Faber and Faber, 1974).

Bergonzi, Bernard, 'Remythologizing: David Jones's *In Parenthesis*', in *Heroes' Twilight* (London: Constable, 1965; reprinted London and Basingstoke: Macmillan, 1980).

Matthias, John (ed.), *David Jones: Man and Poet* (Orono, Maine, 1989).

Ward, Elizabeth, *David Jones: Mythmaker* (Manchester: Manchester University Press, 1983).

Kavanagh, Patrick (1904–67)
Complete Poems, ed. Peter Kavanagh (New York: Peter Kavanagh Hand Press, 1972; reprinted Newbridge, Co. Kildare: Goldsmith Press, 1984).
Selected Poems (London: Chatto and Windus, 1982).

Quinn, Antoinette, *Patrick Kavanagh: Born-again Romantic* (Dublin: Gill and Macmillan, 1991).

Keyes, Sidney (1922–43)
Collected Poems, ed. Michael Meyer (London: Routledge, 1945).

Guenther, J., *Sidney Keyes; A Biographical Inquiry* (London: London Magazine Editions, 1967).

Kinsella, Thomas (b. 1928)
Collected Poems (Oxford: Oxford University Press, 1996).
Poems 1956–1994 (Oxford: Oxford University Press, 1997).

Kipling, Rudyard (1865–1936)
Rudyard Kipling's Verse, 1885–1926 (London: Hodder and Stoughton, 1927).
A Choice of Kipling's Verse, ed. T. S. Eliot (London: Faber and Faber, 1941).
Early Verse by Rudyard Kipling, 1879–1889, ed. Andrew Rutherford (Oxford: Oxford University Press, 1986).
Selected Poems, ed. Peter Keating (Harmondsworth: Penguin, 1993).

Green, Roger Lancelyn (ed.), *Kipling: The Critical Heritage* (London: Routledge & Kegan Paul, 1971).
Keating, Peter, *Kipling: The Poet* (London: Secker & Warburg, 1994).

Larkin, Philip (1922–85)
Collected Poems, ed. Anthony Thwaite (London: Faber and Faber, 1988; New York: Farrar, Straus & Giroux, 1989).
Required Writing: Miscellaneous Pieces 1955–1982 (prose) (London: Faber and Faber, 1983; New York: Farrar, Straus & Giroux, 1984).
All What Jazz: A Record Diary, 1964–6 (jazz music reviews) (London: Faber and Faber, 1970; revised edition, 1985).
Selected Letters, 1940–1985, ed. Anthony Thwaite (London: Faber and Faber, 1992; New York: Farrar, Straus & Giroux, 1993).

Motion, Andrew, *Philip Larkin: A Writer's Life* (London: Faber and Faber, 1993).

Booth, James, *Philip Larkin: Writer* (Hemel Hempstead: Harvester Wheatsheaf, 1992).
Cookson, Linda, and Loughery, Brian (eds), *Critical Essays on Philip Larkin: The Poems* (London: Longman, 1989).
Motion, Andrew, *Philip Larkin* (London and New York: Methuen, 1982).
Rossen, Janice, *Philip Larkin: His Life's Work* (London: Harvester Wheatsheaf, 1989).
Tolley, A. T., *My Proper Ground: A Study of the Work of Philip Larkin and Its Development* (Ottawa: Carleton University Press, 1991; Edinburgh: Edinburgh University Press, 1991).
Whalen, Terry, *Philip Larkin and English Poetry* (London and Basingstoke: Macmillan, 1986; revised edition, 1990).

Lawrence, David Herbert (1885–1930)
Complete Poems, ed. V. de S. Pinto and Warren Roberts (2 vols) (London and New York: Heinemann, 1964; paperback (1 vol.), Harmondsworth: Penguin Books, 1967).
Selected Poems, ed. Keith Sagar (Harmondsworth: Penguin Books, 1972).
Selected Poems, ed. Mara Kalnins (London: Dent, Everyman's Library, 1992).
Phoenix (miscellaneous prose), ed. Edward D. McDonald (London: Heinemann, 1936; reprinted 1961).
Phoenix II (miscellaneous prose), ed. Warren Roberts and Harry T. Moore (London: Heinemann, 1968).
Letters (7 vols), General Editor James T. Boulton (Cambridge: Cambridge University Press, 1979–92).

Moore, Harry T., *The Intelligent Heart: The Story of D. H. Lawrence* (New York: Farrar, Straus & Young, 1955; London: Heinemann, 1955; revised edition, Harmondsworth: Penguin, 1960).
Worthen, John, *D. H. Lawrence: The Early Years: 1885–1912* (vol. 1 of Cambridge University Press biography of Lawrence) (Cambridge: Cambridge University Press, 1991).
Kinkead-Weekes: *D. H. Lawrence: Triumph to Exile: 1912–1922* (vol. 2 of Cambridge University Press biography) (Cambridge: Cambridge University Press, 1996).
(Vol. 3 of Cambridge Univeristy Press biography will be by David Ellis.)

Bannerjee, A. (ed.), *D. H. Lawrence's Poetry: Demon Liberated* (London and Basingstoke: Macmillan, 1990).
Draper, R. P. (ed.), *D. H. Lawrence: The Critical Heritage* (London: Routledge & Kegan Paul, 1970).
Gilbert, Sandra, *Acts of Attention: The Poems of D. H. Lawrence* (New York and London: Cornell University Press, 1972).
Heywood, Christopher (ed.), *D. H. Lawrence: New Studies* (London and Basingstoke: Macmillan, 1987).
Kalnins, Mara (ed.), *D. H. Lawrence: Centenary Essays* (Bristol: Bristol Classical Press, 1986).
Marshall, Tom, *The Psychic Mariner: A Reading of the Poems of D. H. Lawrence* (London: Heinemann, 1970; New York: Viking, 1970).
Vries-Mason, Jillian de, *Perception in the Poetry of D. H. Lawrence* (Berne and Frankfurt/Main: Peter Lang, 1982).

Leonard, Tom (b. 1944)
Intimate Voices: Selected Work, 1965–1983 (Newcastle: Carcanet, 1984).

Levertov, Denise (b. 1923)
Selected Poems (Newcastle: Carcanet, 1986).

Kinnahan, Linda A., *Poetics of the Feminine: Authority and Literary Tradition in William Carlos Williams, Mina Loy, Denise Levertov, and Kathleen Fraser* (Cambridge: Cambridge University Press, 1994).

Rodgers, Audrey T., *Denise Levertov: The Poetry of Engagement* (Rutherford: Fairleigh Dickinson University Press, 1993; Associated University Presses, 1993).

Wagner-Martin, Linda (ed.), *Critical Essays on Denise Levertov* (Boston: G. K. Hall, 1990).

Lewis, Alun (1915–44)

Collected Poems, ed. Cary Archard (Bridgend Glam: Seren, 1994).

Selected Poems, ed. Jeremy Hooker and Gweno Lewis (London: Unwin, 1981).

Alun Lewis: A Miscellany of His Writings, ed. John Pikoulis (Bridgend, Glam: Poetry Wales Press, 1982).

Pikoulis, John, *Alun Lewis: A Life* (Bridgend, Glam: Poetry Wales Press, 1984).

Lochhead, Liz (b. 1947)

Dreaming Frankenstein and Collected Poems (Edinburgh: Polygon, 1984).

True Confessions and New Clichés (Edinburgh: Polygon, 1985).

Bagpipe Muzak (Harmondsworth: Penguin, 1991).

Longley, Michael (b. 1939)

Poems, 1963–1983 (Edinburgh: Salamander Press, and Dublin: Gallery Books, 1985).

Gorse Fires (London: Secker & Warburg, 1991).

Lowell, Robert Traill Spence (1917–77)

Poems, 1938–1949 (London: Faber and Faber, 1950).

Life Studies and For the Union Dead (New York: Farrar Straus & Giroux; paperback, 1968).

Selected Poems (London: Faber and Faber, 1965).

Selected Poems (New York: Farrar, Straus & Giroux, 1976; revised edition, 1977).

Day by Day (London: Faber & Faber, 1965).

Collected Prose, ed. Robert Giroux (London: Faber and Faber, 1987).

Hamilton, Ian, *Robert Lowell: A Biography* (New York: Random House, 1982; London: Faber and Faber, 1983).

Mariani, Paul, *Lost Puritan: A Life of Robert Lowell* (New York and London: W. W. Norton, 1994).

Meyers, Jeffrey (ed.), *Robert Lowell: Interviews and Memoirs* (Ann Arbor: University of Michigan Press, 1988).

Axelrod, Steven Gould, *Robert Lowell: Life and Art* (Princeton: Princeton University Press, 1978).

Crick, J. F., *Robert Lowell* (Edinburgh: Oliver & Boyd, 1974).

Parkinson, Thomas Francis (ed.), *Robert Lowell: A Collection of Critical Essays* (Englewood Cliffs, NJ: Prentice-Hall, 1968).

Perloff, Marjorie G., *The Poetic Art of Robert Lowell* (Ithaca, NY, and London: Cornell University Press, 1973).

Rudman, Mark, *Robert Lowell: An Introduction to the Poetry* (New York: Columbia University Press, 1983).

Tillinghurst, Richard, *Robert Lowell's Life and Work: Damaged Grandeur* (Ann Arbor: University of Michigan Press, 1995).

McAuley, James (1917–76)
Collected Poems, 1936–1970 (Sydney: Angus and Robertson, 1971; reprinted 1994).

MacCaig, Norman (b. 1910)
Collected Poems (London: Chatto & Windus, 1990).
Selected Poems, ed. Douglas Dunn (London: Chatto & Windus, 1997).

Hendry, Joy, and Ross, Raymond (eds), *Norman MacCaig: Critical Essays* (Edinburgh: Edinburgh University Press, 1990).

MacDiarmid, Hugh [Christopher Murray Grieve] (1892–1978)
Complete Poems (2 vols), ed. M. Grieve and W. R. Aitken (London: Martin Brian & O'Keeffe, 1978; Harmondsworth: Penguin, 1985).
Selected Poems (Manchester: Carcanet, 1992).
A Drunk Man Looks at the Thistle, ed. Kenneth Buthlay (Edinburgh: Scottish Academic Press, 1987).
Letters, ed. Alan Bold (London: Hamish Hamilton, 1984).
The Raucle Tongue: Selected Essays, Journalism and Interviews (2 vols), ed. Alan Riach (Manchester: Carcanet, 1996–7).

Bold, Alan, *MacDiarmid: A Critical Biography* (London: John Murray, 1988).

Bold, Alan, *MacDiarmid: The Terrible Crystal* (London: Routledge & Kegan Paul, 1983).
Buthlay, Kenneth, *Hugh MacDiarmid (C. M. Grieve)* (Edinburgh: Oliver & Boyd, 1964; revised edition, Edinburgh: Scottish Academic Press, 1982).
Gish, N., *Hugh MacDiarmid: The Man and His Work* (London and Basingstoke: Macmillan, 1984).
Glen, D. (ed.), *Hugh MacDiarmid: A Critical Survey* (Edinburgh: Scottish Academic Press, 1972).
Morgan, Edwin, *Hugh MacDiarmid* (Harlow: Longman (for British Council), 1976).
Smith, Iain Crichton, 'The Complete Poems of Hugh MacDiarmid' and 'MacDiarmid and Ideas, with Special Reference to "On A Raised Beach"', in Iain Crichton Smith, *Towards the Human* (Edinburgh: MacDonald, 1986).
Watson, Roderick, *MacDiarmid* (Milton Keynes and Philadelphia: Open University Press, 1985).

McGough, Roger (b. 1937)
Blazing Fruit: Selected Poems, 1967–1987 (London: Cape, 1989; Harmondsworth: Penguin, 1990).

McGuckian, Medbh (b. 1950)
The Flower Master (Oxford and New York: Oxford University Press, 1982).
Venus and the Rain (Oxford and New York: Oxford University Press, 1984;
revised edition, Oldcastle, Co. Meath: Gallery Books, 1994).
On Ballycastle Beach (Oxford and New York: Oxford University Press, 1988).
Marconi's Cottage (Oldcastle, Co. Meath: Gallery Books, 1991; Newcastle:
Bloodaxe, 1992).

Docherty, Thomas, 'Postmodern McGuckian', in Neil Corcoran (ed.), *The Chosen Ground: Essays on the Contemporary Poetry of Northern Ireland* (Bridgend, Glam: Seren, 1992).

MacLeish, Archibald (1892–1982)
New and Collected Poems, 1917–1976 (Boston: Houghton Mifflin, 1976).

MacNeice, Louis (1907–63)
Collected Poems, ed. E. R. Dodds (London: Faber and Faber, 1966; New York,
1967).
Selected Poems, ed. Michael Longley (London: Faber and Faber, 1988).
The Strings Are False (autobiography), ed. E. R. Dodds (London: Faber and
Faber, 1965; New York, 1966).

Stallworthy, Jon, *Louis MacNeice* (London: Faber and Faber, 1995).

Longley, Edna, *Louis MacNeice* (London: Faber and Faber, 1988).

Mahon, Derek (b. 1941)
Poems, 1962–1978 (Oxford: Oxford University Press, 1979).
Selected Poems (London: Viking, Gallery, Oxford University Press, 1991).

Mandel, Eli (b. 1922)
Dreaming Backwards, 1954–1981: The Selected Poetry of Eli Mandel (Don Mills,
Ontario: General Publishing Co., 1981).

Masefield, John (1878–1967)
Collected Poems (London: Heinemann, 1923).
Selected Poems (Manchester: Carcanet, 1984).

Merrill, James (1926–95)
The Country of a Thousand Years of Peace (New York: Atheneum, 1959; revised
edition, 1970).
Water Street (New York: Atheneum, 1962).
Braving the Elements (New York: Atheneum, 1972).
The Changing Light at Sandover (New York: Atheneum, 1976–80).
Late Settings (New York: Atheneum, 1985).
Three Poems (Child Okeford: Words, 1988).
The Inner Room (New York: Knopf, 1988).

Kalstone, David, *Five Temperaments* (Bishop, Lowell, Merrill, Rich and Ashbery) (New York: Oxford University Press, 1977).

Moffett, Judith, *James Merrill: An Introduction to the Poetry* (New York: Columbia University Press, 1984).
Yenser, Stephen, *The Consuming Myth: The Work of James Merril* (Cambridge, MA: Harvard University Press, 1987).

Merwin, William Stanley (b. 1927)
Selected Poems (New York: Atheneum, 1988).
Travels (New York: Knopf, 1993).
The Miner's Pale Children (autobiography) (New York: Atheneum, 1970).

Brunner, Edward, *Poetry as Labor and Privilege: The Writings of W. S. Merwin* (Urbana: University of Illinois Press, 1991).
Folsom, Ed, and Nelson, Cary (eds), *W. S. Merwin: Essays on the Poetry* (Urbana: University of Illinois Press, 1987).

Mitchell, Adrian (b. 1932)
For Beauty Douglas: Adrian Mitchell's Collected Poems, 1953–79 (London and New York: Allison & Busby, 1982).

Montague, John (b. 1929)
New Selected Poems (Oldcastle, Co. Meath: Gallery, 1989; Newcastle: Bloodaxe, 1990).
Faber Book of Irish Verse, ed. John Montague (London: Faber and Faber, 1974).

Moore, Marianne (1887–1972)
Complete Poems (London: Faber and Faber, 1968; reprinted, 1984).

Bloom, Harold (ed.), *Marianne Moore: Modern Critical Views* (New York: Chelsea House, 1987).
Diehl, Joanne Feit, *Elizabeth Bishop and Marianne Moore: The Psychodynamics of Creativity* (Princeton: Princeton University Press, 1993).
Holley, Margaret, *The Poetry of Marianne Moore* (Cambridge: Cambridge University Press, 1987).
Miller, Cristanne, *Marianne Moore: Questions of Authority* (Cambridge, MA: Harvard University Press, 1995).
Rotella, Guy, *see under* **Bishop, Elizabeth**.

Morgan, Edwin (b. 1920)
Collected Poems (Manchester: Carcanet, 1990).
Collected Translations (Manchester: Carcanet, 1996).

Morris, Mervyn (b. 1937)
The Pond (London: New Beacon, 1973).
On Holy Week (Kingston, Jamaica: Dangaroo, 1976; Hebden Bridge, 1993).
Shadowboxing (London: New Beacon, 1979).
Examination Centre (London: New Beacon, 1992).

Motion, Andrew (b. 1952)
Dangerous Play, Poems 1974–1984 (London: Salamander Press, 1984; Harmondsworth: Penguin Books, 1985).

Natural Causes (London: Chatto & Windus, 1987).
Love in a Life (London: Faber and Faber, 1991).
Salt Water (London: Faber & Faber, 1997).

Mudie, Ian (b. 1911)
Poems 1934–1944 (Melbourne: Georgian House, 1945).

Muir, Edwin (1887–1959)
Collected Poems, ed. Willa Muir and J. C. Hall (London: Faber and Faber, 1960; revised edition, 1984).
Selected Poems, ed. T. S. Eliot (London: Faber and Faber, 1965).
An Autobiography (London: Hogarth Press, 1954).
Selected Letters, ed. Peter Butter (London: Hogarth Press, 1974).

Butter, Peter, *Edwin Muir: Man and Poet* (Edinburgh: Oliver and Boyd, 1962).
MacLachlan, J. M., and Robb, D. S. (eds), *Edwin Muir: Centenary Assessments* (Aberdeen: Association for Scottish Literary Studies, 1990).

Muldoon, Paul (b. 1931)
New Weather (London: Faber and Faber, 1972).
Mules (London: Faber and Faber, 1977).
Why Brownlee Left (London: Faber and Faber, 1980).
Quoof (London: Faber and Faber, 1983).
Shining Brow (London: Faber and Faber, 1993).
The Prince of the Quotidian (Oldcastle: Gallery, 1994).
The Faber Book of Contemporary Irish Verse, ed. Paul Muldoon (London: Faber and Faber, 1988).

Murray, Les (b. 1938)
Collected Poems (Manchester: Carcanet, 1991; reprinted London: Minerva, 1992).
Translations from the Natural World (Manchester: Carcanet, 1993).
Subhuman Redneck Poems (Manchester: Carcanet, 1996).
The Paperbark Tree (prose) (Manchester: Carcanet, 1993).

Bourke, Lawrence, *A Vivid Steady State: Les Murray and Australian Poets* (Kensington, NSW: New South Wales University Press, 1992).
Ross, Bruce Clunies, 'Les Murray and the Poetry of Australia', in R. P. Draper (ed.), *The Literature of Region and Nation* (London and Basingstoke: Macmillan, 1989).

Nemerov, Howard Stanley (1920–91)
Trying Conclusions: New and Selected Poems, 1961–91 (Chicago: University of Chicago Press, 1991).

Labrie, Ross, *Howard Nemerov* (Boston: Twayne, 1980).
Mills, William, *The Stillness in Moving Things: The World of Howard Nemerov* (Memphis, Tenn.: Memphis State University Press, 1975).

Nichol, b p [Barrie Phillip] (1944–88)
The Martyrology (7 vols) (Toronto: Coach House Press, 1972–).

O'Hara, Frank (1926–66)
Collected Poems, ed. Donald Allen; Introduction by John Ashbery (Berkeley:
    University of California Press, 1971; reprinted 1995).
Selected Poems, ed. Donald Allen (Manchester: Carcanet, 1991).

Feldman, Alan, *Frank O'Hara* (Boston: Twayne, 1979).
Perloff, Marjorie, *Frank O'Hara: Poet Among Painters* (New York: G. Braziller,
    1977).
Ward, Geoff, *Statutes of Liberty: The New York School of Poets* (Basingstoke
    and London: Macmillan, 1993).

Olson, Charles (1910–70)
The Maximus Poems, ed. George F. Butterick (Berkeley and London:
    University of California Press, 1983).
Collected Poems, ed. George F. Butterick (Berkeley and London: University
    of California Press, 1987).
Selected Poems, ed. Robert Creeley (Berkeley and Oxford: University of
    California Press, 1993).

Merrill, Thomas F., *The Poetry of Charles Olson: A Primer* (Newark, London
    and Toronto: University of Delaware Press, 1982).

Ondaatje, Michael (b. 1943)
The Dainty Monsters (Toronto: Coach House Press, 1967).
The Collected Works of Billy the Kid: Left Handed Poems (London and Boston:
    Marion Boyars, 1981).
There's a Trick with a Knife I'm Learning to Do (New York: Norton, 1979).
Left Handed Poems (London and Boston: Marion Boyars, 1981).
Secular Love (New York and London: Norton, 1985).
Rat Jelly and Other Poems, 1963–78 (London and Boston: Marion Boyars,
    1980).
The Cinnamon Peeler: Selected Poems (London: Picador, 1989).

O'Sullivan, Vincent (b. 1937)
Selected Poems (Auckland: Oxford University Press, 1992).

Owen, Wilfred (1893–1918)
The Poems of Wilfred Owen, ed. Edmund Blunden (London: Chatto & Windus,
    1946).
War Poems and Others, ed. Dominic Hibberd (London: Chatto & Windus,
    1973; paperback, 1975).
Complete Poems and Fragments, ed. Jon Stallworthy (London: Chatto &
    Windus, 1986).
Poems of Wilfred Owen, ed. Jon Stallworthy (London: Chatto & Windus, 1990).
The War Poems of Wilfred Owen, ed. Jon Stallworthy (London: Chatto &
    Windus, 1994).

Stallworthy, Jon, *Wilfred Owen* (Oxford and New York: Oxford University Press, 1974).

Hibberd, Dominic, *Owen the Poet* (Basingstoke and London: Macmillan, 1986).
Welland, D. S. R., *Wilfred Owen: A Critical Study* (London: Chatto & Windus, 1960).
White, Gertrude M., *Wilfred Owen* (Boston: Twayne, 1969).

Patten, Brian (b. 1946)
Grinning Jacks: Selected Poems (London: Unwin, 1990; reprinted London: Paladin, 1992).

Paulin, Tom (b. 1949)
Selected Poems, 1972–1990 (London: Faber and Faber, 1993).

Plath, Sylvia (1932–63)
Collected Poems, ed. Ted Hughes (London and Boston: Faber and Faber, 1981).
The Bell Jar (semi-autobiographical fiction, originally published under the pseudonym of Victoria Lucas) (London: Heinemann, 1963; London: Faber and Faber, 1966).
Johnny Panic and the Bible of Dreams (prose) (London: Faber and Faber, 1977).
Letters Home, ed. Aurelia Schober Plath (New York: Harper & Row, 1975).

Stevenson, Anne (and others), *Bitter Fame: A Life of Sylvia Plath* (London: Viking and Boston: Houghton Mifflin, 1989; Harmondsworth: Penguin, 1990).
Wagner-Martin, Linda, *Sylvia Plath: A Biography* (London: Chatto & Windus, 1988).

Barnard, Caroline King, *Sylvia Plath* (Boston: Twayne, 1978).
Bassnett, Susan, *Sylvia Plath* (London and Basingstoke: Macmillan, 1987).
Broe, Mary Lynn, *Protean Poetic: The Poetry of Sylvia Plath* (Columbia: University of Missouri Press, 1980).
Butscher, Edward (ed.), *Sylvia Plath: The Woman and the Work* (New York: Dodd, Mead, 1977).
Holbrook, David, *Sylvia Plath: Poetry and Existence* (London: Athlone Press, 1976).
Markey, Janice, *A Journey into the Red Eye: The Poetry of Sylvia Plath – A Critique* (London: Women's Press, 1993).
Marsack, Robin, *Sylvia Plath* (Milton Keynes: Open University Press, 1992).
Newman, Charles (ed.), *The Art of Sylvia Plath: A Symposium* (London: Faber and Faber, 1990).
Wagner, Linda W. (ed.), *Critical Essays on Sylvia Plath* (Boston: G. K. Hall, 1984).
—— (ed.), *Sylvia Plath: The Critical Heritage* (London: Routledge & Kegan Paul, 1988).

Porter, Peter (b. 1929)
Collected Poems (Oxford: Oxford University Press, 1983).
Fast Forward (Oxford: Oxford University Press, 1984).
A Porter Selected (Oxford: Oxford University Press, 1989).
Possible Worlds (Oxford: Oxford University Press, 1989).
The Chair of Babel (Oxford: Oxford University Press, 1992).

Steele, Peter, *Peter Porter* (Melbourne: Oxford University Press, 1992).

Pound, Ezra (1885–1972)
Personae: The Shorter Poems of Ezra Pound, ed. L. Baechler and A. Walton Litz (New York: New Directions, 1990).
Collected Shorter Poems (London: Faber and Faber, 1952; reprinted 1973, 1984).
Collected Early Poems, ed. M. J. King (London: Faber and Faber, 1977).
The Cantos of Ezra Pound, revised collected edition (London: Faber and Faber, 1975; reprinted London: Faber and Faber, 1981).
The Literary Essays of Ezra Pound, ed. T. S. Eliot (London and New York: Faber and Faber, 1954; reprinted 1974).
Selected Letters, ed. D. D. Paige (London: Faber and Faber, 1971).

Carpenter, Humphrey, *A Serious Character: The Life of Ezra Pound* (London: Faber and Faber, 1988).
Stock, Noel, *The Life of Ezra Pound* (Harmondsworth: Penguin, 1970; revised edition, 1985).

Alexander, Michael, *The Poetic Achievement of Ezra Pound* (London: Faber and Faber, 1979).
Brooker, Peter, *A Student's Guide to the Selected Poems of Ezra Pound* (London and Boston: Faber and Faber, 1979).
Cookson, William, *A Guide to the Cantos of Ezra Pound* (London and Sydney: Croom Helm, 1985).
Davie, Donald, *Ezra Pound: Poet as Sculptor* (New York: Oxford University Press, 1964).
——, *Ezra Pound* (New York: Viking, 1975).
——, *Studies in Ezra Pound* (Manchester: Carcanet, 1991).
Flory, Wendy Stallard, *The American Ezra Pound* (New Haven and London: Yale University Press, 1989).
Gibson, Andrew (ed.), *Pound in Multiple Perspective: A Collection of Critical Essays* (Basingstoke and London: Macmillan, 1993).
Homberger, Eric (ed.), *Ezra Pound: The Critical Heritage* (London: Routledge & Kegan Paul, 1972).
Kearns, George, *Ezra Pound: The Cantos* (Cambridge: Cambridge University Press, 1989).
Kenner, Hugh, *The Poetry of Ezra Pound* (Norfolk, CT: New Directions, 1951; reprinted New York: Kraus, 1968).
——, *The Pound Era* (Berkeley: University of California Press, 1971; London: Pimlico, 1991).
Perloff, Marjorie, *The Dance of the Intellect: Studies in the Poetry of the Pound Tradition* (Cambridge: Cambridge University Press, 1985).

Stock, Noel, *Poet in Exile: Ezra Pound* (Manchester: Manchester University Press, 1964).

Sullivan, J. P. (ed.), *Ezra Pound: A Critical Anthology* (Harmondsworth: Penguin, 1970).

Terrell, Carroll F., *A Companion to the Cantos of Ezra Pound* (2 vols) (Orono: University of Maine; Berkeley: University of California Press, 1980–4).

Raine, Craig (b. 1944)
The Onion, Memory (Oxford: Oxford University Press, 1978).
A Martian Sends a Postcard Home (Oxford: Oxford University Press, 1979).
Rich (London: Faber and Faber, 1984).
The Electrification of the Soviet Union (London: Faber and Faber, 1986).
Haydn and the Valve Trumpet (London: Faber and Faber, 1990).
History: The Home Movie (London: Penguin, 1994).
Clay. Whereabouts Unknown (Harmondsworth: Penguin, 1996).

Raine, Kathleen (b. 1908)
Selected Poems (Ipswich: Golgonooza, 1988; Rochester, Vermont, 1989).

Ransom, John Crowe (1888–1974)
Selected Poems (New York: Knopf, 1969; Manchester: Carcanet, 1991).
Selected Essays, ed. T. D. Young and J. Hindle (Baton Rouge: Louisiana State University Press, 1984).

Reading, Peter (b. 1946)
Collected Poems, 1: Poems, 1970–1984 (Newcastle: Bloodaxe, 1995).
Collected Poems, 2: 1985–1996 (Newcastle: Bloodaxe, 1996).

Redgrove, Peter (b. 1932)
The Moon Disposes: Poems, 1954–1987 (London: Secker & Warburg, 1987).
Under the Reservoir (London: Secker & Warburg, 1992).

Reed, Henry (1914–86)
Collected Poems, ed. Jon Stallworthy (Oxford: Oxford University Press, 1991).

Rexroth, Kenneth (1905–82)
Complete Collected Shorter Poems (New York: New Directions, 1967).
Collected Longer Poems (New York: New Directions, 1968).
Flower Wreath Hill: Later Poems (New York: New Directions, 1974; reprinted 1991).

Rich, Adrienne (b. 1929)
A Change of World (New Haven: Yale University Press, 1951).
Snapshots of a Daughter-in-Law: Poems, 1954–1962 (New York: Harper, 1963).
Necessities of Life: Poems, 1962–1965 (New York: Norton, 1966).
Leaflets: Poems, 1965–1968 (New York: Norton, 1969).
The Will to Change: Poems, 1968–1970 (New York: Norton, 1971).
Diving into the Wreck: Poems, 1971–1972 (New York: Norton, 1973).
Poems: Selected and New, 1950–1974 (New York: Norton, 1975).

The Dream of a Common Language: Poems, 1974–1977 (New York: Norton, 1978).
A Wild Patience Has Taken Me This Far: Poems, 1978–1981 (New York: Norton, 1981).
Sources (Woodside, CA: Heyeck Press, 1983).
The Fact of a Doorframe: Poems Selected and New, 1950–1984 (New York: Norton, 1984).
Time's Power: Poems, 1985–1988 (New York: Norton, 1989).
An Atlas of the Difficult World: Poems 1988–1991 (New York and London: Norton, 1991).
Dark Fields of the Republic: Poems, 1991–1995 (New York and London: Norton, 1995).
Collected Early Poems: 1950–1970 (New York and London: Norton, 1993).
Blood, Bread and Poetry: Selected Prose, 1979–1985 (New York: Norton, 1986; London: Virago, 1987).
Adrienne Rich's Poetry and Prose: Poems, Reviews and Criticism, ed. Barbara Charlesworth Gelpi and Albert Gelpi (New York and London: Norton, 1993).

Cooper, Jane Roberta (ed.), *Reading Adrienne Rich: Reviews and Re-Visions, 1951–1981* (Ann Arbor: University of Michigan Press, 1984).
Keyes, Claire, *The Aesthetics of Power: The Poetry of Adrienne Rich* (Athens, GA, and London: University of Georgia Press, 1986).

Riding, Laura [Laura Riding Jackson] (1901–91)
Poems (Manchester and New York: Carcanet, 1980).
A Survey of Modernist Poetry, with Robert Graves (London: Heinemann, 1927; reprinted New York: Haskell House, 1969).

Wallace, Jo-Ann, 'Laura Riding and the Politics of Decanonization', *American Literature*, vol. 64, no. 1 (March 1992) pp. 111–26.

Robinson, Edwin Arlington (1869–1935)
Collected Poems (New York: Macmillan, 1937).

Barnard, Elsworth, *Edwin Arlington Robinson: A Critical Study* (New York: Macmillan, 1952).
Neff, Emery, *Edwin Arlington Robinson* (London and New York: Methuen, 1948).

Roethke, Theodore (1908–63)
Collected Poems (London: Faber and Faber, 1966; reprinted 1968).

Malkoff, Karl, *Theodore Roethke: An Introduction to the Poetry* (New York: Columbia University Press, 1966).
Parini, Jay, *Theodore Roethke: An American Romantic* (Amherst, MA: University of Massachusetts Press, 1979).
Stein, Arnold (ed.), *Theodore Roethke: Essays on the Poetry* (Seattle: University of Washington Press, 1965).

Rosenberg, Isaac (1890–1918)
Collected Works, ed. Ian Parsons (London: Chatto & Windus, 1979; reprinted 1984).

Cohen, Joseph, *Journey to the Trenches: The Life of Isaac Rosenberg* (London: Robson Books, 1975).
Graham, Desmond, *The Truth of War: Owen, Blunden, Rosenberg* (Manchester: Carcanet, 1984).
Liddiard, Jean, *Isaac Rosenberg: The Half Used Life* (London: Gollancz, 1975).

Sandburg, Carl (1878–1967)
Complete Poems (New York: Harcourt Brace Jovanovich, 1950; revised edition, 1970).

Crowder, Richard, *Carl Sandburg* (New York: Twayne, 1964).

Sassoon, Siegfried (1886–1967)
Collected Poems, 1908–1956 (London: Faber and Faber, 1961).
Selected Poems (London: Faber and Faber, 1968).
Memoirs of a Fox-Hunting Man (London: Faber and Faber, 1928).
Memoirs of An Infantry Officer (London: Faber and Faber, 1930; reprinted 1995).
Sherston's Progess (London: Faber and Faber, 1936).
The Old Century: And Seven More Years (London: Faber and Faber, 1938).
Siegfried's Journey (London: Faber and Faber, 1945).

Sternlicht, Sanford V., *Siegfried Sassoon* (New York: Twayne, 1993).

Schuyler, James (b. 1923)
Selected Poems (New York: Farrar, Straus & Giroux, 1988; Manchester: Carcanet, 1990).

Schwartz, Delmore (1913–66)
Selected Poems (1938–1958): Summer Knowledge (New York: New Directions, 1959).

Atlas, James, *Delmore Schwartz: The Life of an American Poet* (New York: Farrar, Straus & Giroux, 1977).

Scott, Alexander (1920–89)
Collected Poems, ed. David S. Robb (Edinburgh: Mercat Press, 1994).

Scott, Tom (b. 1918)
The Ship, and Other Poems (Oxford: Oxford University Press, 1963).

Sexton, Anne (1928–74)
Complete Poems (Boston: Houghton Mifflin, 1981).
Selected Poems, ed. Diane Wood Middlebrook and Diana Hume George (London: Virago, 1991).

Middlebrook, Diane Wood, *Anne Sexton: A Biography* (London: Virago, 1991).

George, Diana Hume, *Oedipus Anne: The Poetry of Anne Sexton* (Urbana: University of Illinois Press, 1987).
Wagner-Martin, Linda (ed.), *Critical Essays on Anne Sexton* (Boston: G. K. Hall, 1989).

Sisson, Charles (b. 1914)
Collected Poems, 1943–1983 (Manchester: Carcanet, 1984).
God Bless Karl Marx (Manchester: Carcanet, 1988).
Antidotes (Manchester: Carcanet, 1991).
What and Who (Manchester: Carcanet, 1994).
Collected Translations (Manchester: Carcanet, 1996).
Collected Poems (Manchester: Carcanet, 1998).

Sitwell, Dame Edith (1887–1964)
Collected Poems (London: Sinclair-Stevenson, 1957; revised edition, 1993).

Glendinning, Victoria, *Edith Sitwell: A Unicorn among the Lions* (Oxford: Oxford University Press, 1981).

Slessor, Kenneth (1901–71)
Poetry, Essays (etc.), ed. D. Hockell (St Lucia: University of Queensland Press, 1991).

Smith, Iain Crichton (b. 1928)
Collected Poems (Manchester: Carcanet, 1992; paperback edition, 1996).
Selected Poems (Manchester: Carcanet, 1985).
Ends and Beginnings (Manchester: Carcanet, 1995).
The Human Face (Manchester: Carcanet, 1996).
Towards the Human: Selected Essays (criticism) (Edinburgh: Macdonald, 1986).

Alexander, J. H., 'The English Poetry of Iain Crichton Smith', in David Hewitt and Michael Spiller (eds), *Literature of the North* (Aberdeen: Aberdeen University Press, 1983).
Gow, Carol, *Mirror and Marble: The Poetry of Iain Crichton Smith* (Edinburgh: Saltire Society, 1992).
Nicholson, Colin (ed.), *Iain Crichton Smith: Critical Essays* (Edinburgh: Edinburgh University Press, 1992).

Smith, Stevie (1902–71)
Collected Poems, ed. James MacGibbon (London: Allen Lane, 1975).
Selected Poems, ed. James MacGibbon (Harmondsworth: Penguin, 1978).

Smithyman, Kendrick (b. 1922)
Selected Poems, ed. Peter Simpson (Auckland: Auckland University Press, 1989).

Snodgrass, William De Witt (b. 1926)
Selected Poems, 1957–1987 (New York: Soho, 1987).

Snyder, Gary (b. 1930)
Left Out in the Rain: New Poems, 1947–1985 (San Francisco: North Point Press, 1986).
Axe Handles (San Francisco: North Point Press, 1983).

Sorley, Charles Hamilton (1895–1915)
Collected Poems, ed. Jean Moorcroft Wilson (London: Woolf, 1985).
Poems and Selected Letters, ed. Hilda Spear (Dundee: Blackness Press, 1978).

Soutar, William (1898–1943)
Poems of Wiliam Soutar: A New Selection, ed. W. R. Aitken (Edinburgh: Scottish Academic Press, 1988).

Spender, Sir Stephen (1909–96)
Collected Poems, 1928–1985 (London: Faber and Faber, 1985).
Dolphins (London: Faber and Faber, 1994).
World Within World (autobiography) (London and New York: Hamish Hamilton, 1951).

Stallworthy, Jon (b. 1935)
The Anzac Sonata: New and Collected Poems (London: Chatto & Windus, 1986).
The Guest from the Future (Manchester: Carcanet, 1995).

Stevens, Wallace (1879–1955)
Collected Poems (New York: Vintage, 1990).
Selected Poems (London: Faber and Faber, 1953; paperback, 1965).
Selected Poems, ed. Helen Vendler (San Francisco: Arion Press, 1985).
Opus Posthumous: Poems, Plays, Prose by Wallace Stevens, ed. Samuel French Morse (New York: Knopf, 1957; London: Faber and Faber, 1959; revised edition, ed. Milton J. Bates, 1990).
Letters, ed. Holly Stevens (London: Faber and Faber, 1967).

Bates, Milton J., *Wallace Stevens: A Mythology of the Self* (Berkeley: University of California Press, 1985).
Bloom, Harold, *Wallace Stevens: The Poems of Our Climate* (Ithaca, N.Y: Cornell University Press, 1977).
Doyle, Charles, *Wallace Stevens: The Critical Heritage* (London: Routledge & Kegan Paul, 1985).
Gelpi, Albert (ed.), *Wallace Stevens: The Poetics of Modernism* (Cambridge: Cambridge University Press, 1985).
Kermode, Frank, *Wallace Stevens* (Edinburgh: Oliver & Boyd, 1969; revised edition, 1989).
Litz, A. Walton, 'Williams and Stevens: The Quest for a Native American Modernism', in R. P. Draper (ed.), *The Literature of Region and Nation* (London and Basingstoke: Macmillan, 1989).
McCann, Janet, *Wallace Stevens Revisited: 'The Celestial Possible'* (Boston: Twayne, 1995).
Rehder, Robert, *The Poetry of Wallace Stevens* (Basingstoke and London: Macmillan, 1988).

Rotella, Guy: *see under* **Bishop, Elizabeth**.
Vendler, Helen, *Wallace Stevens: Words Chosen out of Desire* (Cambridge, MA: Harvard University Press, 1986).

Stevenson, Anne (b. 1923)
Collected Poems (Oxford: Oxford University Press, 1996).

Tate, Allen (1899–1979)
Collected Poems, 1919–1976 (New York: Farrar, Straus & Giroux, 1977).
The Man of Letters in the Modern World: Selected Essays: 1928–1955 (London: Thames and Hudson, 1957).

Thomas, Dylan (1914–53)
Collected Poems, 1934–1953, ed. Walford Davies and Ralph Maud (London: Dent, 1988; reprinted 1994).
Poems, ed. Daniel Jones (London: Dent, 1982).
Under Milk Wood: A Play for Voices (London: Dent, 1954).
Collected Letters, ed. Paul Ferris (London: Paladin, 1985).

Ferris, Paul, *Dylan Thomas* (London: Hodder & Stoughton, 1977; Harmondsworth: Penguin, 1978).
FitzGibbon, Constantine, *The Life of Dylan Thomas* (London: Dent, 1966).

Ackerman, John, *A Dylan Thomas Companion* (London and Basingstoke: Macmillan, 1991).
Bold, Alan Norman, *Dylan Thomas: Craft or Sullen Art* (London: Vision, 1990; New York: St Martin's Press, 1990).
Davies, Walford (ed.), *Dylan Thomas: New Critical Essays* (London: Dent, 1972).
——, *Dylan Thomas* (Milton Keynes: Open University Press, 1986).
Fraser, G. S., *Dylan Thomas* (London: Longman (for The British Council), 1957).
Hardy, Barbara, 'Region and Nation: R. S. Thomas and Dylan Thomas', in R. P. Draper (ed.), *The Literature of Region and Nation* (London and Basingstoke: Macmillan, 1989).
Kershaw, R. B., *Dylan Thomas: The Poet and His Critics* (Chicago: American Library Association, 1976).
Korg, Jacob, *Dylan Thomas* (New York: Twayne, 1965).
Olson, Elder, *The Poetry of Dylan Thomas* (Chicago: University of Chicago Press, 1954).

Thomas, Edward (1878–1917)
Collected Poems, ed. R. George Thomas (Oxford: Oxford University Press, 1978).
Collected Poems (with Foreword by Walter de la Mare) (London: Faber and Faber, paperback, 1979).

Cooke, William, *Edward Thomas: A Critical Biography* (London: Faber and Faber, 1970).

Thomas, Helen, *Under Storm's Wing* (Manchester: Carcanet, 1988; Paladin/ Grafton, 1990).

Thomas, R. George, *Edward Thomas: A Portrait* (Oxford: Oxford University Press, 1985).

Draper, R. P., 'Edward Thomas: The Unreasonable Grief', in *Lyric Tragedy* (London and Basingstoke: Macmillan, 1985).

Motion, Andrew, *The Poetry of Edward Thomas* (London: Hogarth, 1980).

Scannell, Vernon, *Edward Thomas* (London: Longman (for The British Council), 1962).

Smith, Stan, *Edward Thomas* (London: Faber and Faber, 1986).

Thomas, Ronald Stuart (b. 1913)

Selected Poems: 1946–1968 (London: Hart-Davis, MacGibbon, 1973; Newcastle: Bloodaxe, 1986).

Later Poems: 1972–1982 (London: Macmillan, 1983; London and Basingstoke: Papermac, 1984).

Welsh Airs (Bridgend: Seren Books, Poetry Wales Press, 1987; reprinted 1993).

Collected Poems, 1945–1990 (London: Dent, 1993).

Anstey, Sandra (ed.), *Critical Writings on R. S. Thomas* (Bridgend: Seren, 1992).

Brown, Tony, 'The Romantic Nationalism of R. S. Thomas', in Norman Page and Peter Preston (eds), *The Literature of Place* (London and Basingstoke: Macmillan, 1993).

Davies, William Virgil (ed.), *Miraculous Simplicity: Essays on R. S. Thomas* (Fayetteville: University of Arkansas Press, 1993).

Dyson, A. E. (ed.): *see under* **Gunn, Thom.**

——, *Yeats, Eliot, and R. S. Thomas: Riding the Echo* (Basingstoke and London: Macmillan, 1981).

Hardy, Barbara: *see under* **Thomas, Dylan.**

Ward, John Powell, *The Poetry of R. S. Thomas* (Bridgend: Poetry Wales, 1987).

Thwaite, Anthony (b. 1930)

Selected Poems 1956–1996 (London: Enitharmon, 1997).

Tuwhare, Hone (b. 1922)

Deep River Talk: Collected Poems (Auckland: Godwit, 1933).

MIHI: Collected Poems (Auckland/Harmondsworth: Penguin, 1987).

Short Back & Sideways: Poems and Prose (Auckland: Godwit, 1992).

Manhire, Bill, interview with Hone Tuwhare, *Landfall*, 167, vol. 42, no. 3 (September 1988) pp. 262–81.

Walcott, Derek (b. 1930)

Poems, 1965–1980 (London: Cape, 1992).

Collected Poems, 1948–84 (New York and Toronto: HarperCollins, 1986; London: Faber and Faber, 1992).

Omeros (New York: Farrar, Straus & Giroux, and Toronto: Collins, 1990; London: Faber and Faber, 1990).

Brown, Stewart (ed.), *The Art of Derek Walcott* (Bridgend, Glam.: Seren Books, 1991).
Hamner, Robert, D., *Derek Walcott* (Boston: Twayne, 1981).
——, *Critical Perspectives on Derek Walcott* (Washington, DC: Three Continents Press, 1993).
Terada, Rei, *Derek Walcott's Poetry: American Mimicry* (Boston: Northeastern University Press, 1992).
Todd, Loreto, *Notes on Derek Walcott: Selected Poems* (Harlow: York/Longman, 1993).

Wilbur, Richard (b. 1921)
New and Collected Poems (San Diego: Harcourt Brace Jovanovich, 1988; London: Faber and Faber, 1989).

Michelson, Bruce, *Wilbur's Poetry: Music in a Scattering Time* (Amherst: University of Massachusetts Press, 1991).
Salinger, Wendy (ed.), *Richard Wilbur's Creation* (Ann Arbor: University of Michigan Press, 1983).

Williams, William Carlos (1883–1963)
Collected Poems (2 vols), ed. A. Walton Litz and Christopher MacGowan (New York: New Directions, 1986; Manchester: Carcanet, 1987; London: Paladin Grafton, 1991).
Paterson (New York: New Directions, 1963); ed. Christopher MacGowan (Manchester: Carcanet, 1992).
Selected Poems, ed. Charles Tomlinson (New York: New Directions, 1985; Harmondsworth: Penguin, 1990).
Selected Letters, ed. John C. Thirwall (New York: New Directions, 1957).
Selected Essays (New York: New Directions, 1954).

Mariani, Paul, *William Carlos Williams: A New World Naked* (New York and London: McGraw-Hill, 1981).

Bremen, Brian A., *William Carlos Williams and the Diagnostics of Culture* (Oxford and New York: Oxford University Press, 1993).
Callan, Ron, *William Carlos Williams and Transcendentalism: Fitting the Crab in the Box* (Basingstoke and London: Macmillan, 1992).
Doyle, Charles, *William Carlos Williams and the American Poem* (London and Basingstoke: Macmillan, 1982).
—— (ed.), *William Carlos Williams: The Critical Heritage* (London: Routledge & Kegan Paul, 1980; reprinted 1985).
Litz, A. Walton: *see under* **Stevens, Wallace**.
Markos, Donald W., *Ideas in Things: The Poems of William Carlos Williams* (Rutherford, NJ: Fairleigh Dickinson University Press, 1994; London: Associated University Presses, 1994).

Weaver, Mike, *William Carlos Williams: The American Background* (Cambridge: Cambridge University Press, 1971).

Wright, Judith (b. 1915)
Collected Poems: 1942–1985 (Manchester: Carcanet, 1994).
A Human Pattern: Selected Poems (Manchester: Carcanet, 1992).

Walker, Shirley, *Flame and Shadow: A Study of Judith Wright's Poetry* (St Lucia: University of Queensland Press, 1991).

Yeats, William Butler (1865–1939)
Collected Poems (London: Macmillan, 1950).
Poems, ed. Daniel Albright (London: Dent, 1990; revised edition, 1994).
Variorum Edition, ed. P. Allt and Russell K. Alspach (New York: Macmillan, 1957).
Poems of W. B. Yeats: A New Edition, ed. Richard J. Finneran (London and Basingstoke: Macmillan, 1984).
Yeats's Poems, ed. A. Norman Jeffares (London: Macmillan, 1989; London: Papermac, 1991).
The Works of W. B. Yeats (Ware: Wordsworth, 1994).
Selected Poetry, ed. Timothy Webb (Harmondsworth: Penguin, 1991).
Variorum Edition of the Plays, ed. Russell K. Alspach and Catharine C. Alspach (Basingstoke and London: Macmillan, 1966).
Collected Letters, ed. John Kelly and Eric Domville (Oxford: Oxford University Press, 1985–).
Autobiographies: Memories and Reflections (London: Bracken, 1995).
Essays and Introductions (London: Macmillan, 1961).
A Vision and Related Writings, ed. A. Norman Jeffares (London: Arena, 1990).
The Oxford Book of Modern Verse, ed. (with Introduction) W. B. Yeats (London: Oxford University Press, 1936).

Foster, Roy, *W. B. Yeats: A Life*, vol. 1 (Oxford: Oxford University Press, 1997).
Jeffares, A. N., *W. B. Yeats: Man and Poet* (Dublin: Macmillan, 1996).

Bloom, Harold (ed.), *William Butler Yeats* (New York: Chelsea House, 1986).
Donoghue, Denis, *Yeats* (Edinburgh: Oliver & Boyd, 1971).
Dyson, A. E.: *see under* **Thomas, R. S.**
Ellmann, Richard, *Yeats: The Man and the Masks* (New York: W. W. Norton, 1948; revised edition, 1979).
——, *The Identity of Yeats* (London: Faber and Faber, 1954).
Faulkner, Peter, *Yeats* (Milton Keynes and Philadelphia: Open University Press, 1987).
Fraser, G. S., *W. B. Yeats* (London: Longman (for the British Council), 1962).
Heaney, Seamus, 'Yeats as an Example?' in *Preoccupations* (London: Faber and Faber, 1980).
Jeffares, A. N., *W. B. Yeats: The Poems* (London: Edward Arnold, 1961).
——, *A Commentary on the Collected Poems of W. B. Yeats* (London: Macmillan, 1975).

——, *A New Commentary on the Poems of W. B. Yeats* (Stanford: Stanford University Press, 1984).

—— (ed.), *W. B. Yeats: The Critical Heritage* (London: Routledge & Kegan Paul, 1997).

MacNeice, Louis, *The Poetry of W. B. Yeats* (London: Oxford University Press, 1941; reprinted 1969).

Malins, Edward, *A Preface to Yeats* (London: Longman, 1974).

Meir, Colin, *The Ballads and Songs of W. B. Yeats* (London and Basingstoke: Macmillan, 1974).

Rosenthal, M. L., *Yeats's Poetic Art* (Oxford and New York: Oxford University Press, 1994).

Smith, Stan, *W. B. Yeats: A Critical Introduction* (Basingstoke and London: Macmillan, 1990).

Stallworthy, Jon, *Between the Lines: Yeats's Poetry in the Making* (Oxford: Oxford University Press, 1963).

——, *Vision and Revision in Yeats's 'Last Poems'* (Oxford: Oxford University Press, 1969).

—— (ed.), *Yeats: Last Poems* (Casebook) (London and Basingstoke: Macmillan, 1968).

Unterecker, John, *A Reader's Guide to William Butler Yeats* (London: Thames and Hudson, 1959).

—— (ed.), *Yeats: A Collection of Critical Essays* (Englewood Cliffs, NJ: Prentice-Hall, 1963).

Watson, George, *Irish Identity and the Literary Revival: Synge, Yeats, Joyce and O'Casey* (London: Croome Helm, 1979).

WORKS OF REFERENCE

Drabble, Margaret (ed.), *The Oxford Companion to English Literature* (revised edition) (Oxford: Oxford University Press, 1985).

Hamilton, Ian (ed.), *The Oxford Companion to Twentieth-Century Poetry* (Oxford and New York: Oxford University Press, 1994).

Hawkins-Dady, Mark (ed.), *Reader's Guide to Literature in English* (London and Chicago: Fitzroy Dearborn, 1996).

Kirkpatrick, D. L. (ed.), *Reference Guide to English Literature* (3 vols) (Chicago and London: St James Press, 1984; revised edition, 1991).

—— (ed.), *Reference Guide to American Literature* (Chicago and London: St James Press, 1987).

ANTHOLOGIES OF MODERN POETRY

Adcock, Fleur (ed.), *The Faber Book of Twentieth Century Women's Poetry* (London: Faber and Faber, 1987).

Allott, Kenneth (ed.), *The Penguin Book of Contemporary Verse* (Harmondsworth: Penguin, 1956).

Alvarez, A. (ed.), *The New Poetry* (Harmondsworth: Penguin, 1962; revised edition, 1966).

Burnett, Paula (ed.), *The Penguin Book of Caribbean Verse in English* (Harmondsworth: Penguin, 1986).

Curnow, Allen (ed.), *The Penguin Book of New Zealand Verse* (Harmondsworth: Penguin, 1960).

Doyle, Charles (ed.), *Recent Poetry in New Zealand* (Auckland: Collins, 1965).

Dunn, Douglas (ed.), *Twentieth-Century Scottish Poetry* (London and Boston: Faber and Faber, 1992; paperback edition, 1993).

Ellman, R., and O'Clair, R. (eds), *The Norton Anthology of Modern Poetry* (New York: W. W. Norton, second edition, 1988).

Enright, D. J. (ed.), *The Oxford Book of Contemporary Verse, 1945–1980* (Oxford: Oxford University Press, 1980).

Figueroa, John (ed.), *Caribbean Voices: An Anthology of West Indian Poetry* (London: Evans Brothers, 1966; reprinted 1984).

Geddes, Gary (ed.), *15 Canadian Poets X 2* (Toronto: Oxford University Press, 1988).

Jones, Peter (ed.), *Imagist Poetry* (Harmondsworth: Penguin, 1972).

King, Charles (ed.), *Twelve Modern Scottish Poets* (London: Hodder and Stoughton, 1971).

—— and Smith, Iain Crichton (eds), *Twelve More Modern Scottish Poets* (London: Hodder and Stoughton, 1986).

Larkin, Philip (ed.), *The Oxford Book of Twentieth-Century Verse* (Oxford: Oxford University Press, 1973).

Lindsay, Maurice (ed.), *Modern Scottish Poetry: An Anthology of the Scottish Renaissance, 1920–1945* (London: Faber and Faber, 1946).

Lucie-Smith, Edward (ed.), *British Poetry since 1945* (Harmondsworth: Penguin, 1970; revised edition, 1985).

MacBeth, George (ed.), *Poetry 1900 to 1965* (London: Longman/Faber and Faber, 1967).

Moore, Geoffrey (ed.), *The Penguin Book of Modern American Verse* (Harmondsworth: Penguin, 1954).

Morrison, Blake, and Motion, Andrew (eds), *The Penguin Book of Contemporary British Poetry* (Harmondsworth: Penguin, 1982).

Muldoon, Paul (ed.), *The Faber Book of Contemporary Irish Poetry* (London and Boston: Faber and Faber, 1986).

New Generation Poets. Poetry Review (Special Issue) (London: Poetry Society, 1994).

Parsons, I. M. (ed.), *Men Who March Away: Poems of the First World War* (London: Heinemann, 1985).

Penguin Modern Poets (Harmondsworth: Penguin, 1959–96).

Press, John (ed.), *A Map of Modern English Verse* (Oxford: Oxford University Press, 1969).

Roberts, Michael (ed.), *The Faber Book of Modern Verse* (London: Faber and Faber, 1936; revised edition, ed. Donald Hall, 1965).

Thompson, John, Slessor, Kenneth, and Howarth, R. G. (eds), *The Penguin Book of Australian Verse* (Harmondsworth: Penguin, 1958).

Yeats, W. B. (ed.), *The Oxford Book of Modern Verse* (London: Oxford University Press, 1936).

ANTHOLOGIES OF CONCRETE POETRY

Bann, Stephen (ed.), *Concrete Poetry: An International Anthology* (London: London Magazine Editions, 1967).

Between Poetry and Painting (catalogue of ICA exhibition, 22 October–27 November, 1965) (London: Institute of Contemporary Arts, 1965).

Chicago Review (concrete poetry issue), vol. xix, no. 4 (September 1967).

Riddell, Alan (ed.), *Typewriter Art* (London: London Magazine Editions, 1975).

Sharkey, John (ed.), *Mindplay: An Anthology of British Concrete Poetry* (London: Lorimer, 1971).

Williams, Emmett (ed.), *Anthology of Concrete Poetry* (New York: Something Else Press, 1967).

GENERAL STUDIES OF MODERN POETRY

Bedient, Calvin, *Eight Contemporary Poets* (Tomlinson, Davie, R. S. Thomas, Larkin, Hughes, Kinsella, Stevie Smith, W. S. Graham) (London and New York: Oxford University Press, 1974).

Bergonzi, Bernard, *The Myth of Modernism and Twentieth Century Literature* (Brighton: Harvester, 1986).

Blamires, Harry, *Twentieth-Century English Literature* (London and Basingstoke: Macmillan, 1982).

Booth, Martin, *British Poetry, 1964 to 1984: Driving Through the Barricades* (London and Boston: Routledge & Kegan Paul, 1985).

Brown, Dennis, *The Poetry of Postmodernity: Anglo/American Encodings* (London and Basingstoke: Macmillan, 1994).

Christ, Carol T., *Victorian and Modern Poetics* (Chicago: University of Chicago Press, 1984).

Corcoran, Neil, *English Poetry since 1940* (London: Longman, 1993).

—— (ed.), *The Chosen Ground: Essays on the Contemporary Poetry of Northern Ireland* (Bridgend: Seren, 1992).

Crawford, Robert, *Devolving English Literature* (Oxford and New York: Oxford University Press, 1992).

Davie, Donald, *Under Briggflatts: A History of Poetry in Great Britain, 1960–1980* (Manchester: Carcanet, 1989; Chicago: University of Chicago Press, 1989).

Day, Gary, and Docherty, Brian (eds), *British Poetry, 1900–50: Aspects of Tradition* (London and Basingstoke: Macmillan, 1995).

Draper, R. P., *Lyric Tragedy* (London and Basingstoke: Macmillan, 1985).

—— (ed.), *The Literature of Region and Nation* (London and Basingstoke: Macmillan, 1989).

Easthope, Anthony, and Thompson, John O. (eds), *Contemporary Poetry Meets Modern Theory* (Hemel Hempstead, Herts: Harvester Wheatsheaf, 1991; Toronto: University of Toronto Press, 1991).

Evans, Patrick, *The Penguin History of New Zealand Literature* (Auckland and Harmondsworth: Penguin, 1990).

Fraser, G. S., *The Modern Writer and His World* (London: Derek Verschoyle, 1953); revised edition (London: André Deutsch, 1964).

——, *Vision and Rhetoric: Studies in Modern Poetry* (London: Faber and Faber, 1959).

——, *Essays on Twentieth-Century Poets* (Leicester: Leicester University Press, 1977).

Goodwin, Ken, *A History of Australian Literature* (London and Basingstoke: Macmillan, 1986).

Harvey, G., *The Romantic Tradition in Modern English Poetry: Rhetoric and Experience* (Basingstoke and London: Macmillan, 1986).

Hoffpauir, Richard, *The Art of Restraint: English Poetry from Hardy to Larkin* (Newark, Delaware: University of Delaware Press, 1991; London: Associated University Presses, 1991).

Hynes, Samuel, *Edwardian Occasions* (London: Routledge & Kegan Paul, 1972).

Juhasz, Suzanne, *Naked and Fiery Forms: Modern American Poetry by Women* (New York: Harper & Row, 1976).

King, P. R., *Nine Contemporary Poets: A Critical Introduction* (Larkin, Tomlinson, Gunn, Hughes, Plath, Heaney, Dunn, Paulin, Mills) (London: Methuen, 1979).

Levenson, M. H., *A Genealogy of Modernism: A Study of English Literary Doctrine, 1908–1922* (Cambridge: Cambridge University Press, 1984).

Lucas, John., *Modern English Poetry from Hardy to Hughes* (London: B. T. Batsford, 1986).

MacNeice, Louis, *Modern Poetry: A Personal Essay* (London: Oxford University Press, 1938).

Millard, Kenneth, *Edwardian Poetry* (Oxford: Oxford University Press, 1991).

Page, Norman, and Preston, Peter (eds), *The Literature of Place* (London and Basingstoke: Macmillan, 1993).

Pinto, V. de S., *Crisis in English Poetry, 1880–1940* (London: Hutchinson's University Library, 1951).

Schmidt, Michael, and Lindop, Grevel (eds), *British Poetry since 1960: A Critical Survey* (Manchester: Carcanet, 1972).

Scully, James (ed.), *Modern Poets on Modern Poetry* (New York: McGraw Hill, 1965; London and Glasgow: Fontana/Collins, 1966).

Sisson, C. H., *English Poetry, 1900–1950: An Assessment* (London and New York: Methuen, 1971; Manchester: Carcanet, 1981).

Smith, Stan, *The Origins of Modernism: Eliot, Pound, Yeats and the Rhetorics of Renewal* (Hemel Hempstead, Herts.: Harvester Wheatsheaf, 1994).

Spender, Stephen, *The Struggle of the Modern* (London: Methuen, 1963).

Stead, C. K., *The New Poetic: Yeats to Eliot* (London: Hutchinson's University Library, 1964; Harmondsworth: Penguin, 1967).

——, *Pound, Yeats, Eliot and the Modernist Movement* (London and Basingstoke: Macmillan, 1986; New Brunswick, NJ: Rutgers University Press, 1986).

Thurley, G., *The Ironic Harvest: English Poetry in the Twentieth Century* (London: Arnold, 1974).

Thwaite, Anthony, *Poetry Today: A Critical Guide to British Poetry, 1960–1984* (London: Longman, 1985).

——, *Twentieth-Century English Poetry: An Introduction* (London: Heinemann, 1978; New York: Barnes & Noble, 1978).

Walker, Marshall, *The Literature of the United States of America* (London and Basingstoke: Macmillan, 1983).

Ward, John Powell, *The English Line: Poetry of the Unpoetic from Wordsworth to Larkin* (London and Basingstoke: Macmillan, 1991).

Woodring, Carl, and Shapiro, James (eds), *The Columbia History of British Poetry* (New York: Columbia University Press, 1994).

OTHER WORKS

Atkins, G. Douglas, and Morrow, Laura (eds), *Contemporary Literary Theory* (Amherst: University of Massachusetts Press, 1989).

Brooker, Peter, and Widdowson, Peter (eds), *A Practical Reader in Contemporary Literary Theory* (Hemel Hempstead, Herts: Prentice-Hall/Harvester Wheatsheaf, 1996).

Culler, Jonathan, *Saussure* (Glasgow: Fontana/Collins, 1976).

Newton, K. M. (ed.), *Twentieth-Century Literary Theory: A Reader* (London and Basingstoke: Macmillan, 1988).

Selden, Raman, *A Reader's Guide to Contemporary Literary Theory* (Brighton: Harvester, 1985).

Tallis, Raymond, *Not Saussure: A Critique of Post-Saussurean Literary Theory* (London and Basingstoke: Macmillan, 1988; revised edition, 1995).

Index

A number followed by 'n' signifies a reference to the Notes.

Adcock, Fleur 150, 153–4; 'Advice to a Discarded Lover' 153; 'For a Five-Year Old' 153; 'Going Back' 154; 'Grandma' 153; 'Letter to Alistair Campbell' 154; 'On the Border' 154; 'Settlers' 154

Aiken, Conrad 14

Allott, Kenneth 114, 241n

Ammons, A. R. 26

Angelou, Maya 160, 212, 214–16; *Oh Pray My Wings Are Gonna Fit me Well* 215; 'Africa' 214; 'Artful Pose' 215; 'Calling of Names, The' 214; Mothering Blackness, The' 214; 'On the Pulse of Morning' 214; 'Our Grandmothers' 215; 'Preacher, Don't Send Me' 215; 'Riot: 60s' 214; 'Through the Inner City to the Suburbs' 215; 'To a Man' 214; 'When I Think About Myself' 214

Apollinaire, Guillaume, *Calligrammes* 221

Aristotle 71, 86

Armitage, Simon 161

Arnold, Matthew 161, 242n

Ashbery, John 9, 26, 225–9, 235, 246n; *Double Dream of Spring, The* 228; 'Decoy' 228; 'Farm Implements and Rutabagas in a Landscape' 226; 'He' 226; 'Houseboat Days' 228–9; 'Painter, The' 226; 'Tennis Court Oath, The' 226–7

Atwood, Margaret 160, 200–4, 244n; *Journals of Susanna Moodie, The* 201; *New Poems, 1985–1986* 202; *Power Politics* 200–1; *Survival* 201; 'Aging Female Poet

Reads Little Magazines' 202; 'Galiano Coast: Four Entrances' 203; 'This is a mistake' 201; 'You did it' 201–2

Auden, W. H. 8, 48, 55, 94, 98–107, 108, 110, 111, 113, 114–15, 125, 221, 229, 234, 238n, 241n; *Poems, 1927–1931* (Poem No. xxiii) 101, 240n; *Sea and the Mirror, The* 151; 'Consider this and in our time' 101; 'Good-Bye to the Mezzogiorno' 105; 'Horae Canonicae' 105; 'In Memory of W. B. Yeats' 240n; 'In Praise of Limestone' 105–7; 'Lakes' (No. 4 of 'Bucolics') 105; 'Lay your sleeping head, my love' 101; 'Letter to Lord Byron' 99; '1929' 101; '"O where are you going?" said reader to rider' 101; 'O what is that sound' 102; 'September 1, 1939' 98; 'Shield of Achilles, The' 105; 'Spain 1937' 103–4, 204n; 'This Lunar Beauty' 100–1; 'Wanderer, The' 103

Bach, Johann Sebastian 142

Bann, Stephen 246n

Baraka, Amiri (LeRoi Jones) 212; 'It's Nation Time' 213–14

Barthes, Roland 7, 237n

Baudelaire, Charles Pierre 6

Baxter, James 197

Beethoven, Ludwig van 143

Bergonzi, Bernard 96, 110, 240n, 241n

Berryman, John 26, 75, 144; 'The Hell Poem' 75

Bible, The 14, 17, 89, 146, 177, 189, 190, 191, 212–13

Bishop, Elizabeth 144, 155–60, 192;
'At the Fishhouses' 155; 'Crusoe
in England' 155; 'End of March,
The' 155; 'In the Waiting
Room' 155–7; 'Moose, The' 155,
157–9
Blackburn, Paul 12
'Black Mountain' 116–18, 126–30,
225
Blake, William 85, 109, 127, 130,
146, 149, 189, 191; *Marriage of
Heaven and Hell, The* 214;
Songs of Innocence 149; 'London'
140; 'Tyger, The' 41, 140
Blunden, Edmund 88
Boer Wars, the 3
Boly, John R. 102, 103, 240n
Bomberg, Victor 85
Boulton, James T. 241n
Brahms, Johannes 142
Brathwaite, Edward Kamau 206;
'Horse Weebles' 206
Brecht, Bertolt 71, 103
Bridges, Robert 34
Brontë sisters, the (Anne, Charlotte
and Emily) 161
Brooker, Peter 237n
Brooks, Gwendolyn 212; 'The
Ballad of Rudolph Reed' 213
Brown, Dennis 225
Brown, George Mackay 171
Brown, Stewart 245n
Browning, Robert 34, 35, 61, 75, 149,
151
Bulletin, The (Sydney) 187
Burnett, Paula 244n
Burns, Robert 166, 168, 169

Cairns, Farquharson, 'BarcOde' 225
Calvin, John 169, 173
Campbell, Roy 98
Campion, Thomas 51
Campos, Augusto de 245
Carpenter, Humphrey 240
Carroll, Lewis, *Alice in
Wonderland* 221
Carter, D. N. G. 239n
Cavalcanti, Guido 17
Chaucer, Geoffrey 187

Clampitt, Amy 150, 154–5;
Kingfisher, The 154; *What the
Light Was Like* 154; 'New Life,
A' 155; 'Outer Bar, The' 154;
'Voyages: A Homage to John
Keats' 154–5
Clare, John 161
Clinton, President William
Jefferson 214
Clough, Arthur Hugh 34
Cohen, Keith 246n
Coleridge, Samuel Taylor 25, 26, 89,
122; 'Ancient Mariner, The' 122
Communism 98, 166, 242n
Concrete poetry 167, 194, 221–5,
225, 231, 235
Conrad, Joseph, *Heart of
Darkness* 211
Conservative Party, the 4
Cooley, Dennis 244n
Crabbe, George 161, 178, 181;
Village, The 178
Crane, Hart 155
Crase, Douglas 246n
Creeley, Robert 126, 127–8;
'Don't Sign Anything' 127–8
Cromwell, Oliver 196
Cullen, Countee 212
Culler, Jonathan 6, 237n
cummings, e. e. 219–21, 230, 235;
'here's a little mouse)and' 219;
'(of Ever-Ever Land i speak' 221;
'ygUDuh' 219–21, 245n
Curnow, Allen 196–9, 244n;
Incorrigible Music, An 199; 'Bring
Your own Victim' 199; 'Evening
Light, An' 198, 244n; 'Landfall in
Unknown Seas' 196–7; 'Letters,
The' 199; 'Raised Voice, A'
197–8
Cushman, Stephen 23, 237n

Dabydeen, Cyril 206
Dabydeen, David 206; 'Slave
Song' 206, 244n
Dadaism (and 'neo-Dadaist') 226,
246n
Dante, Alighieri 12, 17, 19, 20, 83,
196, 239n; *Divine Comedy* 12, 20

Davidson, Michael 26, 30, 237n, 238n
Davie, Donald 239–40n
Davies, James A. 243n
Day Lewis, C. 98, 104, 110–12, 115, 241n; *From Feathers to Iron* 241n; *Hope for Poetry, A* 104; *Italian Visit, An* 111; 'As one who wanders' 110; 'Birthday Poem for Thomas Hardy' 110; 'But Two there are' 110; 'Come, live with me and be my love' 111; 'Cornet Solo' 111; 'Innocent, The' 111; 'Nearing again the legendary isle' 111; 'Neurotic, The' 111; 'O Dreams, O Destinations' 111; 'Passage from Childhood' 111; 'Sheep Dog Trials in Hyde Park' 111–12; 'Tempt me no more' 110
Defoe, Daniel, *Robinson Crusoe* 207
Derrida, Jacques 185
Dickens, Charles 14
Donoghue, Denis 65, 239n
Doolittle, Hilda *see* H. D.
Donne, John 1, 2, 72, 100, 178, 234
Douglas, Keith 90, 91–2, 97, 239n, 240n; 'Cairo Jag' 91; 'How to Kill' 91; 'Vergissmeinnicht' 91–2
Dowson, Ernest 118
Draper, R. P. 8, 237n, 242n, 243n, 244n, 245n, 246n
Dryden, John 97, 100, 106
Duffy, Carol Ann 150, 151–3, 154, 155; *World's Wife, The* (Mrs Darwin, Mrs Lazarus, Mrs Midas, Queen Kong, Mrs Tiresias) 151; 'Standing Female Nude' 151–2
Dunbar, William 166, 168
Duncan, Robert 26, 126, 127; 'Apprehensions' 127; 'Sequence of Poems for H. D.'s Birthday, A' 127
Dunn, Douglas 243n
Dyson, A. E. 130, 241n

Eco, Umberto 185
Eliot, T. S. 7, 11–20, 21, 31–2, 33, 35, 38, 51, 58, 59, 60–1, 72, 75, 89, 93, 99, 105, 124, 134, 178, 199, 206, 208, 218, 239n; *Ash Wednesday* 17, 191; *For Lancelot Andrewes* 238n; *Four Quartets* 17–20, 31–2, 76, 191, 238n; *Waste Land, The* 6, 12–16, 17, 19, 20, 25, 31, 58, 88–9, 99, 165, 166, 169, 208, 228; 'Journey of the Magi' 240n; 'Love Song of J. Alfred Prufrock, The' 61; 'Marina' 16, 17; 'Metaphysical Poets, The' 72; 'Preludes' 11, 21; 'Rhapsody on a Windy Night' 30; 'Tradition and the Individual Talent' 15–16, 60
Eliot, Mrs Vivien (first Mrs T. S. Eliot) *see* Haigh-Wood, Viven
Eliot, Mrs Valerie (second Mrs T. S. Eliot) 12
Elizabeth I, Queen 15
Emerson, Ralph Waldo 159
Empson, William, *Seven Types of Ambiguity* 15, 237n
Encounter 98
Evans, Patrick 199, 244n

Fanthorpe, Ursula Askham 150–1, 155; 'Not My Best Side' 151; 'Only Here for the Bier' 151
Fascism 31, 91, 98, 102, 104, 145
Feminism 4, 8–9, 138–9, 143, 144, 155, 189, 192–3, 201–2, 214
Figueroa, John 207, 245n
Finlay, Ian Hamilton 221, 222, 235, 246n; 'Acrobats' 222–3; 'Ajar' 222; 'au pair girl' 222, 223; 'Homage to Malevich' 221; 'To the painter Juan Gris' 221
Flaubert, Gustave 6
Franco, General Francisco ('el Caudillo') 98, 102
Frank, Waldo 239n
Fraser, G. S. 166–7, 229–30, 233; 'To Hugh MacDiarmid' 166
Freud, Sigmund 89, 101
Frost, Robert 33, 35, 44–9, 50, 53, 58, 115; *Boy's Will, A* 45; *Mountain Interval* 46; *North of Boston* 45, 46; *Steeple Bush* 48; *Witness Tree, A* 48; 'After Apple-Picking' 46, 47;

Frost, Robert (*Continued*)
'Birches' 46, 48; 'Death of the
Hired Man, The' 46; 'Design' 49;
'Figure a Poem Makes, The'
44–5, 238n; 'Gift Outright, The'
48; 'Home Burial' 45; 'Importer,
An' 48; 'Mending Wall' 46; 'Most
of it, The' 49; 'Mowing' 45; 'No
Holy Wars for Them' 48; 'Out,
Out –' 46–7; 'Road Not Taken,
The' 46, 47; 'Servant to Servants,
A' 45; 'Snow' 46
Fugitive Movement, the 72
Fuller, John 240n
Fuller, Roy 90, 94–5; *Epitaphs and
Occasions* ('Dedicatory Epistle')
95; 'Autumn 1940' 94; 'During a
Bombardment by V-Weapons'
95; 'Teba' 95; 'Tribes, The' 95;
'White Conscript and the Black
Conscript, The' 95

Gardner, Helen 17, 237n
Garnett, Edward 241n, 243n
Garrioch, Robert 167; 'Embro to the
Ploy' 167; 'To Robert
Ferguson' 167
Gelpi, Albert 237n, 238n
Gertler, Mark 85
Gilbson, Graeme 204
Gibson, James 238n
Gilbert, W. S. and Sullivan, A. 51
Gilmour, Robin 242n
Ginsberg, Allen 212
Glob, Prof. P. V. 184
Goldsmith, Oliver, *Vicar of
Wakefield, The* 14
Gomringer, Eugen 222; 'grow, flow,
show, blow' 222; 'silence' 222
Gonne, Maud 66
Goodwin, Ken 187
Graves, Robert 3, 33, 35, 53–8, 59,
72, 88, 110, 192, 238n, 239n, 241n;
Claudius the God 57; *I, Claudius*
57; *Goodbye To All That* 57; 'Beast,
The' 56; 'Cool Web, The' 54–5;
'Despite and Still' 56; 'Down,
Wanton, Down!' 56; 'Flying
Crooked' 55–6; 'In Broken

Images' 57; 'Outlaws' 54; 'Persian
Version, The' 57; 'Rocky Acres'
54; 'Succubus, The' 56; 'Turn of
the Moon' 56; 'Ulysses' 56
Great War, The *see* World War I
Grieve, Christopher Murray *see*
MacDiarmid, Hugh
Gurney, Ivor 88

Haigh-Wood, Vivien (first
Mrs T. S. Eliot) 15
H. D. (Hilda Doolittle) 40
Hamilton, Ian 72
Hamner, Robert 205, 244n
Hardy, Barbara 174, 243n
Hardy, Emma Lavinia (first
Mrs Thomas Hardy) 38, 39
Hardy, Florence Emily (second
Mrs Thomas Hardy) 38, 39
Hardy, Thomas 8, 33–41, 44, 50, 53,
55, 58, 65, 83, 88, 99, 109, 110, 115,
137, 161, 229, 234, 242n; *Dynasts,
The* 39, 238n; *Jude the
Obscure* 86, 161; *Life of Thomas
Hardy, The* 34, 238n; *Return of the
Native, The* 21–2, 86; 'After a
Journey' 38; 'At Castle Boterel'
38; 'August Midnight, An' 39, 40;
'Beeny Cliff' 38; 'Christmas in the
Elgin Room' 40; 'Convergence of
the Twain, The' 39; 'Darkling
Thrush, The' 40; 'Dream or No,
A' 38; 'During Wind and
Rain' 88; 'His Visitor' 39;
'In Time of "The Breaking of
Nations"' 88; 'Overlooking the
River Stour' 40–1; 'Oxen,
The' 40; 'Phantom Horsewoman,
The' 39; 'Practical Woman,
A' 40; 'Ruined Maid, The' 40;
'St Launce's Revisited' 38; 'Spell
of the Rose, The' 39; 'Thoughts of
Phena at News of her Death'
35–8; 'Under the Waterfall' 39;
'Voice, The' 38
Harris, Max 187
Hayward, John 238n
Heaney, Seamus 8, 159, 160, 161,
181, 182–6, 242n, 243n, 244n;

Death of a Naturalist 183–4; *Haw Lantern, The* 185; *North* 184; *Wintering Out* 184; 'Alphabets' 185–6; Death of a Naturalist 183–4; 'Digging' 183; 'Punishment' 184–5; 'Tollund Man, The' 184

Heath, Stephen 237

Henri, Adrian 235

Henryson, Robert 166, 168

Herbert, George 72, 221; 'Easter Wings' 221

Hewitt, John 181

Hibberd, Dominic 239n

Hitler, Adolf 102, 145

Hodge, Alan 241n

Homer 12, 207–8, 209; *Iliad* 12; *Odyssey* 12, 207

Hope, A. D. 188; 'Australia' 188

Hopkins, Gerard Manley 23, 34, 99, 154, 173, 178, 223; 'Windhover, The' 154

Hopkinson, Abdur-Rahman Slade, 'The Madwoman of Papine' 205–6, 244n

Horace (Quintus Horatius Flaccus) 81

Housman, A. E. 33, 42–4, 55, 58; *Last Poems* 42, 43; *Shropshire Lad, A* 42–4; 'Bredon Hill' 43; 'Into my heart an air that kills' 43; 'laws of God, the laws of man, The' 43; 'Loveliest of trees, the cherry now' 43; 'Oh see how thick the goldcup flowers' 43; 'street sounds to the soldier's tread, The' 42–3; 'Terence, this is stupid stuff' 43–4; ''Tis time, I think, by Wenlock town' 43

Hughes, Langston 212, 215–16; 'Brass Spittoons' 212–13; 'Fortune Teller Blues' 212; 'Listen Here Blues' 212; 'Minnie Sings Her Blues' 212; 'Theme for English B' 216; 'Weary Blues, The' 212, 215

Hughes, Sylvia *see* Plath, Sylvia

Hughes, Ted 6, 50, 54, 65, 91, 118, 130–7, 138, 145, 161, 180, 239n,

241n; *Birthday Letters* 137; *Crow* 132–4; 136, 180, 241–2n; *Gaudete* 130, 134–6; *Lupercal* 130, 132; *Hawk in the Rain, The* 131, 132; *Moortown Elegies* 130, 136; *Remains of Elmet* 130; *River, The* 130, 136; *Wolfwatching* 130; 'Battle of Osfrontalis, The 133–4; 'Bayonet Charge' 130; 'Crow's First Lesson' 133; 'Crow's Nerve Fails' 134; 'Crow's Theology' 133; 'Daffodils' 137; 'Disaster, A' 134; 'Examination at the Womb-door' 133; 'February 17th' 136; 'Fingers' 137; 'Grand Canyon' 137; 'Hawk Roosting' 91, 130–1, 132; 'Horrible Religious Error, A' 133; 'How Water Began to Play' 134; 'Jaguar, The' 91, 130; 'Karlsbad Caverns' 137; 'Lineage' 133; 'Littleblood' 134; 'Martyrdom of Bishop Farrar, The' 130; 'October Salmon, An' 136–7; 'Pike' 130, 132; 'Sheep' 136; 'Thrushes' 132

Hulme, T. E. 40

Hutchinson, George 241n

Hynes, Samuel 35, 238n

Imagism 12, 13, 19, 23, 26, 31, 40–1, 60, 72, 99, 165

Ingamells, Rex 187

Ingersoll, Earl G. 244n

Isherwood, Christopher 104

Jackson, Moses 42

James, Henry 226

Jameson, Frederic 5–6, 237n

Jarrell, Randall 72

Jeffers, Robinson 49–50; 'Apology for Bad Dreams' 50; 'Birds and Fishes' 50; 'Carmel Point' 50

Jennings, Elizabeth 49, 238n

Jindyworobak Movement, the 187, 188

John of the Cross, St (Juan de Yepis y Alvarez) 19

Johnson, Dr Samuel, *The Vanity of Human Wishes* 20

Johnson, Trevor 238n
Jones, David 89–90, 92, 96, 174;
    In Parenthesis 89–90
Jones, LeRoi *see* Baraka, Amiri
Jonson, Ben 115
Joyce, James 5–6, 25, 51, 76, 89,
    94, 206, 207, 208–9, 210, 211;
    Dubliners 76; *Ulysses* 5–6, 25, 89,
    208–9, 210, 211
Jung, Carl Gustav 25, 89
Juvenal (Decimus Junius
    Juvenalis) 42

Kallet, Marilyn 129, 241n
Kavanagh, Patrick 181, 182–3, 243n;
    'Art McCooey' 183; 'Christmas
    Childhood, A' 183; 'Epic' 183;
    'Great Hunger, The' 182–3;
    'Long Garden, The' 183;
    'Spraying the Potatoes' 183
Keats, John 16, 28, 70, 82–3, 86, 100,
    101, 119, 149, 154, 185, 234, 235,
    240n; 'Belle Dame Sans Merci,
    La' 240n; 'Ode on a Grecian
    Urn' 100; 'Ode to a Nightingale'
    16, 86, 101; 'To Autumn' 82–3
Kelly, Robert 26
Kermode, Frank 237n
Kershaw, R. B. 243n
Keyes, Claire 138, 143, 242n
Keyes, Sidney 91, 92; 'War Poet' 92
Kierkegaard, Søren Aabye 98, 103,
    105, 178
King, Edward 72
Kinsella, Thomas 181, 182; 'Tao
    and Unfitness at Inistiogue on the
    River Nore' 182
Kipling, Rudyard 33–4, 50–3, 58,
    81; *Barrack-Room Ballads* 51; *Puck
    of Pook's Hill* ('The Children's
    Song') 51; 'Ave Imperatix!' 52;
    'Boots' 51; 'Danny Deever'
    51; '"Fuzzy-Wuzzy"' 51;
    'Gentlemen-Rankers' 51;
    'Gunga Din' 52; 'McAndrew's
    Hymn' 51; 'Mandalay' 51;
    'Mesopotamia' 52; 'Non Nobis
    Domine!' 51; 'Our Lady of the
    Snows' 52; 'Recessional' 52–3;

'Song in Storm, A' 51; 'Tommy'
    51–2, 53; 'White Man's Burden,
    The' 50–1; 'Widow at Windsor,
    The' 51–2
Klein, A. M., 'Indian Reservation:
    Caughnawaga' 200
Kooning, William de 225
Kreisel, Henry 200
Kroetsch, Robert, *Seed
    Catalogue* 225

Labour Party, the 4
Lampman, Archibald, 'At the Long
    Sault' 200, 244n
Lane, Patrick, 'Mountain
    Oysters' 200
Langland, William 187
Larkin, Philip 3, 8, 35, 37, 42, 44, 55,
    115, 172, 229–35, 238n, 246n; *All
    What Jazz* 230–1; *North Ship,
    The* 35; *Oxford Book of
    Twentieth-Century English Verse,
    The* 230; *Required Writing* 238n;
    'Ambulances' 231; 'Arundel
    Tomb, An' 231; 'Aubade' 234;
    'Building, The' 231, 234, 235;
    'Church Going' 231; 'MCMXIV'
    3; 'Naturally the Foundation Will
    Bear Your Expenses' 231; 'Old
    Fools, The' 231, 234; 'Show
    Saturday' 231; 'Study of Reading
    Habits, A' 231; 'Whitsun
    Weddings, The' 231–4
Lawrence, D. H. 6, 28, 48, 50, 54, 65,
    66, 86, 88, 89, 101, 106, 118–26,
    129, 130, 134, 137, 138, 139, 165,
    170, 239n, 240n, 241n, 243n;
    Apocalypse 120, 241n; *Birds Beasts
    and Flowers* 106, 119, 120; *Last
    Poems* 106, 124–5; *Look! We have
    Come Through!* 118–19; *Man Who
    Died, The* 126; *More Pansies* 125;
    Nettles 125; *New Poems* 119;
    Pansies 48, 125; *Rainbow, The* 165,
    240n, 243n; *Women in Love* 88,
    239n; 'All Souls' Day' 124;
    Almond Blossom' 121–2; 'Baby
    Tortoise' 120; 'Bat' 120;
    'Bavarian Gentians' 124, 241n;

'Beware the Unhappy Dead' 124; 'Fidelity' 243n; 'Fish' 122–4; 'For the Heroes are Dipped in Scarlet' 125; 'Lui et Elle' 120; 'Man and Bat' 120; 'Not I, not I, but the wind that blows through me!' 119; 'Red Geranium and Godly Mignonette' 125–6; 'Ship of Death, The' 101, 124, 134, 241n; 'Snake' 122, 123–4; 'Song of Death' 124; 'Tortoise Family Connections' 120; 'Tortoise Gallantry' 120; 'Tortoise Shell' 120; 'Tortoise Shout' 120, 121

Leggett, B. J. 44, 238n

Lehman, David 246n

Leicester, Robert Dudley, Earl of 15

Lentricchia, Frank 45, 238n

Leonard, Tom 167, 219–20

Leventen, Carol 148, 242n

Levertov, Denise 127, 128–30, 139; 'Tree Telling of Orpheus, A' 128–30, 139

Lewis, Alun 90, 91, 92–4, 95, 97, 174; 'After Dunkirk' 93; 'All Day It Has Rained' 92, 93; 'Burma Casualty' 94; 'Mahratta Ghats, The' 93; 'To Edward Thomas' 92

Lewis, C. Day *see* Day Lewis, C.

Liberal Party, the 4

Lindsay, Vachel 49–50, 214; 'Congo, The' 50, 214; 'Simon Legree' 50

Livesay, Dorothy 200, 244n; 'Fire and Reason' 200

Lodge, David 133, 214–2n

Lodge, Thomas 51

Longley, Edna 91, 239n

Longley, Michael 181

Lowell, Robert 8, 61, 72–9, 133, 138, 144, 148, 239n; *Land of Unlikeness* 72; *Life Studies* 72, 74–7, 78; *Lord Weary's Castle* 72; 'Epilogue' 77–8; 'For the Union Dead' 74; 'My Last Afternoon with Uncle Devereux Winslow' 75–6; '91 Revere Street' 75; 'Quaker Graveyard in Nantucket, The' 72–4; 'Skunk Hour' 76–7, 133

Lucie-Smith, Edward 108–9, 240n

McAuley, James 188

MacBridge, John 67

McCombs, Judith 244n

McCormack, W. J. 237

MacDiarmid, Hugh (Christopher Murray Grieve) 163–6, 167, 168, 174, 178, 195, 242n, 243n; *Drunk Man Looks at the Thistle, A* 163–4; 'Eemis Stane, The' 163; 'Empty Vessel' 163; 'On a Raised Beach' 164–6; 'Watergaw, The' 163; 'Water Music' 163

McDonald, Edward D. 239n

McGough, Roger 235

MacNeice, Louis 98, 107–10, 115; *Autumn Journal* 107, 108; 'Bagpipe Music' 107–8; 'Birmingham' 107, 109; 'Carrickfergus' 107, 109; 'Eclogue for Christmas' 107; 'Habits, The' 109; 'Ode' ('Tonight is so coarse') 108; 'Soap Suds' 109–10; 'Star-Gazer' 109

Mallarmé, Stéphane, *Un Coup de Dés* 221

Mallett, Phillip V. 237n

Mandel, Eli 244n

Manilius 42

Marcus, Mordecai 45, 238n

Mahon, Derek 181

Markiewicz, Con 67

Marsh, Edward 118

Marvell, Andrew 72, 101; 'Definition of Love, The' 101

Marx, Karl (and 'Marxism') 101, 104, 138, 211, 246n

Mason, Ron 197

Masters, Edgar Lee 49

Meanjin 187

Melville, Herman, *Moby Dick* 72, 73

Mendelson, Edward 99, 240

Merril, Thomas F. 241n

Merrill, James 26

'Metaphysical' poets 72, 74, 99, 148, 149

Miller, Russell 237n
Milton, John 12, 19, 72, 89, 176, 208, 211, 245n; *Lycidas* 72; *Paradise Lost* 12, 77, 211, 245n; *Samson Agonistes* 19
Modernism 4–9, 11–32, 33, 35, 38, 40, 41, 45, 53, 57, 58–9, 60, 65, 72, 74, 83, 88–9, 99, 100, 108, 117, 124, 139, 149, 163, 165, 182, 194, 199, 202, 206, 218, 224, 225, 227, 230, 235, 236
Montague, John 181
Moore, Geoffrey 238n
Morgan, Edwin 167, 222, 223–4, 235, 245–6n; *Glasgow Sonnets* 167; *Themes on a Variation* 224; 'French Persian Cats having a Ball' 224; 'jollymerry / hollyberry / jollyberry' 224; 'Newspoems' 224; 'Orgy' 224; 'pomander' 223–4; 'starryveldt' 224; 'Unscrambling the waves at Goonhilly' 224
Moro, Aldo 199
Morrio, Mervyn 206
Motion, Andrew 246n
Mozart, Wolfgang Amadeus 120, 132, 142
Mudie, Ian 187, 188; 'This Land' 188
Muir, Edwin 167–71, 172, 243n; 'Horses, The' 169, 170–1; 'Journey Back, The' 169; 'Labyrinth, The' 169–70; 'Robert the Bruce' 169; 'Scotland 1941' 169
Muldoon, Paul 181, 182; 'More a Man Has the More a Man Wants, The' 182
Murray, Les 188, 193–6, 244n; 'Buladelah-Taree Holiday Song Cycle, The' 194; 'Dream of Wearing Shorts Forever, The' 194; 'Elegy for Angus Macdonald of Cnoclinn' 195; 'Four Gaelic Poems' 195; 'Idyll Wheel, The: Cycle of a Year at Bunyah, New South Wales' 194–5; 'Inverse Ballad' 194; 'Machine Portraits

with Pendant Spaceman' 194; 'Mouthless Image of God in the Hunter-Colo Mountains, The' 194; 'Noonday Axeman' 193; 'Sydney Highrise Variations, The' 194, 195–6; 'Walking to the Cattle Place' 194, 195
Mussolini, Benito 31, 102

Napoleon Bonaparte 146–7
Nash, Paul 85, 89, 239n
Nevinson, C. R. W. 85, 89
New Criticism, the 72
Newlove, John, 'Pride, The' 200
Newton, K. M. 237n
New York School, the 225
Nicholson, Colin 244n
Nietzsche, Friedrich Wilhelm 65–6, 83, 239n

Oates, Joyce Carol 244n
O'Donoghue, Bernard 182, 185, 243n
O'Hara, Frank 225
Olivier, Sir Laurence 246n
Olson, Charles 116–18, 119, 126–7, 128, 129, 137, 138, 139, 212, 219, 241n; 'D. H. Lawrence and the High Temptation of the Mind' 126, 241n; 'Distances, The' 126; 'Kingfishers, The' 126
Orwell, George 104
Owen, Wilfred 3, 80–3, 84, 85–6, 88, 87, 89, 90, 91, 93, 95–6, 173, 184; 'Anthem for Doomed Youth' 82; 'Apologia pro Poemate Meo' 82; 'At a Calvary Near the Ancre' 83; 'Chances, The' 81, 82; 'Dulce et Decorum Est' 80–1, 85, 87; 'From My Diary, July 1914' 96; 'Futility' 83; 'Greater Love' 83; 'Inspection' 82, 84, 96; 'Miners' 82, 85; 'Preface' 80; 'Send-Off, The' 83; 'Soldier's Dream' 3, 82, 86; 'Strange Meeting' 82, 83, 84, 85, 86, 96

Page, Norman 238n
Palmer, Michael 26

Parker, Charlie 235
Parker, Michael 244n
Parzival (epic by Wolfram von Eschenbach) 135
Patmore, Coventry 34
Paulin, Tom 181
Perloff, Marjorie G. 75, 239n
Petrarch, Francesco 82
Picasso, Pablo 27, 89
Plath, Sylvia 137, 144–8, 149, 155, 160, 193, 201, 239n, 242n; 'Ariel' 144–5; 'Arrival of the Bee Box, The' 147, 242n; 'Beekeeper's Daughter, The' 242n; 'Bee Meeting, The' 147, 242n; 'Daddy' 145; 'Lady Lazarus' 145–6, 148, 242n; 'Stings' 146, 147, 148, 242n; 'Swarm, The' 147, 242n; 'Wintering' 147–8, 242n
Plato 71, 189
Poe, Edgar Allan 149, 239n
Pope, Jessie 81
Post-modernism 9, 26, 193, 195, 211, 218, 225
Pound, Ezra 7, 8, 11–13, 20, 21, 31–2, 33, 40–1, 51, 52, 58, 60, 72, 75, 88, 89, 116, 117, 118, 124, 172, 199, 218, 225, 239n; *Cantos* 12, 20, 31, 117; 'E. P. Ode Pour L'Election de Son Sépulchre' 31; 'Hugh Selwyn Mauberley' 88; 'In a Station of the Metro' 12
Projective verse 116–18, 126, 128, 138, 139, 241n
Proust, Marcel 109
Pursglove, Glyn 243n
Pythagoras 71

Rajan, B. 237n
Reed, Henry, 'Naming of Parts' 95
Replogle, Justin 102, 240n
Rich, Adrienne 9, 138–44, 146, 155, 160, 225, 242n; *Time's Power* 141; 'Aunt Jennifer's Tigers' 140–1, 142; 'Blood, Bread and Poetry' 139, 242n; 'Children Playing Checkers at the Edge of the Forest' 225; 'Ninth Symphony of Beethoven Understood at Last as a Sexual Message, The' 143; 'Snapshots of a Daughter-in-Law' 143; 'Solfeggietto' 141–3
Richards, I. A. 72
Riding, Laura 53
Robinson, Edwin Arlington 49–50; 'Mr Flood's Party' 50; 'New England' 50
Roethke, Theodore 75
Rosenberg, Isaac 3, 84, 85, 87, 96; 'Break of Day in the Trenches' 85; 'Dead Man's Dump' 85, 87; 'Louse Hunting' 85
Rosenthal, M. L. 74
Ross, Bruce Clunies 244n
Rudman, Mark 75, 239n
Ruskin, John 34

Sagar, Keith 241n
Sanchez, Sonia 212
Sandburg, Carl 49–50; 'Chicago' 49
Sankey, Benjamin 25, 237n
Sassoon, Siegfried 3, 84, 86, 88, 89, 91, 93, 96; 'Blighters' 84; 'General, The' 84; 'Rear-Guard, The' 84; 'To Any Dead Officer' 84
Saussure, Ferdinand de 6
Shapiro, David 226, 228, 246n
Schuyler, James 225
Schwartz, Delmore 75
Scigaj, Leonard M. 130, 241n
Scott, Sir Walter 166, 168, 169
Scully, James 238n, 241n
Selden, Raman 243
Seneca, Lucius Annaeus, the Younger, *Hercules Furens* 16, 237n
Seymour-Smith, Martin 54–5, 238n
Sexton, Anne 148, 149, 193, 201, 239n; *All My Pretty Ones* 148; *Live Or Die* 148; *To Bedlam and Part Way Back* 148; *Transformations* 148; 'Abortion, The' 148; 'In Celebration of My Uterus' 148; 'Menstruation at Forty' 148
Shakespeare, William 6, 14, 16, 82, 83, 89, 149, 151, 207, 232, 246n; *Antony and Cleopatra* 151;

Shakespeare, William (*Continued*)
As You Like It 151; *Hamlet* 246n;
Henry V 89, 246n; *Othello* 207;
Pericles 16; *Winter's Tale, The* 6;
Sonnet 73 ('That time of year
thou mayst in me behold') 83
Shelley, Percy Bysshe 16, 119;
'Ode to the West Wind' 16
Shklovsky, Viktor 175, 243
Smith, Grover Cleveland 13
Smith, Stevie 148–50, 160;
'After-Thought, The' 149;
'Avondale' 149; 'I Rode with my
Darling' 150; 'Major Macroo'
150; 'Not Waving but Drowning'
149–50; 'Singe Qui Swing,
Le' 149; 'Singing Cat, The' 149
Somme, the Battle of 2
Sophocles, *Antigone* 68
Sorley, Charles 88, 93
Southam, B. C. 237n
Smith, Ian Crichton 163, 171–3,
242n, 243n; 'Deer on the High
Hills – A Meditation' 172; 'Eight
Songs for a New Ceilidh' 173;
'Law and the Grace, The' 173;
'Life, A' 173; 'Old Woman' 173
Snodgrass, W. D. 239n
Spanish Civil War, The 103–4
Speight, Robert 14
Spencer, Stanley 85, 89
Spender, Stephen 98, 104, 112–14,
115; *Dolphins* 113–14; *Poems of
Dedication* 113, 114; 'Dolphins'
114; 'Elegy for Margaret' 113;
'Exiles from their Land, History
their Domicile' 112, 113; 'Fall of a
City' 112; 'I Think Continually of
Those Who Are Truly Great' 112;
'Moving through the silent
crowd' 112–13; 'Letter from an
Ornithologist in Antarctica' 114;
'oh young men oh young
comrades' 112; 'Perhaps' 112;
'Poetes Maudits' 114; 'Spiritual
Explorations' 113; 'Thoughts
during an Air Raid' 112; 'Two
Armies' 112; 'Van der Lubbe'
112; 'Variations on My Life' 113;

'Who live under the shadow of
war' 112; 'Worldsworth' 114
Spenser, Edmund 12, 14; *Faerie
Queene, The* 12
Starkey, Roger 244n
Stead, Alistair 237n
Stevens, Wallace 7, 26–30, 33, 38,
58, 199; 'Anecdote of the Jar'
27–8; 'Bantams in Pine-Woods'
27; 'Chocorua to its Neighbor' 28;
'Credences of Summer' 28;
'Esthetique du Mal' 28; 'Idea of
Order at Key West, The' 27, 28;
'Man with the Blue Guitar,
The' 27, 28; 'Notes Toward a
Supreme Fiction' 26–7, 28; 'Of
Modern Poetry' 29–30; 'Ordinary
Evening in New Haven, An' 30;
'Owl's Clover' 28; 'Sunday
Morning' 28–9; 'Thirteen Ways
of Looking at a Blackbird' 27
Stevenson, Robert Louis 34, 168
Stoppard, Tom, *Travesties* 227
Strachey, Lytton 35, 238n, 37
Stravinsky, Igor 28, 31, 89; *Rite of
Spring, The* 28, 31
Symbolism 26, 99

Tasman, Abel Janszoon 196
Tate, Allen 72, 199
Taylor, Dennis 34, 238n
Tennyson, Alfred Lord 34, 82, 149,
178; *In Memoriam* 82; 'Lady of
Shalott, The' 34
Thomas, Dylan 173–7, 178, 243n;
Deaths and Entrances 174;
18 Poems 175; *Map of Love,
The* 174; *Under Milk Wood* 174,
178; 'After the Funeral' 174;
'Especially When the October
Wind' 176; 'Fern Hill' 174,
176–7; 'Hunchback in the Park,
The' 174; 'Over Sir John's Hill'
174, 177; 'Poem in October' 174;
'Poem on his Birthday' 174;
'Process in the Weather of the
Heart, A' 175
Thomas, Edward 35, 84, 85–7, 92, 96,
99; 'As the Team's Head-Brass' 85,

86, 87–8; 'Lights Out' 85, 86; 'Old
Man' 86; 'Rain' 86, 92
Thomas, R. S. 174, 177–81, 182,
243n; *Minister, The* 178;
'Look' 178; 'Peasant, A' 178–9;
'Pilgrimages' 180–1; 'Postscript'
179, 180; 'Reservoirs' 178;
'Rough' 180; 'Walter Llywarch'
178; 'Welshman to Any Tourist,
A' 178; 'Welsh Testament,
A' 178
Thirties poets 91, 96, 98–115
Tolstoy, Count Leo,
Anna Karenina 86
Traquair, Ramsay 238n
Treece, Henry 243n
Tuwhare, Hone 197

Uccello, Paolo 151

Vermeer, Jan 78
Vergil 12, 83, 208, 245n; *Aeneid* 12,
208, 245n
Vettese, Raymond 168
Vietnam War 5

Wagner-Martin, Linda 242n
Wagner, Richard, *Ring, The* 15;
Tristan und Isolde 15
Wain, John 39, 238n
Walcott, Derek 206–12, 244–5n;
*Antilles, The: Fragments of Epic
Memory* 207, 245n; *In a Green
Night* 245n; *Omeros* 206, 207–12;
'Castaway, The' 207; 'Far Cry
from Africa, A' 245n; 'Goats and
Monkeys' 207
Wallace, Patricia B. 159–60;
242n
'Wanderer, The' (Old English
poem) 240n
Ward, Elizabeth 89, 239n
Warren, Robert Penn 72
Watkins, Vernon 174
Watson, George 13
Webb, Sidney and Beatrice 4
Welland, D. S. R. 239n
Wellesley, Dorothy 96
Weston, Jessie L. 13

Whitman, Walt 21, 32, 118, 119, 127,
149, 155, 194, 215
Widdowson, Peter 237n
Wilde, Oscar *Ballad of Reading Gaol,
The* 42
Williams, William Carlos 7, 8, 20–6,
32, 33, 58, 116, 118, 127, 139, 199,
218, 219; *Paterson* 20, 25–6;
Pictures from Brueghel ('Song')
23–4; 'Complete Destruction'
22–3; 'Overture to a Dance of
Locomotives' 22; 'Pastoral' 21;
'Red Wheelbarrow, The' 22;
'This is Just to Say' 22;
'Wanderer, The' 21
Winslow, Warren 73
Woodcock, George 244n
Wolf, Leslie 246n
Woolf, Virginia, *To the Lighthouse* 89
Wordsworth, William 12, 20, 25, 27,
45, 70, 86, 95, 99, 104, 111, 155, 161,
165, 171, 183, 208; *Prelude, The* 12
World War I 2–3, 4, 15, 80–90, 91,
96–7, 156–7, 188
World War II 2, 3, 4, 5, 90–5, 96–7,
104, 108, 188, 196
Wren, Sir Christopher 211
Wright, Judith 160, 188, 189–93;
Gateway, The 191; *Moving Image,
The* 189; *Phantom Dwelling* 192;
Two Fires, The 189;
'At Cooloolah' 189; 'Bullocky'
189–90, 191, 192; 'Cicadas,
The' 191; 'Phaius Orchid' 191;
'Remittance Man' 190–1;
'Smalltown Dance' 193;
'Summer' 192–3; 'Unknown
Water' 191–2
Wyke, Clement H. 244n

Yeats, W. B. 1–2, 8, 33, 60–71, 72,
78–9, 95–6, 110, 115, 126, 166, 189,
229; *Cathleen ni Houlihan* 67;
Countess Kathleen, The 71;
Crossways 62; *In the Seven
Woods* 62; *Last Poems* 70–1, 96;
Oxford Book of Modern Verse, The
(Introduction) 96; *Responsibilities*
62, 66, 72; *Rose, The* 62;

Yeats, W.B. (*Continued*)
Shadowy Waters, The 62; *Tower, The* 64, 69, 72; *Wanderings of Oisin, The* 62, 63, 71; *Wind Among the Reeds, The* 62; *Winding Stair, The* 64; 'Among School Children' 69–70, 71, 77, 79; 'Balloon of the Mind, The' 62; 'Byzantium' 64, 69; 'Circus Animals' Desertion, The' 62–3, 71; 'Coat, A' 62; 'Crazy Jane' poems 62; 'Dialogue of Self and Soul, A' 64; 'Easter 1916' 62, 67–9, 79, 166; 'Long-legged Fly' 70; 'Man and Echo' 67; 'Meditation in Time of War, A' 62; 'News for the Delphic Oracle' 70–1; 'Sailing to Byzantium' 64–5, 69, 79; 'Second Coming, The' 1–2, 10, 65–6, 79; 'Song of the Happy Shepherd, The' 62; 'Song of Wandering Aengus, The' 62; 'To a Wealthy Man' 62; 'To the Rose upon the Rood of Time' 62; 'Under Ben Bulben' 70; 'White Birds, The' 62

Y Gododdin (Welsh poem) 89
Yorke, Liz 143, 242n

Zytaruk, George J. 241n